To Dad

Lots of love for Christmas 1991

from Michèle and Geoff.

GREAT WESTERN RAILWAY
ENGINE SHEDS

The '47' 2—8—0s were an enduring Old Oak feature, their massive proportions a perfect counterbalance to the vaulting Churchward roofs.

AN ILLUSTRATED HISTORY OF

GREAT WESTERN RAILWAY
ENGINE SHEDS

BY

CHRIS HAWKINS & GEORGE REEVE

LONDON DIVISION

WILD SWAN PUBLICATIONS LTD.

FOR

W. A. CAMWELL

Most plans and elevations contained herein have been made available by the kind permission of British Railways Western Region and are marketed together with a wealth of further material through Railprint Ltd. They remain BR copyright as do the excerpts from the technical press.

Designed by Paul Karau
Printed and bound by Butler & Tanner, Frome

Published by
WILD SWAN PUBLICATIONS LTD.
1-3 Hagbourne Road, Didcot, Oxon OX11 8DP

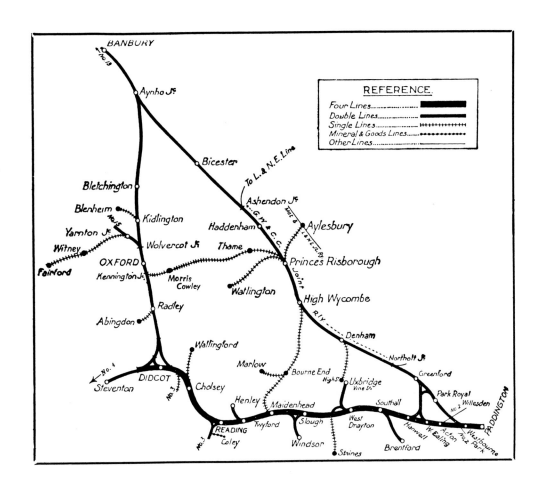

CONTENTS

The 'high and airy' quality of the roundhouse was a principal advantage, seen to greatest effect at Old Oak Common.

INTRODUCTION

Any descriptive approach to the Great Western Railway involves certain difficulties which, if not entirely absent in the case of other companies, may at least seem less pressing. It can be difficult to say anything much new about the Great Western, and next to impossible to be even gently critical without attracting outrage. The fame, prosperity and commercial acumen of the Great Western is not in doubt; along with 'Brunel' it is possibly the only railway term ('Beeching', less pleasantly, might be another) readily springing to the public mind. In 1985 a presenter on the BBC children's television programme *Blue Peter*, on the astounding discovery that the brakes of a restored 14XX 0–4–2T functioned more or less correctly, could assure his young audience with all sincerity 'this is *what made the Great Western best*' [authors' italics].

The literature, accordingly voluminous, varies widely in quality and is nothing if not exhaustive. Reams of text have been devoted to the Great Western, obscure byways no less than the principal services, locomotives and personalities. The Great Western branch is somehow considered quintessential, if not quite of *Merrie England* then certainly of some mystically less troubled epoch; many of the minor engine sheds have thus been investigated in some considerable detail. The coverage intensifies across the Home Counties and the West Country, leaving matters a trifle awkward for a work bearing the title *Great Western Engine Sheds*, especially one beginning with the well-quarried London area.

The GWR *per se* is demonstrably an oddity, a chance of geography and history surviving unscathed where its rivals perished. A queer outcome of Grouping at 1923, companies of wealth, power and influence to rival or overshadow the Great Western disappeared, the ensuing internal strife rending their structures. The GWR was thus relatively free to address itself, without distraction, to the challenges and problems of the time, whilst others floundered in internecine strife. Whether it built to fullest advantage on this wholly enviable position is the question; the comparison has to be made with the 'running departments' of the LMS and LNER, the only concerns of comparable size and complexity.

The various manifestations of Great Western engine shed layout and building design can conveniently be assigned to relatively few 'periods'. They can be grouped essentially (and most usefully) into four: (i) those from the ancient days, often broad gauge and of disparate origins, a handful avoiding by chance the peril of years to survive into the BR period. Few and unimportant. (ii) Dean's northlight pattern buildings, principally dating from the 1880s and 1890s. (iii) Churchward sheds, both straight buildings and the familiar grandiose and lofty

roundhouses. (iv) The 'Loan Act' sheds built with Government assistance in the 1930s.

In this whole process the Great Western can be said only to have roughly paralleled its major contemporaries; for years it lagged behind, forging ahead for a period, only to finally lapse behind mainstream developments. Of the most familiar Great Western engine sheds, most can be found within Groups (iii) and (iv), the Churchward era followed by the 1930s construction period. There have been two principal elaborations of Great Western shed developments, that by Lyons in 1972* and by the RCTS, 1974†. They are related, through an (acknowledged) exchange of information, but vary considerably in their emphasis, the RCTS concerning itself principally with organisation and coding. This account differs quite considerably in its treatment from both these works and it is hoped that the advantages of space afforded herein have allowed a more detailed coverage not possible before.

The sheds are described in their 'Divisional' context, as established shortly prior to Grouping and modified thereafter. Attention is concentrated upon the larger depots, their construction, development and working, from earliest days through to closure under British Railways. The tendency to choose a specific date or year has been resisted; principal sites are those which passed into BR ownership but sheds closed prior to this, predecessors, replaced buildings or whatever, are described as fully as possible at the appropriate point – Westbourne Park and Paddington, for example, are considered to be a part of the story of Old Oak Common.

By the turn of the century the best buildings available to the GWR were certain of the 'Dean' sheds, low and squat with northlight pattern roofs. This was typical contemporary practice, developed principally on the LNWR and Lancashire and Yorkshire Railway; inferior with regard to smoke removal and lighting, the low roofs and beaming suffered overmuch through blast and its corrosive by-products. This became an almost obsessive subject on the Great Western (not that anything much was done about it) and the fruitless search for a system of roofing impervious to decay contributed to the post-Churchward 'stalling' of new building and replacement work, in the 'thirties and after the Second World War. Improved methods of research and materials testing, and experiences gained with concrete in the war, had still not satisfactorily solved the problems by the mid 1950s. Blast, the products of combustion, and the water-retaining qualities of soot layers,

---

* An Historical Survey of Great Western Engine Sheds 1947.
† *The Locomotives of the Great Western Railway. A Chronological & Statistical Survey.*

1

are an appallingly corrosive mix, and engine shed roofs, with troughs and vents and the innumerable accompanying tie bars, beams, hangers and jointing, were uniquely susceptible. The Great Western thought little (probably rightly) of the concrete products of other companies, dating from the '20s and '30s, but correctly attributed the main problems to insufficient attention to detail and the imponderables of relatively new techniques. The company certainly did not solve the problems, however, and conveniently 'talked out' the years until Nationalisation with endless tests and reports. It remained a fascinating research topic spawning a series of discussion papers, but the headlong advance of the type powered through by Churchward was not possible (or desirable, or both) in the 1940s. The GWR, like all institutions, had a tendency to bureaucracy; in its dotage the company still built Churchward locomotives and, although various existing engine shed designs were examined across Britain, all were rejected. None was to be 'taken on board', to be improved and enlarged, in the GW tradition established in the 1900s.

Decades behind its rivals, the GWR only seriously attended to its engine sheds, their layout and construction and their disposition about the system in the period after 1900. Strategically the running department was in a poor state by this time. Other companies from the 1870s had embarked on 'standard ranges' of building, generous new accommodation provided across the networks. Up-to-date practice was put to use, discussed and reviewed in a cross fertilisation of ideas fuelled through a generally accessible engineering press full of regular studies and reports. The insular GWR was little affected by this, and at the end of Dean's long reign a randomly distributed collection of inherited buildings and his rather small and squat designs stood poor comparison with, say, the 'steam sheds' of the LNWR (at least in terms of the scale of provision), the roundhouses of the North Eastern and Midland, and the Scottish companies. At the time even the economically puny LSWR was working out a fine new system of 'standard buildings'. Churchward, by dint of extraordinary effort, turned this situation around.

Churchward's great genius was to take, adopt and improve what was best in existing practice, in a flexible and open-minded way. The contrast between some of the LNWR 'steam sheds' and the high and airy Midland roundhouses was one he could not miss – the main roof, in the case of both the Midland straight sheds and roundhouses, was distanced from the most damaging effects of blast and could be supported on girdering of a bulk to defy corrosion. Churchward took these basic elements, enlarging the floor plan to accommodate a 65 ft. turntable – a 'stretched' Midland shed (their own, enormous, thirty-year programme of new building had only come to its close about the turn of the century) with space appropriate for the larger engine types then

in prospect. Site considerations meant that straight sheds would also be required and these too were marked for the high pitch of the roofs – again 'improved Midland' practice.

The GWR derived enormous benefits from this building on the experience of others, maximising advantage and avoiding some of the pitfalls. By the 1920s, however, the work was considered more or less complete and the running sheds ossified, at least in comparison with (in particular) the efforts its rivals directed at service improvement and mechanisation. Stalwarts would hold that the other companies simply needed to do more to catch up, but this is not the case. The GWR was constantly fiddling with grand plans for improvements, through to its demise, but they almost never included any hint of mechanisation and varied hardly at all from the Churchward turn-of-the-century model.

Internal debate on the relative merits of the two types, roundhouse/straight shed, was never really resolved (see for example, descriptions of Oxford, Reading, Old Oak and indeed others) though BR developments in the late 1950s seem to imply that the roundhouse finally proved to have the most merit.

Provision was almost invariably made for future expansion whatever the building, and a most elegant doubling or quadrupling of accommodation, in the case of the roundhouse model especially, was possible. The Churchward period buildings were laid out to an almost ritually precise formula, with elements of almost military planning. Dean had 'shoehorned' roundhouses into the most unpromising sites (Tondu, Croes Newydd, Taunton), an advantage indeed of the roundhouse principle. Churchward eschewed this. Again previous experience was assimilated and adjudged, disadvantages done away with and advantages honed and highlighted. A cramped site, either with roundhouse or straight shed, was always a cramped site and there were to be no such problems with the new depots, whatever excavation or fill might be necessary. Vast acres were made available and the Churchward sheds set amidst them, with generous approaches, adequate sidings and enough open space about for whatever expansion might one day be conceived.

Far more roundhouses were proposed than were actually completed. In the London operating area alone, three were outlined for Didcot, two at Slough, *four* at Southall (on the Old Oak model) and others in various configurations at places like Oxford and Reading. The GWR Mechanics Institution *Transactions* for 1906 and 1907 review, with unassailable Swindon confidence, the 'Ideal Shed'. . . .

THE IDEAL SHED – Consideration of work performed in and about a Running Shed, as described in the foregoing, enables anyone to grasp the essential elementary requirements of a good shed and Locomotive Yard. In a paper read last Session on 'Locomotive Engine Sheds,' Mr. Arkell dealt fully with their construc-

First days at Old Oak.

Collection E. Mountford

tion, and gave illustrations of the several designs in vogue. Mr. Arkell advocates a straight-through shed as an ideal. There is much in his contention, and the particular form of straight shed he suggests is most convenient, but a round shed is, for many reasons, to be preferred to a straight one. On the ingoing road a pit of sufficient length should be provided to stand the engines waiting their turn to be coaled, and over which the enginemen or turners could make their examinations. Between this pit and the shed should be placed the coal stage, preferably on a loop, so that access might be had directly into the shed on the ingoing road for the convenience of those engines which did not require coaling, but required turning.

The platform of a coal stage should be high enough to allow of the cabs of engines clearing the tips when down, and should be of such an area as to accommodate as many tip wagons as would hold at least one-twentieth of a day's consumption, and long enough to permit of proper mixing.

The elevated road should be high enough, as already mentioned, for the tops of the tip wagons to be level with the floors of the coal wagons. The length of this road to the dead-end beyond the coal stage should be sufficient to hold wagons enough for one day's consumption.

The fire pit should be a fair distance from the stage, and between it and the shed; and at this pit, or at the coal stage, there should be a water crane. If the stage is on a loop, the crane should be put between the loop and ingoing road. The firepit should preferably be lined with fire bricks, as the faces of Staffordshire blue bricks are quickly destroyed by the hot clinkers. This pit should be fitted with a number of hydrants, and these should be well set back in the brick work to protect them from injury. Adjacent to the fire pit, a short dead end siding should be provided, upon which the ash wagons could stand, and pavement should be laid down between the siding and the pit to provide a good bottom for the

ash loaders to shovel on. The fire pit road should converge into the ingoing road outside the sheds, and the points should be as far from the pit as is practicable.

The ingoing road should lead direct to the turntable, and not converge into the outgoing road. The outgoing road should have two or three dead end sidings furnished with pits, over which men could get their engines ready without interference. A road should lead from the outgoing across the ingoing road to the coal stage loop. This should be compounded with the ingoing road, so that an engine requiring coal only could run directly under the tip, through the compound, taking the preference of those engines waiting their turn on the coal stage road, and immediately it was coaled it could run out again on to the outgoing road.

A water crane or cranes should, of course, be provided to serve the outgoing roads. The sand furnace should be placed as near the preparing pits as possible.

The shed described would accommodate from 20 to 30 engines, and it will be seen that all shed operations can be done in proper sequence, and without necessitating a single back shunt, except in the case of engines leaving the shed having to set back on to the preparing pits; but even here there is absolutely no risk of a broadside collision. All our latest sheds are designed more or less on these lines, but the ideal shed and yard occupies a large piece of land, which is, however, unfortunately hardly ever available in practice, and the accommodation provided has, therefore, to be modified according to circumstances.
[Henry Simpson Esq. Vice President, Swindon Engineering Society]

Stourbridge in the mid-1920s was the last of the Churchward buildings and brought to a close a most remarkable period.

It is the sweeping scale of much of the work that remains the most abiding and impressive feature. It is as if British Railways had built two or three dozen Thornabys in the 1950s, and it is a measure of Churchward's power and drive. Much has been made of his position of direct control over the running department but he had still to fight his corner and win the money. Engine running was universally resented as a purely 'spending department', and his political might within the company must have been formidable indeed. The new sheds were sited almost as a military campaign – older constricted places like Bath Road Bristol, Bordesley (Birmingham) Westbourne Park in London, and Stafford Road, Wolverhampton, were rejected out of hand for rebuilding in the new order and these strategically vital areas were re-fashioned comprehensively, St. Philip's Marsh, Tyseley, Old Oak and Oxley replacing or supplementing their predecessors to effectively triangulate the company's network.

The Churchward programme of renewal petered out, with much left undone, in the 'twenties. A gap of several years ensued, until the new impetus provided by the Development (Loans and Guarantees Act) of 1929. A new 'standard' was determined, the 'Loan Act shed' as first identified by Lyons. Expedience determined the type of building employed; it had first of all to be cheap, with a whiff of 'the new' and advanced, with applications readily adaptable to new industry – workshops, etc. There was a need to pitch the grant application fairly precisely; proposals after all were not sanctioned automatically and the approval committee was responsive to projects which could claim wider relevance – a spur to new building applications and techniques. The buildings had parallels elsewhere, in all manner of light industrial settings and on the other railways; the Southern, for instance, had its own 'Loan Act' engine sheds, independently arrived at but bearing many similarities to the Great Western structures. Most of them were built in South Wales, reflecting the upheavals of Grouping, and all tended to be part of a more broad-based programme of alterations in District workings. Care was taken to replicate existing coal stages, purely Churchward features – in the vast reconstruction taking place across Britain in the 1930s. Loan Act funded and otherwise, almost nowhere was there a reversion to this sort of provision. The whole process ended, obscurely, with the reconstruction of Aberystwyth in 1938.

The Churchward buildings, together with the 'Loan Act' sheds, represented a considerable improvement in the depot 'stock' as it were, but, although Old Oak might be held a relative jewel, thoroughly humbling its

The Great Western stages remained little altered, through to the end of steam. After all, as Pellow pointed out (p. 36) 'there was nothing much to go wrong'.
Collection W. Potter

dismal LNWR neighbour, Willesden, such provision must be seen in proper perspective, as relatively uncommon. Old Oak might (rightly) be regarded as monumental but within the London area, for instance, it was balanced by decaying hovels at Reading, Oxford and Didcot. The situation was comparable on the other Divisions. Coaling on the Great Western had long been effected from 'tank over' stages, 'coal holes' on a well-established model (employed by all the major companies) served by earth ramps. Churchward required only to adapt this arrangement to whatever size might be necessary, but experiments only of the most desultory kind were made with mechanical handling. The Great Western before Churchward had been marked by a certain introspection. All the major companies could be fiercely partisan; this was quite normal in the pre-Grouping period, though perhaps on the GWR self-satisfaction, by the end of the nineteenth century, might have become unusually well rooted. Churchward's accomplishments were all the more extraordinary for this; when new buildings commenced under the terms afforded by the 'Loan Act', apart from the requirement to use cheaper materials (contemporary 'factory' type construction), practice did not vary from that established by him. It is hard to avoid the conclusion that an early partisanship had declined through a deserved satisfaction to isolationism and a certain sanguinity.

From the late 1920s a period of revolutionary improvement had been put in motion across great parts of the railway landscape and a great drive initiated to forge new economies in the running and maintenance of engines. A whole British industry grew up for the mechanical handling of bulk materials, and elaborate designs, involving prolonged 'jigging' and 'retarded delivery', were produced to eliminate breakage in soft coal. The Great Western reluctance to mechanise has been ascribed in the unsuitably soft nature of South Wales coal – nevertheless handling (and thereby breakage and dust) problems were overcome at the pits and in ship loading, and other railway companies coped by using hoods and copious slaking with water. Hard coal was also used across much of the Great Western, particularly in the north west and Midlands, and here provision of coal stages was precisely the same. But if the problems of soft coal did indeed prove insurmountable, there was little attempt to mechanise the dreadful job of ash disposal. The railway press throughout the 1930s was much occupied with the varied approaches to this problem, but Swindon, relatively aloof and content with its own learned Engineering Society, hardly gave this particularly unpleasant running shed activity any consideration at all. Similarly ignored in this period was a whole programme of new works intended to rationalise nineteenth century shed layouts. The reduction of unnecessary engine movements was considered a vital part of depot modernisation, and often simple adjustment to allow the 'service-sequence' movement of engines on and off shed could result in substantial savings, in time and thereby money. Less time spent in the stabling, disposal and servicing of engines allowed a reduction in engine stocks and contributed to the continuous driving down of working expenses through the 1930s. Most of this passed the Great Western by, secure in the pre-eminence of Paddington and all its works.

The reading of learned papers, however, was a tradition long nurtured on the Great Western, principally through the agency of the Lecture & Debating Society. Officers were frequently invited to speak and H. G. Kerry delivered a lecture entitled 'The Working of a Locomotive Shed' on 30th January 1947. Mr Kerry was the London Division Locomotive Carriage & Wagon Superintendent and some of his comments are recorded elsewhere in this book – his notes on coal are interesting for the *absence* of references to dust:

> Mechanisation is rather a big subject. So far as the coal stage is concerned, we have no mechanised coal stage as they have on some of the other railways. These big coal-handling plants are very, very good indeed and very efficient. They are mechanical arrangements and they do take the arduous nature out of coaling operations. From that point of view I am in favour of them and I think that we shall be seeing more mechanical coaling plants before long, but they have their disadvantages inasmuch as if anything goes wrong you are 'sunk' unless you have some alternative by which you can carry out the coaling of an engine. Take, for instance, a big plant handling – as we should have to do at Old Oak Common – over 500 tons a day. We could not possibly coal the engines from wagons or from the ground at the rate of 500 tons per day, not by hand or even with a crane.

Mr Benjamin of Swindon asked a range of questions, including one relating to coaling:

> With reference to coal, I understand at Old Oak Common there are about 500 tons a day moved or used. There are a couple of sheds in this country, one on the L.N.E.R., and one on the L.M.S., using about one thousand tons a day and employing mechanical elevators? Where would be the dividing line, or where would we decide to put in mechanical elevators? They take up less room, naturally, but it was a good point you brought up when you said that if anything went wrong you were just dished. Good maintenance prevents this. It seemed to me where you had room the Great Western system of a gradient was better and preferable, but, of course, it all depends on the amount to be handled. Did the speaker not know that we had coal hoists averaging 800 tons/hr. without fear of breakdowns?
>
> MR. KERRY – There are quite a number of points from Mr. Benjamin to keep me for the rest of the evening, so I think we will skip one or two. (*Laughter.*)
>
> Regarding mechanical elevators for coal, there may be depots on the L.N.E.R. and L.M.S. which do one thousand tons a day, but I do not know of them.
>
> MR. BENJAMIN – If they did not, I was wondering why they had installed them.
>
> MR. KERRY – I am afraid I cannot say why they installed them. They have gone in for mechanisation. We shall probably go in for mechanisation to a greater extent than we have done in the past.

Other aids to engine shed working were discussed:

MR. DEAN (Paddington) – I would like to ask Mr. Kerry one or two questions. One, I suggest, is of great importance these days; it is the interior lighting of locomotive sheds. We all must admit, I think, that generally speaking the locomotive sheds are really dismal places as compared with premises of many other commercial firms and undertakings. If we are to invite anybody to work in these sheds – and I know it is very difficult to obtain recruits at the present time – we have got to improve the lighting. I understand this question is being tackled. The point occurs to me, however, that the obvious choice of lighting should be fluorescent, the nearest approach to daylight. How all the fluorescent tubes which will have to be provided are to be kept clean, however, I am unable to say.

That leads me to another point; the extraction of smoke and dust from the shed by electric fans similar to the method employed to extract foul air from a shelter in order to keep the atmosphere as clean as possible. Could not this be arranged in locomotive sheds?

My third question – the mechanical extraction of the very fine ash in the smoke-boxes, the removal of which is now made by hand. I fail to see why one could not use some mechanical contrivance similar to an ordinary vacuum cleaner, which would extract the fine ash, thus avoiding the man-handling. Furthermore, mechanical extraction, it seems to me, would be rather more effective than removal by hand, as obviously one cannot clean away every particle of ash from the smoke-box by hand; further, the cleaner the machine the more efficient it is bound to be.

My final question is in regard to engines stabled in the vicinity of locomotive depots, apparently waiting repair. One often sees a string of these engines which to the layman appear to be deteriorating owing to exposure to the weather. Would it not be better for the engines to be stored away under cover?

Probably the capital cost of such protection would far outweigh the loss due to the slight deterioration.

MR. KERRY – The lighting in the sheds is not always as good as it might be, and it is very difficult to arrange lighting which will give light everywhere it is wanted. That is why you so frequently see a large number of flare lamps about the shed. A man can take this along and put it right on the job he wants to do. It is very difficult to arrange general lighting that will give a man a good enough light to do repairs on an engine: certainly, he cannot get it underneath, not in every pit.

The cleaning of fluorescent tubes would have to be a continuous job at a locomotive shed owing to the amount of smoke and fumes that are about the place. As a matter of fact we are fitting up one pit at Old Oak Common with special pit lighting for examination of engines, and we are also having trolleys on which all sorts of portable lights will be fitted, and these can be used all round an engine. It would be a very expensive job to fit up all pits in the same way, but the idea of this one pit at Old Oak Common is to provide an examination pit where there is light at the sides, so that a man working underneath will get very good light everywhere; but he will still want portable lights.

As to ventilation, there is no doubt about it that some of the sheds are bad, and are very full of smoke. I should be very pleased to get rid of some of it in some way. I do not know that any mechanical appliance for ventilation has been installed. The usual arrangement is to have a long ridge on the roof with louvres, and that should dissipate most of the smoke; but on a damp, foggy day, of course, it just hangs about, and that is where a mechanical extraction plant would be very useful. It would have to be of a tremendous size, because the cubic capacity of a large locomotive shed – I am afraid I cannot work it out in my head straight off – is tremendous, and to change the air, as it would need to be changed to keep it clear, would mean a very big mechanical extraction plant and fans.

As to the mechanical extraction of clinker: the clinker in a fire-box is hard and lumpy, and it would be a practical impossibility to devise a vacuum extractor that would handle that stuff. A lot of the ashes that come from the fire-box of an engine are sold to builders for the purpose of making roads, paths and foundations, and they are in big lumps, as big as a sheet of newspaper, or some of them are. No vacuum plant would pick them up. Smoke-box ashes are quite a different story, and we did have for some time at Old Oak Common a vacuum extracting plant, but that was a fixture, and unless the engine was positioned just in the right spot it could not be used. It was effective; it did the job quite quickly; but it was very, very dirty, although a water spray was fixed at the end of it. This extraction plant consisted of a long horizontal arm pivoted at the centre on a fixed column, one end of the arm going into the smoke-box and the other end being over a wagon on an adjoining road. A steam ejector fitted in the arm would suck up the ashes in the smoke-box and shoot them along the tube into the wagon at the other end. If the wind happened to be in the south or south-west, the tube cleaners were reluctant to use it as they got smothered. If it was blowing the other way and all the dust went over the stock in the yard, that did not matter. (Laughter.)

The other point about the deterioration of engines. We try to avoid having engines standing about outside awaiting repairs, and those were the ones you meant, I think, Mr. Dean, when you were talking?

MR. DEAN – Yes.

MR. KERRY – Those engines you see standing outside the shed are usually awaiting acceptance into the factory, and the idea which the Chief Mechanical Engineer is aiming at is to get an engine straight from a running shed to the factory without any waiting time. At the present time this is not possible because of shortage of staff in running sheds and factories. I do not think it would be desirable, nor do I think it would be economic, to provide covered accommodation for storing these engines.

MR. SMITH (Paddington) – I have got to thank Mr. Kerry for this very pleasant lecture he has given to us, and, like Mr. Cameron, as a member of the operating department of the Chief Mechanical Engineer, and knowing something of the inside working of the sheds, I found the paper – actually I read it in draft – to be so comprehensive as to make it hard to find questions to put to the lecturer. I feel, however, there were some salient features which should be obvious to those who have listened to the lecture, and one important one seems to me to be the fact that we have had mentioned a considerable number of different grades of men in the forty-eight hour shed staff. We have had mentioned the coalman, the fire-dropper, the tube-cleaner, the boiler-washer and the lighter-up. There are a large number of people who have lesser duties to perform – the ash-loader, the boiler-filler, and so on – and I think when one considers the very, very large number of different grades that there are working at a shed, out of the total figure which Mr. Kerry quoted in respect of the 48-hour staff, then it must be obvious that at any time on the shed there must be a comparatively small number in each grade. I bring this out because of very serious operating difficulties which have occurred from time to time due to the absence of, possibly only one or two men in a specific grade during a particular shift. Very considerable difficulties have arisen because of the absence of these one or two men. Although many of these grades may be considered rough and little above that of a labourer's job, nevertheless they are each key jobs and have a definite bearing on the preparation and servicing of a locomotive. I was wondering if Mr. Kerry could give this meeting some indication of what happens if, say, on a given night – it usually happens on a night – we have, possibly, half our fire-dropping strength turn out, and perhaps on that same night we have only half our coalmen turn out? How is the organisation at the shed adjusted to deal with such difficulties which are arising when the engine is in its primary stage, just arrived on shed and

FORM No. 20.   GREAT WESTERN RAILWAY.—LOCOMOTIVE DEPARTMENT.

Coal Consumption Account........................*Division.*   *Four Weeks ended*....................*190*...

Coaling Station.	Running.		Lighting-up Furnaces.		Offices and E'men's Rooms.	Factory Expenses.	Shop Stationary Engine.	Smiths' Fires.	Pumping Engine and Water A/c.			Carriage and Wagon Dept.	Gas Works.		Traffic Dept.			Total Cwts.
	Engines.	Rail Motors.	Engines.	Motors.									Coal.	Oil.	Hydraulics, Hoists, &c.	Steam Cranes.	Steam Boats.	

needing servicing before going in for other preparation duties and leaving the shed again? Mr. Kerry probably has a very adequate answer.

I would also like to make this observation. It was pleasant to see slides showing clean engine sheds and clean engines. I would impress on those who do know the conditions of an engine shed that those illustrations are very different from what we do find now, and that the staff engaged in the sheds have got, to my mind, a filthy and unpleasant job.

MR. KERRY – The filling up of vacancies rests with the foreman, who may have various ways of getting over the difficulty. Pre-war we had a full complement of cleaners who could be used for shed duties, and it was general that at the beginning of each shift, at six, two and ten, the senior cleaners who were not booked up for firing would be watching the shed staff booking on duty to see who was absent, and if Bill Smith, the fire-dropper, or Jack Jones, the coalman had not turned up the senior cleaner was round at the foreman's office at high speed and telling the foreman, 'So-and-so has not arrived. That is my job for to-day', because it gave him extra money. We have not got the cleaners now, but we have tried to get over the difficulty by having physically suitable shed labourers booked on the various shifts who are capable of performing any shed operation and can fill any vacancy in emergency. It is not always possible to do that. If we have not sufficient men to book on as spare or stand-by men, then we have to withdraw men from other less essential jobs, and the cleaning up and the sweeping of the shed has to be neglected in order that the main servicing operations of coaling and fire-dropping can be carried out. At Old Oak Common we have six coalmen on each shift. If one man fails to come in we have lost a sixth of our potential output for that shift. If we have two coalmen failing to turn up we have lost one-third of our potential output. Unless those men can be replaced, we can say that instead of putting on 170 or 180 tons of coal on a shift it is coming down to 120 or even 100 tons.

I am glad Mr. Smith mentioned the slides. I should have said when we had the interior views of the sheds on the screen that those photographs were taken, certainly in the case of the round shed at Ebbw Junction, before the shed had been occupied or used at all. For that reason, that slide was about forty years old, but it gave an illustration of what the shed was like in its very best condition before any engine had been inside it.

CHAIRMAN – Ladies and Gentleman, I do not want to damp down the enthusiasm of others who may wish to join in this debate, but I feel that a number of you may have a journey to make this evening and be confronted with transport difficulties arising from what happens to the engines in the sheds under difficult weather conditions. (*Laughter.*)

I think the residue of my function this evening must be discharged in this way. Firstly, to congratulate the several speakers upon the clarity of their thought, the readiness of their expression and the obvious interest they have all displayed in the subject. Secondly, to congratulate Mr. Kerry upon his replies. When I find

myself in the position of giving a paper I always try to give all the answers at the end. It gives me time to think. But Mr. Kerry is so much a master of his subject that he can produce answers on spontaneous reaction, and in language which even the Goods Department can understand. (*Laughter.*) I do most warmly congratulate Mr. Kerry on his answers to the debate. I always think that the real test of a paper is whether a man can stand up to questions? I think he has stood up to them excellently, and I think you will all agree with me we have had a most informative and instructive evening. (Applause.)

The meeting terminated with a vote of thanks to the Chairman.

The Swindon Engineering Society discoursed at length upon Great Western running procedures. The *Transactions* for 1906–1907 reveal the great complexity of the work and the close detail control exerted. Everything was recorded, on forms and documents precisely defined. The 'Coal Stack Book' was particularly imposing, a system which could account almost for the very dust off the coal stage floor. A packet of fags to the coalmen could still work wonders, however, an ancient system to confound the labyrinthine 'Coal Account'. Witness its operation, through Simpson's exhaustive dissertation:

COAL ACCOUNTS, – Amount required at each depôt arrived at from actual experience, and a distribution list compiled in Chief Running Superintendent's Office for guidance of Coal Distribution Inspector in coal district.

FORM 16 – Daily advice of coal invoiced to each depôt, station, and date inserted in Divisional Office as wagons are received. Details transferred to Form 17, and completed Form 16 then forwarded to Chief Running Superintendent.

A daily telegraphic advice is sent to Chief Coal Inspector at Pontypool Road from large depôts, but at the smaller places a printed form is sent at each week end, shewing number of wagons sent away during week, colliery to which they were sent, and number on hand. This acts as a further guide to distribution in addition to list previously mentioned.

FORM 18. – Daily return of wagons on hand, received and forwarded. Only guide to stock on hand other than that in stack. Details of wagons received transferred to book, Form 19; forms then passed forward to Running Superintendent.

A book shewing 'wagons received' is kept, columns being provided for date, station, wagon number, and contents. Particulars abstracted from Form 18; station and date entered on Form 16. From this book a ready and valuable means is obtained of tracing wagons which may get out of course.

FORM 17. – Four-weekly statement compiled and retained in Divisional Office. Dates received, number of wagons, and weight of contents entered in column on left-hand side of form. A column is provided for each station, where the weight of coal in wagons sent to different stations is recorded.

Numbers and weights of wagons advised as despatched to division each day entered together, and a daily total of quantity made. The weight of coal in each wagon is shewn in station column to which it is sent. Quantity of coal despatched to division, also each depôt in the division, either daily or monthly, can then be readily arrived at. At each coaling place a book is provided, framed with spaces for wagon number, quantity of coal put on, number of engine, and engineman's signature. This book is in duplicate, one portion being sent to Divisional Office, the other being retained at the station for reference.

All coal received at each depôt has to be accounted for on this form, enginemen signing for that used on engines daily, and a weekly form sent in, certified by foreman, for any used for other purposes. Coal put to stack is also shewn daily. A daily total is made of that used on running engines, which is transferred to book framed to suit. Daily totals are cast at end of week, and figure obtained is used for calculating wages of coalmen paid at piecework rate, etc.

Particulars of coal used for purposes other than running – e.g., pumping engines, cabins, offices, etc., transferred to a manuscript form (Sundry Coal Account). Details of coal put or taken from

coal stack entered in coal stack book. Forms then passed over to Accounts Office.

COAL STACK BOOK. – Printed book giving date coal put to stack, name of colliery, wagon number, and weight of coal. The details are abstracted from daily coal return. Totals cast and stock arrived at at end of each four-weekly period. Books kept at each foreman's office and at Divisional Office, one acting as a check on the other. Separate account kept for each stack.

FORM 20. – Monthly return of all coal used in division, giving particulars of charges, sent to Accounts Office. Compiled from returns previously mentioned.

COAL SUPPLY: STOCK ON HAND. – Required for statements for Board entries made for each Loco. Depôt, giving estimated weekly consumption, stock in hand 6 p.m. on the Saturday on ground and in wagons, also quantity put to or taken from stock during week. Supplied to Running Superintendent weekly.

FORM 21 BOOK. – Furnished from each depôt weekly. Last-mentioned return stock on hand weekly compiled from this. At the end of four-week period it is passed forward to Accounts Office with Form 22, in which it is incorporated.

FORM 22. – Compiled from forms mentioned. Forwarded at end of four-weekly period to Accounts Office.

FORM 23. – Compiled in Accounts Office and sent to Divisional Office, but it is usual to compile a trial statement in Divisional

---

FORM No. 21.

GREAT WESTERN RAILWAY.

LOCOMOTIVE DEPARTMENT.

....Station,

................................190

Monthly Return of ACTUAL Stock of UNCHARGED Coal and Coke on hand at Midnight on Saturday.. 190

	COAL.		COKE.		REMARKS.
	Tons	Cwt	Tons	Cwt	
Stacked (Coal 40, Coke 80, cubic feet per ton) ..					
On Coal Stage, and in Tube or Baskets, not charged					
Standing in Tenders, not charged					
Ditto in Wagons :—					

No.	Tons	Cwts	No.	Tons	Cwts
			Brought forward		
Carried forward ...			Total Uncharged) Actual Stock f		

Mr............ ....
Loco. Superintendent.

....Coalman.

....Foreman.

....Station.

To be sent to Swindon on Thursday, after the close of each four-weekly period.

FORM No. 22.

G. W. R.—LOCO. DEPT.

....District.   Four Weeks ending.................190...

COAL RETURN.

ADVICES		STATION.	RECEIPTS.	STOCKS (Cwts.) Saturday, 6 p.m.			
Date.	Cwts.		Cwts.	Stacks.	On Stage and Tenders (uncharged).	In Wagons.	TOTAL.
M.							
Tu.							
W.							
Th.							
F.							
S.							
M.							
Tu.							
W.							
Th.							
F.							
S.							
M.							
Tu.							
W.							
Th.							
F.							
S.		Total Received					
M.		Add—					
Tu.		*Wagons advised, but not received					
W.		*Detailed List to accompany Return.					
Th.		Less—					
F.		Wagons advised, but not received,					
S.		previous Return..					

TAKEN FROM STACK.		ADDED TO STOCK.	
Station.	Cwts.	Station.	Cwts.

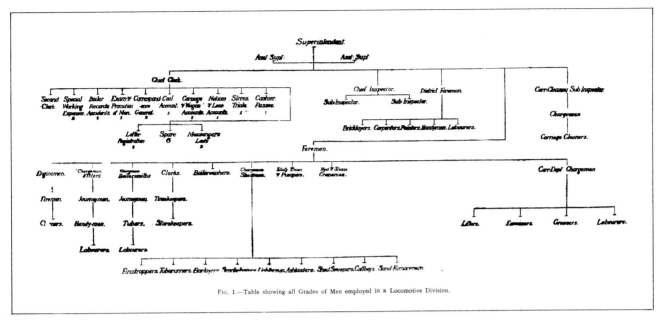

Fig. 1.—Table showing all Grades of Men employed in a Locomotive Division.

Office and look into any serious differences before rendering monthly returns. The undercharge or overcharge is due very largely to the fact that it is impossible to retail coal out to measure which has previously been advised by actual weight in bulk.

NOTE – Quantities are, unless otherwise stated in forms shewn, in cwts.

Procedures in the 'Ideal Shed' were detailed thus:

THE DIVISIONAL SYSTEM. – It is the work of a Divisional Superintendent that will be dealt with particularly in this paper. A sort of genealogical tree is shown in Fig. 1. From this will be seen the chain of responsibility from the Superintendent down to the call-boy, and we will consider the duties of each in detail.

It will simplify matters if we trace the operations of the staff from the time an engine approaches a running shed to its going out again to work a train.

EXAMINATION BY ENGINEMEN. – Upon arrival outside the shed, the engineman, or engine-turner who relieves him, should make a careful examination of engine, and, before going off duty, book all the defects he discovers. The engine is then left at or near the coal stage in charge of the shed turner or, as he is sometimes called, pilotman, who sets it in the proper position for coaling.

COALING. – The engineman or fireman has, before leaving his engine, locked up his tools, and chalked on one of the boxes the quantity of coals he requires for his next trip.

QUALITIES OF COALS. – As a rule, the best bituminous South Wales coal is used on engines intended for fast and heavy passenger trains, and a mixture of hard Yorkshire, North Wales, or Staffordshire, with second grade South Wales coal for trains of less importance. What is known in South Wales as smokeless steam coal is of no use whatever for locomotive purposes, on account of its dry character. It is very rich in carbon, and its calorific value is exceedingly high. With a steady, continuous draught, such as is obtained in steamboats, it gives the best of results; but in locomotives, where the draught is intermittent, the punching effect of the blast produces the same result as poking an anthracite fire. On the other hand, when a bituminous coal is used, the punching of the blast has the desired effect of keeping the fire open, and turning the binding qualities of the coal to the best advantage. Hence it is that the finest coals we obtain from South Wales are those cut in the Western valleys of Monmouthshire and others, such as Cilely, of similar quality. The Northern coals have different characteristics altogether. These are not so rich in carbon, but more so in hydrogen, and are therefore swifter burning. For light work, the hard coal makes an ideal fuel, and a mixture with a slower burning coal, such as Cilely, gives excellent results for heavy work. Instructions are given to the coalmen to put on suitable coal for particular trains, but, owing to the inadequate accommodation on the stage, or irregular supply of first and second grade coal, it sometimes, though fortunately not very often, happens that a shunting engine gets best coal, whilst an express engine gets such a quality as to render the lives of the engineman and fireman not exactly a bed of roses. This results in loss of time during journey, which involves much correspondence and explanation. The cost of coaling locomotives varies from 2¼d. to 3½d. per ton. The lowest prices are paid at up-to-date tipping stages, where the wagon flaps can be dropped clear of the stage, and the tops of the tip wagons are no higher than the bottoms of the coal trucks. The coal can then be practically tumbled out of the trucks into the tip wagons, and labour is reduced to a minimum. The highest prices obtain at those stages where the coal is shovelled into tubs, the tops of which usually stand as high as the tops of the wagons, and the tubs have to be lifted by a hand crane before being tipped on to the tenders or bunkers. This is obviously a two-handed job, and accounts for the high cost of coaling. It will be seen, therefore, how necessary it is to have a well designed coal stage, both on account of the cost and expedition in dealing with the engines. A good, roomy platform is also necessary, as this enables the coalmen to fill a large number of tip wagons whilst there are no engines about, and facilitates the proper mixing of the coal.

The cost of coal on the GWR system amounts to more than half a million pounds per annum; hence it is an important part of the Chief Loco. Superintendent's duty to advise his Directors as to the making of contracts, and the Chief of the Running Department exercises an equally important duty in arranging for the proper distribution of the coal. It might be possible to find on the market a particular coal which would give very good all round results, but if a large Railway Company purchased that coal, and no other, the effect would be to enhance its price, and would put the Railway Company at the mercy of the market in the case of a strike or other dislocation of trade at the particular group of collieries from which the coal was drawn. It is, therefore, good policy to obtain the supply from as large a number of areas as possible. This, also, ensures getting the best possible value for money.

CLEANING SMOKEBOX. – After the engine has been coaled, it is taken by the shed turner beyond the coal stage, where the turner's mate, or a boy appointed for the purpose, cleans out the smokebox, and, to prevent smothering the engine with dust, the ashes are plentifully sprinkled with water. In up-to-date sheds hydrants are fixed for this purpose, and in some cases a shallow pit is provided, into which the ashes are dumped.

FIRE DROPPING. – The engine is then taken to the fire pit, where one fire dropper stands on the footplate and another in the pit. A couple of firebars are either pulled up by the former or knocked up by the latter, and the fire is pushed out into the ashpan, by means of a pricker, by the man on the footplate, whilst the one in the pit waters it from a hosepipe and rakes it out. At some sheds the practice is to 'clean the fire' – that is, to shovel all (or as much as can be got at) of the clinker out through the firehole by means of a clinker shovel. This is really the better, though more costly, because the firebox is not cooled down so suddenly as it is by 'dropping'; consequently there is less liability to cause leakage of tubes, stays, and foundation rings. When the Author was in charge of Stourbridge shed most of the engines at that station had foundation rings of only $\frac{1}{2}''$ in thickness, and, as they were constantly troubled with leaky corners, the practice of dropping was abandoned, and that of cleaning the fires adopted, with most excellent results, as the leaky foundation rings were practically

cured. At Stourbridge the engines did only a small mileage, consequently the amount of dirt and clinker in each firebox after a day's work was inconsiderable, and, as they only had about 25 engines steamed per day, there were no difficulties in the way of fire cleaning. The results justified the slight extra expenditure. When, however, the Author was appointed assistant to Mr. Read at Newport, he found the fireboxes at Pontypool Road, after a few days' work, so full of dirt and clinker that it was impracticable to clean the fires. As an experiment, he timed one of the shunting firemen, and found that, by working hard, this man cleaned a box in 20 minutes, and, even after that, a turner pulled out about six shovels full from the back corners. The conclusion the Author came to was that fire cleaning was advantageous, but not always practicable, more especially where there were 100 or more engines steamed every day.

A careful engineman always brings his engine to the shed with the fire as low as possible, and with very little unconsumed fuel in the firebox; but the more clinker there is in the box at the end of a day's work the higher is the proportion of unconsumed fuel, and this constitutes an absolute waste. Unimportant as this fact appears, there is no doubt that it has some bearing on high consumption.

TUBE RUNNING. – After the fire has been dropped or cleaned, as the case may be, the engine is taken to the shed to be stabled.

Firedropping on *County Wicklow*. This was achingly hard work, dragging out through the firehole the hot and smoking firebox residue. This is an exceptional occasion, fires were thrown out by the firepit, near the coal stage and dumping it so close to the shed would normally bring the foreman's wrath. It was, after all, dangerous and dirty so near the building and consequent removal was made awkward and time-consuming.

British Railways

If the shed happens to be a straight one, it is necessary to have the tubes 'run' at once, because, after it has been put into position, another engine may be put in front of it, and render the operation of tube cleaning impracticable. If, however, the shed is a round one, the operation may be performed at a convenient time to the tube cleaners. To run a set of tubes takes from 40 to 60 minutes. The tubes are cleaned by means of a long rod, about $\frac{3}{8}''$ diameter, with an eye in the end of it through which is threaded a piece of canvas.

Cleaning tubes by means of a steam jet has been in vogue for some time at Paddington, and, it would appear, with good results; although, when a blocked tube is encountered, steam and soot blow back into the cleaner's face. Steam cleaning in large sheds is more economical than rod cleaning, as it takes only 20 minutes or so to clean a set of tubes by this method, and the tubes are swept out very much better; but the corks which form on the tube ends in the firebox are not so effectively removed as by a rod. Corked tubes prevent an engine steaming much more than do dirty tubes, and it is just a question whether a small amount of soot uniformly distributed in a tube does not rather assist the generation of steam, and maintains the tube at a more uniform temperature, thus reducing the risk of leakage.

On the whole, therefore, rod cleaning is more efficient, but steam cleaning is the cheaper. At Paddington a small vertical boiler supplies the steam, and this system is much better than having a cock on each engine, as all careful enginemen bring their engines to the shed low in fire and low in steam, so that by the time an engine is coaled and the fire cleaned there is not always enough steam left for tube cleaning.

CLEANING. – The cleaner or cleaners next take the engine in hand. The best system of cleaning is, in the Author's opinion, for each cleaner to follow his own engine. He then takes more interest in his work, and is alone responsible for the cleanliness of the particular engine he follows, and if the engineman finds he does his work well, every encouragement is given him.

Gang cleaning, on the other hand, affords no special inducement to a lad to exert himself. In fact, he takes about as much interest in his work as a man takes in a hired bicycle. The best *method* of cleaning is that inaugurated on the GWR by Mr. Armstrong at Paddington, and adopted to a great extent in the Swindon Division. Mr. Armstrong has his engines cleaned with cleaning oil and water, and uses absolutely no tallow, as he considers that it has a detrimental effect on the varnish. In the Swindon Division, generally speaking, a little tallow is put on the cleaning plates of the barrel and firebox only, these being the hot parts. The quantity of stores used varies according to the size of the engine cleaned. The following tabulated statement shews, approximately, the stores allowed: –

Class of Engine	Sponge or Cotton Cloths each	Cotton Waste, lbs.	Tallow oz.	Cleaning Oil, pints
0–6–0 T	8 to 12	1 to $1\frac{1}{2}$	$1\frac{1}{4}$	$\frac{1}{4}$
0–6–0	12	$1\frac{1}{2}$	$1\frac{1}{4}$	$\frac{1}{4}$
2–4–0	16	2	$1\frac{1}{4}$	$\frac{1}{4}$
4–4–0 T	16	2	$1\frac{1}{4}$	$\frac{1}{4}$
2–2–2	16	2	$1\frac{1}{4}$	$\frac{1}{4}$
2–4–0	16	2	$1\frac{1}{4}$	$\frac{1}{4}$
2–4–2 T	24	3	$1\frac{1}{4}$	$\frac{1}{4}$
4–4–2 T	24	3	$1\frac{1}{4}$	$\frac{1}{4}$
4–4–0	23	3	$1\frac{1}{4}$	$\frac{1}{4}$
2–6–0	24	$2\frac{1}{2}$	$1\frac{1}{4}$	$\frac{1}{4}$
2–8–0	32	4	$1\frac{1}{4}$	$\frac{1}{4}$*

* The same stores are allowed for the different types of 'Atlantic' passenger engines.
Two galls. of petroleum are allowed per week to each chargeman to help with the cleaning oil on dirty engines.
Three Bath bricks allowed to each chargeman for each turn of duty, and 3 galls. of cleaning oil, which would average about $\frac{1}{4}$ pint per engine.

BAR LAYING. – If it is not necessary to do any repairs to the firebox, the firebars, which were knocked out by the fire droppers, are laid generally about three hours before the cleaner has finished his work. This is done either with a long pair of tongs from the outside or a bar-boy who goes inside, lays the bars, rakes off the accumulation of ashes from the top of the brick arch, and sweeps the corks off the tube plate. The lighter-up then throws a few shovels full of coal round the box, and afterwards one or two scoops of fire into the centre.

SAND FURNACE. – Many sand furnaces are constructed on wrong principles. These have a firebrick lined furnace, above and below which ovens are fixed, into these the wet sand is thrown, and there lies sodden until all the moisture is eliminated. The sand furnaces used on the GWR have a hot chamber between the furnace and the chimney, and above this chamber there is a receptacle for the wet sand. In the roof of the hot chamber one or more gratings are fixed, through which the sand falls gradually, and is dried thoroughly in detail by the hot gases passing through the chamber. These furnaces are automatic in action, and dry at least five times the quantity of sand as the old fashioned oven furnaces would with the same expenditure of fuel.

LIGHTING UP, – Lighting up is essentially a two-handed job, and in sheds too small to justify the employment of two lighters up on each shift it is usual for the cleaner to carry the fire. On an average, it takes about three hours to make steam; and it is, therefore, usual to light up about four hours before the booked time of train. When steam is up the engineman and fireman take charge of their engine; but of their duties the Author will not now speak, as this branch of running work has already been fully dealt with by Mr. R. H. Smith in the excellent paper he read before this Society last session. But to complete the cycle of shed operations, it may be well to mention that the fireman rakes the ashpan out, fills the sand boxes, attends to glands, and takes water. As a rule, water is taken when the engine is coaling, or having the fire dropped; but, in the case of a saddle tank engine, it is essential that water be taken when the engine is leaving the shed, and not before, because, after standing in a saddle tank for any length of time, the water becomes too hot to be picked up by the injectors.

FORM No. 1.   GREAT WESTERN RAILWAY.

Return of Boilers Washed Out in.....................................District

        W.E. Saturday........................ ....190...

Date.	Station.	Engine.	By whom Washed out.	By whom Examined.	Remarks as to Dirt, &c.

WASHING OUT is a most important operation, and one which should be followed up very closely by the management. Two men comprise a 'set' of washers-out, and a set can wash a boiler out in from two to five hours, according to its size. The washers-out first take out all plugs and hand-hole covers. They then very carefully swill out as much of the deposited sulphates, carbonates, etc., as is possible, this being assisted by a vigorous working with rods. After the scale has been removed, the boiler is examined by means of a light, preferably by a boilersmith, who certifies it as 'clean and in good order.' The plugs are then tallowed or greased with a heavy lubricating oil and replaced, as also are the hand-hole covers and any of the lead joints on the latter which may be defective are renewed. In most divisions the foremen are responsible for the washing out, but in the Swindon Division a return on the form shewn is sent to the Divisional Office weekly by each foreman. These lists give the numbers of all engines washed out, and a book is kept

Britain's railways developed a paternalism of monolithic proportions, a cradle to grave approach for both men and plant, in stark contrast to the diversified industries of today, interdependent upon a multitude of suppliers and contractors. Nothing, however prosaic, was obtained 'outside' that could be supplied centrally or on the railway itself. Victorian railway practice spanned a wealth of peculiar and long-lost trades and skills, practices bound by absolute rules and standards no matter how trifling the article to be produced. Firelighters for engines were a typical example:

Lighting-up of Locomotives

About five hours before an engine is due to leave the shed, a lighter-up will attend to this part of its preparation for the road.

'He will arrive on the footplate with shovel, coal pick, short pricker, fire lighters and oily waste. The first operation (after seeing that there is sufficient water in the boiler) is to break up enough coal to line the sides of the firebox, leaving a space in the centre of the box to place the fire-lighter, which is a frame-work of sticks. Having done this, he ignites the piece of oily waste, which has been inserted into the fire-lighter, and the latter is then placed in the centre of the firebox in the space left for it. In some cases more than one lighter is used, regard being paid to the interval of time before the engine is due off the shed, temperature of the boiler and size of the firebox.

'Medium-sized lumps of coal are next carefully placed around and on top of the lighters, and the dampers are opened. The engine can now be left for about an hour without further attention. When from 40 to 60 lbs pressure is showing on the steam gauge, the lighter-up or steam-raiser will close the dampers and the engine is ready for the fireman when he books on duty.'

The shop illustrated is probably Swindon, though it could be one of the regional wagon shops. Damaged planks and headstocks were discarded as wagons came in for repair, to form the raw material of firelighters. These lads are wagon repair apprentices, obviously posed for some demonstration purpose. The process by which the 'framework of sticks' was arrived at is shown neatly, from the splitting of old planks, to the jig (two types) and the finished article. The 'carrying tube' is an unnecessary refinement, it would after all weigh more on its own than any ten firelighters. Wheelbarrows were always used in the sheds. Similarly, the highly specific 'placing' iron — a fireman's shovel was far more adaptable in the confines of the footplate. The whole process is a demonstration of the principle of putting nothing to waste — the shop is divided by a wall of old lamp oil or paraffin barrels, with sundry bits of wood and iron draped around the wall. Firelighters were made on a far greater scale than this, and a gang of lads would be employed. A shed the size of Slough had them in wagonloads, while Old Oak almost warranted a train. London area firelighters all came from the West London wagon works. *British Railways*

in the Divisional Office which shews at a glance how many days have elapsed since one wash out to another. It has been often found that when an engine fails owing to tubes leaking the failure has occurred after it has run over six trips, and this is due to the dirty condition of the boiler and the concentrated condition of the water, which cause over-heating of the plates. When, therefore, a tube failure occurs the wash-out book is examined, and if it is found that the boiler is fairly clean, the boiler card, to which reference will be made later, is examined, and if it is ascertained that according to the reports the firebox is in good condition, a special examination is made by the chief boilersmith, or, in serious cases, by the Superintendent or one of his assistants, the idea being that no failure can take place without some cause, and the cause may be one or more of the following: –

1. Abuse of the engine in working.
2. Neglect in washing out.
3. Bad workmanship.
4. Indifferent examination.

5. The formation of dirt, generally between the tubes, which cannot be removed by the washers out.

The following up of these matters carefully has had a marked effect on the number of tube failures.

As a rule, each boiler is washed out after running for six working days, but at Reading, where the water is exceptionally hard, five, and, in some cases, only four, trips are allowed.

REPAIRS. – The engineman, before going off duty, books any repairs necessary, and in large sheds it is usual to book fitters' work in one book and boilersmiths in another. The leading fitter and boilersmith then distribute the work among their staffs. These books are ruled as shewn: –

FORM No. 2.

Date.	No. of Engine.	Work required on Engine.	Driver's Signature.	Date Finished.	Fitter's or Boilersmith's Name.	Remarks.	Foreman's Signature.

The Great Western left a wealth of specially posed photographs and their interpretation amounts almost to a minor art form. No. 3607 and its attendant wheelbarrows seem to be an illustration of the efficacy of 'the bundle' compared to scrap timber scoured from all over the shed.　　*British Railways*

Generally speaking, one fitter and labourer can keep ten engines going, so far as small ordinary running repairs are concerned, but the number of boilersmiths and tubers depends not so much on the number of engines as upon the quality of the water used; so that in South Wales, where the water is nearly all 'surface' and comparatively free from impurities, one boilersmith can keep from 50 to 100 boilers going, whereas, in the Swindon Division, quite three times as many men are required. When, however, softening plants are in more general use, it will be possible to fix the number of engines per boilersmith as easily and accurately as for a fitter. At first sight, one would think that the running shed maintenance, so far as fitters' work is concerned, of our very large goods engines would be more costly than that of the small ones, but this is found in practice not to be the case, because, in the first place, the adequate bearing surfaces, padded axleboxes, accessibility of parts for cleaning, oiling, etc., and the good design of details, reduces the amount of fitting work. In the second place, the heavy duty of the big engine boilers very quickly reduces the stay heads and renders necessary heavy firebox repairs, which cannot be undertaken in a running shed under ordinary conditions. In other words, the running life of a big engine is dominated by the boiler, and engines of this sort have to be sent into the factory long before the engine itself is run down – that is, before it has reached that stage of its existence up to which it can be profitably maintained by ordinary running shed fitting. In the Author's opinion, every shed which stables a number of big engines should be furnished with a lift of such capacity that the boilers of these engines could be readily lifted out of the frames and the stays below the fire line renewed. The Author further feels confident that if this were done we should have no difficulty in getting upwards of 60,000 miles out of our large goods engines, and great economy effected.

Although the engineman is responsible for the upkeep of his engine, examinations are made periodically by the fitters and boilersmiths.

BOILER REPAIRS. – The practice in the Swindon Division is for a boilersmith to make a thorough examination of each boiler once a month, generally when it is washed out. He can then examine the water ways and is better able to test the stays, since the boiler is empty. In addition to the thorough monthly examination, the stays of each boiler which has a higher working pressure than 150 lbs. per square inch are hammer-tested once a week. A report of all boilers examined is made out weekly by the boilersmith on the form shewn. This is signed by the foreman and boilersmith.

The forms are sent to the Divisional Office, and are dealt with by the clerk as shown on the diagram. He enters the dates of the examinations in a book, which shows whether a longer period than that specified has elapsed between each examination. He then reads carefully over each report, and ticks off those which record 'clean and in good order.' Once a week he reads the reports to the Superintendent, or, in his absence, to one of the Assistant Superintendents, who enters the condition of each boiler on a card (Fig. 3). It will be seen by the system of hieroglyphics a large amount of information is compressed into a very small space, and the whole history of a boiler is recorded from the time it leaves the factory up to the time it goes in again. The specimen card shewn is that for engine No. 2762. This engine left the factory on the 4th March 1903. Nothing of note occurred to the box during that year, but on the 13th January 1904, the stay heads were slightly reduced. Fifteen new stays were put in on the 27th of January 1904. The stays were reported reduced on the 19th April, and on the 12th May a crack had developed in the right-hand flange of the tube plate; also, the top flange of back plate had dropped down near the second crown bars. On the 23rd August the tubes were dirty, and the casing plates were corroded near the foundation ring. It will be noticed there is a discrepancy in the sizes of the crack in the right-hand flange of tube plate, the May examination shewing this as 5" long and 19" from foundation, whilst that of August gives it as $5\frac{1}{4}$" long and 21" from foundation. These figures cannot be reconciled, but there is some excuse for the boilersmith, because it is most difficult to accurately determine the length and position of corner cracks without very carefully scraping the surface of the copper from the foundation ring upwards. On the 30th August, 1904, 84 new tubes were put in to replace those taken out to facilitate the removal of dirt, and this time, also, the sides were found to be slightly bulged. Twelve more stays were put in on the 11th April, 1905, and on the 12th September another crack had developed on the tube plate, this time in the left-hand flange, and the sides which had been previously reported as 'slightly bulged' were reported as 'bulged'. On the 17th October the tubes were again reported dirty, and after the engine had been kept running as long as it consistently could be in this condition, it was sent to the factory for general repairs on the 31st January, 1906. This card gives a good idea of the wear and tear of a locomotive firebox in ordinary service.

In addition to the ordinary shed examinations others are made by the boiler inspector, who is directly under the Chief of the Running Department. He pays flying visits all over the line, and generally selects the worst boilers for inspection. He renders excellent service and, owing to his wide range of operations, he is often able to give good advice to the local boilersmiths.

Generally speaking, the stays give more cause for anxiety in a running shed than any other part of the boiler. Stay heads reduce very much more quickly when hard water is used, and this is due to the fact that the temperature of the firebox plates is raised very much higher. Personally, the Author does not consider that a reduced stay head *per se* is in any way dangerous, the only useful function of the head being to protect the edge of the hole in the plate through which the stay is screwed. It is obvious that, with a firebox plate of reasonable thickness, the shearing strength of the thread is greater than the tensile strength of the stay. Consequently, if the stay is tight in the hole, it is perfectly safe, even without a head at all. Firebox plates, of course, reduce particularly below the fire line, but this reduction is much less marked in the immediate vicinity of the stays than it is between them, so that,

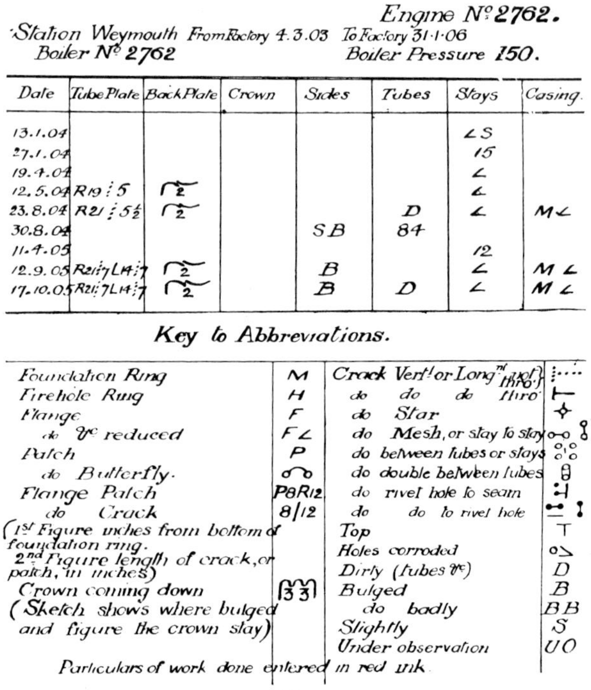
Engine No. 2762.
Station Weymouth From Factory 4.3.03 To Factory 31.1.06
Boiler No. 2762 Boiler Pressure 150.

Date	Tube Plate	Back Plate	Crown	Sides	Tubes	Stays	Casing.
13.1.04						∠S	
27.1.04						15	
19.4.04						∠	
12.5.04	R19 : 5	2				∠	
23.8.04	R21 : $5\frac{1}{2}$	2			D	∠	M∠
30.8.04				SB	84		
11.4.05						12	
12.9.05	R21 : 7 L14 : 7	2		B		∠	M∠
17.10.05	R21 : 7 L14 : 7	2		B	D	∠	M∠

Key to Abbreviations.

Foundation Ring	M	Crack Vert! or Long! not thro'	
Firehole Ring	H	do do do thro'	
Flange	F	do Star	
do &c reduced	F∠	do Mesh, or stay to stay	
Patch	P	do between tubes or stays	
do Butterfly.		do double between tubes	
Flange Patch	P8R12	do rivet hole to seam	
do Crack	8/12	do do to rivet hole	
(1st Figure inches from bottom of foundation ring. 2nd Figure length of crack, or patch, in inches)		Top	T
		Holes corroded	
		Dirty (tubes &c)	D
Crown coming down (Sketch shows where bulged and figure the crown stay)	3 3	Bulged	B
		do badly	BB
		Slightly	S
		Under observation	UO

Particulars of work done entered in red ink.

FIG. 3.

The dull task of washing out was ceaseless work and most sheds had a special area set aside, the universally termed 'washout'.

L & GRP, courtesy David & Charles

even in an old firebox, there should be always plenty of thread. The real danger of reduced stay heads lays in the fact that when the head is gone, the hole corrodes, and the thread is ruined. And again, with long or heavy service, the plates bulge between the stays, and this tends to open the stay holes on the water side of the plate. These two evils render stays unsafe, so that it is always advisable whenever the plates are badly bulged or the holes badly corroded, to renew the stays immediately, or send the engine to the factory. If stays leak when the boiler is well up in steam, this indicates that they are loose in the holes, but mere leakage when the fire is out, and the steam going back, should cause no concern; but if, when so leaking a stay be struck, and the water gushes out more freely, we may conclude it is loose, and therefore unsafe. Broken stays sometimes give trouble, and these are generally due, not to tensile strain, but to the bending moment set up by the expansion of the plates. In the old-fashioned boilers, broken stays are usually found in top front corners, but in modern boilers in the curved part of the side plates. With pressures varying from 150 lbs. to 225 lbs. per square inch, a broken stay is a source of considerable danger. Hence it is necessary to hammer test each stay in boilers working at these high pressures at least once a week. Up to within the last few years the Author had never seen a broken stay unless it had snapped off next the casing, and this is where one would naturally expect the breakages to occur, having regard to the nature of the strains put upon the stays; but latterly several had come under his notice broken either next to, or actually inside, the firebox plate – clearly indicating that some causes have been operating which have seriously weakened the copper. This weak-

ening can only be attributed to the high temperatures to which the stays are subjected.

Leaky tubes provide more work for running shed boilersmiths than anything else. Leakage is brought on by one cause, and one cause only, *i.e.*, 'high temperature.' Most people would put this differently, and say, 'sudden expansion and contraction,' but, in the Author's opinion, this reason is not accurate. It is quite possible to have sudden expansion, or sudden contraction, or both, without leakage; and it is possible for the tube plate to be raised slowly to a very high temperature, and lowered again slowly, when the tubes will leak because the plate has been distorted by the high temperature. If we take a plain piece of copper plate, or bar, make it red hot, and then cool it, either slowly or suddenly, it will contract, and resume its original shape and dimensions; that is, of course, if it is of uniform structure. It does this, because its expansion has been in every way free and unrestricted. These conditions do not obtain in a locomotive firebox, for it is more or less rigidly tied to the casing, and the expansion is, in consequence, restricted. The copper has to 'go' somewhere, and as it cannot 'go' freely it becomes distorted. It never 'comes back' quite to its initial condition, but in a clean boiler, well designed and constructed, the slight distortion of the plates will have very little detrimental effect except around those stay holes which are below the fire line. If the temperature has been excessive the distortion will be of such a serious character as to make it impossible for the copper to assume anything like its original condition when the plates cool down a little, and, consequently, the tubes, in particular, leak. It must be admitted that sudden cooling will aggravate matters, but the real origin of the mischief is the high temperature. The object, therefore, of both the designers of locomotive boilers and those responsible for running and maintaining them should be to so arrange matters that it would be impossible to attain excessive temperatures. Some few years ago it became the practice to crowd as many tubes as possible into the tube plate to obtain greater heating surface, and this involved a mesh of only $\frac{7}{16}$ths of an inch. The result was that the circulation was choked, and steam was generated so rapidly at the tube plate that the water was literally forced away from it. This caused the plate to become over-heated, and, consequently, leaky tubes and cracked meshes were an every-day experience. It may be accepted as an axiom that a cracked mesh indicates too narrow a mesh, and a wider one would increase the efficiency of the boiler, although it decreased the heating surface. The meshes near the top corners of the tube plate should be wider than other meshes, because at three points the expansion of the plates meet with the more or less rigid resistance of the side and top flanges. In Mr. Churchward's large boilers the area of the firebox tube plate has been enlarged to the limit, and the true secret of efficiency has been exploited, that is, free circulation. If it were only possible to carry the sides of the firebox down straight instead of curving them inwards to clear the frames, we should have a boiler perfect in every respect as a steam generator. A boiler may be perfect in design, but even then trouble may arise if it does not receive proper and careful attention. Washing out must be done regularly and thoroughly. If any dirt forms between the tubes it should be at once removed, and this can only be done by taking a few tubes out. The stays must also receive careful attention, particularly those below the fire line, and any which are broken or defective at once renewed either by ordinary or steam-tight stays.

In the Swindon Division, dirt forms very quickly in the water spaces between the tubes owing to the hard water drawn from the chalk and Oolitic formations, so that it is necessary to take out and replace a large number of tubes annually. There are about 490 engines in the Division, and in 1903 14,871 tubes were renewed at an approximate cost of £3,718. In 1904 10,735 tubes were renewed at a cost of £2,684. In 1905 8,309 tubes at a cost of £2,077. It will be seen that the cash saving on the transaction for 1905 as compared with 1903 was £1,641; and if Mr. Churchward continues his present policy of providing softening plants at the various watering stations the expenditure under this head will almost reach vanishing point. Since 1903 steel tubes exclusively have been used on the GWR, and have given excellent results except, in one respect, that is, many of the tubes corrode badly circumferentially, generally close up to the smokebox tube plate, and 'pit' badly also. The same trouble with steel tubes was noticed about twelve years ago but, strange to say, the furrowing took place at the firebox end.

The practice of ferruling has been almost abandoned on the GWR, the tubes being rolled and beaded, our present method being rendered practicable by the use of mild steel tubes.

Corner patches are sometimes put on in Running Sheds. These should be studded on by countersunk fine threaded studs, and the stud holes should be tapped through both patch and plate. It is of no use putting a corner patch on unless it extends down to the foundation ring, because, if this is not done, the fire, continually impinging on the bottom seam of the patch, burns it and causes it to leak. Half tube plates were at one time put in on the GWR, and are even now on some railways, but there is no real economy in this, because the tubes never remain staunch, and the tube plate becomes distorted so badly in the seam as to become almost dangerous.

ENGINE REPAIRS. – Turning our attention now to the fitters' work, we find that the chief causes of failure on the road are hot boxes and hot big ends. Hot boxes may be due to any one or combination of the following circumstances: –

1. Shortness of oil.

2. Dirty trimmings or pads.
3. Bad fitting – *i.e.*, too tight on collars or not properly bedded down on the crown.
4. Bad adjustment of springs, throwing too much weight on a particular box.
5. Dirty white metal.
6. Box not made hot enough when the metal is run into the recesses, causing the metal to be laminated, and, therefore, easily 'picked up' by the journal.
7. Boxes fitting too tightly in horns.
8. Dust, when boxes are not shielded and padded.
9. Water getting into boxes and preventing trimmings from syphoning.
10. Hot weather lowering the viscosity of oil.
11. Running tender first for long distances with ordinary soft journals.
12. Bad design of box.

It will be seen that hot boxes are preventable, and the remedies are in most cases obvious, although, once the metal has been disturbed, it is most difficult to assign the cause of heating.

No bearing surface should be in contact with its journal, but the two should be perfectly separated by a film of oil, and this can only be attained by using oil of sufficient viscosity. Consideration of the conditions under which this film is caused and maintained led Mr. Dewrance to design a box which took its oil from the sides instead of the crown. The universal practice has been to have a single groove in the crown, but Mr. Dewrance abandoned this, and substituted two grooves, one on either side of the crown, his idea being to have a perfect film instead of a broken one at the crown, where experiment has shewn that the highest fluid pressure is attained. This arrangement for a box, whose only function is to 'carry,' is fairly good, but in the case of driving boxes fitted to axles the wheels of which are coupled, the idea is, in the Author's opinion, wrong. In the case of an ordinary 'carrying' axle, the weight supported by the journal acts vertically downwards, and to cut a groove in the crown would mean taking away the bearing surface from the very place where it is required. On the other hand, owing to the thrust and pull of the connecting rod in the case of a driving box, very much more pressure is thrown on the brass at the sides than at the crown, and, with side grooves, the brass is robbed of bearing surface just where it is most wanted. Hence, driving boxes should have one groove only, and that one in the crown. Even in 'carrying' boxes it is usual to give only a small amount of bearing surface at the crown, and, if two grooves are provided, this surface lies between the inner edges of the grooves. Below the outer edges of the grooves the brass is eased, and, therefore, there is a great risk of losing the oil, owing to its running out of the groove, and between the eased part of the box and the journal. The practice of cutting oil ways to convey oil from the groove is to be deprecated, because they are not necessary, and certainly facilitate the blockage of the groove with metal if the box runs hot.

HOT BIG ENDS are caused by: –
1. Shortness of oil.
2. Plug trimmings too tight.
3. Plug trimmings too short, not reaching to the journal, and thus delivering the oil between the strap and brasses instead of on the journal.
4. Insufficient side play.
5. Little ends set up badly, causing spring on rod.
6. Dirty or laminated metal.
7. Increase of boiler pressure, causing too much pressure per square inch of bearing area.
8. Brasses not allowed sufficient bearing surface by fitter.
9. Collar radii of journal too large, thus robbing the bearing surface.

The importance of giving ample bearing surface to a big end will be realised when we consider that the pressure on a crank journal

Traditional pose at Old Oak.

is, in many instances, much greater than the weight on an axlebox. There is no doubt but that the reciprocating character of the pressure is the great safeguard of big ends, because this gives time for the oil to form a proper film on each brass alternately before the pressure is applied. The correct method of fitting big and little end keys is worthy of note. These should on no account be allowed to bear in the straps, and if the key holes in the straps are cut back there will never be trouble with loose keys or shouldered and broken bolts.

INJECTORS. – Injectors, clack boxes, and injector pipes require constant attention. Feed pipes drawing air frequently cause the failure of injectors, and although this is so obvious it is not by any means commonly known.

EXAMINATIONS. – Periodical examinations are made of the valves and pistons, feeds and strums, steam and vacuum brake apparatus, and safety valves. A sharp eye is kept on the tyre flanges by foremen, enginemen, and leading fitters, and as soon as a leading flange becomes at all sharp or deep, it should be trimmed up on a ground lathe or by a tool which can be secured to the leading brake hanger or in some other suitable manner. Whenever a big end is taken down or an engine lifted, the axles are carefully examined, and a report of their condition is sent to the Chief Superintendent on the form No. 4.

GENERAL REPAIRS. – Attached to many of our large sheds is a small shop in which general repairs are undertaken, and on some railways they differentiate between light and heavy repairs, but the GWR only differentiate between those engines which require more than, or less than, a fortnight's repair. The Author does not think that general repairs should be undertaken at an out-station unless there is sufficient accommodation to permit of at least four engines being on the stocks at a time, as this is the lowest number which can be dealt with economically, and even then facilities should be provided for taking boilers out of frames when necessary. Old and worn out glands should never be bored out and bushed, because the difference in the cost of a gland so treated and a new one is so slight as not to justify the risk of a weakened gland breaking. If underhung axleboxes knock in the horns, these should not have brass liners pegged on, but should be scrapped, and new boxes fitted. When an engine is sent to the factory, a full report of repairs necessary is forwarded to the Chief of the Running Department, and sent by him to the Locomotive Works Manager. The following is a specimen report (Forms 5, 6 and 7). This is signed by the foreman and countersigned by the Divisional Superintendent. A report of work done (Forms 8 and 9), other than small running repairs, to each engine is sent in by the Works Manager or the Divisional Superintendent; if the work has been done at an out-station, to the Chief Locomotive Superintendent, so that he may have a complete record of the repairs done to each engine.

H. G. Kerry's lecture of 1947 outlines changes in the repair procedures over the half century since Simpson's day:

MECHANICAL REPAIRS. – The next point to be dealt with is the mechanical and boiler repairs to engines when they are in the shed.

The driver, when booking off duty, has to report any known defects on engines in the special report book provided for that purpose, and these reports are handed over to the fitting or boiler staff according to the defect. Some of these defects are of a minor character and can be attended to while the engine is being got ready for its next turn of duty, while others are of such a nature as to make it necessary to book the engine back in order that the work can be completed. Such things as hot axleboxes cannot be dealt with in the shed itself, but have to be attended to in a special shop which is provided with a hoist to lift the engines and so get the wheels and axleboxes clear of the engine. All large sheds have

FORM No. 4.

GREAT WESTERN RAILWAY.

LOCO. DEPT.,........................... ....STATION.

Report of Loco. Axles examined, Wheels changed, &c.,

Week ending.................................190...

Date.	Engine or Tender.		Marks on Axle.			Ma-terial.	Dia. of wheels.		Thickness of Tyres.	Particulars of Condition of Axle, and Repairs to Wheels or Axles.
	Taken from	Put under	No.	Date.	Maker.		Ft.	In.		
										Signature..............

a lifting shop, but engines from smaller depots have sometimes to be sent to a parent depot for this work to be carried out. These are normal running repairs which form part of the everyday work of a locomotive shed.

Apart from repairs we have a system whereby the boilers and all the parts of an engine are examined periodically. Such a system has existed in various forms for very many years, but the arrangements have been recently overhauled and made much more comprehensive.

You will probably be aware that a boiler explosion on a locomotive is a very rare occurrence and very stringent regulations are laid down to make quite sure that all boilers are thoroughly and regularly examined. In outside firms all boilers are insured and the Insurance Companies employ boiler inspectors whose duty it is to examine, at stated intervals, all the boilers insured by that company. In the railway industry, however, we are our own Insurance Company and we employ our own boiler inspectors, and our standard is at least as high, is not higher, than the Insurance Companies'.

When I was transferred to the running department in 1924, I went to a division (the Cardiff Valleys Division) which was composed entirely of the South Wales Railways, there being no Great Western engine sheds or engines in the division. The division included the old Taff Vale, Rhymney, Barry, Cardiff and parts of the Brecon & Merthyr Railways. Each of these railways had its own system for examinations and repairs, but as it was obviously very desirable that all engines should be dealt with alike, it fell to my lot to introduce, by gradual stages, the Great Western system as it then was. The staff in that division were very co-operative, and from that aspect the task was made very much easier.

In order to try and bring the practice of all these railways into line, I instituted a weekly meeting with the divisional mechanical and boiler inspectors, with the idea of keeping a close check on the condition of all the engines in the division, which at that time numbered nearly six hundred. Conditions in the Cardiff Valleys Division were very suitable, as the division was, and still is, a self-contained unit, there being very little through working into other divisions. The whole of the system of engine repairs and examinations was based on the boiler inspectors' reports, as these could be relied on to be carried out at proper intervals. On this was built a system whereby all the mechanical examinations were linked up with the boiler examinations and carried out at stated intervals.

This system was built up over a number of years, but by the end of 1935 it was working satisfactorily and smoothly and the

FORM No. 5.

G.W.R.

....190...

Report of Repairs to Boiler on No..............Engine,

from.................................Station.

BOILERSMITHS' WORK.

PART OF ENGINE.	REPAIRS REQUIRED.
Boiler Barrel ..	Barrel of boiler requires cleaning and examining.
Outside Firebox ..	Casing plates grooved badly by foundation inside, waterways also eaten away by mud plug holes near foundation, all mud plugs to be re-tapped.
Inside Firebox ..	Mesh cracks showing in both top corners of tubeplate between the tubeholes, both flanges of backplate showing bad cracks, stayheads reduced all round firebox and require renewing.
Tubes ..	Tubes dirty in boiler, require renewing; several slightly reduced on ends in firebox; tubes slightly pitted.
Smokebox ..	Smokebox drawing air both sides, baffleplate burned away, requires renewing.
Ashpan, Dampers and Rods	Ashpan eaten away badly at bottom, requires renewing, sides very thin; dampers require setting in on bottom drawing air; rods want examining.
Framing and Cross Stays	Framingstay loose, requires rivet taken out and renewing; several loose rivets in framing require examining.
General Condition of Boiler	Tubeplate seam leaking badly at bottom of boiler; seams back of firebox leaking both sides; boiler will have to be taken out of framing to do repairs.
Miscellaneous ..	Please have all other necessary repairs done.

Signed,

FORM No. 6.

G.W.R.

....190...

Report of Repairs required to No..................Engine,

from.................................Station.

FITTERS' WORK.

PART OF ENGINE.	REPAIRS REQUIRED.
Wheels, Axles and Axleboxes	Wheels and axles examined, axle boxes re-lined and new bushes in outside rods.
Framing	Framing examined.
Springs	Springs examined and adjusted.
Cylinders	Slide valves and ports re-faced, new rings in both pistons, and pistons examined; cylinder cocks ground in.
Motion	Big and little end brasses, eccentric straps, motion blocks, quadrant blocks, lifting links, weigh bar, shaft, bearings and reversing lever, lining up; motion bars closing.
Injectors, Clacks and Waterways	Both injectors and clacks changed and pipes cleaned out.
Brake Gear	All brake gear examined, new bush in vacuum pump, pumps cleaned out and clacks re-faced.
Draw Gear	Draw gear examined.
Sandboxes and Gear	Sandboxes cleaned out and gear examined.
Boiler Mountings ..	Both whistle valves ground in and steam valves and gauge frame changed.
Steam - heating Apparatus	
Regulator	Regulator valve and rod and steam pipe in boiler and smokebox examined.
Feed Valves, Strums and Connections	Feed valves, strums and connections examined.
Water Pick-up and Gear	
Safety Valves ..	Safety valves examined.
Ejectors, Pipes and Connections	Ejector box changed and pipes and connections cleaned out.
Miscellaneous ..	Leading guard irons, buffers and blower pipe in smokebox examined.

Signed,

FORM No. 7.

G.W.R.

....190...

Report of Repairs required to No..................Tender,

from.................................Station.

FITTERS' WORK.

PART OF TENDER.	REPAIRS REQUIRED.
Wheels, Axles and Axleboxes	Wheels turned, axles examined and axleboxes re-lined.
Framing	Framing examined.
Springs	Springs examined and adjusted.
Sandboxes and Gear	Sandboxes cleaned out and gear examined.
Brake Gear ..	Brake gear examined, and new bolts, brake blocks, and brake screw and nut wanted.
Vacuum Pipes and Connections	Vacuum pipes and connections examined and cleaned out.
Dragbars, Couplings and Screw Connections	Dragbars, couplings and screw connections examined.
Steam - heating Apparatus	
Tank	Tank examined.
Feed Valves, Strums and Connections	Feed valves, strums and connections cleaned out.
Water Scoop ..	
Miscellaneous ..	Intermediate and trailing buffers examined.

Signed,

G.W.R.

....190...

Report of Repairs required to No..................Tender,

from.................................Station.

BOILERSMITHS' WORK.

PART OF TENDER.	REPAIRS REQUIRED.
	Tank and shovel plates repaired.

Signed,

FORM No. 8.

G.W.R.

Report of Repairs done to No..........Engine at.............Station.

BOILER WORK.

Date came in Shop......................................190...

Date finished ....190...

Name of Leading Man...

Tubes	
Inside Firebox	
Outside Firebox	
Boiler Barrel	
Remarks ..	

Signature...

FORM No. 9.

G.W.R.

Report of Repairs done to No..........Engine at.............Station.

FITTERS' WORK, &c.

Date came in Shop......................................190...

Date finished ....190...

Name of Leading Fitter..

Wheels	
Springs	
Framing	
Cylinders	
Motion	
Miscellaneous ..	

Signature...

GREAT WESTERN RAILWAY—LOCOMOTIVE DEPARTMENT.

CLASSIFICATION OF WORK.

In accordance with Circular No. 3/478 B.

Swindon, March, 1883.

FIRST CLASS.
(10 hours per day.)

All work over the Metropolitan & District Railway.
London and Suburban Passenger Service.

MAIN LINE PASSENGER TRAINS between

Paddington	and Aylesbury
"	Slough
"	Reading
"	Oxford
"	Wolverhampton
"	Swindon
"	Bristol
"	Exeter
"	Gloster
Reading	" Slough
"	Trowbridge
Oxford	" Wolverhampton
Swindon	" Bristol
"	Taunton
"	Weymouth
"	Neath
"	Carmarthen

Bristol Suburban Service

Bristol	and Frome
"	Chippenham and Salisbury
Yatton	" Taunton, Exeter, & Newton Abbot
Yeovil	" Witham
Taunton	" Durston or Weymouth
"	Exeter, Newton Abbot, & Plymouth
"	Barnstaple
Plymouth	" Minehead
"	Penzance
Gloucester	" Launceston
Cheltenham	" Neath
"	Hereford
Newport	" Chipping Norton Junction
Cardiff	" Nantyglo and Blaenavon
"	Portskewett
"	Worcester
Neath	" Swindon
Llanelly	" New Milford
"	Llanidlo and Llandovery
Leamington, Birmingham, Wolverhampton, Stourbridge, and Dudley Local Service	
Birmingham	and Reading
"	Hereford
"	Oxford via Worcester
Wolverhampton	" Chester and Birkenhead
"	Birmingham
"	Oxford
"	Hereford
"	Chester
"	Birkenhead
"	Birmingham and Worcester
Chester	" Hereford
"	Ruabon
"	Birkenhead and Manchester
Birkenhead	" Birmingham
Wellington	" Crewe
"	Shifnal, Buildwas, and Craven Arms
Corwen	" Ruabon and Dolgelly
Stourbridge	" Worcester
Leominster, Ludlow, and Wooferton, and Birmingham and Wolverhampton	
Worcester	" Wolverhampton and Birmingham
"	Didcot
"	Hartlebury and Shrewsbury
"	Stratford and Leamington
"	Malvern
Hereford	" Oxford
Evesham	" Abergavenny & Newport
Ross	" Cardiff
Merthyr	" Pontypool Road & Swansea
"	Swansea

SECOND CLASS.
(10 hours per day.)

THROUGH GOODS TRAINS, between

Paddington	and Devizes
"	Worcester
"	Wolverhampton
"	Swindon
"	Weymouth
"	Bristol
"	Gloucester
"	Penarth
Reading or Basingstoke	" Wolverhampton
Swindon	" Aberdare
"	Weymouth
"	Exeter
"	Aberdare
"	Cardiff
"	Neath
"	Wolverhampton
Didcot or Oxford	" Wolverhampton
Oxford	" Taunton
"	Paddington
"	Pontypool Road
Bristol	" Bristol
"	Wolverhampton
"	Weymouth
"	Neath
Exeter	" Plymouth
Plymouth	" Gloucester
Gloucester	" Penzance
"	Reading
"	Neath or Swansea
"	Llanelly
"	Milford
Bullo	" Worcester
Cardiff	" Salop or Birkenhead
"	Worcester
Neath or Swansea	" Wolverhampton
"	Pontypool Road
"	Bristol
Birmingham	" Milford
"	Banbury & Oxford
"	Tenbury
"	Crewe & Shrewsbury
"	Hereford & Pontypool Road
Bordesley	" Paddington
Wolverhampton	" Banbury
"	Birkenhead
"	Chester & Manchester
"	Oswestry
"	Ruabon & Wheatsheaf
"	Crewe
Shrewsbury	" Pontypool Road
"	Hollingswood & Crewe
"	Wednesbury & Hereford
Chester	" Manchester and Birkenhead
Birkenhead	" Pontypool Road
Stourbridge	" Buildwas
Worcester	" Wooferton
"	Oxford
"	Birmingham
"	Dudley & Wolverhampton
"	Crewe
Hereford	" Pontypool Road
"	Pontypool Road & Shrewsbury
Pontypool Road	" Worcester & Dudley
"	Grange Court or Gloucester

THIRD CLASS.
(10 hours per day.)

LOCAL GOODS TRAINS between

Paddington	and Didcot
Reading	" Trowbridge
Oxford	" Taplow via Thame
Didcot	" Bristol
"	Gloucester
Swindon	" Yeovil
"	Salisbury
"	Bullo
"	Bristol
Bristol	" Frome
"	Salisbury
Yatton	" Witham
Wells	" Chippenham
Yeovil	" Durston or Witham
Taunton	" Tiverton
"	Barnstaple
"	Dunball
"	Minehead
Exeter	" Plymouth
Plymouth	" Truro
"	Launceston
Truro	" Penzance
Gloucester	" Hereford
"	Sharpness
Cheltenham	" Chipping Norton Junction
Newport	" Nantyglo and Blaenavon
Cardiff	" Gloucester
" or Neath	" Nantymoel
"	Tywith
"	Whitland
Swansea	" Stormy
"	Llantrissant
"	Tredegar
Llanelly	" Llandilo and Llandovery
Leamington	" Banbury
Birmingham	" Leamington & Honeybourne
"	Dudley & Stourbridge
Wolverhampton	" Shrewsbury
"	Stourbridge, Kidderminster & Bordesley
"	Walsall
Gobowen	" Ruabon & Owestry
Corwen	" Ruabon & Dolgelly
Chester	" Shrewsbury
Chester or Birkenhead	" Stations in North Wales Colliery District
"	Warrington
Chester	" Helsby & Birkenhead
Stourbridge	" Stoke & Round Oak
Worcester	" Honeybourne & Hatton
"	Moreton
"	Henwick & Malvern
Hereford	" Grange Court & Monmouth
Pontypool Road	" Monmouth & Chepstow
"	Newport
"	Aberdare & all Stations on the Taff Vale Extension
"	All Stations on the Monmouthshire Section
Newport	" ditto
Aberdare	" Aberdare
Merthyr	" Swansea
"	Hirwain & Swansea

BRANCHES.
(Specially dealt with under Clause 4 of Circular).

West London Lines (Goods trains)
Brentford
Uxbridge
Henley
Windsor
Great Marlow
Aylesbury
Basingstoke
Wallingford
Abingdon
Fairford
Didcot & Newbury
Faringdon
Highworth
Cirencester
Malmesbury
Calne
Camerton
Portland
Bridport
Radstock & Mells
Weston
Clevedon
Chard
Tiverton
Culm Valley
Moretonhampstead
Teign Valley
Kingswear
Ashburton
Burngullow
Portreath
Cornwall Minerals
Falmouth
St. Ives
Bullo
Wye Valley
Ely Valley
Swansea & Morriston
Carmarthen & Cardigan
Milford
Garnant
Mountain
Maesteg
Ogmore
Porthcawl
Black Mill Extension
Garw
Minsterley
Bromyard
Alcester
Oswestry
Brymbo
Summerhill
Hooton & Helsby
Hooton & Parkgate
Stourbridge
Halesowen
Chipping Norton
Ludlow & Clee Hill and Local trains, Ludlow, Wooferton, & Tenbury
Kington
Eardisley
Presteign
New Radnor
Pontnewynydd & Blaensychan
" Gellydeg
Aberbeeg & Ebbw Vale
Cwm Bargoed
Quakers Yard & Merthyr
Dare & Amman
Hirwain & Merthyr
Golden Valley
Bala & Festiniog

general condition of the engines in the division was good. At the beginning of 1936 I was transferred to London, where I found, of course, that the Great Western system of examination had been in operation for many years and was working reasonably well. I did, however, superimpose my own ideas on top of this scheme, as I had done at Cardiff, but from my point of view the results were not so satisfactory, as the division was not self-contained.

Practically all the engine working, including freight, was balanced so that the total number of engines out of course was never very large. The war, however, altered all this. The flow and direction of freight traffic changed, Government stores and troop trains were numerous in all directions, and the general rhythm of the pre-war balanced working was to a very large extent destroyed. As a result, engines were not returned to their home depots regularly and, in order to regulate them, the Chief Mechanical Engineer and the Superintendent of the Line jointly set up the engine control organisation. From the shed maintenance point of view, however, the most serious effect of the out-of-course working was the difficulty in maintaining the engines in good repair and carrying out examinations regularly. This problem became so serious that the Chief Mechanical Engineer deputed one of his assistants to go into the whole matter, with the result that a very comprehensive scheme was evolved to cover all contingencies. It was a source of a good deal of satisfaction to me to find this scheme was based on that in operation at Cardiff, but it went a good deal further. Very elaborate schedules were worked out and the method of recording examinations greatly improved. Detailed instructions covering all examinations were issued and a small book printed for the guidance of all running-shed fitters. When sufficient skilled staff become available to operate the scheme fully, there is no doubt that the general condition of Great Western engines will be even better than they were in the years prior to the war. Despite what anybody says, Great Western engines are still the best cared for in the country.

When examinations are carried out in the sheds, certain roads in the shed are usually set aside for them. Boiler inspectors usually make their examinations after an engine has been washed out. For this purpose all the wash-out plugs and mudhole doors are left out so that they can make a thorough internal examination of all stays and waterways. Stays are found all round the sides of the firebox and have a screw thread at both ends, one end screwing into the outside plate and the other into the inner copper firebox. There is a water space all round the firebox and the function of the stays is to support the firebox and prevent, like other stays we have heard of, bulges in places where they shouldn't occur! These firebox stays are subject to very considerable stresses and the boiler inspector has to make a close examination to make quite sure they are not broken or wasted away. He does this by inserting mirrors and lights in plug-holes at various places. He also goes round each stay end with a hammer and gives this a smart tap and he can tell from the resultant sound whether the stay is broken or not. He also has to see that the spaces between the tubes in the boiler barrel are clear. If they are not, a few tubes have to be taken out to clear the dirt from the spaces. He also has to make a close examination of all the boiler plates, firebox and tube-plate, to see that there are no cracks in the plates or that they are not reduced in thickness. He also has to see that the tubes are not what we call pitted, that is, corroded in very small spots, which may in time turn into tiny pin-holes or even cause the collapse of a tube.

In addition to the thorough examination given to a boiler by the inspector, the shed boilersmith has to make an examination each time the boiler is washed out. You can see from this the stringent nature of the examinations.

Other examinations which have to be watched carefully are those for the safety valves, those things right in the middle of the top of the boiler and which make such a pleasant, soothing noise just outside your office window. Judging by the complaints I receive these noises seem to cause more disturbance in the after-noons. Then there is the water gauge on the back of the boiler inside the cab by which the footplate crew can see the level of the water in the boiler. This fitting is most important and is subject to frequent examination to make sure that it is functioning properly.

Examination of pistons and valves, connecting and coupling rods, injectors and ejectors, brake and spring gear, water pick up gear and scoop and, last but not least, the automatic train control apparatus, all have to be carried out, as well as lots of other parts of the locomotive which I have not mentioned.

As stated earlier on, most large sheds have a lifting shop attached to them, where hot axleboxes can be attended to and wheels changed. A few of the biggest sheds have a well-equipped repair shop in which quite substantial repairs can be done. Old Oak Common is one of the depots so equipped, and a considerable amount of work is done in this shop. Engines, which would otherwise have to be sent to Swindon for what, to them, would be a light repair, can be dealt with, leaving Swindon free to concern itself with major repairs.

Henry Simpson concluded his paper 'The Work of a Running Department' at a Swindon meeting of Tuesday 6th November 1906 and the following extract illumines some of the working background to Divisional operations:

WORKING OF TRAINS. – So far as goods trains are concerned, the working arrangements are made by the Traffic Officers. The existing service has grown up to meet the requirements of the traffic, and from time to time meetings are called by each Divisional Traffic Superintendent to discuss the working and loading of the goods trains in his Division. The Superintendents of adjacent Divisions are invited to these meetings, and a representative from the Chief of the Loco. Running Department, together with the Divisional Loco. Superintendent, also attend. Various suggestions are made for improving the train service. The loading of each train is carefully considered, and in some cases new trains are proposed. The Locomotive Officers are in a position to say whether or not the suggested alterations are practicable from a locomotive point of view, and sometimes they themselves make suggestions with the object of saving power, and these are considered by the meeting. Minutes are drawn up by the Divisional Traffic Superindent at whose office the meeting is held, and these are sent to the Superintendent of the line, who, if he approves, recommends the General Manager to put on any new trains which may have been recommended, and the necessary alterations are made in the service books. The through goods trains are worked by second-class enginemen, and, generally, they have tender engines. Most of these trains are 'double home.' For example, a train from Swindon to Exeter is worked through to its destination, and the men take rest at Exeter, returning to Swindon the next day or night, as the case may be, with the balancing train. On alternate days Exeter men work to Swindon, where they take rest, and return to Exeter working their balancing train. The effect of this arrangement is that at every Loco. Depôt Mondays, Wednesdays, and Fridays are looked upon as 'our' days, and Tuesdays, Thursdays, and Saturdays are looked upon as 'foreigners'' days.

The local goods trains are worked by third-class men, and are almost invariably 'single home' jobs – that is, the men take rest at their home stations. Shunting engines are worked by the lowest grade of Enginemen, known as turners or pilotmen. In addition to shunting, this grade does most of the relief work, although at some stations, where the relief men have to frequently do long distance work, third-class men are employed. Relief work is most irregular, and is, of course, provided for the purpose of keeping the hours of the train men within reasonable limits when trains are running late, owing to fog, congested state of the line, or other causes.

ENGINE DIAGRAMS. – The provision of power for working the passenger service is dealt with solely by the Chief of the Running

FORM No. 10.   G.W.R.—LOCO. DEPT...DISTRICT.

Working of.................Engines..................................190...

Class of Engines................................   Class of Men { Engineman ....
                                                                { Fireman ....

No. of Train.	Reference to Service Books.			Time of		From	To	Time Booked out.		Miles.	Days booked to run marked "R."							Time Paid.
	bk.	page.	col.	dep.	arr.			H.	M.		S.	M.	Tu.	W.	Th.	F.	S.	Hours.

Department, with the exception of the Birmingham local service, which is arranged by the Divisional Superintendent at Wolverhampton, and also the whole of the Severn and Wye service, both goods and passenger, which is dealt with by the Traffic Manager and the Divisional Superintendent at Swindon. Mr Waister has in his office an expert who schemes out the most economical arrangement of engine power by means of diagrams. Generally there are three sets of these diagrams issued annually to meet with the changes in the train service, and, in addition, small diagrams shewing the excursion and special workings are issued at holiday times. If these diagrams are not drawn out, a lot of light mileage would be caused, and this would involve the Company in unnecessary expense. Many years ago the late Mr. Joseph Armstrong was Locomotive Superintendent of the Shrewsbury and Chester Railway, and when that line amalgamated with the Shrewsbury and Birmingham there was naturally one Superintendent too many, and the Directors decided that the one who could make the best and most economical working arrangement for the amalgamated lines should be retained. Mr. Armstrong, who was essentially a splendid 'Running' man, was selected. He continued in that office until the amalgamated lines were taken over by the GWR, when he was appointed Divisional Superintendent at Wolverhampton, and shortly afterwards became the Chief Locomotive Superintendent of this line. This little historical fact is mentioned to shew the importance of being able to make good and cheap working arrangements. The diagram shewn (Fig. 4) gives the engine working, both goods and passenger, on the Severn & Wye Joint Line. A map is also given (Fig. 5) of the Severn & Wye Joint Line to shew the routes covered by the trains. The engine working of the S. & W. Line is arranged at a meeting called by the Traffic Manager and attended by the Divisional Loco. Superintendent, the Chief Clerk to the Traffic Manager, and the Chief Traffic Inspector.

The method of constructing the diagram is as follows: – First, the timetables are gone carefully through, and the names of all those stations at which trains terminate are noted down. A number of vertical lines are drawn to represent railway stations, and those stations which appear to be likely to have many engines running to and from during the day will require two lines each. In the diagram under consideration, only Lydney Junction and Coleford Junction are so treated. Each of the other stations is represented by one vertical line only. When two lines are used, the arrival times are always shewn between them and the departure times outside them. The arrival times of all trains from stations to the left of a two line station are entered adjacent to the left-hand line, whilst the arrival times of all trains from stations on the right are entered adjacent to the right-hand line. The departure times are dealt with in a similar manner, and a mere inspection of the diagram, therefore, indicates the direction in which a train is going, irrespective of the times. When a single vertical line represents a

Severn & Wye Joint Rly.

FIG. 5.

station, the arrival and departure times can be shewn on whichever side of the line suits the convenience of the diagram maker.

Having drawn the vertical lines, and entered at the top of them the names of all the stations which have been noted, the next thing to do is to enter all the trains in order as these appear in the timetables, and represent them by horizontal lines, which should at first be drawn in pencil. The next operation is most important – viz., the coupling up of the horizontal lines with the vertical or diagonal lines to represent the working of the engines. It is obvious that an engine must start from a Locomotive Depôt and finish at one. In the particular case under consideration there is only one Locomotive Depôt – viz., Lydney Junction. The starting of an engine is represented by a square above the horizontal line representing the train, and the finishing up of it is indicated by an arrow. If the men are relieved, this is shewn by a circle. It must not be supposed that the way in which the lines have been joined up is the only or best one, and it should be borne in mind that the specimen diagram is only intended to indicate the elementary principles of diagram making. As mentioned before, this is expert work, and there are all sorts of conditions to be taken into consideration, such as short margins, suitability of engines for particular work, etc., which complicate matters considerably.

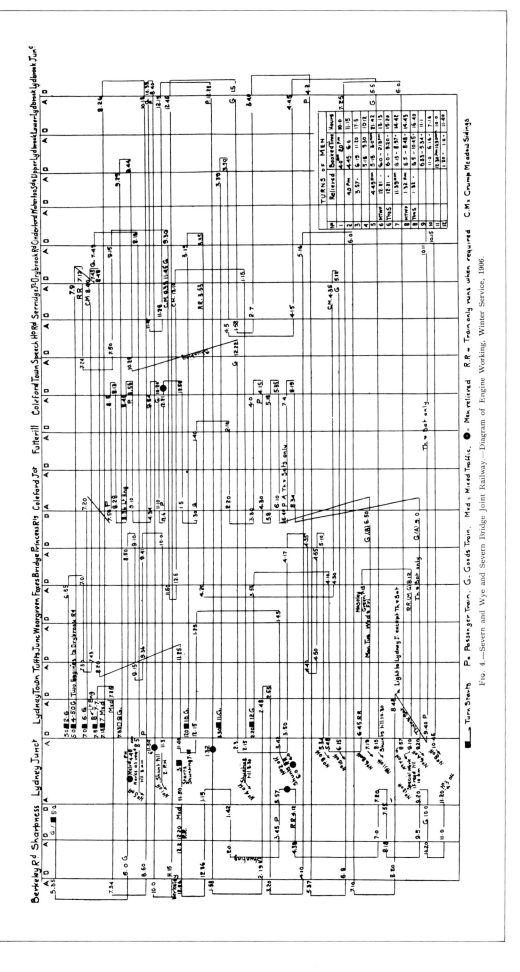

Fig. 4.—Severn and Wye and Severn Bridge Joint Railway.—Diagram of Engine Working, Winter Service, 1906.

LINK SYSTEMS – The turns of duty of the men are arranged by the loco. foreman. He knows from the diagram what trains he has to run, and, for convenience of reference, the working of all trains, goods and passenger, is shewn on Form No. 10. He arranges his enginemen, according to their grades, in suitable 'links.' Take, for example, the second-class engineman at Swindon. The second class trains starting from this station run to Wolverhampton, London, Aberdare, Llantrissant, Neath, Cardiff, Weymouth, Taunton, Yeovil, Hereford, and Exeter. There are 22 sets of second-class men employed, and if they were all of the same character, these men would form one big link, and work all the trains round in turn. This would be the fairest to the men, because they would each make practically the same time, taking all the year round, and would be treated with absolute impartiality. However, the Aberdare and Cardiff trains have to be worked by big engines, whereas the Wolverhampton, Exeter, London, etc., are worked by small tender engines, and the Yeovil and Hereford trains by tank engines. Hence, the 22 sets of second-class men are divided into four links – one link, comprising 13 sets of men, working the Wolverhampton, Exeter, Taunton, Paddington, Weymouth, and Neath trains; one link, comprising four sets of men, working the Aberdare and Cardiff trains; one link, comprising three sets, working the Hereford and Yeovil trains; and one link, comprising two sets, working the Llantrissant trains. To ensure each man getting his proper turn, the foreman has either a foreman's day book or he makes a diagram for each link in the form shewn on Fig. 6.

LINK DIAGRAM. – The specimen diagram represents the method adopted for working the men in the Wolverhampton link. The lower part shews the daily turns of each of the 13 men. Taking for example turn No. 1, it will be seen that on Sunday the men work 'up,' that is, they are returning home from Exeter, after working the 7-55 a.m. from Swindon to Exeter on the Saturday in the previous week, when they were doing No. 13 turn. On Monday they are off duty, and on Tuesday work the 2-20 a.m. to Wolverhampton, coming 'up' home again on Wednesday. They work the 2-20 a.m. to Wolverhampton again on Thursday, back Friday, and to Wolverhampton again on Saturday, 'up' on Sunday, and they then take the 9-55 p.m. on Monday to Neath, because they are then off turn No. 1, and on to No. 2. Each man should, in his proper turn, work each of the 13 trains, and to ensure this being done, the foreman makes use of the top portion of the diagram. Here the letters A, B, C, etc., represent the names of the enginemen. In the actual diagram the names are of course entered, and not letters. I have substituted letters for names to make the diagram clearer. The horizontal row of figures represents the numbers of turns, whilst the vertical row represents the weeks. A pin, or drawing pin, is placed in the number which indicates the current week's working. Supposing it is in No. 6, the foreman then allots the first turn to engineman (I), the second to engineman (J), and so on. On Saturday, when the duty sheet is made out for the following Sunday and Monday, the foreman puts the pin in No. 7 week, and then Turn No. 1 is allotted to engineman (H), Turn No. 2 engineman (I), and so on. It will be seen that so far as the regular trains are concerned, there is no difficulty in dividing the work out fairly among the men, but in the case of special and conditional trains, the foreman finds it most difficult to do this. As a class, enginemen and firemen know less of the amenities of life than any other section of the community. Their hours of duty and rest are irregular, and they never know what it is to have a decent square meal whilst they are at work. They sometimes come on duty, expecting to arrive at a certain destination, but owing to fogs or other causes they never reach it, having to put in for rest at some station out of course, and possibly do not return to their home station again for some days. If a man books off say at 7 p.m., he may be called for duty again at 4-0 a.m. the next day, and he is prepared for this, but he may not be required until much later. If however a foreman keeps in touch with the traffic inspectors,

Diagram showing working of men in 2nd Class Link Swindon. Wolverhampton, Exeter, Taunton, Paddn, Weymouth & Neath Trains

— Weekly Turn Number —

Weeks	1 Eman	2 Eman	3 Eman	4 Eman	5 Eman	6 Eman	7 Eman	8 Eman	9 Eman	10 Eman	11 Eman	12 Eman	13 Eman
1	A	B	C	D	E	F	G	H	I	J	K	L	M
2	M	A	B	C	D	E	F	G	H	I	J	K	L
3	L	M	A	B	C	D	E	F	G	H	I	J	K
4	K	L	M	A	B	C	D	E	F	G	H	I	J
5	J	K	L	M	A	B	C	D	E	F	G	H	I
6	I	J	K	L	M	A	B	C	D	E	F	G	H
7	H	I	J	K	L	M	A	B	C	D	E	F	G
8	G	H	I	J	K	L	M	A	B	C	D	E	F
9	F	G	H	I	J	K	L	M	A	B	C	D	E
10	E	F	G	H	I	J	K	L	M	A	B	C	D
11	D	E	F	G	H	I	J	K	L	M	A	B	C
12	C	D	E	F	G	H	I	J	K	L	M	A	B
13	B	C	D	E	F	G	H	I	J	K	L	M	A

Order of working for 13 weeks.

— Daily Turns of Men —

	1	2	3	4	5	6	7	8	9	10	11	12	13
Sunday	Up	Up	Down				p.m 5.30 London						a.m 7.40 Reading
Monday	Off	p.m 9.55 Neath	p.m 11.30 for 1.0 Whpton	a.m 5.15 Exeter	p.m 11.45 Taunton	a.m 11.45 Weymo	Down	a.m 10.15 Whpton	p.m 5.5 Exeter	p.m 9.40 Whpton	p.m 7.45 London	a.m 5.55 Whpton	Off
Tuesday	a.m 2.20 Whpton	Up	Up	Up	Up	Up	noon 12.0 London	Up	Up	Up	Down	Up	a.m 7.55 Exeter
Wednesday	Up	p.m 11.30 for 1.0 Whpton	p.m 7.45 London	a.m 7.50 Exeter	p.m 9.40 Whpton	a.m 11.45	Down	a.m 10.15 Whpton	p.m 5.5 Exeter	p.m 11.45 Taunton	p.m 9.55 Neath	a.m 5.55 Whpton	Up
Thursday	a.m 2.20 Whpton	Up	Down	Up	Up	Up	noon 12.0 London	Up	Up	Up	Up	Up	a.m 7.55 Exeter
Friday	Up	p.m 7.45 London	p.m 11.45 Taunton	a.m 7.50 Exeter	p.m 9.55 Neath	a.m 11.45 Weymo	Down	a.m 10.15 Whpton	p.m 5.5 Exeter	p.m 9.40 Whpton	p.m 11.30 for 1.0 Whpton	a.m 5.55 Whpton	Up
Saturday	a.m 2.20 Whpton	Off	Up	Up	Up	Up	Off	Up	Up	Up	Up	Up	a.m 7.55 Exeter

FIG. 6.

and exercises good judgment, he can, and mostly does, make such arrangements as put the men to the least possible inconvenience, and on the other hand, generally speaking, the men pull together well with the management, and do all they possibly can to meet the exigencies of the traffic.

DUTY SHEET. – Each day the foreman makes out and exhibits the duty sheet, Form No. 11, shewing the working for the following day. The information on this sheet is not only necessary for the enginemen and firemen, but it is useful to the lighters up, washers out, fitters, and boilersmiths, and these men have to keep in touch with the sheet, noting any alterations which have been made; and if a fitter or boilersmith finds that he cannot complete the work which he may be doing on a particular engine before the time at which it is marked to go out, he at once notifies the foreman, so that arrangements can be made for another engine to replace it.

EXHIBITION AND DISTRIBUTION OF NOTICES. – A very important part of a foreman's duty is to exhibit and distribute the notices appertaining to reduction of speed, no water, single line working, special trains, etc. All notices which involve the safe working of the line are signed for by the enginemen affected. This not only impresses on the men the importance of the notice, but it forms a record, and shews that each man concerned has been supplied with a copy.

Form No. 11.

GREAT WESTERN RAILWAY.

Shed Notice of Duty to be performed by Enginemen.

....Station................... ...day,................... 190 ..

ENGINE.	ENGINEMAN.	FIREMAN. N.B.—The blanks show that the Firemen work with same Engineman as on previous days.	TRAIN.				Remarks and Special Instructions.
			Time of Departure.	a.m. or p.m.	From	To	

STATISTICAL INFORMATION. – There is, perhaps, more statistical information prepared in the Running Department than in any other. This is due to the fact that the men employed in the Running Department are, unlike those employed in factories, spread over a large area of country, and are not under the immediate eye of the management. And again, in a factory the cost of making or repairing an article can be laid down very definitely – so much for labour, so much for material, and so much for factory expenses – but in the Running Department the cost of working is a much more complicated matter, and unless a Divisional Superindent had a mass of statistical information provided for him, it would be impossible to keep any check on the working expenses. In the Swindon Division there are 270 forms used, many of them relating to working expenses. Many of these, together with a description, will be found in the appendix. Each engineman, in addition to making out a daily ticket, which gives full particulars of the times and loads of the trains he has worked, makes out a weekly mileage ticket, upon which he enters the number of trips, shunting, empty mileage, ballasting, piloting, and train mileage, and the starting and finishing times of each turn of duty. These tickets furnish the necessary data for compiling the mileage and engineman and fireman's times. The coalmen record the quantity of coal in cwts. put on each engine, and this is usually signed for by the engineman. A complete record is also kept of the quantity of coal used for other purposes.

STORES. – Nothing whatever is given out from the Stores unless a requisition, duly signed by an authorised person, is handed in. This requisition states clearly for what purpose the article or articles are required, that is for locomotive or rail motor car, running oil and tallow, running tools and sundries, boilerwashing, cleaning, coaling, shed tube running, fire dropping, smoke boxes, lighting up, shed labouring (such as sweeping up and ash loading), offices and stores, water pumping, repairs to water appliances, repairs to locomotives and tenders, rail motor cars, buildings and turntables, coal expenses (such as coal stacking), sundries, credits (such as materials supplied to other departments).

TIMEKEEPING. – The time of the mechanical, cleaning, and shed staffs is recorded in practically the same manner as similar work is done in the factory, but all men are rated at 10 hours per day, except the mechanics and their labourers. The time of each man is charged properly to the section of work upon which he is engaged. For instance, a cleaner may be engaged tube running, and his time would be charged, not to cleaning, which is his usual work, but to shed attendance on engines, or a shed labourer may be employed stacking coal, and his time would be charged to coal expenses. Again, a fitter may examine a locomotive belonging to a trader to ascertain whether it is fit to travel on its own wheels over the main line. His time would be debited against the Goods Department through credits. A return of engines cleaned and lighted up is compiled once every four weeks. It will thus be seen that the cost of all labour and material can be appropriated to the proper charges, and the necessary work of compilation is done

partly in the divisional offices and partly in the general offices of the department. The Divisional Superintendent is furnished once every four weeks with a statement of the miles run, coal and oil consumed, and the number of pounds of coal per mile and pints of oil per 100 miles for each engine in his division. The corresponding figures for the previous four weeks are also given. On this statement the engines are grouped together in links, and the average consumption of coal per mile and oil per 100 miles is given, so that it can be readily seen which men are above and which below the average. Each half year a statement of a similar character is supplied, and it is upon economical working, as shewn by this sheet, that the first and second class enginemen are paid their premiums. Each first and second class engineman is recommended by the Divisional Superintendent once every six months for a premium, provided that his general conduct has been good, and he has not had it deferred for misconduct. The chief of the Running Department will grant a premium to each man so recommended, who is either below or next above the average in his link, but if his cost of working is higher than that of the man who is next above the average he is called upon for an explanation, and if this is unsatisfactory his premium is deferred for one, two, three or more months, according to circumstances. If, however, his engine has been rough, as compared with others in the link, or his conditions of work have been exceptional, the chief of the Running Department grants it. These premiums are well worth having, being £5 for six months, and if one if deferred only for one month it means a loss of rather more than 16s.

ABSTRACT BOOK. – Once a month, what is known as the abstract of working expenses book, is entered up in the General Offices. In this the total mileage run, passenger, goods, trains for other companies, ballasting, rail motor cars, light miles (these include banking, traffic shunting, and empty), number of locomotives in district, number in working order, and number under repair, similar information being given for motor cars, number of engines, and motor cars in steam, average number of miles per engine in steam, and per motor car in steam, quantity of coal consumed by engines, motor cars, sand furnaces, offices, etc., pumping engines, smiths' fires, etc., and hydraulics, consumption of coal in lbs. per mile for both engines and motor cars. The whole of the wages paid are also abstracted, and appropriated to the several charges, and the average wages paid to each class of men, together with the cost per mile of each class of work, is entered, for comparative purposes. The cost of all the Stores consumed is likewise appropriated to the several charges. It will be seen that this book forms a complete record of the work done in a Division, and the cost of doing it, and a Divisional Superintendent can see at a glance whether his Division is being worked, as a whole, more or less economically than previously, and it is an important part of his duty to watch the fluctuations in this book, and take every precaution against extravagance.

DISSECTION OF EXPENDITURE. – The abstract book does not, however, reveal the particular part of the Division where serious fluctuations in expenditure take place. It is therefore necessary to obtain information of a more local character. To show what can be done in this direction, consideration will be given to coal and oil, the cost of which is such a serious item. The fact has already been mentioned that the monthly consumption statements shew the engines and men grouped together in links, and that the consumption is shewn for both the current and previous months. This is done for comparative purposes, but it is found from experience that the only true comparison is that made with the corresponding period of the previous year. A special book is used in the Swindon Division, which is framed in such a way as to show at a glance the average consumption, month by month, and year by year, of each link in the Divisions (Fig. 7). All the links which show increases over the previous year are noted, and the monthly consumption statement is then examined to ascertain which men in these links are above the averages, and they are asked for an

King George V at Old Oak, its daily progress dogged by the Abstract Book, at the heart of a form-filling empire.   *Collection Peter Winding*

Fig. 7

WORKING EXPENSES.

CONSUMPTION OF FUEL PER MILE AND OIL PER 100 MILES.

Didcot Main Line Goods Link.   Goods Engines.

Abbreviation.	Year	Jan. 10th.		Feb. 7th.		March 7th.		April 4th.		May 2nd.	
		Coal.	Oil.	Coal.	Oil.	Coa .	Oil.	Coal .	Oil.	Coal.	Oil.
D2	1902	53·9	4·73	50·8	5·00	53·5	5·05	50·5	5·34	52·3	5·07
	1903	56·7	4·86	57·8	5·01	53·0	5·00	54·9	5·48	51·3	4·95
	1904	50·9	3·94	52·4	3·85	49·5	3·34	49·9	3·60	50·3	3·83
	1905	50·4	3·79	54·9	4·05	51·9	3·88	52·1	4·08	52·4	3·88
	1906	48·1	3·69	48·0	3·67	47·3	3·57	47·1	3·59	44·4	3·58

explanation of their high consumption. The foremen are also asked to express an opinion as to the increase in the average of the link. When the statements of the men are received in the Divisional Office they are examined, and in the case of an unsatisfactory explanation a record is made on a card against the uneconomical man. This method of dissecting the accounts can be carried to any length, and applies to both wages and stores as well as coal, but it is unnecessary to point out that the more refined the accounts the greater the cost of keeping them. The reason why coal in particular was selected for dealing with in this way was that coal is, next to the wage of enginemen and firemen, the heaviest item of expenditure, and indeed in some divisions it is the heaviest. The consumption in pounds per mile in the Swindon division is about

36.2, and at the low estimated cost of .06d. per lb., a difference in consumption of only 1lb. per mile would represent a cash gain or loss of at least £170 per month.

Of late years the number of engine miles and train miles per hour per man have been abstracted, and these figures are most interesting. In the Swindon Division for month ending August 15th, 1906, the number of engine miles per hour per man equals 7.28, whilst the train miles per hour per man equals 6.07. The great difference between these figures arises from the fact that the engine miles include light miles, banking, and traffic shunting at four miles per hour. This mileage ranks as 'empty', and the percentage of empty to total engine miles is about 17%. One would imagine that a much greater average speed than 7.28 miles per hour would be attained, but this figure compares most favourably with other divisions, more especially those in which the percentage of passenger mileage to goods is low, because a high percentage of goods miles means a slower average speed of running, and also a largely increased empty mileage. Useful as is this miles per hour figure, practically the same information is given in another form, and in greater detail in the abstract book, as 'cost of enginemen and firemen in pence per mile' for both passenger and goods. It is obvious that as the cost per mile goes up the miles per hour go down, and *vice versa*, and the cost per train mile is really a more valuable figure than the 'miles per hour'; but to demonstrate to any officer outside the Loco. Department that a particular section of the line is badly congested, or to impress upon them the importance of improving the methods of dealing with the traffic, the 'miles per hour' is much more useful, and would appeal with much greater force than any other figures.

A few particulars of the mileage and cost of operating the Swindon Division for month ending the 15th September, 1906,

G.W.R. Engineman's Mileage Ticket. W.E. _____ 190 __ Station _____ Engineman _____

Day of Week	Between	And	Engine	No. of Trips	Train Miles.		Piloting.	Empty Miles.		Shunting at 4 Miles per hour.			Ballasting, &c.		Fireman's Name	Booked Time of Starting of Train.	Actual Time of Arrival of Train.	Time in Hours.	Lodging Money.	REMARKS.

SUMMARY OF TIME AND LODGING MONEY.

NAME.	Hours.	Rate.	Lodgings Amount
Engineman			
Fireman			

Divisional Superintendent.

W.E. _____ Station _____ Engineman _____

Engine _____

Train Miles.		Empty.		Shunting.		Total.
Pass.	Goods.	Pass.	Goods.	Pass.	Goods.	

FORM 14.

may prove interesting. There were 431 engines in the division, of which 412 were in working order and 19 under repair, and there were also nine motor cars. The total mileage run was 857,978. The total quantity of coal consumed was 299,504 cwts., and of this 268,385 cwts. were used by locomotives and 4,134 cwts. by cars. The consumption of coal by passenger engines per train mile equals 31.34, and that of goods 40.00. The average consumption per engine mile equals 36.20.

Fig. 8 gives the divisional expenditure under all heads, the cost of coal being assumed as 10/- per ton. The grand total of nearly £20,000 per month is made up of numerous items, which require the watchful care of the Divisional Superintendent and his staff; and it is obvious that with such an enormous expenditure the commercial part of the Superintendent's duties are quite as important as the engineering part.

CLERICAL STAFF. - Turning now from statistics to the members of the staff who do their share – that is the divisional share – in preparing them. On the genealogical tree [p. 9] the chief clerk comes first. He should have had considerable experience of Running work. He knows the duties of all the clerks under his control, and divides the work amongst them as equitably as he possibly can, taking care to have men employed as far as practicable on work for which they have a special aptitude. He deals with a large amount of the correspondence himself, and generally takes up some speciality such as, for instance, Carriage and Wagon work. He follows up the routine work, and generally gets everything cleared up day by day. He scorns 'repeats', and only gets one when there is some good cause for delay in replying to a letter. In short, he saves his Superintendent from a lot of worry over routine matters and details.

The second clerk keeps in touch with the work of the chief clerk, so that he can at any time take his place. He deals with some of the correspondence, and takes up some particular section or sections of the work according to circumstances. In the Swindon Division, he deals with engine failures and special train working. All the other clerks work either single-handed or in couples. When in couples, there is always one in charge. Immediately on the right of the second clerk will be seen 'special and working expenses'. This man dissects the consumption statements in the manner already described, and he also gets out all special statistical information which the divisional superintendent or the chief officers may require. His duties are onerous and varied. The next clerk to the right keeps the boiler records (which were described in the last paper), and makes out all the accident reports. Still again to the right will be found a single-handed job, that of examining the eyesight of cleaners and dealing with the promotion of men, advanced rates of wages, premiums, etc. Next are three correspondence clerks. They deal with general correspondence, and are experts at shorthand and typewriting. The senior of the three goes through the more important letters with the superintendent daily. He also attends some of the more important joint enquiries, and types seven copies at once of the evidence of the men concerned as fast as it can be dictated. The next job is the coal account, which is single-handed, and involves the preparation of numerous returns. Two men are employed on Carriage and Wagon accounts, and these also deal with the advances of carriage examiners, etc. One man deals with notices of special trains, also the accounts which are rendered by or against the Locomotive Department. Stores trials, etc., is a single-handed job performed by a man who makes a speciality of storekeeping. Frequently as many as fifty articles are on trial at a time; it will be seen, therefore, that keeping a proper record of these forms an important part of his duties. The cashier in the Swindon Division deals also with the applications for passes, and by means of a card system he can at once see whether or not an applicant for a pass is entitled to it. Letter registration is an important duty, though for some reason or another most people look upon it as simple routine work, calling for no special use of brains and judgment; but the way letters

FIG. 8 (see p. 55).

LOCOMOTIVE DEPARTMENT.
DIVISIONAL SUMMARY OF MONTHLY EXPENDITURE.

CHARGE.	WAGES. Cost.	WAGES. Cost per Train Mile.	STORES.	COAL.	TOTAL.
	£ s. d.	d.	£ s. d.	£ s. d.	£ s. d.
LOCOMOTIVES — Enginemen and Firemen—Passenger	2228 12 10	1·59	494 12 2	6814 8 6	14037 17 8
Ditto Goods	4500 4 2	3·08			
Boilerwashers	174 17 10	·06	5 19 4	—	180 17 2
Foremen and Inspectors	192 18 6	·06	—	—	192 18 6
TOTAL	7096 13 4	2·49	500 11 6	6814 8 6	14411 13 4
Cleaning	791 7 10	·27	147 14 2	—	939 2 0
Coaling	161 3 4	·05	·1 3 6	—	162 6 10
Shed	594 3 9	·20	15 19 5	10 10 6	620 13 8
Shunting	3 9 9	—	—	—	3 9 9
TOTAL	8646 18 0	3·03	665 8 7	6824 19 0	16137 5 7
RAIL MOTOR CARS — Enginemen and Firemen	133 17 10	1·14	14 7 4	103 8 6	251 13 8
Boilerwashers	4 10 7	·03	0 10 2	—	5 0 9
Foremen and Inspectors	4 0 0	·03	—	—	4 0 0
TOTAL	142 8 5	1·21	14 17 6	103 8 6	260 14 5
Cleaning	9 16 0	·08	3 9 8	—	13 5 8
Coaling	4 17 7	·04	1 2 9	—	6 0 4
Shed	4 1 11	·03	—	—	4 1 11
TOTAL	161 3 11	1·37	19 9 11	103 8 6	288 2 4
Time and Storekeeping	168 3 1	·05	3 18 9	—	172 1 10
Water Pumping	113 19 1	·03	18 9 10	106 3 6	238 12 5
Water Repairs	98 5 4	·03	9 5 7	—	107 10 11
TOTAL WORKING EXPENSES	9188 9 5	3·09	716 12 8	7034 11 10	16939 13 1
Repair to Engines and Tenders	970 10 6	—	509 3 6	19 0 6	1499 4 6
Do. Rail Motors	16 15 9	—	9 13 1	—	26 8 10
Do. Buildings, Locomotive	63 11 2	—	10 18 7	—	74 9 9
Do. Buildings, Rail Motors	—	—	—	—	—
Coal Expenses	5 11 3	—	0 3 4	—	5 14 7
Factory Expenses	384 7 1	—	—	—	384 7 1
Sundries	102 18 8	—	23 5 11	—	125 14 7
Credits	342 7 11	—	41 19 0	162 17 6	547 4 5
TOTAL	11074 11 9	—	1311 16 1	7216 9 0	19602 16 10

referring to the same subject sometimes get registered under two or three different references leads the Author to think that none but experienced clerks should be employed on this work. The six spare men, shewn on diagram, are not waiting round for a job, the word 'spare' merely indicating that they are not told off for any specific work.

Simpson elaborated the Divisional system in both of his papers of 1906, parts of which have been reproduced; the system can be seen to have been well established by that time:

IN the early days of railways each Company had a small capital and only a few miles of line, but it was very soon found to be to the mutual advantage of small Companies to amalgamate. From these amalgamations have sprung such gigantic corporations as the Great Western, North Western, and Midland Railway Companies. With these changes have come modifications in the organisation of the Locomotive, Carriage, and Wagon Departments. On a railway of from 50 to 200 miles of line the function of the Chief Locomotive Superintendent was essentially that of a Running Superintendent. He was responsible for the running and the repairing of the engines under his control. He would undertake general repairs; but if he required a new boiler, crank shaft, or pair of cylinders he would order these from the engine builders. His responsibilities were, in short, about the same as a present day

Divisional Superintendent. His engines were built by private firms, and most of you are aware that even now we have engines running on the Great Western which were originally built by such firms as England, Sharp, Stewart, Slaughter, Gruning & Co., Wilsons, Beyer, Peacock & Co., and others. Within the last few years some consternation was caused among the Locomotive Superintendents at a meeting of the Institute of Mechanical Engineers by the suggestion that the true function of a Locomotive Superintendent was to see to the running and repairing of Locomotives, but that the designing and building should be left to private firms. This suggestion was made by a representative of a private firm, and was not endorsed by the Locomotive Superintendents present. No matter how clever the engineers of private firms may be, it would be impossible for them to build such engines as are at present running on the Great Western Railway unless they had actual experience in running, and were in a position to develop in directions which the working of the engines indicated. Now-a-days the Chief Locomotive Superintendent of a great railway is responsible for the designing, building, and running of all locomotives, as well as the designing and repairing of the carriages and wagons. One of his principal assistants is the Chief of the Running Department. The organisation of this department is not the same on all railways. On the L. & N.W., for instance, there are two Superintendents – one is at the head of the Northern, and the other of the Southern Division – and these officers have foremen at the different sheds under their control. The Locomotive Running Department is altogether distinct from the Carriage and Wagon Department, and under a different set of officers. On our line the Chief of the Running Department has an assistant and seven Divisional Superintendents. The author does not propose to discuss the relative advantages and disadvantages of the different systems, but will content himself by saying that the Running Department of the Great Western is the most economical of the great trunk lines.

FOREMEN. – Each division is sub-divided into districts, over each of which a foreman has charge. On the G.W.R. these are usually promoted from the grade of enginemen. On the L. & N.W. Railway and some other lines they are usually men who have been pupils or apprentices. The Author considers the G.W. system the better, because the most important part of a foreman's duty is arranging the working of the engines, and his training as an engineman renders him more competent to do this work than a man who has spent his time in a factory and drawing office. An assistant foreman, however, should be appointed at all large sheds who has been either a pupil or an apprentice. Such a man could follow up thoroughly the shed work and repairs, and thus leave the head foreman free to do the arranging. Sometimes, when the line is very congested and the demand for engines and relief excessive, it is impossible for a foreman to follow up the mere routine work as closely as it should be followed up, so that if he had a competent assistant it would relieve him considerably. The assistant could pick up the work of the head foreman, and his detail knowledge of running work would make him well fitted to become an Assistant Superintendent, and finally a Superintendent.

The longevity of the debating habit affords the great benefit of a considerable continuity in the story of these 'Locomotive Sheds', at least as seen from 'above'. Mr. W. N. Pellow, M.Inst.Mech.E., M.Inst.Loco.E., was Motive Power Superintendent, Western Region by 1952 and in a paper to the Society, 'The Work of the Motive Power Department', felt the need to refer back to Simpson's early work:

CHAIRMAN: Ladies and gentlemen, tonight it is our great privilege and pleasure to listen to a lecture by Mr. Pellow, our Motive Power Superintendent, who is so well known to us. Unlike Mr. Pellow, I have no impassioned speech to deliver tonight, so, therefore, I will immediately call on him to deliver his lecture. (*Laughter and Applause.*)

MR. PELLOW: Mr. Chairman, ladies and gentlemen, I should take it as a favour if somebody in the rear rank would indicate presently whether or not you can hear me. I gather that the acoustics are not too good, and if you have any difficulty do not fail to hold up your hand or give some kind of signal if you cannot hear what is being said.

Mr. Grand said this was going to be a lecture. Well now, I am not so sure about that. When I was here a fortnight or three weeks ago, one of the gentlemen who was speaking at that time started his reminiscences and talked about a paper read to the Society twenty or more years ago relating to Storekeeping. A predecessor of mine, a Mr. Henry Simpson, prepared a paper, and delivered it before the Swindon Engineering Society quite forty-six years ago. It ran to one hundred and six pages, plus a lot of appendices, took two evenings to deliver, and quite a lot of time to discuss. It was very full of all sorts of details: it went into such matters as the size of spanners, and the details of all kinds of appliances, and described scores of various forms that had to be filled in. Its title was 'The Work of the Running Department,' and was regarded almost as a text book by the young locomotive engineers of that period.

I am not going to attempt that to-night in the time at my disposal, so I rather thought the right thing to call this paper was 'Some Notes on the Work of a Motive Power Department' instead of a full blooded lecture.

In the ears of the older members of our Society, the term 'Motive Power Department' may sound rather strange, whilst in the case of the younger members, they may be interested in some degree to hear a little of how the work of the Locomotive Department was organised in past years, and the present Department came into being.

HISTORICAL. Since the date of nationalisation of the Railways of this country, development has tended toward a form of standardisation. Whilst this trend is still going on, the present position is that the railway system of England and Wales, with Scotland, has been divided into six geographical Regions.

The old G.W.R. system, plus the addition and subtraction of certain 'bits and pieces' has come to be known as the Western Region of British Railways. It is of this particular Region and its Motive Power Department that I would like to speak tonight.

During the period of the old G.W.R. regime, which, by the way, continued for well over a century, the term Motive Power was not used, neither was there a separate Department as such. There was a section of the Chief Mechanical Engineer's Department, known as the Locomotive Running section.

Throughout the time of the G.W.R. the successive Mechanical Engineers were responsible, not only for building and heavy repair of their locomotives, but also for the 'day by day' maintenance and running of the engines.

Sir Daniel Gooch was 'the first of the few' Mechanical Engineers so far as the G.W.R. at was concerned. His title at the time was 'Locomotive-Carriage and Wagon Superintendent.' He held office from 1837 till 1864 and was then followed by: Mr. Joseph Armstrong 1864–1877, and finally Mr. William Dean 1877–1902, each one carrying the original title.

In 1902, Mr. G. J. Churchward was appointed Locomotive-Carriage and Wagon Superintendent, at Swindon, but in 1916 the title was changed to Chief Mechanical Engineer, and that title Churchward held till he retired in 1921, being followed by: Mr. C. B. Collett 1921–1941, and as you know, Mr. F. W. Hawksworth 1941–1949, and during all this time the Locomotive Running Section was under the Mechanical Engineer.

In process of time, these gentlemen had additional responsibilities laid on them until, at a certain period of Mr. Collett's time, and right down to the time of Mr. Hawksworth's retirement, the Chief Mechanical Engineer was responsible to the General Manager and to the Board of Directors for: –

(1) Construction and repair of Locomotives, and running of same.
(2) Construction and repair of all types of Carriages and Wagons.
(3) The cleaning and lighting of coaching stock.
(4) All matters relating to Electrical Engineering.
(5) Machinery of all kinds, Pumps and Hydraulic work, Turntables, etc.
(6) Maintenance of cranes – lifts – hauling and lifting tackle, Wire Ropes, Chains, Slings, etc.
(7) He also had Docks Mechanical Installations under his care and
(8) Locomotive Water Supplies – Mains, etc.

There is reason to believe that fairly early on the need was felt for Assistants to the Chief of this Department.

Sir Daniel Gooch at the start, appears to have conducted the business of his Department personally, but as the line grew in size, and the number of Depots increased, there is a record that he appointed what he called Divisional Assistants.

For some time the line was divided into two parts, known as the 'Northern Division' and the 'Southern Division' with a Divisional Supt. in each.

This arrangement lasted from about 1854 to 1884. Then a new post was created, known as 'Locomotive Running Superintendent'; and subsequently 'Loco Running Assistant to Chief Mechanical Engineer.' This office was at Swindon, and the post was filled in succession by: –

Mr. Thomas Simpson (who was a product of the Wolverhampton works of those days) 1885–1897, Mr. W. H. Waister 1897–1912, Mr. W. H. Williams 1913–1919, Mr. J. A. Robinson 1919–1920, Mr. H. Simpson 1920–1922, Mr. C. Crump 1922–1931, Mr. F. C. Hall 1931–1941, and then myself.

All these gentlemen had been trained as Mechanical Engineers.

Early in 1922, a Board Minute was drawn whereby the officer filling the post was to be designated 'Locomotive Running Superintendent and Outdoor Assistant to C.M.E.'

In this capacity the individual was responsible to the Chief Mechanical Engineer for: –

(1) The 'day by day' maintenance of Locomotives and Boilers.
(2) Day by day repairs to Carriage and Wagon Stock.
(3) Carriage Cleaning and Lighting.
(4) General supervision of outdoor staff and machinery, etc.
(5) Liaison with other Departments.

He was jointly responsible to the Chief Mechanical Engineer and the Superintendent of the Line for such items as: –

(1) Allocation and distribution of Engine Power,
(2) Preparation of working diagrams for engines and men, both Passenger and Freight.
(3) Examination of Daily Records of work done.
(4) Rostering of hours of duty and allocation of enginemen to depots.

Under him there were the nine Divisional Assistants to the Chief Mechanical Engineer, and these were co-ordinated by the Loco. Running Superintendent.

On occasions he had a very full day's programme.

FIG. 1. This was the set-up just at the time the last Chief Mechanical Engineer finished his term of office, and before the split-up of the department came. We had the Board of Directors, the General Manager, and then the Chief Mechanical Engineer. Under him there were the Loco Works Managers, with their Assistants. The Carriage and Wagon Works Manager with his Assistants, and the Docks people on the other side. The Principal Assistant,

by the way, in the absence of the Chief Mechanical Engineer, carried on the business of the whole department. But generally speaking, the Chief Mechanical Engineer dealt directly with the people in the main workshops.

From the C.M.E. we have got this line to the Loco Running Superintendent and his two Assistants (one for loco matters, and one for carriages), dealing directly with the nine divisions into which the line had been split up. These persons here were all reporting under various headings, which I have already mentioned.

We have also the Electrical Assistant with three districts throughout the line, and, of course, the Chief Draughtsman, Chief Chemist, and so on.

That was the general set-up, and you will see in a moment how subsequently the Motive Power side came off that fairly easily so far as general arrangements were concerned.

At the beginning of January, 1950, the existing state of affairs was altered. The old Chief Mechanical Engineer's Department ceased to exist on the retirement of Mr. Hawksworth, and was divided up under the following headings: –

(1) Mechanical and Electrical Engineer's Department.
(2) Carriage and Wagon Engineer's Department.
(3) Docks Mechanical Engineer's Department.
(4) Motive Power Department.
(5) Chief Accountant's Department.

The responsibility for Carriage Cleaning was placed on the Operating Superintendent. Thus the Chief Mechanical Engineer's Department, which comprised a total of something like 46,500 persons of all Grades, was split up into six Departments. The Motive Power Department took over approximately 24,000 persons out of that total.

FIG. 2. In this diagram we have the Railway Executive Officers, with our Chief Regional Officer, then the Motive Power Superintendent and his assistants. On the right are the various assistants in the Head Office: the Staff Assistant and Chief Clerk dealing with the various clerical units, the Mechanical Assistant, a General Assistant, and Fuel Supply Assistant, with locomotive running inspectors, and mechanical inspectors and others. They in turn still govern the nine sections, or districts as they are now called, rather than divisions. The old offices which were divisional offices with an officer in each, and an assistant in every one except Oswestry, are now the District Offices.

You will notice here that at the high level we have two gentlemen at the Railway Executive who are interested. They can, and do, on occasions deal direct with the Motive Power Superintendent, both from the point of view of operating matters or mechanical and electrical engineering matters; but the main source is through the Chief Regional Officer and straight down through the Motive Power Superintendent to his District Officers and men.

In this way the Motive Power Department, Western Region, British Railways, came into being, with the existing Locomotive Running Superintendent at its head, but bearing the new title of Motive Power Superintendent, and now responsible to the Chief Regional Officer and the Railway Executive.

At the latter high level two of the functional members of the Railway Executive take a very lively interest in the work of the Department, viz: –

(1) The Member for Operating, and
(2) The Member for Mechanical and Electrical Engineering.

The former gentleman is very concerned to see that all Traffic offering is moved currently on the Railway, whilst the latter gentleman is watching to see that the locomotives are not maltreated and that they are properly maintained in as good a state as possible, to do the work required of them, also to receive suggestions in regard to improvement in types and things of that kind.

FUNCTION. The duty of a Motive Power Superintendent has been described as being 'to provide the necessary Motive Power of

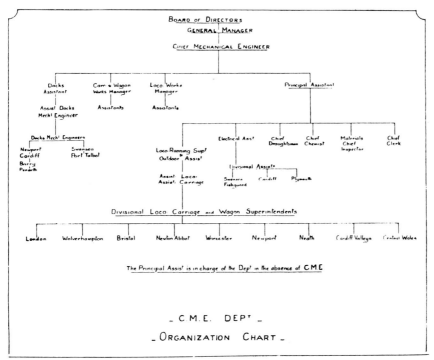

FIG. 1

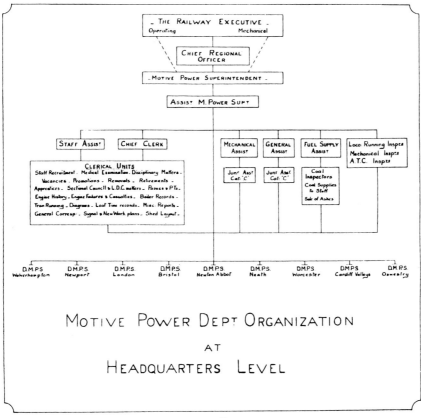

FIG. 2

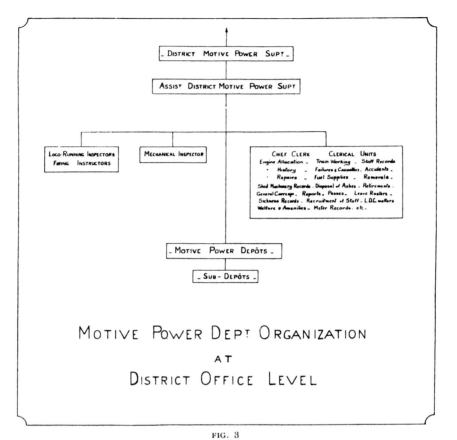

MOTIVE POWER DEPT ORGANIZATION
AT
DISTRICT OFFICE LEVEL

FIG. 3

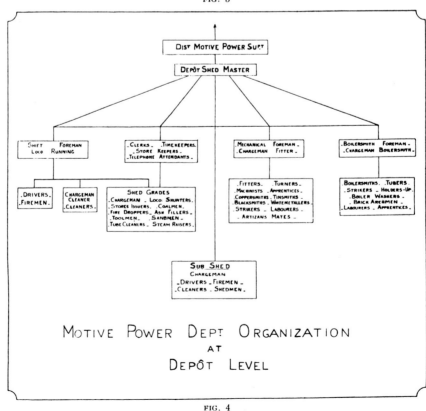

MOTIVE POWER DEPT ORGANIZATION
AT
DEPÔT LEVEL

FIG. 4

suitable types, and in good working order, at the right time and place to work to the requirements of the Operating Superintendent.' (*Laughter.*)

At the same time he must see to it that the locomotives for which he is responsible are maintained in a manner satisfactory to the Mechanical Engineer.

The Motive Power Department, Western Region, is operating daily roughly 3,600 locomotives, whilst there is a total stock of about 3,850 at the moment, I think. This entails the employment of approximately 24,000 persons of all grades. The total mileage run by the engines is about 98,500,000 per annum, made up roughly: –

(1) Passenger   45,300,000
(2) Freight   50,100,000
(3) Departmental   3,100,000

These are approximate figures.

The amount of coal used on locomotives is about 45,000 tons per week all the year round, or about 2.1/3 million tons per annum, Western Region alone.

These are somewhat astronomical figures, but they do give you some indications of work done for other departments and the Public.

ORGANISATION. On the question of organisation at Motive Power Headquarters, in addition to the Motive Power Superintendent, the following persons have their respective responsibilities: –

(1) The Assistant Motive Power Superintendent.
(2) Staff Assistant to Motive Power Superintendent.
(3) Mechanical Assistant to Motive Power Superintendent.
(4) General Assistant to Motive Power Superintendent.
(5) Fuel Supply Assistant to the Motive Power Superintendent.

The Motive Power Department, Western Region, have the whole line divided into nine Districts, mentioned previously, with a responsible officer in charge of each. In the Districts there are a number of Loco. Depots and Sub-Depots in charge of officials known as Shed Masters.

FIG. 3. This is the general lay-out to-day of the District Motive Power Superintendent's office. A D.M.P.S. with assistant D.M.P.S., certain Inspectors and Firing Instructors and a Chief Clerk handling all clerical work dealing with engine allocation within his own province; and that in turn is used as the general organisation to deal with the Motive Power depots and sub-depots.

Sub-depots are generally not in charge of Shed Masters but someone of a lower category, and they are subsidiary to the main depots.

FIG. 4. In this diagram we see the general arrangement as it should be at a Motive Power Depot. The District Motive Power Superintendent is responsible for the district, and he has under him a Shed master at each Main Shed who, in turn, has all these people gathered under him. You have the Shift Foreman for Locomotive purposes, who in turn looks after Drivers and Firemen, Cleaners and various shed grades. Of course, there are the clerks, typists, storekeepers, and so forth; and on the other side there is a Mechanical Foreman or a Chargeman Fitter as the case may be, and a Boilersmith Foreman or Chargeman, under whom are working all the artisan staff as required.

At the Sub-Depôt these people are working day to day with the main depot as their parent, and any repairs or alterations to working are dealt with by the main shed organisation.

It will be appreciated therefore, from what I have said, that the Shed Masters work and responsibility is all focussed at District Office, while the District Officers in turn focus on Headquarters.

The Motive Power Superintendent and his Principal Assistant, whilst dealing with numbers of items in detail, have to see that each of the Sections is operating efficiently, and of course, in addition keep in touch with other Departmental Officers, and matters in which they are jointly concerned.

It is also necessary to visit frequently and report to the Chief Regional Officer, who gives direction on matters of principle and policy.

Subsequent questions revealed some aspects of the New Order to be less than heartily endorsed. Familiar themes remained popular:

I have tried in some fashion to give you an idea of what goes on in a Motive Power Department. My time has been limited, and I fear that I have not fully covered the subject. If, however, it has interested the members to any degree, and if I have been able to help you to understand to some extent, at least, some of the problems and trials which confront those men who day by day, night after night, have to carry on the work of the Motive Power Depots, sometimes under great difficulty, and with a shortage of experienced Staff in nearly all grades, I do not think this evening's talk will be entirely wasted. I feel that the middle-aged Supervisors that we have in all groups, are doing a good job of work, and are still striving to carry on our old traditions, because they have had enough years of service to remind them of the conditions which existed before the War caused so much upset and dislocation, and they realise that some of those standards have been lowered to-day. This does not tend in the right direction, and the Supervisors know that better results can be obtained if all the Staff would co-operate, but it is often an uphill fight, and these Supervisors should be encouraged and supported as much as possible.

Finally, I would like to record my thanks to my Assistants who have helped me in collecting some of the facts and information which have gone into the 'build-up' of these notes ... and I must thank the Mechanical and Electrical Engineer for the making up and supplying of the slides which have been used in connection with this Paper. (*Applause.*)

CHAIRMAN: Now, ladies and gentlemen, as is our usual custom, the meeting is open for discussion.

MR. GARDNER (Chief Accountant's Department, Swindon): Mr. Chairman, I was very interested in Mr. Pellow's slides of the two types of shed, the straight one with the dead end and the round one. I wonder if he could help by telling us some of the factors which govern the decision as to whether to have a straight one with a wall at the end or a round one? From the amateur's point of view the round one seems to have all the advantages of easy mobility of locomotives.

CHAIRMAN: Mr. Pellow proposes, ladies and gentlemen, to deal with the questions at the end. I think he is probably very wise. (*Laughter.*) Now what is the next one?

MR. DASHWOOD (Chief Accountant): Mr. Chairman, there are two very short questions, short as time is getting on. The first is: you have seen and heard of the disintegration of a powerful department which operated successfully for over one hundred years. (*Hear, hear.*) I do not know whether it is fair to ask the speaker whether he commends this disintegration ... (*Laughter*) ... either from the point of view of economy or of efficiency. The other question – and this is something outside my real sphere – is that I do remember in connection with coal consumption two schools of thought in regard to the firing of a locomotive, whether it should be a convex fire or a concave fire. I wonder whether Mr. Pellow could tell, us whether any solution of that problem has been reached? (*Laughter.*)

MR. MATTHEWS (Operating Superintendent): This is not a question, Sir, exactly, but I am confused with admiration (even more than ever before) of my friend, Mr. Pellow, and I think I am safe in saying that, having learned so much about locomotives when I knew absolutely nothing, on behalf of my department I can promise him there will not be any criticism of his department whatsoever, at least not until tomorrow morning. (*Laughter.*)

Mr. S. G. Ward (Regional Staff Office): Mr. Chairman, ladies and gentlemen, I would like to ask Mr. Pellow what is, perhaps, a rather personal question if he does not mind. Is he really satisfied with his title and that of his department? They are, respectively, Motive Power Superintendent and Motive Power Department. Some time ago I read a couple of books by a prominent Civil Servant – written, I think, largely for the benefit of Civil Servants – in praise of the use of plain words. I am rather intrigued as to whether 'Motive Power Department' describes in the plainest and most straightforward way the function of this department.

Previously, as Mr. Pellow tells us it was known as the Locomotive Running Department and, earlier, the Locomotive Carriage and Wagon Department. Why not simply call this department the Locomotive Department or the Locomotive Running Department? Why 'Motive Power'? I took the trouble to look up in my dictionary the meaning of 'motive'. Among the definitions I found this: 'tending to initiate movement'.

But I assume Mr. Pellow's department is out to do rather more than that. I also looked up 'locomotive' in the same dictionary, and that included: 'having the power of or given to locomotion, not stationary.' That is surely, more apt?

Can Mr. Pellow point to any practical, psychological or other advantage as a result of the adoption of this designation. How did the 20,000 odd members of his staff react to it when they suddenly found themselves translated? I have heard men express themselves rather forcibly about the condition of certain blank engines or locomotives Do they now speak of this 'so and so instrument of motive power'? (*Laughter*.)

Chairman: We may have to rule some of that out in the end.

Mr. Taylor (Architect's Office, Paddington): I should like to ask Mr. Pellow how it is that locomotives are withdrawn from service. It seems to the amateur enthusiast that it is done in a rather haphazard way, though obviously it is not. For example, 'Saint' class locomotives started to be withdrawn out of the service years ago, but I know of one of them which was recently overhauled and, even though it has survived its brothers by 15 years, I am told by the drivers it puts up a magnificent performance and it is quite as good as the latest 'Castle' engine. (*Laughter*.) I should be interested to know how this engine survives and why it does so well when many others of its type were withdrawn.

Mr. Wallington (Mechanical and Electrical Engineer's Department, Swindon): Mr. Chairman, I should like to ask Mr. Pellow if any difficulty is experienced with engine crews, who have been used to the G.W.R. type of locomotive, with controls on the right-hand side, when they are transferred to the new standard locomotive, with all controls on the left. In view of the fact that their aspect of signal gantries, junctions, etc, is different, do they have to re-learn the road?

I must say I have experienced considerable difficulty in driving cars on the continent in countries where the rule of the road is the reverse of that here. My reactions tend to become subconscious in this country and unless I keep very wide awake abroad, there is the tendency to do the wrong thing in an emergency.

The road and rail problems are of course not quite the same, but I should be interested to know whether any difficulties have arisen.

Secondly, with reference to Diesel and other locomotives, where the prime movers are made by outside firms, I gathered from Mr. Pellow's remarks, that our crews are given a certain amount of instruction in carrying out running repairs.

Are running emergencies and adjustments of every kind dealt with by our men, or are certain more intricate parts of the mechanism sealed, and arrangements made that they shall only be dealt with by experts?

Mr. Bowles (Chief Regional Office): I was very intrigued by the picture Mr. Pellow showed us of a clean engine. (*Laughter*.) You will remember that the picture portrayed a number of industrious young men polishing an engine. I want to ask him whether the picture was specially taken for this occasion. (*Laughter*.)

Mr. Hens (Operating Department, Reading): Some of our engine schedules seem to be designed with one eye on the need to return the engines to their home depots once a week for washing out. If there is a temporary alteration in the flow of traffic, the wagons stop where they are and the engine goes home 'light' to be washed out. Can there be some relaxation of this instruction? I know it was not very successful when it was tried out during the war, but is it likely to give better use of engines, if we try again under peace time conditions?

Mr. Woodbridge (Signal Engineer): I notice our friends in the Locomotive Department have made a move towards modernisation by putting the driver on the left-hand side, as one of the previous questioners said. I would like to ask Mr. Pellow what his views would be on what is again, I am afraid rather a frivolous suggestion.

Mr. Pellow: Did you say 'right' or 'left'-hand side?

Mr. Woodbridge: Left-hand side?

Mr. Pellow: Thank you.

Mr. Woodbridge: This is a frivolous suggestion, but in the diesel car they now put the driver in front of the engine. Why is not the steam engine designed that way round? (*Laughter*.)

Mr. Abraham (Motive Power Supt. L.M. Region): Mr. Chairman. May I ask Mr. Pellow a point about the photographs? He showed one of a round shed completely empty, and another one of a straight shed. Is that due to all the locomotives allocated to those sheds being out in traffic and held by the Operating Department ... (*Laughter*) ... or is it because the availability at these sheds is so excellent that they were all revenue earning?

There are two other small points I should like to mention. One is that I feel, although Mr. Pellow has given a most excellent general idea of the duties of the Motive Power Department, he did not give us sufficient idea of the fact that he has to work to a fixed budget and that, although this work has to be done every year, he has to keep within his budget. Secondly, it is most important that he should get the co-operation of his staff under him and all the other departments who are helping him. I should think those two items might have been stressed a little bit more in the paper.

Mr. Pearman (Operating Department, Paddington): The first fact I would like to mention is that drivers of the new engines are going to be situated on the left-hand side of the cab. Will this have any bearing on the question of signal siting?

The second point is that in my travels round the old Great Western Railway – and latterly round the Western Region – I have noticed no sign of large mechanical coaling plants such as one sees on the London Midland and the London North Eastern. I wonder whether the installation of these would reduce in a way the average turn-round of six hours?

Thirdly, it might be rather impertinent and I might get into trouble over it, but I would like to ask why the London–Birmingham trains no longer do it in two hours. (*Laughter*.)

Chairman: Shall I ask Mr. Pellow to try and answer some of these questions now, because there are some quite good ones here. (*Laughter*.)

Mr. Pellow: Ladies and gentlemen, the question box is filling up very well. Mr. Gardner said, I think, he should like to know the factors governing the selection of types of shed. One of the factors, of course, is the size and shape of the land at your disposal; and, naturally, there other items or factors which one cannot always lay down at a meeting of this kind. I rather fancy that what you have got in mind, Mr. Gardner, are the advantages or disadvantages of a 'straight' as against a 'round' shed.

Mr. Gardner: Yes.

Mr. Pellow: That would take another paper to decide, I think, but all practical locomotive men will tell you that there are decided advantages in many ways with a round-house type of shed because, having got your machines in the shed, you berth them in such a way that each one is on its own separate road. It is there and it need not be interfered with in any way by other movements throughout the time it is in the shed.

In the case of a 'straight' shed, of whatever number of roads or dimensions you always have certain difficulties whether it is a 'dead end' or whether it is a 'through' shed where you can get out at the other end. You may have two or three or even four, or maybe more engines, one behind the other, in succession on a particular road. If repairs have to be done, such as anything in the nature of dealing with tubes or flues, you must separate your engines and so provide a space to give head room for the tools to be used. Furthermore if you have fitters or other artisans at work underneath, they are always on tenterhooks because of the possibility that somebody is going to move another engine on the same road, and possibly make contact and move the engine on which they are engaged.

On the other hand, if you have a 'round-house' shed practically filled with engines, and then by some mischance, act of God or providence or something like that your turntable breaks down, well, you have got all that power locked in. It has happened to me more than once, and on those occasions you do not bless a round-house type of shed. (*Laughter.*)

Mr. Hedges here will remember that there was a committee some years ago which went into the pros and cons at some length. I think there is a lot to be said for a rectangular shed; 'straight' so far as the shed itself is concerned, but with means of access down the sides. In other words, your approach roads run down on the outside of the shed and you fan off in the same way as you would park cars, in 'herring-bone' fashion. By that means you can stable each locomotive on a separate road, and at the same time have access to each without the risk of heavy stoppage due to turntables breaking down, or any of that trouble, because each would be in its own stall. But it would be a heck of a cost, and I think that is the trouble to-day.

Mr. Dashwood asked: 'Is disintegration good or bad?' Well, that is a difficult question, Sir. (*Laughter.*) Am I bound to answer that one.

CHAIRMAN: Not a bit. (*Laughter.*)

MR. PELLOW: Disintegration. I should say from my own point of view, has not been good. It has had the effect of breaking up a department that was welded together and doing perfectly good work. From all that I have seen of it so far, it has cost us more in supervision, if not in other ways. Whereas the department was run under one flag with one man in charge, we now have at least five departments, each with a man in charge: not necessarily all on the same wage or salary, worse luck! (*Laughter.*) In sum total, however, I must say the salaries are greater and cost must be higher.

Regarding the firing of a concave or a convex fire, Mr. Dashwood, we used to call it a 'haycock' fire. It is really a pile, but in these days of 'little and often' the great point is to cover the firegrate and not allow any holes to get in the fire, whether in the corners or in the middle. With the old type of Great Western firegrate, where the front section was on a slope, our best means was, and still is to fire the coal just under the door, and allow the hot fire to work gradually down to the front end of the firebox and under the underside of the brick arch, rather than to throw green coal right down to the front end. I do not know whether one of my inspectors is going to give me a pasting over that answer. (*Laughter.*)

Mr. Matthews, I am very glad to know I have got at least one friend in the audience.

Mr. Ward queried the use of the term 'Motive Power' – Well – What's in a name? It is as good as anything else is it not?

I heard the department called 'Motor Power Department' the other day.

When my title was Loco Running Supt. some of my friends said they never saw me run in my life! After all, the tendency to 'initiate movement' is there, with the greater tendency to keep it going, and improve upon it. (*Laughter.*)

As far as the reaction of the men is concerned 'by and large' I would say that they have taken to it just as they have in other instances in years gone by, when they had to take to certain other adjustments and alterations, such as the amalgamations in 1921-22. There may have been – and there probably are – numbers of men who make remarks which are not printable from time to time. But that may be due to a loss of a turn of duty, or somebody stepping in front of them, or even to bad digestion. I would not like to be too definite.

Then we have Mr. Taylor's question on how and why engines are withdrawn from service. I am not quite sure what you are driving at, Mr. Taylor, but take the class of engine thay you mentioned, the 'Saint' class, the old Churchward two-cylinders, which in their day were very fine machines, but have become out-moded with the loads that we have to haul to-day. Age, of course, has a great deal to do with it. The Accountant knows more about the financial side than I do; but it was quite a number of years ago that it was decided that these engines would have to go out of the service because of age, and the cost of renewals. But like a good many other things, they did not all fail in the same way or at the same rate. The earlier engines which came out of the service more quickly probably did so because of at least two reasons – either the cylinders broke down, or the frames gave way, and were not worth the expense of repairing. What was more likely, the boiler was in a very poor state, and we did not have at that time enough spare boilers of the type to carry on, thus making it not worth while to go for another heavy repair. The engines of that type which are still left in service are being worn out as rapidly as possible. If there is any one of them coming up for consideration for a heavy repair by the Mechanical Engineering Department, which is in such a state that it is not worth the spending of the money necessary for another repair (which means it must get the mileage in again to make it financially worth while running for about two and a half to three more years). That is the general system underlying condemnations. Engines are not necessarily condemned in a full group, neither are they condemned on paper alone – condition at time of shopping enters into the case. With a list of six or eight engines built early in the group some of the early engines may possibly have a fair 'life' to run out while later ones may be in worse condition.

Mr. Wallington wanted to know if there was any difficulty with men working on right or left-hand sides. I would say not, Mr. Wallington. We have had a number of engines with the left-hand side drive at various times. During the war we had quite a fleet of them running, and then they were taken away again. Now we have got some coming back to us, as the new B.R. Standard engines are left-hand drive. If I may couple this with the question of some other gentleman farther down, Mr. Woodbridge talked about drivers on the left-hand side and Mr. Pearman did also. The driver is all right. He has got a position to take up, and except that he probably will be working his regulator more now with the right hand than he would in former days (because it is normal to keep his left hand on the regulator handle with right-hand side driving. I think, while he is looking out to the front.) I do not think there is anything in it as far as he is concerned. But some of the firemen may find it difficult if they get their sternposts round the wrong way while firing on the right. (*Laughter.*) I have seen a number of our drivers working quite easily and comfortably on the left-hand side.

From the point of siting signals, probably most of you railwaymen know it is a Recommendation of the Ministry, of many years standing that, as far as possible, all signals should be sited on the left-hand side of the track to which they apply, except in those cases where you have them on a gantry high enough to clear your loading gauge, when you may put them over the centre of the track or towards the right. In those instances, I would say a left-hand side drive is an advantage to the driver because he personally would be in a position to pick up and see the signals himself. After all, the driver is responsible for observing the signals, although he does get a good deal of help from his fireman if the fireman is a practised hand, and a proper fireman.

From that point of view I have no quarrel with the average – or the greater proportion of – our men do not grumble, and do not forsee any difficulty in driving on the left-hand side.

With regard to Mr. Wallington, I might say he must remember this. Although he found difficulty in driving a motor car on a public road, on the Continent, a locomotive driver is constrained to run in a certain track by the flanges of the wheels of his engine, and he has nothing to do with the steering, so he would not go across to the other side of the road on that account. (*Laughter*.)

Mr. Bowles mentioned the cleaning of the engines. The photograph which you saw was an old photograph taken just before the war when we had a lot of cleaners. (*Laughter*.)

Then there was Mr. Hens, was it, on the question of return of engines for boiler washing? It is policy, and the proper thing to do, in spite of your thinking, that there is at times something queer, and loss of time, etc., involved by this practice. In the end, taking the thing by and large, the proper place for an engine to be serviced is at its home depot, with its own shed men and its own artisans, who should, and do know, of the peculiar points of that engine. They are in a better position to deal with these idiosyncracies. I would say every time that the proper thing is to fetch an engine back to its own home station for servicing generally, as well as regular boiler washing.

Mr. Abraham wanted to know why the photographs of the 'round' and 'straight' sheds showed the sheds completely empty of locomotives. Although they may have given you rather a misguided impression of my availability figures the engines were just not there. In each case the shed was in process of being handed over that week by the contractors, and we thought it was a grand opportunity to get a general view of the shed without the interruption of all the 'bits and pieces' which generally strew themselves round a locomotive shed whether it is in my region or yours, Mr. Abraham. (*Laughter*.)

I think that is all, gentlemen, unless you would like to ask some more. Oh! Mr. Pearman mentioned the driving on the left-hand side and signals too. I see he also asked about mechanical coaling plants. You are quite right. I would say from my own experience of years that I wanted to see coaling plants put in and established at some of our depots earlier on, but the policy in those days was that there was an element of doubt about it. Any kind of mechanical coaling plant is liable to break down. We have heard of some very sticky times in the sheds of other people where such things had been installed. My old Chief Mechanical Engineers, from Mr. Churchward downwards held that, by and large, the elevated road with a means of dealing with at least two if not three wagons of coal, was ideal from the point of view of mixing various grades of coal and the least cost in running; after the first cost had been incurred in building it. There was nothing much to go wrong. Your coal wagons were placed at a certain height in relation to the coaling deck by means of line laid on an incline. More than half the coal falls out by gravity, or is just scraped out of the wagon into tubs on wheels. It is wheeled across the steel platform, and, again gravity does its work and the coal falls into the tender or bunker of the locomotive. From that point of view the wear and tear and general upkeep are infinitesimal I should say, as against the general run of coaling plants, and mechanical devices, as we know them to-day.

On the other hand, when there is a run of engines following close behind one another and only one or two men in the coaling gang, you cannot coal any faster than those men can work. They have to fill the tubs and empty them, and with the big tenders taking five and a half or, say, six tons of coal as a maximum, I should say (and I think my analysis figures show) that quite often it is a half-hour to three-quarters job coaling them; whereas I understand that with a mechanical coaling plant you can get your five tons down in a minute or a minute and a half, and your engine is in position, filled, and out again inside five minutes, on the average. From that point of view you do get a quicker turn-round.

CHAIRMAN: Ladies and gentlemen, it is my privilege now at the end of the evening to express, on behalf of you all – and myself particularly – our very grateful thanks to Mr. Pellow for his most interesting paper.

I think some of his charts of the new organisation may have given us food for thought. They have given me especially food for thought, when I realise some of the implications of the dotted lines ... (*Laughter*) ... none of which, ladies and gentlemen, after four years do I understand. (*Laughter*.) Still, that is neither her nor there. (*Laughter*.)

I was also intrigued about the coal used. I thought that was very interesting indeed, not only about the quantity we use, but the type of coal we are getting, which is one of our great difficulties at the present time, and to which there does not seem to be much solution. There is one thing I would say in regard to that, and I believe Mr. Pellow will agree with me. If you pick up the British Transport statistics we issue every month, price one shilling now – we used to give them away free in the old days (*Laughter*) – Western Region consumption per pound per engine mile is the lowest of any region still. So it does not seem to matter whether we burn rubbish or not.

I was also intrigued, Mr. Pellow, if I may mention one thing from a personal point of view, about your tribute to the Inspectors; because I think that is a very worthy tribute and one which should be paid and re-paid and made quite clear many more times than it is. (*Hear, hear*.) I believe, Sir – and I am going to say this straight in front of you, despite the fact that you are our guest tonight— I believe they are the backbone of your department.

MR. PELLOW: I am sure they are.

CHAIRMAN: And I am quite sure they keep you in order. (*Laughter*.)

I have no more comments, except that I notice Mr. Pellow evaded very skilfully answering the last question tonight: 'When are the Birmingham trains going to run the journey in two hours?' (*Laughter*.) Although it is against the rules, I am going to make him get up and answer that one. (*Laughter*.) Otherwise I am not going to propose a vote of thanks. (*Laughter and applause*.)

MR. PELLOW: I am very sorry, Sir. I put that one down in such small writing ... (*Laughter*.)

CHAIRMAN: We have heard that one before, too.

MR. PELLOW: The two hour running time would depend on a great number of conditions. I should be likely to cause a riot here if I said all I would like to say about it, but in short if we were given the conditions we had at the time we were running the trains in two hours, we would run them again now. (*Laughter and applause*.)

CHAIRMAN: Let me say I do not think he deserves the vote of thanks I should like you all to give him anyway. (*Prolonged applause*.)

MR. DASHWOOD: Ladies and gentlemen, it is my pleasure to ask you to accord to Mr. Grand – who, I might say, has come here tonight at some inconvenience – the heartiest vote of thanks possible. His interest in this Society is synonymous with his interest in all other Great Western activities ... (*Hear, hear*) ... and we could not have a finer Chief Regional Officer than we have. I give you Mr. Grand. Ladies and gentlemen will you accord him a vote of thanks. (*Loud applause*.)

CHAIRMAN: Thank you very much, gentlemen.

CODINGS

Codings have exercised an almost magical influence over the years, with endless and sometimes tedious debate as to the exact arrangement of letters, the precise date of their introduction, withdrawal and alteration. The very existence of some is a source of dispute. This sort of thing is, of course, the case with other railways besides the GWR, a peculiar desire for order on the part of enthusiast adherents which has more than once manifested itself in the *invention* of entire coding systems, where a company unobligingly made no use of them. The Great Western codes in particular have exerted an inordinate degree of interest; Lyons covers the subject and the RCTS have published a comprehensive review. Collett incidentally, called them 'brands', an apt term in that their principal function was, after all, to stop engines straying. In the 'twenties the system involved marks 'in the cab of the locomotive engine'. Collett chided his Divisional Superintendents with a circulated reminder that brands on transferred locomotives were not being altered promptly, if at all:

'Considerable difficulty is being experienced owing to the fact that many engines bear several station brands in the cab, and scarcely a day passes without enquiries reaching these offices to ascertain the home station of some engine.

It is important that all old brands should be effectively removed before new ones are painted on, and I shall be glad if you will please give definite instructions for this to be done.'

'Coding' is a subject owing a great deal more to enthusiast observation than to real railway practice. It was, after all, a subjective matter, logical enough at first examination but intrinsically silly. Single numbers had to be learnt, or could be wrongly translated. The GW letter codes theoretically were an abbreviation making confusion impossible, but was SHL immediately obvious as Southall, were OXF and OXY easily distinguishable? Old Oak was PDN, with scant logic, and both Bristol sheds apparently were BL. In addition to all this there is supposed to have been a numerical code as well, each Division sharing a digit, prefixed by a number representing the *approximate* respective places of each shed in the alphabet. The GW thus went one better than its rivals yet again, acquiring two daft systems instead of one.

Areal extent of the Districts/Divisions and their status one to another changed over the years, some of it bravely pieced together by RCTS workers from inadequate and partly contradictory records. There is a wealth of tantalisingly brief detail, the principal feature of the years before the First World War emerging as a sprawling Swindon District, occupying the heartland of the GWR. Simpson conveniently provides a measure of its extent in 1906, reproducing one of the forms beloved of the Running Department:

This was an extraordinary position, compressing the Districts at the extremities, London, Wolverhampton and Bristol. 'London', the subject of this book, amounted to little more than the metropolitan approaches.

The whole lot was rearranged around the time of the Great War and the familiar seven Divisions instituted, the bloated Swindon divided up principally between London and Bristol. This system, together with those Welsh Divisions added at Grouping, form the basis of this series of descriptions. The 'London Stations', then:

Old Oak:	PDN
Southall:	SHL
Slough:	SLO
Reading:	RDG
Didcot:	DID
Oxford:	OXF

Setting aside idiosyncracies such as the 'alphabetic' code, the Great Western system seems almost designed to defy any subsequent rationale. The most logical procedure was to list depots 'outwards' from Paddington. This gives the entirely sensible listing, Old Oak Common, Southall, Slough, and beyond, with their appropriate outstations.

The problem arises in the attempt to match lists across time – responsibility for the small sheds in the Division tended to alter over the years and frequently two (or more) main sheds were intermittently or even coincidentally involved. Some points are flatly inexplicable – witness the placing of Marlow under Reading in the 1938 'Summary of Allocation of Engines for All Purposes (page 371). There is no further evidence for this relationship, and scant logic. Wallingford and Lambourn, furthermore, are seen to have been 'swapped' between Reading and Didcot at different periods, for no clear reason. This account has settled firmly on the geographical approach, ignoring further peculiarities such as the BR coding, placing Slough as 81B before Southall at 81C. The LMS-derived system had much to commend it, but, wincing under the hated 'Motive Power' label, the Western was hardly disposed to see much logic in it. A casual clerical error emanating from somewhere outlandish like Derby seems the likeliest culprit.

FORM No. 17.

GREAT WESTERN RAILWAY.—LOCOMOTIVE DEPARTMENT.
COAL RECEIVED —SWINDON DISTRICT.

	COAL ADVICES.				Date Received.	WEIGHTS (CWTS.) RECEIVED AT EACH STATION.																												
Date.	Colliery.	Wagon No.	Weight T. C.	Daily Total. T. C.		Reading.	Basingstoke.	Wallingford.	Didcot.	Abingdon.	Winchester.	Oxford.	C. Norton Jnc.	C. Norton.	Woodstock.	Banbury.	Faringdon.	Swindon.	Chippenham.	Malmesbury.	Box.	Colchester.	Tetbury.	Brimscombe.	Gloucester.	Cheltenham.	Bullo Pill.	Lydney.	Trowbridge.	Frome.	Marlborough.	Salisbury.	Yeovil.	Bridport.	Weymouth.
	Brought forward.																																		
	Carried forward..																																		

Churchward's *Great Bear* suitably posed against the vast tank of 'the largest depot of its type in Great Britain, and probably the world'.

Collection R. C. Riley

OLD OAK COMMON

The Old Oak tank was certainly an enormous structure, an illustration of the 'strategic' principles developed in the planning of the depot. Provision was made on a generous rather than sparing scale whether it be accommodation or services. Planning dated back to at least 1899; on 20th December Churchward declared to the Traffic Committee in reference to an earlier minute of 4th October: 'in connection with the general scheme for improving the accommodation at the Paddington end of the line which involves the removal of the Locomotive Depot at Westbourne Park, it is necessary to provide in lieu thereof Engine Shed accommodation at Old Oak Common, Estimated Cost £70,000, exclusive of excavation . . . Approved'. *British Railways*

The Great Western had long made use of the roundhouse arrangement, low square buildings roofed in a northlight pattern enamoured of William Dean. Churchward's reign ushered in a wholly different style, high airy buildings quite clearly reminiscent of long-standing Midland Railway practice. Churchward had taken this well established model, developing and improving upon it, and dispensing with the last vestiges of decoration.

MR 'square' roundhouses (see *LMS Engine Sheds Vol. II,* WSP, 1981) were quite sufficient for that company's 0–6–0s and 4–4–0s,, but by the turn of the century Churchward had much more substantial engines in mind. The older square roundhouses had the classic number of roads, 24, but enlargement to 28 had already begun before Churchward (or rather his officers) determined upon a rectangular disposition. This allowed a more generous measure of stabling accommodation towards the corners with a quite considerable area for attention and fitting work at the extremities.

Old Oak Common was a magnificent affair, a quite extraordinary step in this late period. Compared to its major contemporaries, giants like the LNWR and the Midland, accommodation in the GW running department had been neglected,

allowed really to deteriorate quite badly. Great Western locomotives in the capital stabled in a ramshackle conglomeration of buildings, impossibly arranged, at Westbourne Park, hardly better than the Brighton's ancient and eccentric premises at New Cross. Speedy reform of this dismal situation – numbers of new sheds both roundhouses and traditional straight buildings – punctuated the years to Grouping, a time when construction on the Midland, LNWR, the L & YR and other major British companies, had largely come to an end. This situation, extraordinary in itself, was made more remarkable by the establishment only then of a proper system of outstation repair shops. Churchward, able to draw upon the best of British and American practice, laid the basis for a comprehensive engine running and repair system. Final touches were not made until the 1930s but the system owed everything to Churchward and is a measure of his achievement as telling as the efforts directed at locomotive design.

Despite a relative tardiness in this field the Great Western, with a capacity for publicity seemingly unique, contrived to appear in a pioneering light. Paget, General Superintendent of the Midland and for long an enthusiastic (if frustrated) innovator, delivered a paper in 1910 before the Insti-

tution of Mechanical Engineers, in praise of GWR developments:

English Running-Shed Practice
By Mr. CECIL W. PAGET, General Superintendant, Midland Railway, Derby. [*Not all Fig. Nos. have been reproduced*]

The running-sheds in England are of two types: –

(1) Those in which the roads are laid parallel, usually called straight sheds.

(2) Those in which the roads radiate from a centre turntable, called round sheds.

The straight sheds are economical in first cost and maintenance, but unless they are of the type known as 'through sheds' they are awkward to work; the latter class are necessarily draughty.

The centre turntable type, though more expensive to build, possesses considerable advantages of working because engines can be easily got in and out without moving others. The radial arrangement of the pits also lends itself better to lighting and convenience of getting about. There is plenty of room towards the end of the pits for fitters to work at the bench between two engines, and the work of washing out boilers, swilling out pits, and general cleaning can be done without inconvenience. To set against these advantages, there is the objection that when the turntable requires lifting for repairs it throws the whole of the pits served by it out of use whilst the repairs are going on.

Paget's Fig. 1 & 2, a comparison of the 'Through Type' and 'Turntable Type', and a detailed illustration of the latter. The relative merits of the two principles occupied the Great Western at intervals through to its extinction in 1948 and indeed beyond.

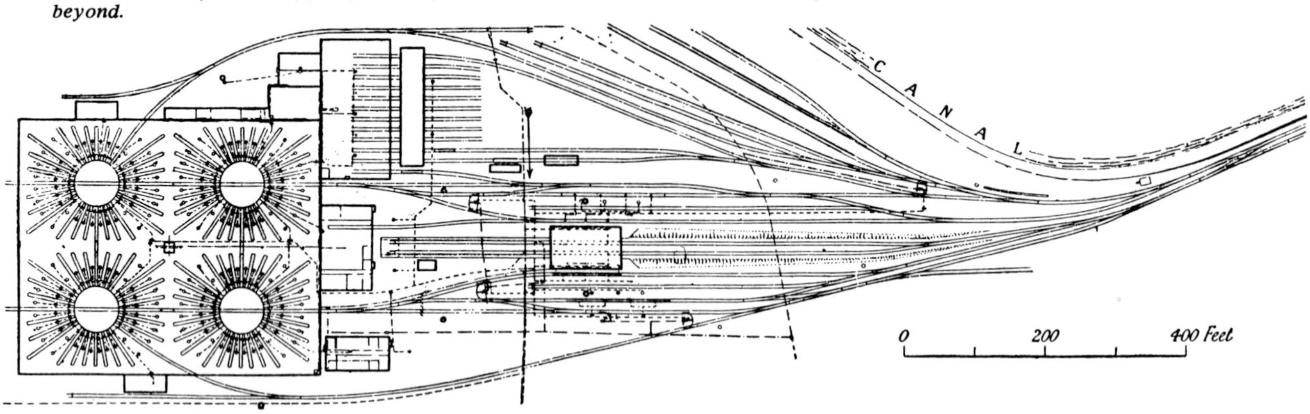

Fig. 1.—Turntable Engine-Shed and Yard, G.W. Ry., Old Oak Common.

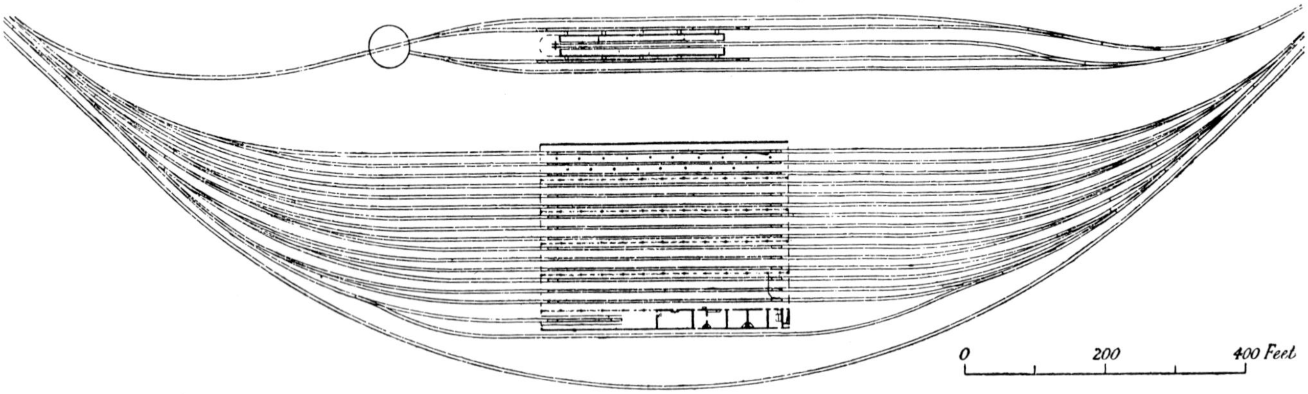

Fig. 2.—Through-Straight Type Engine-Shed and Coal-Stage, L. and South Western Ry., Eastleigh.

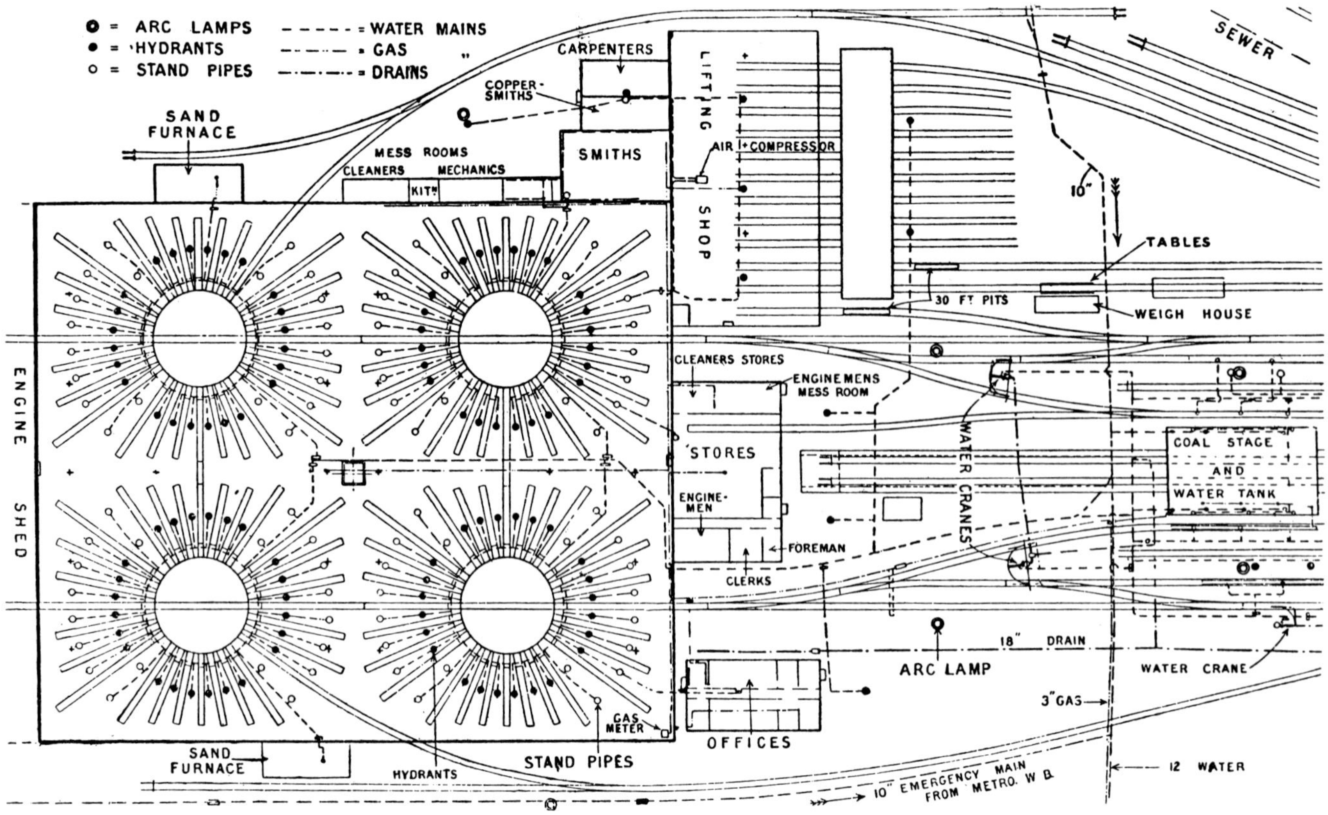

Fig. 3.—Turntable Engine-Shed and Yard, Great Western Ry., Old Oak Common.

Plans are shown of two of the most recent sheds built in this country: – Figs. 1 and 3. The Great Western Sheds at Old Oak Common – centre turntable type. Figs. 2 and 5. The L. and South-Western Shed at Eastleigh – through straight type.

The necessary offices, stores, mess-rooms and lavatories should be conveniently placed, and reference to the plans will show their arrangement in the two sheds referred to, which may be taken as examples of the latest British practice. Illustrations are also given of a typical mess-room, fig. 7, and lavatory, fig. 8. The lavatory illustrated is equipped with shower baths and a separate locker provided for every man employed at the shed. The cleaners, and particularly the enginemen, appreciate and regularly use the lavatories and shower baths.

Attached to every shed of any size are sheer-legs capable of lifting one end of an engine so that the wheels and axle-boxes may be removed for examination or repairs. These legs were made almost universally at one time of wood, and of the tripod type, the single leg on one side of the rails being of extra strength and carrying the lifting gear. The disadvantage of this type, of which many are still in existence, is, that now that so many engines have extended cabs, the legs have to be of great height in order to allow of the trailing wheels being taken out, as the cab top has not room to rise between the frame of the legs. This difficulty was sometimes overcome by forming the top of the legs of bow-shaped iron castings, whilst two wooden struts were placed on either side. The most modern construction is, however, to use a framework of steel joists, the top cross-girders and gussets leaving sufficient head room for any contingency. To some modern examples is attached a small jib-crane, which is of use in taking off the bogie-frame for examination, loading wheels, etc. A capacity of 15 tons used to be looked upon as amply sufficient, but the large increase in the weight of engines in recent years had led to stronger legs being required, and the more modern ones are capable of raising 35 to 40 tons. The load is usually lifted by hand by means of a crab or train of wheels operating a chain or wire rope, which works round a sheaf or set of blocks. In some cases, where hydraulic power is available it is employed, but the more modern method, where current can be obtained, is to use an electric motor.

The position of the sheer-legs relative to the shed depends largely upon local circumstances, but in sheds where the pits radiate from the table and the building is a square one a set of legs is usually fixed on one of the longer roads, that is, one of the roads leading to the corners of the shed, as better work and more care are probable where men can work without being exposed to the weather. In all cases, whether outside or indoor, the legs are placed over a pit which is usually 2ft 10in deep below rail-level.

Very little tackle of a special nature is required by shed fitters, but amongst those things which must be always at hand are jacks – hydraulic and bottle – for lifting

engines to change bearing springs, etc., lever and stands, to allow of axle-boxes being tried up the horn plates, wood blocks to act as temporary axle-boxes, clamps to draw engine and tender together to facilitate uncoupling, iron lorries to put under engine when the bogie has been removed, wood blocks to pack engine on, etc., as well as a good supply of ordinary shop-tools. If not attached to the sheer-legs a small crane is useful to lift a bogie-frame off the axles when required, whilst a pair of two-hundredweight pulley-blocks are

often employed to allow of the boxes being tried on the axles.

Despite claims, when Old Oak Common opened on 17th March 1906, it was not the 'largest' shed of its kind in the country, 'if not the world'. Its modernity, the Churchward 'leap frog' of absorbed technical experience, was, however, fully deserving of a widespread and detailed coverage in the technical press:

The Great Western Railway's New London Locomotive Depot.
Description of the Newly Opened Engine Sheds at Old Oak Common.

On 17th March, a new locomotive depôt in connection with the Great Western Company's Paddington terminus was brought into use. This depôt, which has been under construction for some three or four years, is situated about three miles west of Paddington, at Old Oak Common, Acton, on a large area of land to the north of the main line, where are located extensive siding accommodation, carriage sheds, &c.

The old engine sheds at Westbourne Park are now being dismantled in connection with the improvement of the lines to and from the Paddington station. In passing, it may be noted that the new depôt is the third to be provided at Paddington. The first, which was no doubt erected in the later 'thirties,' was a wooden circular shed situated somewhere in the vicinity of the present Paddington goods station.

This was superseded about the year 1852, when the present Paddington Station was contructed, by the Westbourne Park depôt. This consisted of two sheds which were always known respectively as the 'broad gauge shed' and the 'narrow gauge shed,' notwithstanding that the broad gauge ceased to exist some 14 years ago. The broad gauge shed was the older of the two; it was 650 ft by 71 ft, of the 'straight' type with four roads passing through it. The narrow gauge shed was 135 ft by 90 ft, and consisted of two bays each containing three roads. The first bay was built in 1861–2 and the second was added in 1873 to meet the demand for additional accommodation. There were also at this depôt, workshops, stores and offices for the divisional locomotive superintendent, the office being, for a short time, occupied by Sir Daniel Gooch in his early days.

Originally there was a coal stage of the type having cranes and swing tubs. This was on the site now occupied by the up and down relief lines at Westbourne Park Station, in connection with the provision of which, in 1876 or 1877, it was demolished, and an up-to-date stage substituted. There were two turntables at the Westbourne Park locomotive depôt.

The Old Oak Common locomotive depôt presents an imposing appearance, as will be seen from the general view of the buildings.

It is the largest of its kind in Great Britain and possibly in the world. The various buildings are of red Staffordshire bricks, and the total area (approximate) is 215,000 sq ft. Here are now accommodated locomotives appropriated to Paddington, together with those from other stations working to and from the London terminus.

By the courtesy of Mr. G. J. Churchward, Chief Mechanical Engineer of the Great Western Railway, we are able to give a plan and elevation of the various buildings, and also a plan showing the general lay-out of the yard and its connections with the running lines. The depôt was designed by Mr. G. J. Churchward, and was erected by Mr Walkerdine of Derby, under the superintendence of Mr. Walter Armstrong, New Works Engineer of the Great Western Railway.

The shed proper is designed on the internal turn-table principle with radial pits, a design which, while not so economical in the matter of space as others, enables engines to be worked in and out of the shed in a rapid and convenient manner. The internal dimensions are 444 ft by 360 ft. There are four 65 ft electrically-operated tables of the under-girder type, each serving 28 roads, accommodation being provided for 112 locomotives (one half tender engines, the other half tank), for each of which there is a separate smoke shoot.

The above mentioned electric turntables have been supplied by Ransomes & Rapier, of London and Ipswich, and are suitable for a working load of 114 tons, and a test load of 140 tons, distributed. The tops are decked all over with timber. Chequer plates are provided between the rails, $\frac{5}{16}$ in thick. The load and moving part of each table revolves on hardened steel centres which work in a bath of oil arranged so as to be dust proof.

The turntables are equipped with two hinged tractors, placed diagonally one at each end of the main girders, arranged to turn the table at a speed of one revolution in $1\frac{1}{2}$ minutes. Each tractor is driven by a 5 b.h.p. motor, suitable for a continuous current of 550 to 600 volts, a solenoid brake being fitted to each motor.

The controllers of the turntables are of the British Thomson Houston Company's R. 28 type, continuous current rheostatic control-

Continued on page 49

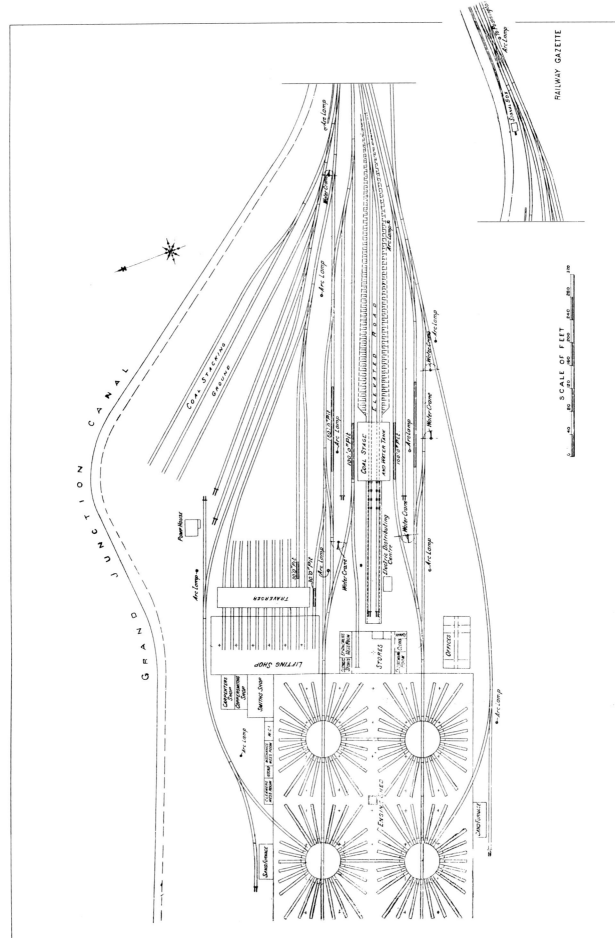

General Plan showing Layout of Yard of Great Western Railway's New London Locomotive Depot.

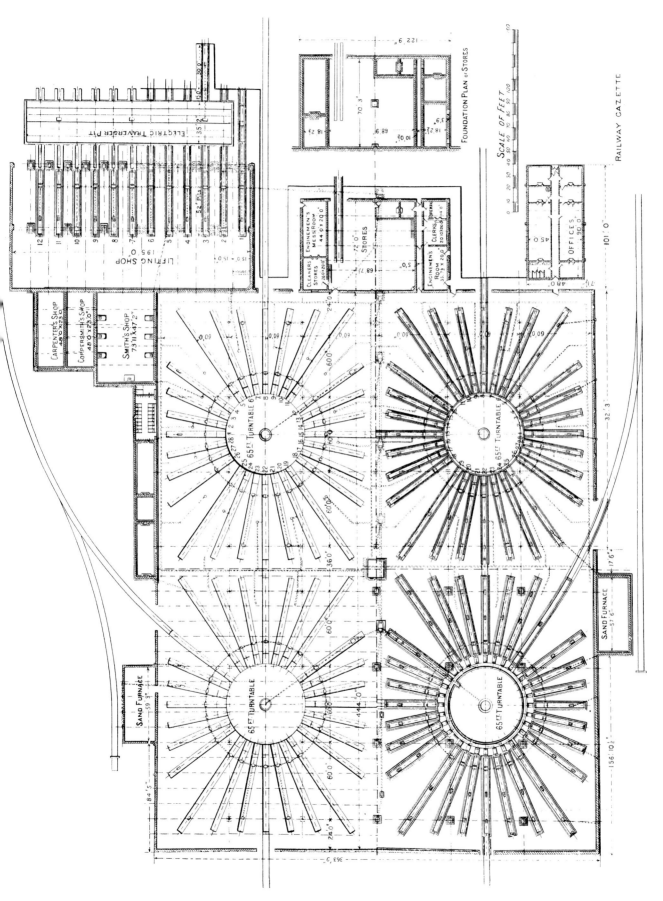

General Plan of Engine Shed, Repair Shops, Offices, &c.—Great Western Railway's New London Locomotive Depot.

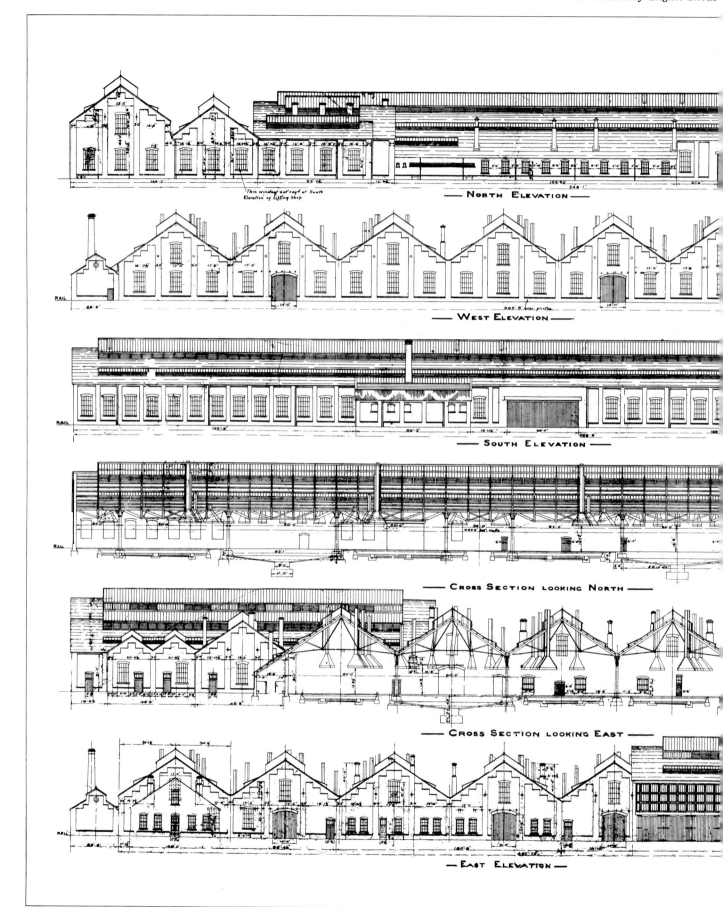

— North Elevation —

— West Elevation —

— South Elevation —

— Cross Section looking North —

— Cross Section looking East —

— East Elevation —

Old Oak structural detail. Churchward, it seems, could wrest money from his masters more or less at will, though in truth the Great Western had already come to the very zenith of its power and prosperity. On 22nd July 1902 he reported that the vote of £70,000 'had lapsed' and that 'we should now proceed with as shown on plan . . . £110,000 . . . due to addition of machinery and internal fittings which were not included in the former vote.' The Directors agreed to this, apparently without demur and on 3rd December 1903 authorised acceptance of W. Walkerdine's tender of £40,313 'for Engine Shed at Old Oak Common'. By 12th April 1905 various amendments had been agreed 'and additional work had been carried out by the Contractor at a cost of £2,500'.

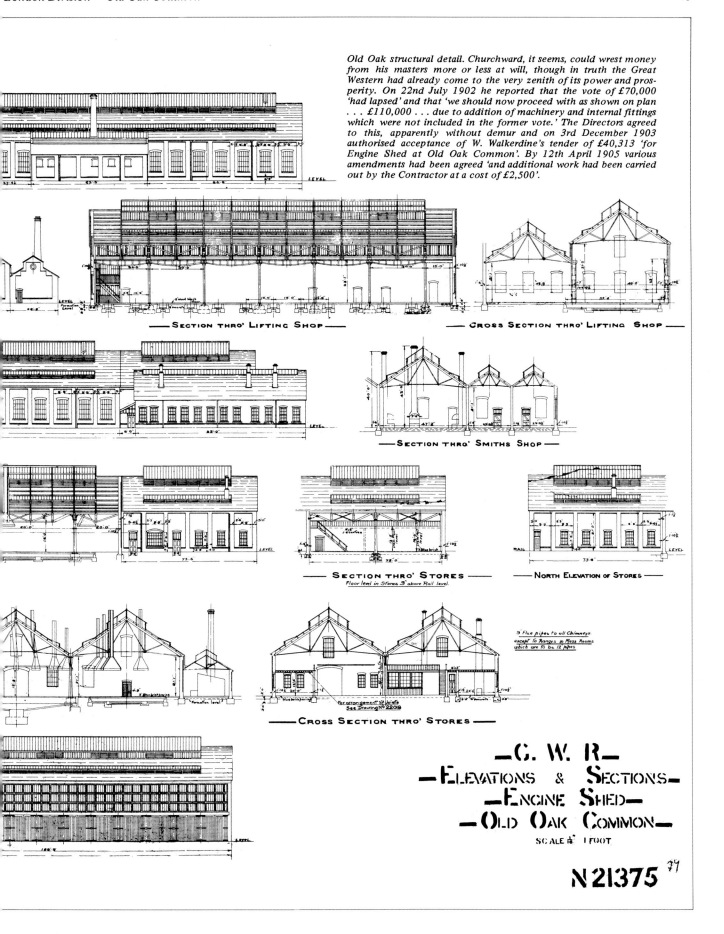

SECTION THRO' LIFTING SHOP

CROSS SECTION THRO' LIFTING SHOP

SECTION THRO' SMITHS SHOP

SECTION THRO' STORES
Floor level in Stores 9" above Rail level.

NORTH ELEVATION OF STORES

CROSS SECTION THRO' STORES

G. W. R.
ELEVATIONS & SECTIONS
ENGINE SHED
OLD OAK COMMON
SCALE ⅛" 1 FOOT

N 21375

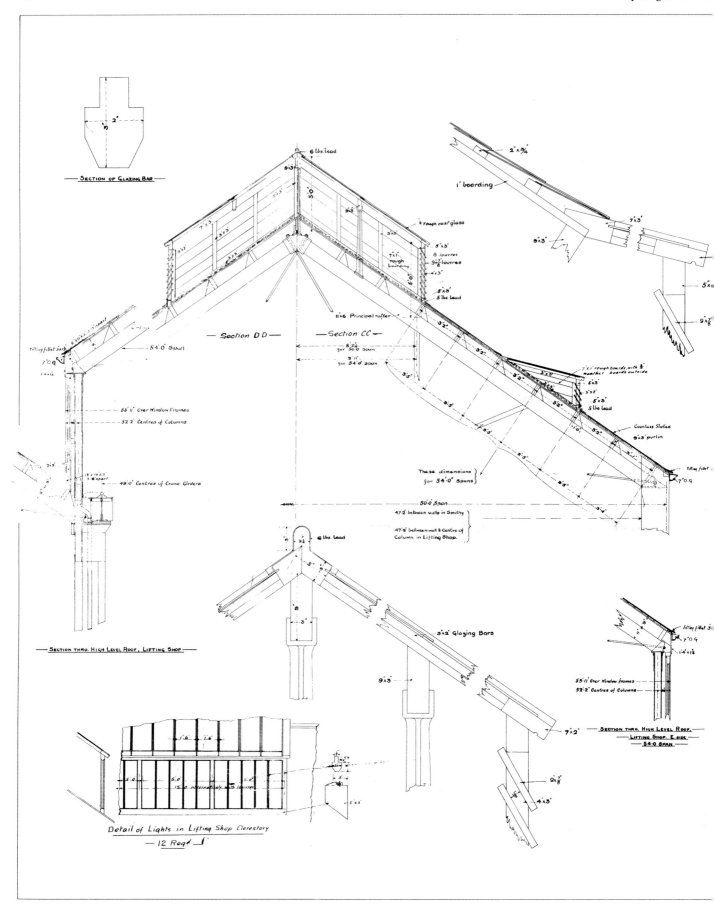

— Section of Glazing Bar —

— Section D D —   — Section C C —

Section thro. High Level Roof, Lifting Shop —

Detail of Lights in Lifting Shop Clerestory
— 12 Req'd —

Section thro. High Level Roof,
Lifting Shop. E. Side.
— 54·0 Span —

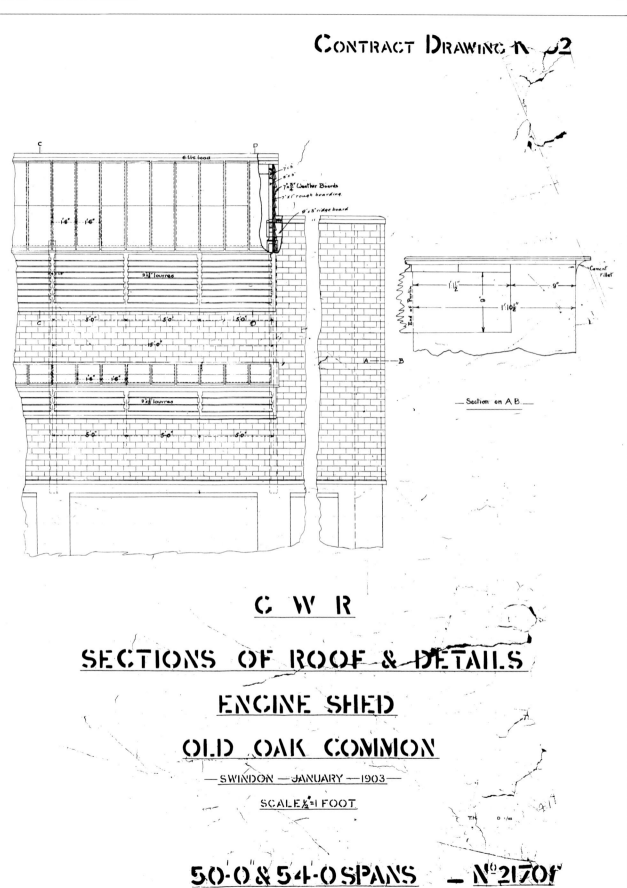

C W R

SECTIONS OF ROOF & DETAILS

ENGINE SHED

OLD OAK COMMON

— SWINDON — JANUARY — 1903 —

SCALE ½=1 FOOT

50-0" & 54-0 SPANS _ N° 2170f

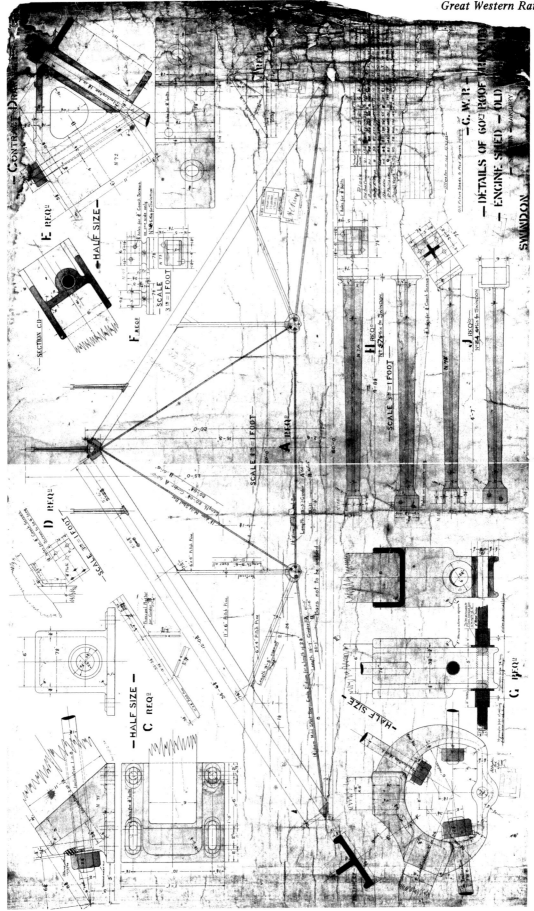

'60 ft Roof Principal' of 1903, adaptable throughout the roundhouse and associated parts (see elevation, page 44) and standard for any number of buildings.

lers. These are fitted with a magnetic blow-out device, which will ensure prompt disruption of the arc formed on opening the various circuits without any injury to the contacts. They have five points forward and five reverse, with one handle, forward and reverse.

The roof is the trussed type, carried by pitch-pine principals, 60 ft span – with steel tie-rods – on steel girders, mostly 60 ft span, supported on cast-iron columns. The height from rail level to shoe of principal is 21 ft 1 in. The walls are of red brick throughout, 1 ft 10½ in thick at the piers 1 ft 6 in at the panels, and inside are whitewashed.

It is evident that in designing the depôt Mr Churchward had in mind the modern practice of carrying out at the district sheds a large proportion of the repairs required by locomotives, thus rendering unnecessary their frequent going into the central repair shops. This is fully recognised in America, where the engine houses of to-day are much more in the nature of repair shops than they are of simple storage buildings for locomotives. At Old Oak Common the lifting and repair shop is replete with every convenience. It adjoins the eastern wall of the main building, and is generally similar to it in design. The internal dimensions are 195 ft by 101 ft, and there are twelve 52 ft pits. The span of the crane is 49 ft, and it runs transversely to the pits. The shop is fully provided with electrically-operated machinery, while outside, parallel with the shop, is an electric traversing table capable of dealing with 80 tons. It is 35 ft long and moves on seven rails.

As shown in one of the accompanying illustrations the equipment of the fitters' and machine bay (195 ft by 45 ft) includes a 30-ton electric overhead travelling crane, supplied by Vaughan & Son, Ltd., West Gorton, Manchester. This crane, which has a span of 49 ft is of the three motor type, having separate motors for each of the individual movements, hoisting, cross traversing and longitudinal travelling. Hoisting is effected through specially flexible plough steel wire rope, an auxiliary barrel independent rope and hook being provided for rapidly lifting light loads up to 6 tons. Spur gearing only is employed in reduction of speed between the motor and the hoisting barrels. An improved automatic brake with solenoid release is embodied in the hoisting gear, which, though offering no resistance to hoisting, automatically comes into action whenever current is cut off from any cause, and so sustains the load. The makers' patent device for prevention of overwinding and also of over-lowering is incorporated in the hoisting mechanism.

All the motions of the electric travelling crane are controlled from the driver's cage fitted at one end, in which are placed the tramway type motor controllers and a compact switchboard. Wide platforms extend along the full length of the crane on both sides, thus permitting ready access to all parts. The electrical equipment of the crane is designed for a potential of 630 volts, continuous current.

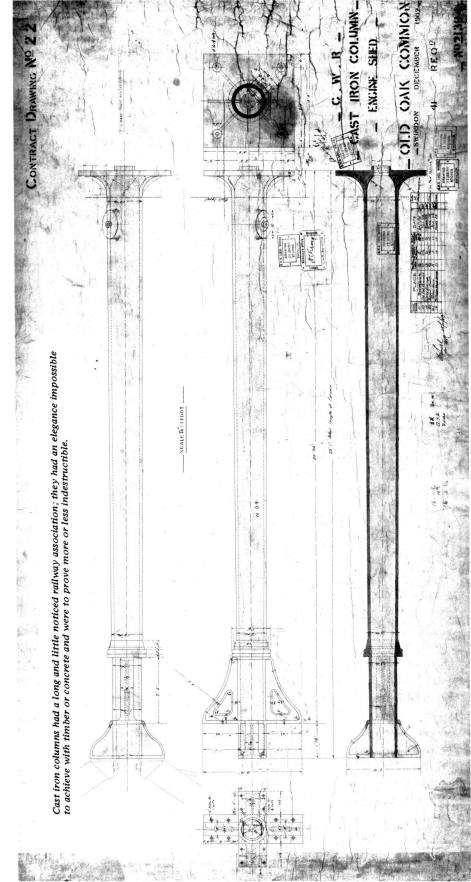

Cast iron columns had a long and little noticed railway association; they had an elegance impossible to achieve with timber or concrete and were to prove more or less indestructible.

Old Oak amidst the last of the builders' clutter. Much of the construction is visible before the intrusion of engines and the blackening of the timbers. The hydrants still require their rather pleasantly curved tap fittings, parts designed to swivel for the most convenient attachment of the water pipe. Contrary to a lot of experience elsewhere, the timbers on demolition were found to be in excellent condition, fuelling fires all across Acton and put to use in all manner of fencing, garages, extensions and garden sheds. The timber and glass cabin was known as 'the Central Office', home of the shed fitter. He walked around the shed 'inspecting things', usually with cleaners in tow ready for their allotted tasks. He was the sole protector against a variety of 'big-wigs' and was idolised by 'his boys' when staving off various unwelcome jobs or changes.

British Railways

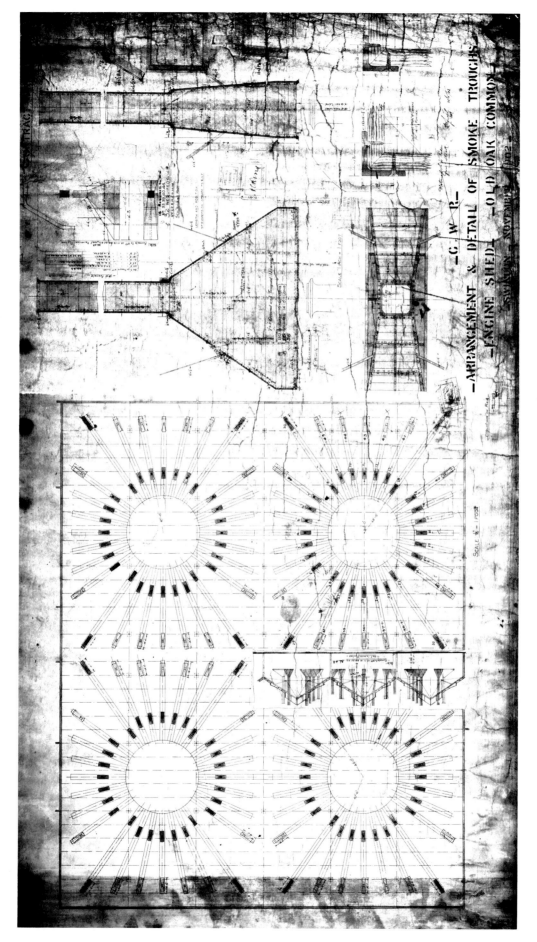

Working drawing of smoke troughs, issued in 1902 and variously amended through to the following year.

'The Factory', the London Divisional Shops, still in use for diesels today, and little altered in its essentials. Orders were placed on 5th October 1904 for both traverser and overhead crane, 'Recommended £2,070 for provision of electric traversing tables at each of the Locomotive Depots at Bristol, Newton Abbot and Newport Dock Street . . . All Ransomes and Rapier, plus one at Old Oak Common (cost included in £110,000) . . . for sum of £2,760.' And again: 'Old Oak Common. Orders placed. Messrs. Vaughan & Son 130 ton electrically driven crane £1,025. Messrs. Ransomes & Rapier, four 65 feet Turntables, £3,900. Approved.' Later, on 10th May, the costs of the Vaughan crane were amended to £1,106 and the Ransomes and Rapier traverser specified at 80 tons, cost £712. 'An electrically driven wheel lathe' was ordered from Beyer Peacock £625 . . . 'Turntables at Old Oak Common will be electrically driven . . . further £1,240 for tractors from Ransomes & Rapier'. It was a shed job to get the engines up to the traverser, made awkward by the need to disconnect the tenders of larger engines. This was done by the 'weighbridge blokes' who arranged for the subsequent transfer of the engine and the removal or storage of the tender, using a system of capstans. The fitting roads were numbered 1 to 12, south to north.

British Railways

The crane is designed to operate at the following speeds:-

Hoisting	30	tons at	4 ft	per minute.	Slow gear.
,,	15	,,	8 ft	,,	Quick gear.
,,	6	,,	20 ft	,,	Small barrel.

Cross traverse 100 ft per minute.
Long travel 250 ft.

Locomotive department officers will quickly gain an idea of the amount and nature of repair work that can be performed at Old Oak Common without sending engines to Swindon from the following list of the principal machine tools in the fitters' and machine bay:—

4 lathes.
2 wheel lathes.
2 buffing machines.
2 shapers.
2 drilling machines.
1 automatic cold sawing machine.
1 slotting machine.
1 punching and shearing machine.
1 screwing machine.
1 drill slotter.
1 grindstone.

There is to be a compressed air plant, made by the Consolidated Pneumatic Tool Co., Ltd., for the pneumatic tools which will be largely used at the Old Oak shops.

The smiths' (74 ft by 47 ft), coppersmiths' and carpenters' shops (each 61 ft by 23 ft) are exceedingly well appointed. The former contains seven hearths, a fan, and a power hammer, each driven by an independent motor: the carpenters' shop is equipped with an electrically-driven circular saw bench and a 'general joiner.'

A subsidiary building contains the stores and shed foreman's office. Its dimensions are 117 ft by 72 ft and there are two floors. A portion of the ground floor is set apart for messrooms and lavatories for the men, and offices for the chief running-shed foreman. The remainder comprises the stores, a feature of which is a gallery running round the walls by means of which the storage accommodation has been much increased.

The depôt being the head-quarters of the London divisional locomotive superintendent, Mr John Armstrong, a block of offices (90 ft by 45 ft) containing seven rooms has been erected for his use. Mr W. Russell, late of Swindon, is the Assistant Divisional Superintendent.

The coal stage is conveniently placed and may be regarded as the best practice in the facilities afforded for rapid coaling of engines. It is situated on the south side of the main building and is 104 ft by 59 ft 6 in. There are four double and two single tips and two elevated tracks for coal wagons, supported on brick arches. The tracks are laid on a gradient of 1 in 80 so that the empty coal wagons can be let down by gravity as required. Beneath the stage are rooms for the coalmen and lavatory accommodation.

At so large a depôt an ample water supply is most essential for washing out and filling up boilers, &c. A water tank of 290,000 gallons capacity has been built over the coal stage from which the whole of the buildings and yard are supplied. The tank is made in four sections and so arranged that each can be cut off from the others for cleaning or repairs.

Carpenters Shops. One of their lesser-known engine jobs was the replacement and repair of engine footboards, items subject to a heavy use.

'View of part of Machine Shop', regimented rows of vices and everything precisely ordered. 'The Factory' men were wholly separate from the shed fitters and the latter were regarded by enginemen (probably through a more regular contact) as somewhat more accomplished in the setting of valves and other 'running' tasks.

Old Oak nearing completion. The land had lain some yards above the main line and a considerable excavation was necessary to reduce the site to 'level ground'. On 16th May 1900 the Locomotive Committee heard that 'the material required to be removed at Old Oak Common . . . is about 240,000 cubic yards . . . Estimated cost £20,000 . . . Approved'. The *Great Western Magazine* of April 1940: 'Old Oak Common, the Company's principal London locomotive and carriage depot, was, as its name suggests, common land for many decades. In the Middle Ages, the common was part of the lands granted to Eustace, Bishop of London, by one Peter, presumably the manorial lord. Newcourt's *Repertorium*, published in 1708, has this on the subject:— "Peter, the Son of Aulf, gave to Eustace, Bishop of London, forty acres of arable land in Acton, in the field called Pulla, he paying yearly to the said Peter one pound of cumin-seed, which, after the death of the said Bishop, the Dean of S. Paul's accustomed to pay yearly to the said Peter; but he afterwards, for the health of his soul, remitted and quit-claimed to God and the Church of S. Paul, and to William de Sanctae Mariae Ecclesia, the Dean of the same, and to his successors, the said yearly rent of cumin-seed, and such homages and reliefs as his predecessors were used to pay him." The chief purpose of the common, while it was tenanted by the bishop and his successors at cumin-seed rent, appears to have been as a feeding ground for the bishop's pigs, and in this connection it is notable that pig-breeding was carried on in the area until recent years. A more modern historian than Newcourt, one Baker, in his work on *Acton*, says: "The Old Oak Common was evidently lost to the public through neglect in exercising the right to use it." *It is unlikely that the Great Western Railway will lose it for this reason!*

British Railways

The distributing main is 15 in diameter and is carried from the coal stage to supply five 8 in swinging-jib water cranes in the yard and thence into the shed, where it is led round the turntables with branches to supply hydrants and standpipes fitted with M.F.B. hose connections. The hydrants are placed between each pair of roads and are used for filling and washing out boilers, &c, as well as being available in case of fire.

At present 154 engines are stationed at Old Oak Common. This total is made up as follows:—

Passenger engines with tenders	58
Passenger tank engines	25
Goods engines with tenders	33
Goods tank engines..	38
	154

Of course, in addition to above, engines from other sheds put up at Old Oak whilst waiting in London between journeys.

From the foregoing it will have been noted that a feature at Old Oak Common is the part played by electricity, which is, we believe, being used for motive and lighting purposes to a greater extent than at any other depôt of the kind in the country.

At present, current is being generated by temporary apparatus, but it will, in the course of a few months, be obtained from a new generating station now being erected by the Great Western Company in connection with the electrification of the Hammersmith & City Railway lines. This generating station is situated only a short distance from the locomotive depôt. There are two main circuits, viz.: 600 volts, direct current and 220 volts three-phase alternating current, the former being used principally for power purposes. At the switchboard these are divided into four circuits for direct current, and two circuits for alternating.

In addition to a clerical staff of 25 the number of men attached to the Old Oak Common locomotive depôt is 786. This total is made up as follows:—

Inspectors	2
Foremen	6
Drivers	184
Firemen	184
Fitters	48
Cleaners	110
Labourers	75
Firedroppers	11
Miscellaneous	166
Total	786

Old Oak Common sheds being two miles further from Paddington than the old Westbourne Park sheds, complete revision of the method of working light engines and empty trains in and out of the terminus has been made necessary. Previously the train-engines invariably ran light between the Westbourne Park sheds and Paddington Station, and the empty trains were hauled in and out by pilot, or shunting, engines. Strange as it may seem, the removal of the locomotive depôt to Old Oak Common has lessened the light engine-mileage! The working time tables have been so arranged that the passenger train-engines in many cases work empty trains in and out of the terminus. The Old Oak Common Carriage sidings adjoin Old Oak Common engine sheds, and in many cases the train-engines, running tender first, haul into Paddington the carriages of the train due out of Paddington immediately preceding theirs. Thus the train-engine of the 11 a.m. ex Paddington takes in to the terminus the coaches for the 10.50 a.m. ex Paddington. As an example in the other direction, we find that the coaches of an up-train due at Paddington at 5.30 p.m. are worked back to the sidings by the train-engine of the train due at Paddington at 5.10 p.m.

Shunting-engines are still used to marshall and haul in and out of Paddington some of the trains, but though the locomotive depôt is 2 miles further from Paddington than formerly, yet by the method of working above described three shunting engines less are used

than formerly. This shows that real economy in railway operation is being practised on the Great Western.

To facilitate the working of empty coach trains and to reduce as far as possible the occupation of the lines, light engines are allowed to be worked at the rear end of trains of empty coaches between Paddington and Old Oak Common. It is also arranged that when two or more engines happen to be standing on the down engine line waiting to go to Old Oak, they must be coupled together and worked through as one. The pilot or shunting engines engaged solely in working empty coach trains to and from Paddington each carry a big numbered disc to correspond with their numbers as shown in the working time tables.

(*The Railway Gazette*, June 1st 1906)

Old Oak Common lay yards from Willesden, the major London shed of the London North Western Railway, a conjunction (a word defined, amongst other things, as an *apparent proximity of two heavenly bodies*) hardly welcomed by LNWR men. J. M. Dunn, in his splendidly jaundiced autobiography, *Reflections on a Railway Career* recalls a visit by the railway chronicler E. L. Ahrons ('trained at Swindon and a good GW man'). The pair moved onto Old Oak, to see 'Young Armstrong' (R. J. Armstrong, Divisional Superintendent), the differences between the two establishments, Dunn glumly notes, being 'positively startling'. Rightly he pointed out the great disparity in the relative ages of the two sheds, but it reads, then as now, somewhat lamely.

WEEK DAYS ONLY. **UP TRAINS.** (PASSENGER & GOODS).						WEEK DAYS ONLY. **DOWN TRAINS.** (PASSENGER & GOODS).					
Time Train due Paddington	Time Coaches leave for Old Oak	Time Coaches leave for West London	Coaches worked down by	Time Train Engine leaves Paddington for Old Oak	Platform Train arrives at Paddington	Time of Train from Paddington	Time Coaches leave Old Oak	Time Coaches leave West London	Coaches worked up by	Time Train Engine leaves Old Oak	Platform Train starts from at Paddington
	a.m.	a.m.					p.m.	p.m.		p.m.	
7.57 a.m. Passr.	—	8.5	Pilot **No 7**	To Yard for 8.25 out	8	5.32 p.m. Pass.	Formed at Padd. (due 5. 2 p.m.)	—	—	From Yard due 4. 2 **SX** 4.57 **SO**	5
.8. 0 ,, Goods	—	---	---	8.20		5.35 ,, ,,	Formed at Padd. (due 4.17 p.m.)	—	—	5.15 **C**	3
8. 5 ,, ,,	---	---	---	8.20 **C**		5.40 ,, ,,	—	4.45	Pilot **No. 12**	‡ 5.15	4
8.23 ,, Passr.	—	8.50 **C**	Pilot **No. 3**	To Yard.	8	5.45 ,, ,,	—	5. 0 **C**	,, **No. 6**	5.15 **C**	1
8.30 ,, ,,	—	8.50 **C**		*8.50	9	5.50 ,, ,,	4.50	—	6.10 p.m. Padd. Train Engine	, 5.35	2
8.49 ,, ,,	8.55		Train Engine due 8.23 a.m.	To Yard.	6	5.52 ,, **SX**	5.10 **C**	—	6.53 p.m. Padd. Train Engine	5.25 **C**	5
8.52 ,, ,,	—	9 15 **C**	Pilot **No. 5**	To Yard for 9.15 out.	7	5.55 ,, Goods	—	—		5.25 **C**	
8.58 ,, ,,	9.25 **C**	—	Train Engine due 8.49 a.m.	To Yard	8	6. 0 ,, Pass.	—	5. 0 **C**	Pilot **No. 6**	5.30 **SO**	1
9. 5 ,, ,,	---	9.15 **C**	Pilot **No. 5**	*9.20	9	6. 5 ,, ,,	Formed at Padd. (due 4.57 p.m.)	—	•	From Yard due 4.57 **SX** 5. 2 **SO**	4
9.15 ,, ,,	9.25 **C**	—	Train Engine due 8.49 a.m.	To Goods.	8						
9.27 ,, ,,	9.35 **C**	—	Train Engine due 9.15 a.m.	To Yard for 10.5 out	6	6.10 ,, ,,	—	5.25	Pilot **No. 7**	6. 0 **C**	3
9.30 ,, ,,	9.35 **C**	—		To Yard	8	6.15 ,, ,,	—	5.10 **C**	6.53 p.m. Padd. Train Engine	6. 0 **C**	5
9.32 ,, ,,	---	9.50	Pilot **No 10**	*9.50	9	6.30 ,, ,,	—	5.50	Pilot **No. 5**	6. 0 **C**	1
9.37 ,, ,,	To Yard (out 10.5 a.m.)	---		To Yard for 10.58 out	7	6.32 ,, ,,	5.55 **C**	—	9.30 p.m. Padd. Train Engine	From Yard due 5. 2 **SX** 5.30 **SO**	5
9.43 ,, ,,	—	9.55	Pilot **No. 9**	To Yard	6	6.35 ,, ,,	—	5.45	Pilot **No. 3**	From Yard due 4.52	2
9.48 ,, ,,	10.5 **C**	—	Train Engine due 9.43 a.m.	10.10 **C**	8	6.50 ,, ,,	—	6. 0	Pilot **No. 11**	‡ 6.30	3
9.53 ,, ,,	—	10.10	Train Engine due 9.30 am., then to Shed.	*10.10 **C**	9	6.53 ,, ,,	5.55 **C**	—	9.30 p.m. Padd. Train Engine	---	5
9.54 ,, ,,	10.5 **C**	—	Train Engine due 9.43 a.m.	To Yard	7	7. 0 ,, ,,	6.15	—	Pilot **No. 4**	From Yard due 6.30 p.m.	1
10. 3 ,, ,,	To Yard. (out 10.58 a.m.)	—	---	To Yard for 10.40 out	6	7. 8 ,, **SX**	6.35 **C**	—	8.10 p.m. Padd. **B**	From Yard due 6.38	5
10.10 ,, ,,	—	10.25	Pilot **No. 1**	To Yard	9	7.12 ,, **SO**	6.35 **C**	—	Train Engine	Ex Aldgate	5
10.15 ,, ,,	—	10.30	,, **No. 4**	*10.30	8	7.25 ,, ,,	Formed at Padd. (due 6.38 p.m.)	—		From Yard due 6.35 p.m	2
10.25 ,, ,,	---	10.40	Train Engine due 9.54 am., then to Shed.	*10.40	9	7.30 ,, ,,	—	6.45	Pilot **No. 1**	‡7.15	1
10.29 ,, ,,	10.45	—	Train Engine due 10.10 a.m.	To Yard for 12.32 out	6	7.45 ,, ,,	—	6.50 **B**	,, **No. 9**	‡7.15	3
10.35 ,, ,,	—	10.50	Pilot **No. 11**	*10.50	8	7.45 ,, Goods	—	---		7.15	
10.40 ,, ,,	—	10.55	,, **No. 3**	To Yard	7	7.50 ,, Pass.	6.35 **C**	---	8.10 p.m. Padd. Train Engine	From Yard due 7.28	5
10.42 ,, ,,	To Yard (out 11.38 a.m.)	—		*10.50	6	8.10 ,, ,,	—	7.15 **B**	Pilot **No. 8**		1
10.48 ,, ,,	—	11. 0	Pilot **No. 7**	*11. 0	9	8.10 ,, Goods	—	—		7.40	-
11. 5 ,, ,,	11.15 a.m.	---	Train Engine due 10.40 a.m.	To Yard for 12.30 out	8	8.15 ,, Pass.	Formed at Padd. (due 7.24 p.m.)	---		From Yard due 7.47	4
11. 7 ,, ,,	—	11.35	Pilot **No. 8**	*11.35	7	8.30 ,, ,,	Formed at Padd. (due 7.28 p.m.)	—	—	From Yard due 7.24 **SX** 7.28 **SO**	3

* These engines run to Subway Junction only, for the purpose of turning.   ‡ These engines work from Green Lane only, after being turned.

The new arrangements for pilot and empty stock working, a much lauded feature of the new depot. Late running ruined this, of course, and a loco foreman was stationed in the carriage sidings to organise whatever corrective action might be necessary.

The 'four turntable unit' laid out and essentially complete. The tracks exiting at the rear of the building, shown on contemporary plans, were not put in, though the doors remained for any extensions which might become necessary. Proposals only arose some years on, a 'future extension' at the rear amongst the earliest in March 1927. The proposal envisaged a further set of four turntables and would have required some alterations both to the LNW loop line and to Old Oak Common Lane. It was modified to a pair of turntables only in late 1935. Accommodation was a particularly pressing problem in the war and in 1943 wholly radical ideas involved a new traverser-served fitting shop at the rear, fourteen roads backing onto the existing shed wall (and taken through where they corresponded to the two exits above), with smithy at the north end and machine shop at the south. Roads on the opposite side of the traverser were to be for 'tender work'. 'The Factory', meanwhile, would be converted into a straight shed with four additional roads, all for washout work and replacing the carpenters, coppersmiths and smiths shops and the various mess rooms of 1906 on the north side of the depot. 'The Factory' would also be extended out over the old traverser, which would be removed and a new 65 ft turntable put in to provide connection with the exit road on the 'washout' table. None of all this was ever carried out and the rear of the shed remained much as it is seen here, a quiet grassy space, a useful path out of the depot. Old springs were dumped on rails in this area, the new ones also stockpiled in lines parallel to the rear wall but inside the shed. *British Railways*

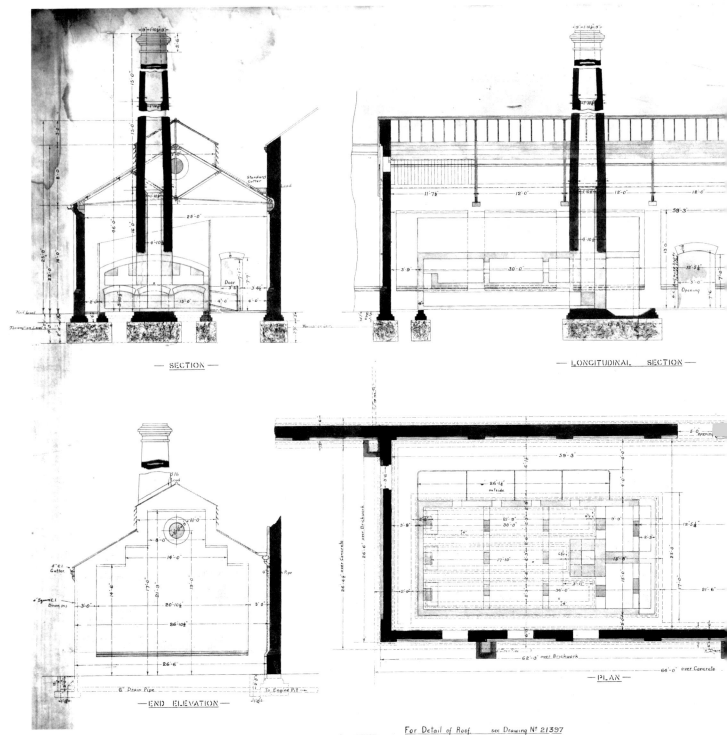

— SECTION —

— LONGITUDINAL   SECTION —

— END   ELEVATION —

— PLAN —

For Detail of Roof.	see Drawing Nº	21397
Furnace	,,	21398.
Sand Bin	,,	21400.
Coal Bunker	,,	21399.
Furnace Doors	,,	21415.
Brick for Dº	,,	21416 Shop Copy Nº 10821.

— G. W. R. —
— SAND FURNACE HOUSE —
ENGINE SHED — OLD OAK COMMON

— SWINDON — SEPTEMBER –1902 —
— SCALE ¼ IN = 1 FOOT —

Nº 21399

The sand furnace on the south side of the shed went out of use after a few years and was long put to sundry purposes. Part of it became the First Aid Post and the 1940s proposals detailed a smoke trough and pit to be installed, the approach road to the erstwhile rear traverser passing through the building. It is one of the few parts of the original building to survive today.

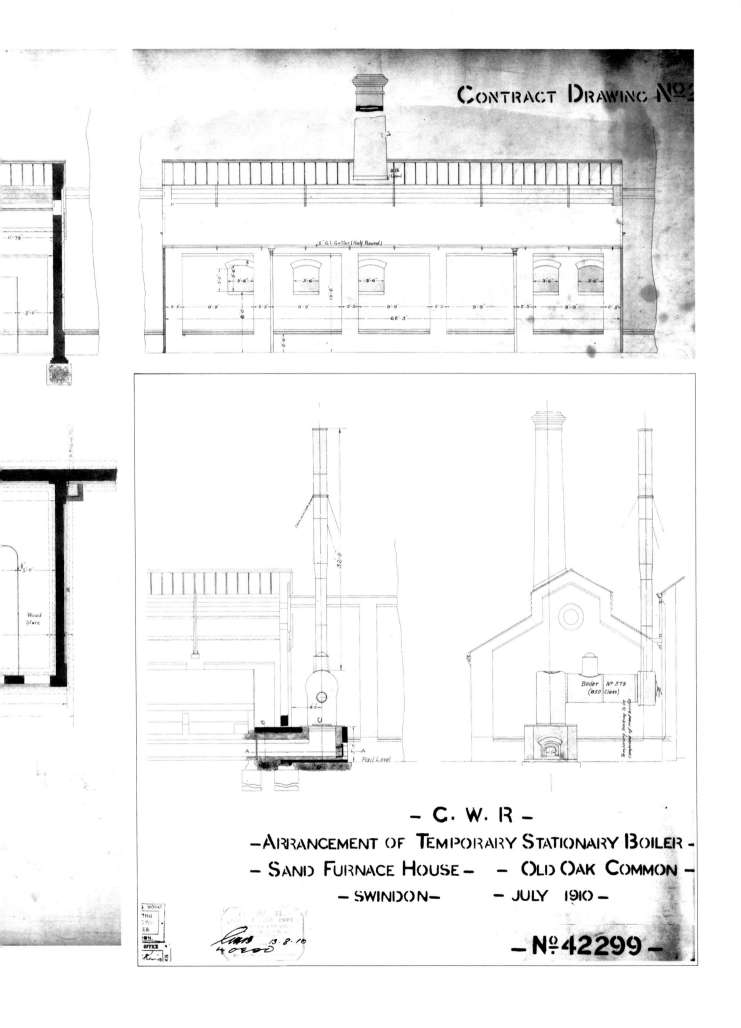

- C. W. R -

-ARRANCEMENT OF TEMPORARY STATIONARY BOILER -

- SAND FURNACE HOUSE -   - OLD OAK COMMON -

-SWINDON-   - JULY 1910 -

- N.º 42299 -

The new depot was, of course, celebrated in the Great Western house magazine, together with a convenient appraisal of past developments at Westbourne Park. This account of the new depot is of a more popular nature, for consumption by both company servants and, to an extent, the travelling public . . .

New Locomotive Depôt at Old Oak Common.

By A. J. L. White.

For some three or four years past extensive engine sheds have been in course of erection by the Company at Old Oak Common, about three miles West of Paddington. This great undertaking has now been consummated and was opened for service on 17th March, superseding the sheds at Westbourne Park, which are to be dismantled in the near future, in

connection with the improvement of the lines to and from Paddington station.

THE WESTBOURNE PARK DEPÔT.

In the March MAGAZINE reference was made to the last of the broad-gauge engines, and, for associations' sake, before proceeding to describe the Old Oak Common depôt I will briefly mention the buildings at Westbourne Park, where, on numerous occasions, the old 'Lord of the Isles' and 'North Star' sheltered, and where their successors have been 'stabled' and 'groomed.'

Names have a curious habit of clinging, and it is significant that, right down to the period of the transfer, the sheds at Westbourne Park were always spoken of as the 'B.G.' (Broad Gauge) and 'N.G.' (Narrow Gauge) sheds. Their history is substantially as follows:

The Broad Gauge shed (*i.e.*, the main building), 650 feet by 71 feet, was built about 1852

in substitution for a wooden circular shed at Bishop's Road, here illustrated, which formed part of the first Paddington terminus. The original four inside roads were, of course, broad gauge, and so remained until about 1869, from which time they were gradually modified by the addition of the third rail as the narrow gauge requirements increased and those of the broad gauge decreased.

The narrow gauge shed, *i.e.*, the smaller one, near the north-west corner of the broad gauge shed was 135 feet by 90 feet, and consisted of two bays, each containing three roads. The first or southern bay was built in 1861–2, in connection with the opening of the third rail into Paddington in the latter year and the second was added in 1873, doubling the accommodation.

The workshops, stores and offices were in a building parallel with the broad gauge shed, on the north side. This building was erected concurrently with the broad gauge shed in

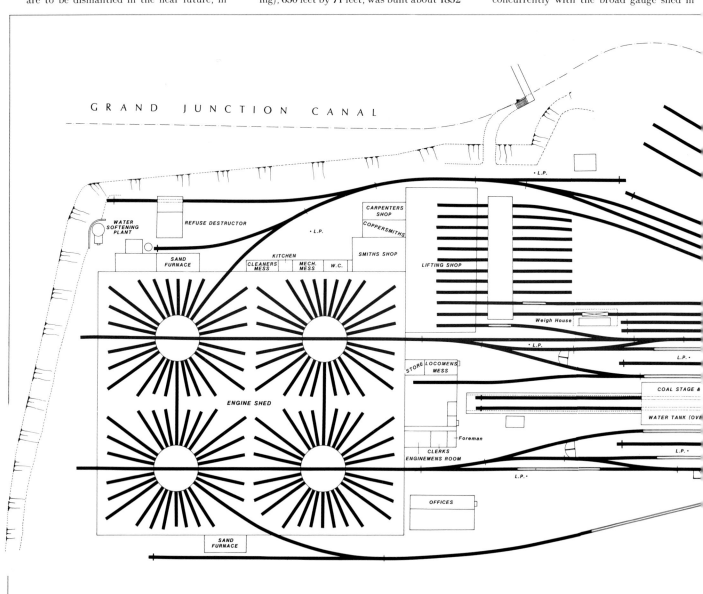

1852, and it is of interest to recall the fact that the offices were used for a year or two by Mr. (afterwards Sir Daniel) Gooch, who moved thence with his staff to the general offices at Paddington.

Originally there was a coal stage of the old type with cranes and tubs of the swing pattern. This stood on the site of the present up and down relief lines at Westbourne Park Station, and was surmounted by a clock tower, with large four-dial turret clock. It was demolished to make room for a relief line 1876 or 1877, when a more up-to-date stage was provided.

A turntable, believed to have been forty-two feet in diameter, was at the west end of the broad gauge shed, and was remarkable as being the only one actuated by steam on the line, and probably in the country. The engine and boiler were in a small house alongside, power being transmitted by a chain, which passed round the periphery of the table, and a horizontal sprocket wheel in the engine shed. This table was taken out about the year 1883,

and replaced by the one which may be seen at the present time. There was also a 40 ft hand turntable, manipulated by means of a pair of winches. This was probably put in when the narrow gauge shed was built, and was in 1895 replaced by a 55 ft surface table.

THE OLD OAK COMMON SHED

As previously indicated, this shed has been constructed for the accommodation of engines appropriated to Paddington, together with those from other depôts working to and from that station. It is situate on the up side of the main line to London, three miles from the terminus, between West London Junction and Acton, and is the largest of its type in Great Britain, and probably in the world. The inside measurements are 444 feet by 360 feet; it is designed on the 'internal turntable' principle, having four 65 ft tables (actuated by electric tractors) of the under-girder type, each with twenty-eight radiating roads, representing a total of 112 engine pits.

This form of construction is not quite so economical in the matter of space as the 'straight' shed with parallel roads, but is much more convenient for getting engines in and out without having to move others – a consideration of vast importance at a busy depôt. The roof, which is of the ordinary trussed type, affording excellent lighting, is carried by pitch pine principals 60 feet span, with steel tie rods. The principals are carried

by steel girders, mostly 60 feet span, supported on cast-iron columns. The height from rail level to shoe of principal is 21 feet 1 inch. It has been found that this form of roof resists corrosion by gases from locomotives much better than a roof with iron principals. The walls are of red brick throughout, the inside being whitewashed. Accommodation is provided for fifty-six tender and fifty-six tank engines.

Next to the engine shed, the most important building at a locomotive depôt is the Lifting and Repair Shop. The one at Old Oak Common is quite up-to-date from the point of view of adaptability, and is replete with every convenience. It adjoins the eastern wall of the shed and is 195 feet by 101 feet inside, with twelve pits 52 feet long, being in design generally similar to the main structure. The fitters' and machine bay is 195 feet by 45 feet. The shop is equipped with an electrically driven overhead crane, 23 feet above rail level, of thirty tons capacity, operated by electric motors. The span of the crane is 49 feet, and it runs transversely to the pits. Modern, electrically operated machinery has been installed, and there is excellent accommodation for the foreman and clerks. Outside, parallel with the shop, is an electrically operated traversing table, capable of dealing with a working load of eighty tons; it is 35 feet long, and moves on seven rails.

The smiths', coppersmiths' and carpenters' shops are exceedingly well appointed. The

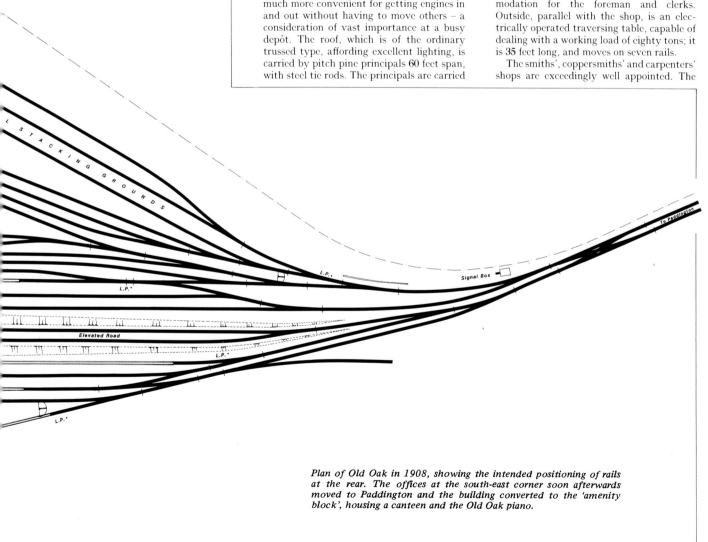

Plan of Old Oak in 1908, showing the intended positioning of rails at the rear. The offices at the south-east corner soon afterwards moved to Paddington and the building converted to the 'amenity block', housing a canteen and the Old Oak piano.

former contains seven hearths, while the latter is equipped with electrically driven wood-working machinery.

An important building is that containing the stores, shed foreman's office, etc. It is 117 feet by 72 feet and has two floors. A portion of the ground floor has been appropriated for messrooms for enginemen, etc., and offices for the chief running shed foreman and staff. The remainder has been laid out as stores, and by ingenious planning a gallery has been provided round the walls, thus appreciably increasing the accommodation.

An admirably arranged block of offices (90 feet by 45 feet) has been erected at the eastern corner of the shed for the superintendent of the division (Mr Jno. Armstrong) and his staff. There are seven rooms of varying sizes, with an overhead room for correspondence, etc.

The coal stage is conveniently placed, and may undoubtedly be regarded as the height of perfection in the practice of coaling engines as obtaining in this country. It is situated on the south side of the main building and is 104 feet by 59 feet 6 inches. Four double and two single tips are available, and there are two elevated roads for wagons, supported on brick arches. These roads are on a gradient of 1 in 80, so that wagons can be let down by gravity as required. Beneath the stage are rooms for the coalmen, together with lavatory accommodation. A water tank, capacity 290,000 gallons, is built over the coal stage and is the source of supply for the whole of the buildings and the yard. A special feature of the tank is that it is made in four sections, so arranged that either can be cut off from the others for cleaning or repairs. The distributing main is 15 inches diameter and is carried from the coal stage to supply five 8-inch swinging-jib water cranes in the yard and then into the shed, where it is laid round the turn-tables with branches to supply hydrants and stand-pipes, which are of the Metropolitan type. The hydrants are placed between each of the roads and are used for filling, washing out boilers, etc.; they are also available for fire purposes.

Next to the arrangement of the depot, the outstanding feature is undoubtedly the extent to which electricity has been employed for motive and lighting purposes. At present the power is being generated by temporary apparatus, but will eventually be obtained from the Company's Park Royal Station. There are two circuits, viz., 600 volts direct current, and 220 volts alternating current, the former being used principally for power purposes. The switchboard is divided into four circuits for direct current and two circuits for three-phase alternating current. The 30-ton overhead crane is actuated by three motors, viz., for travelling, traversing and lifting, wire ropes being employed for the latter purpose. The crab is also fitted with a light lift, operated from the lifting motor by means of a clutch. Attached to the winding gear is an automatic switch to prevent over-winding.

Arc lamps (10 amp.) double carbon, open type, are employed for lighting, some being on the direct and others on the alternating current circuit, the former (forty-eight in

number) burn twelve in series and the latter (twenty-five in number) burn five in series, each group on the alternating series being fitted with a patent compensator, allowing one or more of the groups to burn at a time.

The depôt was designed by Mr. G. J. Churchward. Locomotive Superintendent, the contractor being Mr. Walkerdine of Derby, who carried out the work under the superintendence of Mr. W. Armstrong, New Works engineer.

Thanks are due to Mr. A. Beasley, chief clerk to the locomotive superintendent of the Paddington division, for information as to the old sheds at Westbourne Park and for the illustration of the original round house.

On 15th January the periodical Locomotive Department Conference was held at the Old Oak Common shed, and Mr Churchward very readily fell in with a suggestion I made that he and his officers should be photographed in the shed, and the photograph reproduced in the MAGAZINE is a memento of the first official visit.

For reference purposes we append a schedule of the shops, etc., with principal dimensions.

Beginnings

Both of the main accounts thus far transcribed felt compelled to mention the original shed at Paddington. A major depot was obviously necessary at the London end of the line from the very first and the 'Paddington' (a term variously in use long after the establishment of Old Oak Common) shed's evolution was always associated with important enlargements of the terminus and its approaches. The Bishops Road, or Bishops Bridge Road, crosses the lines on a great iron girder bridge and the original, albeit temporary, Paddington terminus lay at first on the west side of its forerunner, 'Bishops Walk'. Associated with this first terminus of 1838 was a fairly elaborate engine shed, a wooden 'polygon' with longitudinal sections appended. Workshops were built separately on the north side but within a short period lack of space prompted the provision of a larger turntable and a set of shear-legs, a short

Building.	Dimensions, &c.
Engine Shed - - - - - -	444' × 360'.
Span of roof principals - - -	60'.
Height to shoe of principal - - -	21' 1".
Walls—Thickness - - - -	Piers 1' 10½"; Panels 1' 6".
Lifting and Repair Shop - - - -	195' × 101'.
Stores (including Shed Offices) - - -	117' × 72'.
Smiths' Shop - - - - -	74' × 47'.
Carpenters' Shop - - - - -	61' × 23'.
Coppersmiths' Shop - - - - -	61' × 23'.
Sand Furnaces (2) - - - - -	59' × 25'.
Offices—General - - - -	90' × 45'.
Coal Stage - - - - - -	104' × 59' 6".
Tank—Capacity - - - - -	290,000 gallons.
Coal Tips - - - - - -	4 double; 2 single.
Total Area of Buildings - - - - (approximate)	215,000 sq. ft.

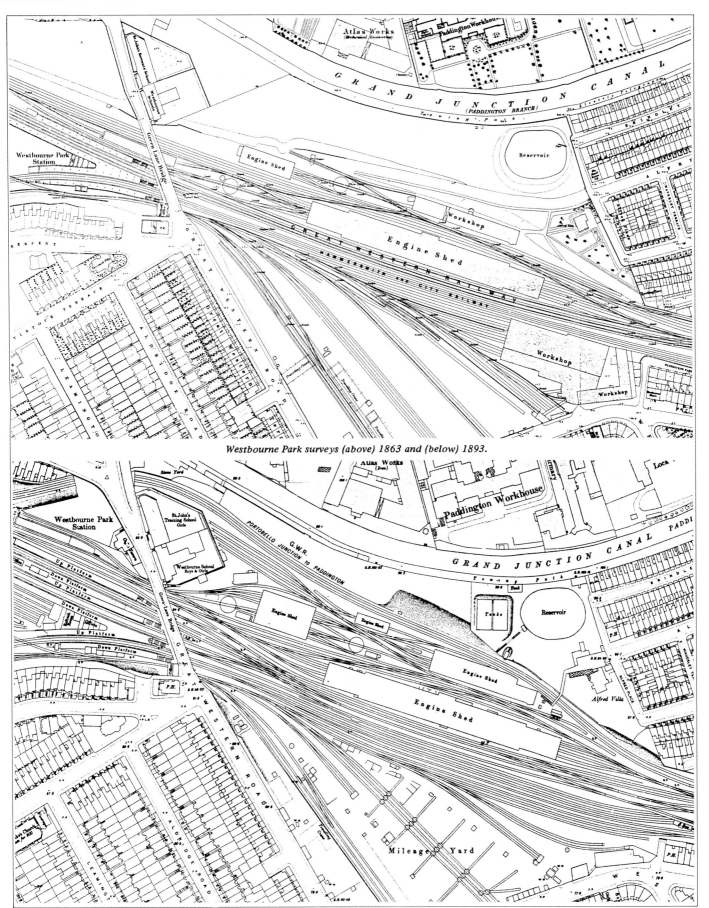

Westbourne Park surveys (above) 1863 and (below) 1893.

ENGINE SHED *(Sketch Plan to be attached).*

	"B.G." Shed (so called)	"N.G." Shed (so c
How built (Stone, Brick or Wood)	Brick & Slate	Brick & Slate
Inside dimensions. Length	663'· 0"	147'· 0"
Breadth	{ Middle sec: 68'· 6" } { End Secs: 56'· 6" }	84'· 0"
Height to top of roof ridge	{ Middle sec: 35'· 0" } { End Secs: 33'· 3" }	26'· 0"
Do. do. wall plate	21'· 0"	16'· 6"
Cubical contents	About 562,000 cft.	About 260,000 cf
Style of Roof (Gable, Hip Gable or Saw-tooth)	Gable	Gable, 2 spar
Roof principals (Material)	Iron	Iron
If fitted with Smoke Troughs	{ Troughs removed Nov. 1900. The chimneys only now remain }	Yes
Date built, or date Shed was first used	About 1862	{ South Span 1862 } { North " 1873 }
Length of each Line used for running Engines	4 lines, 663 ft each = 2652 ft	6 lines 147 ft each = 8
Do. do. do. repairs	Variable *×*	Variable *×*
Engine Pits—Length of each used for running Engines	4 pits 663 ft each	6 pits 140 ft each = 8
Do. do. do. repairs	Variable *×*	Variable

× *Engines are repaired on running lines as required*

SHOPS OR OFFICES OUTSIDE THE SHED.

	3	4	5	
How built (Stone, Brick or Wood)	Brick & Slate	Brick & Slate	Brick & Slate	Bric
Inside dimensions. Length	91'· 0"	61'· 0"	50'· 0"	{ See atta ta Of
Breadth	23'· 6"	24'· 0"	18'· 0"	
Height to top of roof ridge	29'· 6"	23'· 8"	17'· 0"	
Do. do. wall plate	22'· 6"	16'· 0"	17'· 6"	
Cubical contents	About 55,000 cft.	About 30,000 cft.	about 12,600 cft.	About
Style of Roof (Gable, Hip Gable or Saw-tooth)	Saw-tooth	Gable	Gable	Gab
Roof principals (Material)	Wood	Iron	Wood	
Date built, or date opened	1878 (?)	1882 (?)	1894	{ 1852 { addi date
Length of Line used for repairs	91 ft.	—	—	4 l
Do. Engine Pit used for repairs	73 ft.	—	—	4 pits
	Lifting, or "Shear-Legs" Shed	Sand House & Enginemens cabin	Running Foremen's office	Shop off

7. Small cabin at Paddn. Pass. yard 80 yards West
of Bishops Road bridge; for use of pilot
enginemen. Dimensions: 7 ft. long, 6 ft wide
height to ridge 10 ft.; to wall plate 7 ft 6 ins. Gable
roof Built of Brick & Slate. (About 367 cft.)

LOCOMOTIVE DEPARTMENT.

Engines at *Paddington (Westbourne Park)* **Station.**

OUTSIDE SHED.

Lines available for standing Engines ... { One line N. side of B.G. Shed, 468 ft. All other outside lines are required for circulation of engines; standing coal trucks &c. but are when available used as required for standing engines; all lines being practically full at times (e.g. Sunday night) when few engines are at work

Engine Pits—length of each ... { B.G. Shed, east end, 60½, 68, 65, 38½ ft; west end, 24½, 26½, 18½ ft; N.G. Shed, east end 50, 01, 29½, 50 ft, at coal stage 149 ft; "Long-pit road 224 ft. = Total 924 ft.

Do. at Station ... { Paddⁿ Passr Statn 1 pit 36 ft for pilot engs. At Westbourne Park (H & C. Joint) two pits 26 ft each. These latter at "hot water" pits grated over, for empty tanks of condensing engines only.

ENGINE TURNTABLES.

	No. 1.	No. 2.
Diameter ...	45 ft	55′·6″
Length of Rail ...	{ 45 ft with hinged extension rails }	55′·6″
Girders (Material) ...	{ W.I. Full circle decked over with timber }	W.I. (or steel)
How turned ...	{ Small vertical engine & boiler in house on table }	Hand levers { This is a balance table, with girders above rail level, and shallow pit. }
Where fixed ...	Near west end of N.G. Shed	Near east end N.G. Shed
Date fixed ...	1882 (?)	1896
Maker ...	G.W.R. Swindon	G.W.R. Swindon

COAL STAGE.

Sketch and size ... See Sketch plan attached (7)

Number of Cranes or Tips ... Four Tips

How built (Stone, Brick or Wood) { Brick up to stage floor; Corrugated iron above; Iron curved roof with lean to extension over coal-truck road on N. side (The latter now building: Feb. 1901)

Date built ... About 1882

SAND FURNACE. *in building described on other side (4)*

Outside dimensions of Furnace length, 30 ft breadth, 15 ft height { 11·6 Front 9·0 back

Brief description and Sketch Elevation of Furnace } a structure of rail iron & plates, lined firebrick. Two arched flues in & upon which is dried & drawn by side doors into bin

Date built ... 1882 (?)

Where situated ... In building described on other side (4) near N.W. corner of N.G. Shed

Date Certified 12 Feb 1901 _____ Superintendent's Signature.

" " _____	_____	"	"
" " _____	_____	"	"
" " _____	_____	"	"
" " _____	_____	"	"
" " _____	_____	"	"

Westbourne Park.

1. "Broad Gauge" Engine Shed. (Pulled down May '06)

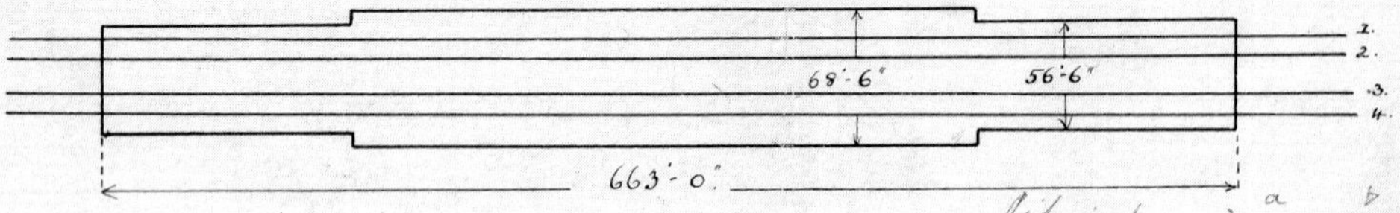

68'-6"   56'-6"

663'-0"

Pits:- 1 — 302.9 — 334.9
       2 — 304.3 — 344.9
       3 — 304.3 — 334.9
       4 — 304.3 — 334.9

a   b

2. "Narrow Gauge" Engine Shed.

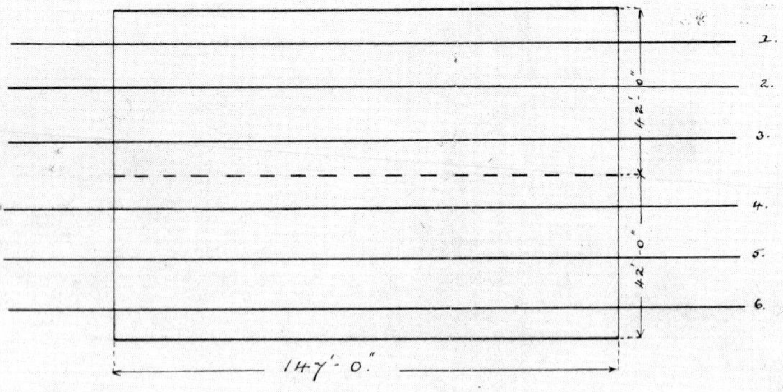

line over pits

1.
2.
3.
4.
5.
6.

137 ft.

42'-0"

147'-0"

3. "Shear-Legs", or Lifting, Shop.

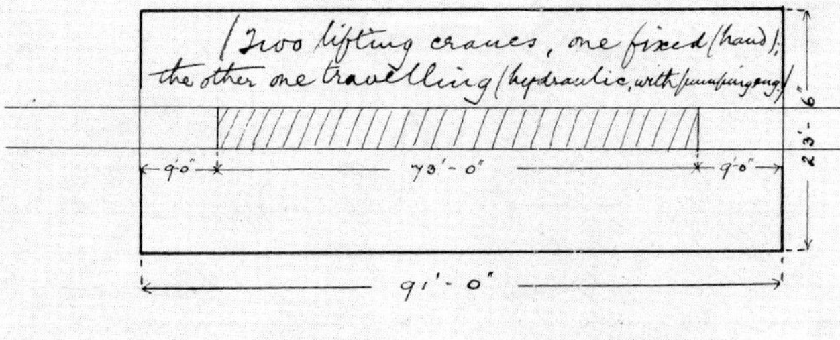

(Two lifting cranes, one fixed (hand), the other one travelling (hydraulic, with pumping engine)

9'-0"   73'-0"   9'-0"

23'-6"

91'-0"

Pit 74.
(Repairs)

4. Sand House and Engineman's Cabin.

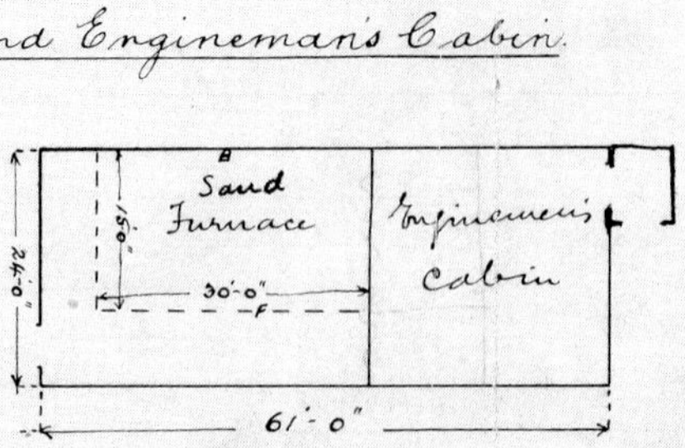

Sand Furnace

30'-0"

Engineman's Cabin

24'-0"

61'-0"

Heights.
Sand House etc.
To ridge. 23'-8"
" wallplate 16'-0"
Sand Furnace.
Front 11'-6"
Back.   9'-0"

Particulars of Shed Accommodation – Paddington

5. Running Foremen's Office

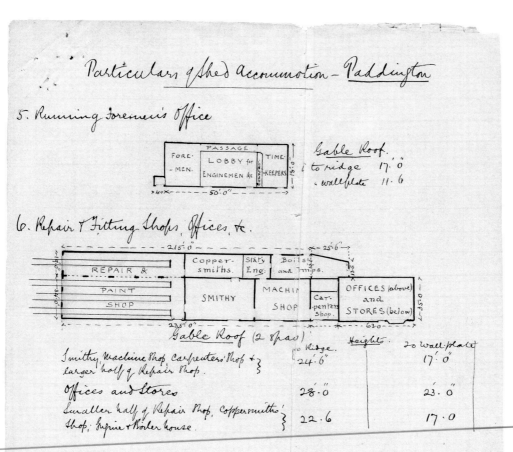

Gable Roof.
to ridge   17'·0"
wall plate   11·6

6. Repair & Fitting Shops, Offices, &c.

Gable Roof (2 span)

	Heights.	
	to Ridge.	to Wall plate
Smithy, Machine Shop, Carpenters' Shop & larger half of Repair Shop.	24'·6"	17'·0"
Offices and Stores	28'·0	23·0
Smaller half of Repair Shop, Coppersmiths' Shop, Engine & Boiler house.	22·6	17·0

7a. Coal Stage.

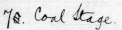

Structure above stage floor is iron. The lean-to extension of the roof is in course of erection [Feb 1907]. It is of corrugated plates carried on tubular pillars, no wall at rear.

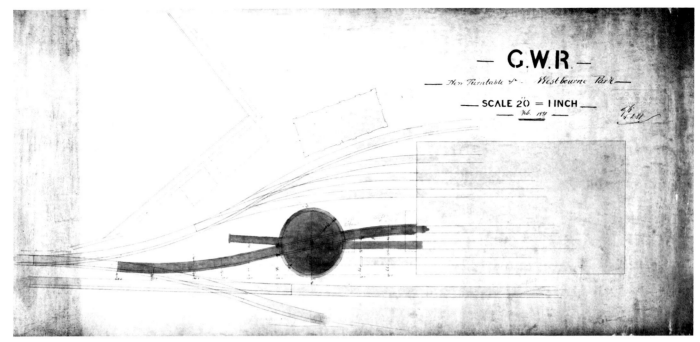

Outside the lengthy 'Broad Gauge Shed'.

Westbourne Park though all manner of additions had obviously taken place in the first years. Two turntables were soon in use, later further altered and the whole cluttered site was arranged in a most awkward fashion. The main building, the 'broad gauge' shed of four roads, was of an extraordinary length, making for a most inconvenient working. In this respect did it resemble the contemporary Bordesley shed (forerunner of Tyseley). The exact arrangements were tabulated by Armstrong, for the authorities at Swindon, and certified on 12th February 1901.

'Replete With Every Convenience'

The completion of Old Oak (conjoint improvements took place, like new arrangements for carriage stock) allowed the immense traffic-goods mineral and passenger funnelling eastward to London – to be dealt with as expeditiously as may be. The Great Western routing had developed into a firmly bifurcate pattern, with Old Oak the strategic point. A substantial proportion of the larger passenger engines (the former inhabitants of Westbourne Park) were thus based at the new shed along with many 'suburban' tanks, numbers of shunting engines and a considerable goods fleet.

Something like a hundred locomotives could be put under cover at Old Oak, an impressive gathering with individual locomotives immediately accessible – the great advantage of course of the roundhouse arrangement. Generally the two turntables

distance to the west. Reconstruction and enlargement at Paddington required removal of this 'Engine House' and its appendages, to the nearest conveniently available site, Westbourne Park. The new shed may have come into operation as early as 1852 though this date is open to question. The new terminus, on the grand scale originally envisaged by Brunel, first came into use in 1854 and the depot at Westbourne Park may have come properly into use around 1854/1855.

Both the accompanying plans are reproduced from Ordnance Survey material which may not have kept precisely 'up-to-date' with the advancing mixed gauge – very likely official GW surveys too became rapidly out of date. Westbourne Park was a crowded, bustling site and minor alterations, official or otherwise undoubtedly at times escaped the eye of Swindon. In the 1860s most routes were still broad gauge – Birmingham, Weymouth and South Wales were all broad gauge until the 1870s, which explains the paucity of mixed gauge in the earlier plan. Most narrow gauge locos were in the north and the Midlands.

Little is really known of early events at

At so long a distance in time, it is impossible to arrive at any detail of the shed working at Westbourne Park, though a glance at the plans reveals obvious complications and drawbacks. The scattered buildings had to accommodate whatever machinery was necessary and the 'particulars' of the previous page give some notion of the disposition of the buildings and their use. Stanier was at Westbourne Park as Assistant Divisional Superintendent from 1903 and his views on running shed practice must reflect his experiences there. On 26th February 1907 he reported to the Swindon Engineering Society:

'Boilerwashing is usually done with the simplest of tools, a bent and a straight nozzle with two or three lengths of split-pin wire being the usual outfit. The steam car boilerwashing nozzle consists of a length of gas pipe, about 6 ft. long, which will pass through a mud plughole in the top tube plate, and having a slot about 1 $1/4''$ x $1/8''$ in the side of the pipe at the bottom, the end being blocked up. On the pipe there is a threaded thimble, which screws into the mud plughole, and in which the gas pipe can be revolved, and at the top a swivel connection, to which is screwed the water pipe. It will readily be seen that when the water is turned on it issues with some force from the slot, and will drive all sediment and scale in front of it, from between the tubes just above the crownplate where it is deposited.

'A similar device could, the Author thinks, be used for clearing scale from between the tubes of a loco boiler, but it would be necessary to modify the tube arrangement a little, perhaps, and also to put one or two mud plugholes around the centre of the smokebox tubeplate.

'Screwed thimbles are also an advantage to boilerwashers, as they protect the mud plugholes from damage.

'When the London division headquarters were at Westbourne Park, they were able to utilize the hot water returning from the condenser at the Electric Light Station, Paddington, with great advantage to the boiler maintenance, and the amount of coal used for lighting up.

'A boiler could be washed out while it was still hot without damage, and there is no doubt the scale and sediment was cleared out more effectually.

'This advantage was greatly missed when the depot was moved to Old Oak Common; so Mr. Jno. Armstrong, the Loco Superintendent of the Division, suggested that some injectors should be tried for washing out purposes. An injector was mounted on an iron barrow and

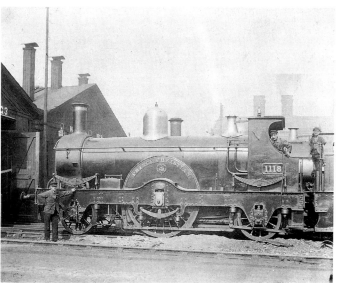

fitted with a water valve and a standard vacuum pipe to connect to the ground hydrants, and with a steam valve and pipes to connect to a shunting engine, the shunting engine having been fitted with a T piece under the regulator box, allowing the portable injector to be connected up to the same point as the engine's injector steam valve, without interfering with the engine's injector connections. As an engine always returns to the shed with steam in the boiler, it was proposed to utilize this steam, not only to increase the pressure of the washing out water, but to heat it; a temperature of 80° to 120° F. being easily obtained. This arrangement has now been working satisfactorily for some time.'

Collection W. A. Camwell and Collection J. E. Kite

Passenger engines arrived at the Old Oak Common stage tender first out of Paddington and coaled before setting back (after turning) to take advantage of the 'fire pit'. Passenger engines used the south side, goods the north, but coal was issued regardless of the work to be done, at least from the 1930s onwards. Only wholly special occasions like 'Royals' might demand a specially chosen coal. At the end of the GWR's existence, Mr. H. G. Kerry was Divisional Locomotive Carriage and Wagon Superintendent for the London Division. On 30th January 1947 he described 'The Working of a Locomotive Shed' to the Great Western Railway (London) Lecture and Debating Society. Naturally enough, his illustrations were concerned with Old Oak:

'I think the best way to deal with the sequence of operations is to follow an imaginary engine from the time it arrives at the shed after having completed a trip, to the time it is ready to leave for its next trip.

'When engines arrive at Old Oak Common shed they are segregated into two sections, the first being the larger passenger engines. This segregation takes place at the signal box known as the loco shed box, which controls all movements in and out of Old Oak loco shed.

'The coal stage at Old Oak Common is a double-sided one, and all the big passenger engines are dealt with at the south side of the stage and all the goods and tank engines at the north side of the stage.

DISPOSAL OF ENGINE BY FOOTPLATE STAFF

'We will follow a large passenger engine onto the south side of the coal stage when it arrives from Paddington after having completed a trip, shall we say, from the West of England.

'The driver and firemen on this engine will make it secure on the coal stage road; that is, they put the engine in mid-gear, open the cylinder cocks, screw the hand brake on the tender hard on, and make sure there is plenty of water in the boiler. Having left the engine secure, the driver and fireman proceed to the time office, where the driver reports in the proper book any defects which he has discovered on the engine. This book is known as the repair book.

'He then makes out what is known as his daily record, which is a record of all he has done on his turn of duty with that particular engine.

'This record is handed to the timekeeper in the shed office and is checked over by the shed foreman's staff before it is forwarded to the divisional office and finally passed to the statistical office at Swindon.

'The driver, having completed his daily record and any other reports, books off duty with his fireman.'   *National Railway Museum*

Above right and opposite: Albert Brassey and Albion at the coal stage on 25th April 1925. Kerry:

'There are three projections from the side of the coal stage which look like "sentry boxes" — these are called coal tips. At the bottom of these projections are hinged flaps. On the first projection the flap is up, and on the second projection the flap is down. On the coal stage itself there are a number of four-wheeled iron trolleys or boxes, each of which will hold 10 cwt. of coal. The height of the coal-stage floor is so arranged that, when the coal-wagon doors are open, the flap of the door will rest on top of the trolleys. Coal is shovelled by hand from the wagon into

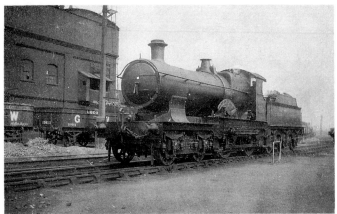

the trolleys and pushed across the iron floor of the coal stage to the coal tips on the side of the stage. When the trolley is pushed against the hinged flap on the tip, the flap falls down and the trolley is pushed out onto the tip until the wheels come up against the curved stops which can be seen on the flap which is down. The front end of the trolley is hinged at the top and is kept closed by a simple catch which is operated from the back end of the trolley. When the trolley is over the engine tender, the catch is released and the trolley is lifted from the back end. The front plate of the trolley swings outward from the top hinge, and the 10 cwt. of coal slides straight onto the tender. The operation is quite simple and, as there is nothing mechanical in the arrangement, there is nothing to go wrong. The work, however, is very arduous and very dirty, but water sprays are provided on the coal stage to minimise the dust as far as possible.

'I wonder if any of you have thought of the quantity of coal that is shifted by each individual coalman on a coal stage at a busy depot? In these days of domestic fuel rationing, we are rarely overburdened by the quantity of coal that is delivered at our houses, but if by some mischance nobody happens to be at home when the coalman calls and a few hundred-weight is dumped in the wrong place, we think we have a big job of work to do when we have to set to and shovel it up and put it in the right place. How the majority of us would feel if we were suddenly faced with three 10-ton wagons to unload in eight hours, I leave to your imagination! Yet this is what a coalman on the coal stage at Old Oak Common occasionally does! Twenty-five tons per shift per man is quite common, and if the amount drops down to twenty tons a shift per man, the coalman does not think much of his piecework balance. In one 24-hours recently, 535 tons of coal was actually put on engines from the coal stage at Old Oak Common. This work was done by eighteen coalmen, six working on each shift, and it works out at a fraction under thirty tons per man per shift. If that is not a good day's work, I do not know what is!'   *Collection Peter Winding*

on the south side were kept for passenger engines whilst those engaged on freight and shunting work were attended to in the other half of the building. The coal stage, aligned as it was on the depot approach, was properly positioned to administer the appropriate grades of coal, the finest to first rank express engines, the quality diminishing accordingly down to shunting tanks. This practice had ceased, by the outbreak of the Second World War at least, and bulk supply was undifferentiated except for special workings – 'Royals', etc. Two roads swung either side of the main building to provide independent access to the two 'rear' roundhouses. That through the south wall (or rather the spur off it) long provided a resting place for visiting 4700 2–8–0s from Exeter or Plymouth, with several stabled in line during the day.

Old Oak's great attraction, of course, lay in the wealth of express power – for a time London had No 6000 *King George V* 'and all the odd numbers except 6017/6019 (Stafford Road), Laira having contented itself with those of even number, from 6002 with the exception of 6018, the Newton engine. When the second batch came out, Wolverhampton got 6005 and 6007 from London and 6014 from Laira.' Of some 150 engines stationed at Old Oak in the beginning, a little over one-third comprised passenger tender types, 2–4–0s and 4–4–0s, whilst the first of a great succession of

4–6–0s were put to work, from their earliest days in traffic. The passenger engine allocation by 1947 (approaching 100, of a total complement of nearly 250) was characterised by 'Castles', 'Kings' and 'Halls'. Through the meticulous recording and kindness of Mr. V. R. Webster it is possible to relate details of engines actually present at Old Oak at certain times. In the 1920s and 1930s it was possible to obtain possession of an 'open shed pass' and on presenting oneself to the shed foreman and upon payment of 1/- towards the benevolent fund, obtain access to the shed. Old Oak in those days could conveniently be visited by the simple (and wholly illegal) expedient of boarding a rake of empty carriages departing Paddington, alighting at Old Oak carriage sheds and walking across the stock lines to the roundhouses. Return to Paddington was the reverse procedure, the visitor having simply to ascertain where the next up empty stock train lay. The procedure required some degree of influence and simply presenting oneself at the entrance was the only method open to most of the hopeful. There was a little-known entrance off the canal towpath, on the north side but for most it was necessary to purchase a copy of the *GWR Magazine* (*WR Magazine* in the '50s) from the gatekeeper at Old Oak Common Lane. The shed foreman nevertheless remained a formidable obstacle. On the day of the F.A.

Cup Final, 21st April 1928, when Huddersfield lost to Blackburn Rovers the following were noted at Old Oak Common:

4–6–0		
	6000	*King George V*
	6001	*King Edward VII*
	6002	*King William IV*
	6006	*King George I*
	6010	*King Charles I*
	4016	*Knight of the Golden Fleece*
	4074	*Caldicot Castle*
	4077	*Chepstow Castle*
	4079	*Pendennis Castle*
	4080	*Powderham Castle*
	4081	*Warwick Castle*
	4092	*Dunraven Castle*
	5003	*Lulworth Castle*
	5011	*Tintagel Castle*
	5012	*Berry Pomeroy Castle*
	4004	*Morning Star*
	4005	*Polar Star*
	4014	*Knight of the Bath*
	4015	*Knight of St. John*
	4019	*Knight Templar*
	4022	*Belgian Monarch*
	4033	*Queen Victoria*
	4036	*Queen Elizabeth*
	4039	*Queen Matilda*
	4045	*Prince John*
	4047	*Princess Louise*
	4049	*Princess Maud*
	4056	*Princess Margaret*
	4065	*Evesham Abbey*
	4066	*Malvern Abbey*

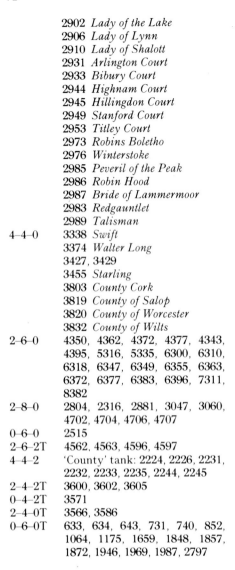

	2902 *Lady of the Lake*
	2906 *Lady of Lynn*
	2910 *Lady of Shalott*
	2931 *Arlington Court*
	2933 *Bibury Court*
	2944 *Highnam Court*
	2945 *Hillingdon Court*
	2949 *Stanford Court*
	2953 *Titley Court*
	2973 *Robins Boletho*
	2976 *Winterstoke*
	2985 *Peveril of the Peak*
	2986 *Robin Hood*
	2987 *Bride of Lammermoor*
	2983 *Redgauntlet*
	2989 *Talisman*
4–4–0	3338 *Swift*
	3374 *Walter Long*
	3427, 3429
	3455 *Starling*
	3803 *County Cork*
	3819 *County of Salop*
	3820 *County of Worcester*
	3832 *County of Wilts*
2–6–0	4350, 4362, 4372, 4377, 4343, 4395, 5316, 5335, 6300, 6310, 6318, 6347, 6349, 6355, 6363, 6372, 6377, 6383, 6396, 7311, 8382
2–8–0	2804, 2316, 2881, 3047, 3060, 4702, 4704, 4706, 4707
0–6–0	2515
2–6–2T	4562, 4563, 4596, 4597
4–4–2	'County' tank: 2224, 2226, 2231, 2232, 2233, 2235, 2244, 2245
2–4–2T	3600, 3602, 3605
0–4–2T	3571
2–4–0T	3566, 3586
0–6–0T	633, 634, 643, 731, 740, 852, 1064, 1175, 1659, 1848, 1857, 1872, 1946, 1969, 1987, 2797

On further visits in 1928 the engines noted were, of course, much the same, though more unusual types in July included petrol engine No. 13 (the Park Royal Loco), 0–4–2T No. 216, condensing 0–6–0Ts Nos. 633, 642 and 643, outside-framed 0–6–0Ts Nos. 740, 1052, 1060, 1062, 1064, 1081, 1152, 1175, 1241, 1248, 1567 and 1651, Dean Goods 0–6–0s Nos. 2484, 2515 and 2570, No. 4000 *North Star*, 'Saints' Nos. 2901 *Lady Superior* and 2903 *Lady of Lyons*, condensing 2–4–0Ts Nos. 3567, 3568, 3570 and 3591 and 'Bulldog' 4–4–0s Nos. 3374 *Walter Long* and 3407 *Madras*.

Apart from the host of big passenger types, other, less grand, engines characterised Old Oak Common through more or less to the 1960s. The 6100 2–6–2Ts had appeared in 1931 and remained the mainstay of London Division secondary work until the end of steam. The lighter 4575 2–6–2Ts had been put on the Old Oak

Continued on page 84

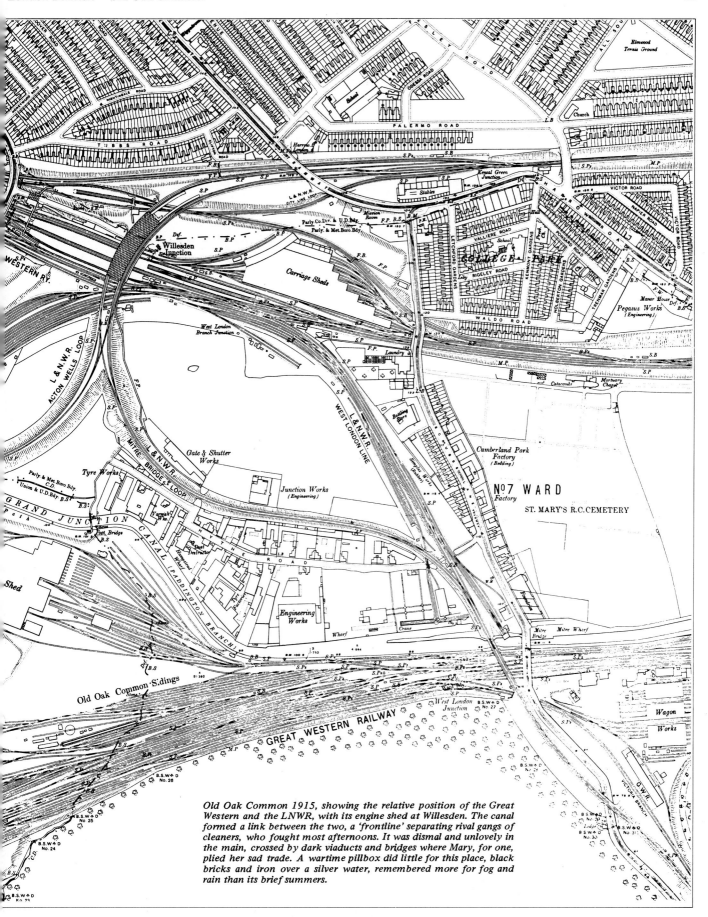

Old Oak Common 1915, showing the relative position of the Great Western and the LNWR, with its engine shed at Willesden. The canal formed a link between the two, a 'frontline' separating rival gangs of cleaners, who fought most afternoons. It was dismal and unlovely in the main, crossed by dark viaducts and bridges where Mary, for one, plied her sad trade. A wartime pillbox did little for this place, black bricks and iron over a silver water, remembered more for fog and rain than its brief summers.

0–6–0T No. 642 at Old Oak on 24th April 1920. The engine beyond would be Brighton 0–6–0 No. 527, one of three loaned (see the RCTS *Chronological and Statistical Survey*) to the GWR in March 1920 and put to work at Old Oak. No. 527 returned to the LBSCR a year later.

H. C. Casserley

No. 9703 on 13th September 1936. Anything with a pipe along the boiler was a 'Tunnel Motor' whether pannier tank or '35'. The feed pump at the front was for use in the tunnels instead of injectors but the fitters never did get the hang of them and often they didn't function at all. The condensers were simply ignored in any event.   *Collection Peter Winding*

No. 3592 in 'The Washout'. The '35s' worked much of the passenger traffic out of Paddington until the '61s' allowed most to be pensioned off but they retained a foothold in the Division through World War Two and beyond. Stanier recalled his Westbourne Park days: 'When he was in London, considerable trouble was experienced with the driving and trailing axle boxes of the Metro class engines. These engines had very hard work to do, and were timed on some of the Slough and Paddington trains 18½ miles in 24 minutes, with 10 eights load, and these boxes continually ran hot about the horizontal centre line. The boxes were fitted as supplied from Swindon, fairly close to the journal to below the horizontal centre line. With underhung boxes the tendency was to pull the sides of the box in, and if they started fretting a little, they had a tendency to close in, and run hot very quickly. The practice now was to put a clearance for about half an inch above the centre, and to scrape away on each side, so that the slight expansion of the box and axle owing to ordinary running was compensated by the clearance, and there was no tendency to pinch the journals. Very good results were obtained from the practice. They are remembered chiefly for the restricted cabs – 'slightly unbelievable' engines; a '35' was put on the Guinness shunting at one time – 'not enough room to turn a shovel'.   *Collection R. C. Riley*

Tanks on the goods engine side of the coal stage, Nos. 633 and 643. The coal 'Tally Clerk' lived in a room on the 'goods side', supremo of a system dedicated in part to confounding the company's attempts at strict control of coal, both its quantity and delivery. A fireman signed for x buckets and inquired less than closely into the correlation between 'chit' and actual delivery. The hoists on many stages were electrically driven, a feature introduced principally to speed up coaling during the war but moving parts and coal lumps are very carefully worked out are markedly incompatible. The Old Oak hoists frequently stuck and they were knocked off by engines, coal flying everywhere. All three delivery points could only be used when tanks were taking coal, for two tender engines together more or less precluded use of the middle station. The rate at which engines could be processed through the coal stage depended upon grades like the firedroppers — the rate of pay and thus the progress depended upon a continuous process of negotiation, dependent upon number of engines, disasters in various places about the yard, the weather, the numbers of staff available or the mental state of the foreman. All these factors and more determined how many engines for the purposes or rates of pay would be classified as "rough 'uns".

Collection J. E. Kite

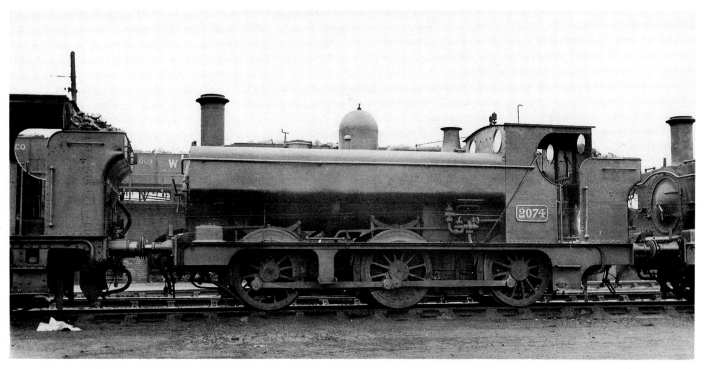

No. 2074 in 1932. There were innumerable duties for such engines, and pannier tanks of every description skittered about the Division in a constant, unceasing activity. Old Oak and Paddington are rightly remembered for the glittering array of express power and finely turned out engines, even on commuter work, but it was these 0–6–0 tanks, '57s' increasingly from the 1930s, that kept the railway, in London more so than most other districts, on the move. They shuffled here and there, little noticed, simple machines put to a more varied use on the GWR than that to be found almost anywhere else.   *Gordon Coltas*

'County' tank No. 2239 on 1st April 1933.   *A. W. Croughton*

No. 4706 in original condition, on 'the 47 Road' at Old Oak. They were parked outside in this fashion for convenience, their great length making it slightly awkward to stable in the shed. It simply became accustomed practice to put them down this side of the shed and no one would be in any doubt if he were directed 'over on the 47'. The road into the 'top passenger' was considered an exit, like its similar loop on the 47. The shed men could never be quite sure of the proper observation of this fact, and customarily placed a red stop light on the road.

Collection J. L. Smith

No. 4908 *Broome Hall* on the north side at Old Oak, 3rd June 1933. Final preparation involved checking and oiling, and varied from one man to the next. For many it demanded an absolute exactitude, the reassurance of the ritual whilst most arrived at some variation acceptable both to driver and fireman — witness the warming of drivers' oil cans, by firemen at Southall, for instance. Good tools were valued possessions and anything desirable soon vanished. An old and cherished shovel or a well-kept lamp would have to be secreted away at the end of a turn and the first job the next day would be to retrieve it. Favourite 'hidey-holes' were provided in 'the stockpile', the coal stack, and firemen picking over it, sometimes in mounting anxiety, were a familiar sight. When the stack was lifted it was revealed as an Aladdin's Cave of tools and lamps, long squirrelled away and lost.   *Collection Peter Winding*

No. 4961 *Pyrland Hall* on 8th September 1934, fully coaled and appropriately positioned to leave the shed.   *Collection Peter Winding*

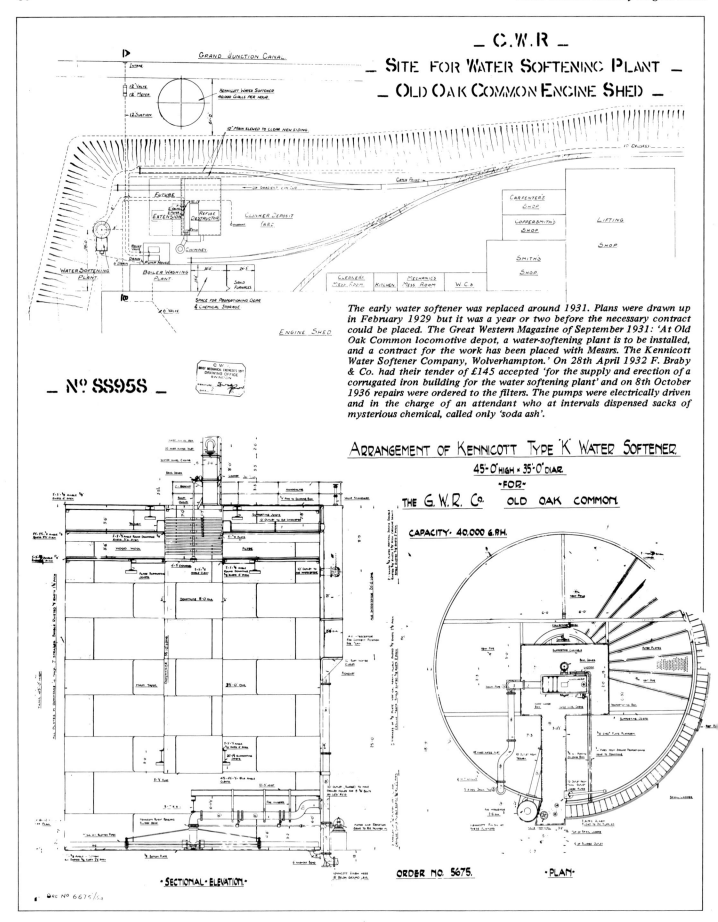

_ C.W.R _
SITE FOR WATER SOFTENING PLANT
_ OLD OAK COMMON ENGINE SHED _

_ Nº SS95S _

The early water softener was replaced around 1931. Plans were drawn up in February 1929 but it was a year or two before the necessary contract could be placed. The Great Western Magazine of September 1931: 'At Old Oak Common locomotive depot, a water-softening plant is to be installed, and a contract for the work has been placed with Messrs. The Kennicott Water Softener Company, Wolverhampton.' On 28th April 1932 F. Braby & Co. had their tender of £145 accepted 'for the supply and erection of a corrugated iron building for the water softening plant' and on 8th October 1936 repairs were ordered to the filters. The pumps were electrically driven and in the charge of an attendant who at intervals dispensed sacks of mysterious chemical, called only 'soda ash'.

ARRANGEMENT OF KENNICOTT TYPE 'K' WATER SOFTENER.

45'-0" HIGH × 35'-0" DIAR

-FOR-

THE G.W.R. Cº   OLD OAK COMMON

CAPACITY. 40,000 G.P.H.

ORDER Nº. 5675.   · PLAN ·

· SECTIONAL · ELEVATION ·

No. 2987 *Bride of Lammermoor* and 4059 *Princess Patricia* on 1st May 1937. *Collection Peter Winding*

No. 3336 *Titan* in the early 'thirties. 'An hour before the engine is due off the shed to take up its working, a driver and fireman book on duty to prepare the engine. About a quarter of an hour before the engine is due to be at the shed "exit" signal, the engine is taken outside the shed to the water column, where the tank is filled right up and any last-minute lubrication is carried out. After this, the engine moves up to the shed signal and is ready to leave to take up its working.'

V. R. Webster

King Edward III undergoing preparation at Old Oak. Staff standards, as with much else, were rigidly defined, if applied with a certain lack of depth (a man was deemed literate if he could correctly write 'The Driver must obey all Signals'). The following is from the Mechanics Institution *Transactions* 9th January 1906, by R. H. Smith and has in part the distinct air of a stock buying guide: 'SELECTION OF MEN – It is perfectly safe to say that fully ninety per cent of locomotive drivers commenced their railway career as engine cleaners. Promotion to first grade of firemen is followed strictly on the principle of seniority, but each man must fulfil the following qualifications:– (1) Must bear a good character, and be recommended by Foreman and Superintendent respectively. (2) Must be over 18 and under 21 years of age. (3) A servant of the Company not less than four months. (4) Able to read and write distinctly. (5) Must be 5 feet 4½ inches or over in height, and weight in proportion; not less than 34 inches round chest; have sound teeth. (6) Able to pass an exceptionally strict eyesight test and medical examination.'

L & GRP, courtesy David & Charles

The 'streamlined' engines at Old Oak on 17th July 1935, (top) 6014 *King Henry VII* and (above) 5005 *Manorbier Castle*. It was an abysmal attempt at streamlining and rightly regarded as 'a bit of a joke'.

W. Potter

ECS trains from about 1924, but lacked versatility. They left for more rural careers as the 6100 tanks became available and ever afterwards were a rarity in the Division. The big 'Prairies' (power class 4 in BR days) could handle both a heavy empty train and a smartly timed commuter service. Condensing tanks were also an abiding feature; by the 1920s and into the 1930s there were ten small engines fitted with (largely unused) condensing apparatus, 633 class 0–6–0Ts Nos 633, 634, 641 and 642 and Metro 2–4–0Ts Nos. 3567, 3568, 3570, 3586, 3591 and 3592.

The equipment was intended for meat workings – the 'Tunnel Motors' – through to the GWR goods station beneath Smithfield Market. Trains were formed of a dozen or so covered vans, usually hauled by 0–6–0Ts but also by the 2–4–0Ts which otherwise took their part in the general suburban working. These trains were heard and felt rather than seen, part of a little known and seldom penetrated world, quite out of time even in that distant era, though in truth steam locomotives remained in use in the tunnels well into BR days. These 0–6–0Ts and 2–4–0Ts seemed suited to the fume-laden catacombs; primitive of aspect (they were completely cabless, a feature *preferred* by the men, it was said) their route lay via the Inner Circle lines to Farringdon Street, where a crossover existed to the widened lines just before the station. After that they halted in Aldersgate station to set back across the eastbound line, pulling forward again into a maze of arches and dripping brickwork, the cramped accommodation that formed the goods station. 0–6–0 pannier No 8700 appeared with condensing gear in March 1932 and in 1933 Nos. 9701–9710 were built, throwing the old condensing tanks out of use – all had disappeared by March 1934 and the panniers, with distinctively enlarged tanks, were familiar Old Oak features well nigh to the end.

The 'Tunnel Motors' were part of a local goods link that included another awkward job, coal trains to Hammersmith (Metropolitan). Various old tender engines were put on these turns and their often less than perfect brakes could make it a hectic night indeed. Old Oak men under these circumstances could find the precise positioning required at the Met signals (for the track circuiting) next to impossible. No. 10 Rillington Place was a landmark of more note and its malign presence was known to all the crews.

The *Railway Observer* of July 1933 gives the Old Oak allocation as:

13,111,633/4/41/2/3, 1716, 1836, 1903/35/ 46/96, 2026/38/74, 2222/32/5/46/50, 2362/ 70, 2443, 2611/36/68, 2805/16/36/44/7/55/6/ 9/67/77/9, 3407, 3567/8/70/86/91/2, 3610, 4003/5/7/35/50/2/7/71 – 6/8/83/93/8, 4331/ 41/5/63/4/5/84/97, 4703/5, 4902/5/8/21/2/

44/7/51/7/60/5/7/73/5/7/85/7/8, 5000/1/3/5/ 6/7/11/2/6/8/22, 5323/47, 5715/7/27/37/45/ 50 – 4/7 – 67/72/3/9/98/9, 5901/14/22/5, 6000/1/3/5/7/13/5/21/6 – 9, 6100/1/3/5/7/ 8/11/8/20/33/4/7/41/6/8/52/5/7/8/9, 6307/ 14/30/2/54/92, 7312, 7708 – 13/7/8/31 – 4/ 50/78/89/91/9, 8320/9/32/3/73/88, 8700/27/ 9/33/45, 9306/7/8/9/10/2/4/5.

So, both passenger and goods engines could be found in abundance at Old Oak Common, the former *Great Western* to the end of steam, and the latter, although predominantly 2800 and 4700 2–8–0s, augmented in BR days by WD 2–8–0s, 9Fs, and even Stanier 8Fs. Three of the LMS-designed engines were transferred from St. Philip's Marsh, Nos. 48410, 48412 and 48431 in the early part of 1960, whilst others could be found there in these last years. USA 2–8–0s designed for Europe worked from Old Oak in the war, as well as the home-grown Austerity engines; Nos. 7094, 7377 and 7492 were all 'received' in September 1944, with others arriving, often 'destined for Longmore' (sic). The bogie problems with the 'Kings' in 1956 perforce brought all sorts of foreigners – BR Pacifics had already become familiar, if not exactly admired on the Western Region; several examples were based on Old Oak and the 1956 intruders were ushered in and out as quickly as possible. The 'Kings' were largely withdrawn for remedial work at the end of January 1956, replacements including BR 4–6–0s Nos. 73085, 73088, 73110 and 73114 from the Southern Region and Pacifics Nos.

46210 *Lady Patricia*, 46254 *City of Stoke-on-Trent* and 46257 *City of Salford* from the LMR. The 'Kings' in fact came to be concentrated at Old Oak in their twilight years but, along with many of their contemporaries on other Regions, were eliminated from London in the early 'sixties. Steam power went first from the main express duties and towards the end they had been increasingly put to work on the Birmingham line. 'No less than 17' of the class were at Old Oak by early 1960 and a veritable Indian Summer ensued during electrification on the main line out of Euston. Delays were rife during the construction work and the GW main line proved a useful alternative.

The great terminal stations, particularly in London, generated an endless round of empty stock working with Old Oak a servicing and maintenance centre for passenger stock as well as locomotives. Vast new sheds opened in 1905, in advance of the engine shed proper, a scheme dating from 1898 but deferred in part and not fully completed until 1940. The original building was no less than 1,000 feet long and 296 feet wide, twenty roads under four great roof spans. Under government-aided work beginning in November 1935, two further bays were added, giving another twenty covered roads. Lifting equipment and wheel lathe, etc. were provided and the concluding remarks of the *Great Western Magazine* of April 1940 are of no little interest in connection with the engine shed:

Improved Accommodation at Old Oak Common

New Carriage Lifting and Painting Shop and extension of existing Carriage Shed

P.W. staff at work between stock movements. Deftness and alertness were prerequisites on this job, for three or four pilots could be engaged simultaneously and trains moving slowly could be lethally quiet. Each engine (they were part of the 'Pilot Link', '57XX' and '87XX' 24 hours a day) had specific roads, three or four each, and was forbidden to stray beyond these strict bounds. In the distance is Kensal Green Gasworks, an Old Oak job until converted to a storage depot.
British Railways

For the first steps in connection with the improvement of access between Paddington and Old Oak Common, it is necessary to go back to 1898, when the Directors had under consideration schemes which included provision of extensive carriage sheds on the north (up) side of the main line at Old Oak Common. Work on the approved scheme was deferred, however, for about five years, and the sheds were not opened until 1905.

A further development was initiated in November, 1935, under the schedule of new works to be undertaken by the Company by arrangement with H.M. Government, when the Directors authorised an extension of the carriage shed, a re-arrangement of the carriage sidings and the provision of a carriage-repairing depot at Old Oak Common. The completion last year of this work has brought about the consummation of the scheme as a whole.

Excavations for the carriage sheds were taken hard up against Old Oak Common Lane, then a dirt road rutted by carts and horses. The building was available for use from 1905 and, along with the engine shed, planning work dated back to the late 1890s. In 1901 Dean had pointed out to the Locomotive Committee that seven pits would be required at the carriage shed 'to be constructed at Old Oak Common'.
British Railways

Extension of Carriage Shed

The original carriage shed was 1,000 ft long by 296 ft wide, and covered 20 roads under 4 bays with 5 roads in each. This shed has now been extended by another two bays on the north side, and places under cover a further 10 roads. The shed, as enlarged, has a total roofed area of 439,310 square ft, and provides accommodation for 420 coaches. The extension, which is 940 ft long by 148 ft wide by 17 ft to eaves, and is covered by two pitched roofs having each a span of 74 ft, as well as

affording protection from the weather for additional coaches, also provides improved facilities and amenities for the carriage-cleaning staff, and enables such work as battery-charging to be done more conveniently.

The roof covering consists of Robertson's protected metal V-beam sheeting, with four sections of glazing, 8 ft deep, in each roof. Movable gangways, travelling the entire length of the roofs, are provided for the purpose of cleaning the glazing.

Similar sheeting is provided for the side coverings, supported on horizontal angle rails and rolled steel joist uprights, the material

having been re-used from existing adjoining sheds. The gable ends from the eaves are covered with asbestos-cement corrugated sheets.

The roof coverings are carried on steel lattice purlins supported on roof trusses at 20 ft centres, and these in turn are fixed on 14 in by 6 in steel stanchions.

New Carriage Lifting and Paint Shop

The new carriage repair depot has also been provided, and will be brought into service as opportunity permits in the present circumstances. It is in two sections. The lifting

The carriage shed and roundhouses at Old Oak lay some distance apart, separated by a raised area of ground, reminiscent of the original 'common' and derelict with the detritus of the earlier construction work. For the new paint and lifting shop, completed in 1939, this last portion of the raised site had to be removed and the work through 1937 rivalled that of over thirty years before. It differed little, the earth shifted principally through shovel and wheelbarrow, the banks cut forward and temporary sidings laid in below. Much of the spoil went to make up embankments on the Central Line at places like Ruislip.

British Railways

Both this view and that opposite are dated 23rd April 1937. Work carried on with little hindrance, the new points laid in and the existing lines adapted for the temporary sidings. The various pilots continued to serve the main carriage shed, on the left, and operation of the engine shed was unaffected. The great breadth of the yards at Old Oak is apparent from the above and to walk from the engine shed across to a pilot engine in the carriage yards, or farther still to the goods yards, some beyond the main line, was no small matter. Walking time was strictly laid down, and men were forbidden to cross either the yards or the main line. The proper route was via the rear of the carriage shed, or Old Oak Common Lane, and time was allowed accordingly per turn. Such niceties were cheerfully ignored, by and large, particularly at the end of a shift, and no one, in any normal circumstance, took the 'long way round'. There was even a boarded crossing over the main line, scarcely free of the tramp of engine crews' boots, yet still, absurdly, barred to them. The double coal stage at Old Oak, like all such ramps, was reliant upon gravity, and runaways were inevitable and regular occurrences. Catchpoints were supposed to avert the worst consequences but, in the pell-mell of Old Oak, incidents occurred. More than once, with the points off and little time to see properly to brakes and loads, wagons ran off, reaching as far (to enormous consternation) as the Kensal Green Gasworks. *British Railways*

shop is 412 ft in length, 70 ft in width, and 32 ft to eaves, with three 350 ft dead-end roads, the area beyond the roads being occupied by the machine shop. This shop includes in its equipment two electrically-driven wheel turning and grinding lathes, and two travelling electric hoists for use with the lathes, an axle journal polishing machine, a vertical drilling, boring, tapping and studding machine, a "Rotax" power grinder, and a 36-in single-wheel wet tool grinder.

To lift coaches off the bogies, two 20-ton electric overhead travelling cranes, each with a 67 ft span, have been installed. These cranes traverse the full length of the shop, and are similar in design and operation to those at the new carriage shed at Caerphilly, described in our February issue.

The second section adjoining the lifting shop on the north side is the carriage paint shop, 592 ft long by 70 ft wide, 18 ft to eaves, with three 552 ft roads. This has been erected close to the engine shed and the large nest of sidings in the marshalling yard. These sidings have been rearranged and extended and lie between the shop and the carriage shed.

The roof-covering of the paint shop consists of Robertson's protected metal sheeting with four lengths of glazing 10 ft deep. The steel

construction comprises 5 in by 3 in by $\frac{3}{8}$ in purlins with roof trusses at 12 ft centres.

The building is constructed of 9-in brick panel walls built in between steel stanchions at 12 ft centres, with a deal floor laid on concrete.

The steam-heating arrangement, a special feature of the shop, is referred to later.

Running Maintenance Work at Old Oak Common

The staff at Old Oak Common includes examiners, carriage fitters, coach body makers, coach trimmers, plumbers, electricians, and carriage cleaners. The examiners report matters that need attention, whereupon the carriage fitters see to any necessary mechanical adjustments of the undergear, steam heating, pipes and radiators; the coach body makers look after the doors, windows, locks, ventilators, etc., and the trimmers make good any wear in upholstery. The plumbers attend to water tanks in the roofs, wash basins, and lavatories; the electricians look to the lights; while carriage cleaners sweep out and clean the compartments and wash down the exteriors of the coaches.

There is, however, an operation – tyre turning – which so far has not been carried

out at Old Oak Common. In the past it has been necessary to send vehicles to Swindon for this purpose, but the provision of the new lifting shop will enable tyre-turning also to be done at Old Oak Common, with a saving of time and of the running of empty mileage to Swindon. The new depot will thus be able to cope with all details of running maintenance.

Other Features

Hydrants are provided at the carriage shed and yard and new lifting and paint shop for use in case of fire. Ground hydrants have been installed for coach washing; and overhead hydrants for filling the water tanks of coaches.

Facilities are provided for charging train lighting batteries while in position on the coaches, by means of portable charging sets which are connected to electric power plugs situated at convenient points in the shed and sidings. These charging sets convert the current, which is taken from the supply main at 230 volts A.C. into 25/35 volts D.C., for charging the carriage lighting batteries.

A boiler-house has been built in which are installed three Lancashire boilers fitted with mechanical stokers. The new boiler-house

Old Oak was but one more complex of yards serving the London approaches. It was an ancient system, already (this view is dated 22nd October 1936) tedious and expensive to work. Old Oak Middle Box stood opposite the shed and an examination of the photograph will reveal much of the signalman's attention to be taken up with the endless movement of pilots and their trains. To the right of the box is the Middle Yard, whilst beyond, towards Paddington, lies (named with customary obscurity) 'Aberdare' Yard. The third of the down yards, 'Kimberley', lay at the country end of the 'Middle' sidings, and each accounted for yet more Old Oak pilot engines. A further tank was put to work in the up sidings – the fully occupied tracks to the left. The site saw an appalling accident when an up train ran into a platelaying gang in fog, killing five men.

British Railways

supplies steam for heating the carriage, paint and lifting shops. The system is of the overhead unit-heater type, thermostatically controlled, The unit heaters consist of a steam radiator through which air is blown by electrically-driven fans. The units are placed near the roof of the shop and the hot air is blown down, causing a constant circulation.

In addition, a steam pipe is laid from the boiler-house to the stop blocks at the ends of fifty-six of the roads in the carriage shed and sidings north of the shed, provision being made for coupling up to the steam heating system in the carriages, so that trains waiting despatch from the depot are warmed preparatory to being coupled to train engines.

The Old Oak developments, as we have seen, fortuitously afforded a measure of economy in the working of empty stock, using train engines. but pilots were, of course, still required and remained an abiding feature. Pannier tanks there were in abundance and these remained prominent amongst the steam pilots (ten, still, in 1958). 5700 pannier tanks could be found on the ECS trains more or less from their appearance in numbers from the 1930s, and were augmented after Nationalisation by both the 9400 engines and the big 1500 outside cylinder tanks. These were amongst the last, in the 'sixties, when diesel hydraulic Type 2 diesels inherited what remained of the work.

Widening of the approaches, including a flyover, had streamlined movements between Old Oak Common and Paddington and an endless procession of empty stock trains made their way back and forth. The *Railway Gazette* (see page 55) made much of the novel practice, introduced as Old Oak came into use, of working empty stock with train engines. While this practice did prove a useful economy, it could never be extended to more than a small minority of trains. Conventional pilots, (the 'up and down link', in Old Oak's precisely descriptive parlance) were in charge of most of the work, though for jobs like Swindon and return, for instance, it made sense to 'tack on' a bit of ECS work at the end or beginning of the turn. The flyover, despite its sharp curves and steep gradients, presented few problems to anyone familiar with the road but it was poorly maintained, and later singled. Both it and the carriage lines had a 15 mph speed restriction, cheerfully ignored if one wanted to 'get home quick'. Train engine working of empty stock ('tender jobs') only really became significant on summer Saturdays. The practice declined still further with the arrival of DMUs-based at West London Sidings and under the control of Old Oak at first and later dispersed to Slough, Southall and Reading.

Despite this elaborate provision, with the Westbourne Park site cleared it was still

2−4−0T passing under the 'overhead bridge', erected to facilitate the movement of empty stock between Paddington and Old Oak.
C. L. Turner

The 'London Division', in a running sense, existed essentially to serve the great terminus and goods depot at Paddington, channelling traffic into the capital; Old Oak was rightly renowned for its express work, but the constant to and fro of empty stock and the endless freights and shunts (much of it at night) is in many respects the more remarkable feature. The 'Up and Down Link' reflected the levels of this work in Paddington and helped mark the station somewhat apart from other London termini − nowhere else (excluding Liverpool Street before electrification) could such a concentration of small tanks be observed, a memorably fussing style of working. London remained the 'Paddington Division' in much internal communication and the Old Oak enginemen's trade union branch was always 'Paddington 20'. The train is a classic Old Oak working, empties for the 10.30 'Limited', brought in from the great yards by one of the shed's innumerable panniers.
British Railways

No. 3303 *Sir Lancelot* in March 1932, withdrawn some weeks previously and put to use as stationary boiler. The purpose-built boiler at the engine shed was designed in addition to supply steam to the carriage shed but in the event of failure an engine was simply coupled up. From the 'thirties at least, a separate, condemned engine was placed over by the carriage sheds. The stationary boiler, and the sand furnace, had always been a locoman's responsibility and this remained the case until negotiated away to some local advantage, the job passing to a carriage cleaner. *S. W. Baker*

necessary to have a turntable close to the terminus, for 'visiting' locos on particularly tight turnrounds. Its development can be plotted in a series of minutes dating from the establishment of Old Oak: '4th July 1906 ... when the Turntables at Westbourne Park Locomotive Depot have been taken out there will be no turning accommodation in the vicinity of Paddington and that as the absence of such accommodation would cause great inconvenience ... recommend the installation of a 65 ft turntable near Ranelagh Bridge, on the south side of Royal Oak Station ... estimate £5,085 ... turntable authorised for Hereford 19th July 1905, be used for Ranelagh Bridge and another turntable used for Hereford'.

'27 February 1907. Ranelagh Bridge – now desirable to have a shunting neck, £280'.

On 6th June £325 was authorised for 'corrugated iron huts for enginemen' and a water crane with hydrants (total £325), and on 9th October electric lights and a 22,000 gallon tank were approved, at £720. This latter item is mentioned again on 11th December when 'in providing a water tank in connection with the construction of a turntable near Ranelagh Bridge, Padding-ton, the Locomotive Superintendent reported that it is necessary also to install an additional engine jet ... £315'.

A minor depot in its own right, Ranelagh Bridge appears thus to have come fully into use some time in 1908, a busy servicing point until well into diesel days. (As steam passenger work into Paddington declined, the 'table was removed and sidings laid in, giving no respite to the long-suffering

'County' tank No. 2243 after performing a similar function, on 6th October 1935.

V. R. Webster

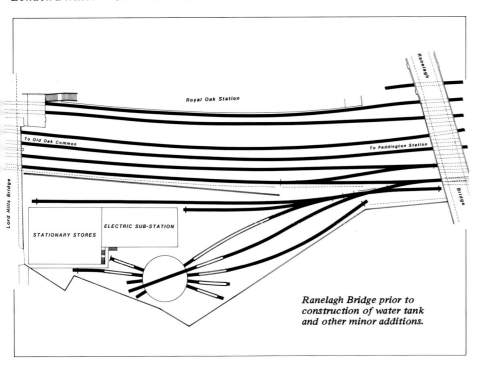

Royal Oak Station

To Old Oak Common

To Paddington Station

Lord Hills Bridge

Ranelagh Bridge

STATIONARY STORES

ELECTRIC SUB-STATION

*Ranelagh Bridge prior to
construction of water tank
and other minor additions.*

Acton Garden Village had been built for GW footplate staff, compelled to live within a defined 'calling out' area and other grades were only allotted tenancies if there were no footplatemen on 'the list'. Those working on the 'white paper' were placed on call for periods of 48 hours and if not used were paid for 8 hours in 24. This practice disappeared during the war, but, with daily suspensions common for the most trivial offence, it was doubly useful to live close. The path down into the depot was for years a cinder zig-zag track and a large board at the top prohibited cycling. Luckless offenders could be met at the bottom by the chief foreman, a daunting figure, stalking the shed most mornings. Inevitably the miscreant would be 'asked' to make his way back up to the entrance and 'read the notice'. Having done so and returned all the way to the bottom of the zig-zag, the offender would promptly be sent away for the day with loss of pay. 'I think you might like to go home' was a verdict no-one argued with. Lateness over 15 minutes meant similar punishment, though a good clerk (and there were plenty) would 'hold the book' for as long as he dared. It was a crude discipline considered specially suitable for the cleaners, admittedly a wild bunch given to swimming in the canal and indeed the main coal stage tank. Cleaners, as they rose in seniority in preparation for firing duties, were at any slack times assigned to labouring jobs, an attractive prospect for it brought a considerable increase in daily pay. Promotion, sometimes agonisingly slow, at times exhilaratingly swift, was dependent largely on external factors, through fireman, the different links, passed fireman, etc, and in its essentials no different on the GWR than on any other major railway. Some luck was needed however to spend an entire career in one's 'home town'.

The GWR, unlike the other companies, had an 'all line' system and when a man became eligible for promotion to a senior position, he went wherever the next vacancy occurred. Everyone had a registered number and perusal of the seniority lists, with men's ages, would reveal a person's likely destination in the next year or two. In order to return, the deportee would have to await a vacancy at Old Oak – as the senior applicant he would automatically be rewarded with the position. Return was fairly straightforward at such a large depot; indeed the next normal vacancy might well occur 'in house' as it were and a man could progress through the grades without leaving Old Oak. It would, though, be a matter of some chance to get back to a shed such as, say, Aylesbury. The system ended with BR.

residents of the adjacent terraced houses.) 'Repairs' to the 65 ft 'table were authorised in November 1919, a total of £950.

Ranelagh Bridge at its peak could be a very busy place indeed, and extremely smart work was required to return engines to traffic. The turnround time was seldom generous. The pilot (the 'target' engine, lurking in a siding) taking away the empty carriage stock would follow the train in, often before it had come fully to rest, and the train might well stand at the platform for only seven to ten minutes. Incoming 'foreign' engines off, say, the 10.00 a.m. from Wolverhampton, would be released, crossed over to Ranelagh, were turned, watered and given a 'once over', all in time to return with the 11.10 a.m. Similarly, the 5.50 p.m. Oxford arrival went back on the 6.55 p.m. down train; the 9.00 a.m. arrival was on an even tighter schedule, returning on the 9.45 a.m. Worcester express. West of England expresses up from Newton Abbot or Plymouth retired to Old Oak, but after some attention, a little 'topping up' or whatever, would often work a fill in turn to Reading. Thus the up 'Torbay' engine (a 'King', say) due in at 3.45 p.m. might reappear for the 5.37 p.m. down semi-fast, its first stop Langley, 16.2 miles in 17 minutes, (Schedule = 19 mins, depart-depart).

The dead end siding at Ranelagh Bridge, nearest the main line, was ever the resting place of the down pilot, from about 1932 almost invariably a 'Castle'. A fascinating place, noisy and crowded, the depot lay partly hidden by an ugly brick office block which, in addition to providing a fine over-head view, housed for many years the British Transport Historical Records, on which this account is largely based.

Life at Old Oak

Great Western mystique had little meaning in the workplace itself; at Old Oak Common the work was hard and dirty, ill rewarded and, for much of the time, subject to a crushing discipline. Men, despite an often fierce pride in the job and a real reverence for the old boys' almost unnatural mastery of the steam locomotive, often held 'the company' and its overseers in contempt. This largely applied however to 'organisation men', and many supervisory staff, where personal contact was possible, earned respect and even admiration. With others it was the reverse.

It is of course impossible to be wholly definitive or objective about this, with much of it essentially a political view; descriptions of the often foul working conditions elicit the response that all such individual trades had their fearsome aspects, stoically borne by an accommodating workforce. Maybe, but a simplistic view ignores much of what we are concerned with; the trains did not run without people, people with all the hopes, fears, prejudice and shortcomings of this and myriad other societies before or since. Cleaner boys at Old Oak, for instance, regarded LMS contemporaries at the ancient Willesden shed with derision, and confrontations – running battles – were not unknown. The thousands who worked at both establishments necessarily lived close about, with their families.

No. 5012 *Berry Pomeroy Castle*, having arrived at Old Oak and taken coal preparatory to turning for smokebox and firebox attention. This engine is thought to have come up from Plymouth, and the crew, if working through with the engine, would necessarily lodge at Old Oak. Before the hostel was put up, men took private digs, often run by widows to make ends meet, in the closely packed little streets on the far side of Old Oak Common Lane. Lodging was generally disliked, except by those who preferred to be away from home as much as possible; Wolverhampton and Bristol men could usually get a turnround for home at Ranelagh Bridge but Laira, Newton Abbot and South Wales men stayed over in London. Lodging increased dramatically during the war but declined sharply afterwards. Wartime experience with 'half way' crew changes enabled the Western Region to dispense with many lodging turns on freights and subsequently much of it disappeared from the passenger working.

Roger Carpenter

ASLEF came to represent most of the footplate staff at Old Oak, though NUR men transferring in from the provinces tended to keep their original membership, for reason of benefit funds etc. There were, however, dozens of other unions on the railway, many of them represented at Old Oak, from the shop staff, mechanical and otherwise through the various grades to the labourers. Disposal on the GWR was performed not by engine crews or a shed link but by a separate group of labouring staff – the tubers and fire droppers, often relatively elderly men, having by far the worst of it. Tubes were blown out by steam from cocks on the smokebox, the engines usually positioned by the coal stage, where the fires were also dropped. Grates were cleaned using 10 ft irons, ash pans raked out and the whole area, particularly on a warm day, was a place to be avoided. The hot suffocating fumes from the ash and clinker mingled with the choking black smokebox char and dust gusted at random in the wind. The whole process was truly appalling; the miserable unfortunate stood beneath the engine with head between the frames, raking the ashpan whilst endeavouring to ensure the damper doors remained open, otherwise one was forced to climb out and up into the cab to reset them.

Condensing tank No. 3567 on 8th July 1933. Generations of various engines were customarily labelled 'Tunnel Motors', of primitive aspect even after receiving all-over cabs. The '35s' in particular were awkward to work – 'like standing up in a wardrobe' – and, if anything, the engines without cabs were preferred on the 'Met jobs'. Nos. 3568 and 3592 were given cabs in 1932 and never appeared on the Smithfield meat trains again, lying out of use at Old Oak by March 1934. When entering a Circle Line station in the quiet and calm of mid-morning, it was almost possible to sense the recent passage of a GW train, through a distinctive aura of Welsh coal. Those who sought these exquisite pleasures could even experience them above ground; over certain gratings in the Marylebone and Euston Roads the trains were readily heard and smelt and indeed a faint whiff of steam would sometimes trail out, unnoticed by nearly all, to lose itself amidst the clatter of trams and horses.
V. R. Webster

Smokebox cleaning on 9th March 1935. This was the infamous 'vacuum cleaner' installed on the passenger side of the coaler; hitched up to the cock on the smokebox, steam from the engine was used to provide a suction. It was awkward to use and the finer ash billowed up and around the receiving wagon alarmingly (see Kerry's comments, page 6).
S. W. Baker

All this enveloped in clouds of fume, probably taking the skin off knuckles on split pins and standing on hot ashes.

South Wales coal produced an inordinate amount of ash except the best, Ebbw Vale, which 'opened up like a cauliflower'. South Wales coal, in truth, did not take kindly to mechanical handling, though other steam coals, notably the north-east, had similar properties and were dealt with on a large scale without too many problems. The Southern used Welsh (and the softer Kent) coal and was happy to provide mechanical coalers at various locations. Almost any coal so handled needed a liberal dousing to reduce dust, but the GWR kept strictly to the old methods, even at places like Old Oak It would never change to other coals of course – most GW Directors had always been deeply involved in the South Wales collieries – but the old wheeled iron tubs

remained a burden to the end. Things could always have been worse of course, and memories remained at Old Oak of the 'Reparations Coal', lignite imported from Europe in the late 1940s.

Firemen on the GW signed for each tub of coal loaded (ten 'Woodbines' could ensure an arrangement to everyone's satisfaction) and at Old Oak, at least, often did the job themselves. That way it was possible to choose the smaller lumps and avoid having to break it up on the tender. Working engines at the coal stage was the most junior footplate duty at the shed; the yard pilot, a pannier, fed the coal stage but also ran trips with coal wagons to and from Acton or Old Oak yards. It was a considerable hoist onto the ramp itself and the trap points at the bottom were not always set properly. There were stories at Old Oak of more than one runaway on this job.

Sunday engine movements about the shed were performed mostly by 'ill health' men barred from the main line and forbidden to pass the shed limits signals.

The shed itself was always very well maintained with labourers constantly sweeping and tidying. Successive waves of immigrants were available for 'the dirty jobs' – young Irish men over very many years and in the time (dis) honoured fashion of such things some of the most unattractive and arduous tasks became the lot of a subsequent group – West Indians and other Commonwealth citizens. Old Oak was, of course, an industrial centre of some considerable magnitude and lay, until recent times at least, in an area of London undergoing a relative boom. This made staffing difficult with higher wages available all along the Western Avenue and in many other concerns locally. The railways,

Smokebox attention under publicity conditions.

Collection Alec Swain

No. 5045 *Bridgwater Castle* on 11th September 1937. Its name was altered to *Earl of Dudley* some days afterwards. The smokebox cock seen to advantage (left) is connected up for steam lancing of the tubes. Kerry detailed the procedure as carried out in ideal fashion, though this was less than frequently the case. When a few "rough 'uns" were lined up, tube cleaning could become a very perfunctory task indeed: 'When the smokebox has been cleaned out, a start can be made on the tubes. This is done by what is called a 'steam lance', and this consists of a steel tube with a tapered end which is small enough to enter the ends of the boiler tubes in the smokebox. This lance is coupled up by a flexible pipe to a steam cock on the front of the smokebox, and is fitted with a wooden handle very much like the handle of an ordinary garden fork, so that the man handling it can do so without burning his hands. The lance is inserted in the mouth of each tube and the jet of steam blows right through the tube into the firebox, removing any soot in the tube in the process. In some cases, the tubes are so badly blocked up that the jet of steam will not clear them – with the result that the tube has to be cleaned by means of a long, flexible, steel rod, which is pushed through the tube from the smokebox end.'   *V. R. Webster*

in relative decline and with an increasing inflexibility, drew in these new workers. They were, it need not be said, lowly paid in time-honoured fashion.

The myriad grades and trades at a depot the scale of Old Oak was, of course, an intimidating prospect in itself – 'fitters', for instance, were strictly separated, those in 'The Factory' enjoying a higher status than those employed in the shed. They were something of an élite having to serve a lengthy apprenticeship – successfully concluded, the newly qualified man was then required to *leave* the railway, for a minimum of two years. A post was then guaranteed if the person wished to return to the GWR. Only the war meant a relaxation of such strictures, and a number of fitters mates were 'made up' without the benefits of a full apprenticeship. Non-footplate engine cleaning staff, a grade employed exclusively on the (Great) Western Region were another institution, taken on in the summer only. Many came back year after year, supporting families and homes and turning to labouring jobs when necessary. Labourers, loading ashes for instance, worked on piece rates and one

giant could fill three ten ton wagons in a shift. This was a quite spectacular feat and if ever such manual labour could be elevated to an art this was it. Art it was held to be in certain writings and documentary film in the 1930s, and during the war, but it was not possible to mask for long the brutal nature of the work. Able neither to read nor write as often as not, the man's labour went to the benefit of his mates, falsifying the returns, at least until 'rumbled' by the engine crews.

The war economy, notching remorselessly upward, demanded ever more manpower, brought from all over the system. Boys who had hardly stepped beyond the confines of their valley or rural parish were pressed into service – away from their villages and the chapel, many had in effect the time of their lives; they were rowdy if uncomplaining and existed in indescribable squalor. Lodgings locally were out of the question, with many families already doubling up, and as these blinking innocents began to arrive wartime Direct Labour took a hand. Conditions at Old Oak had always been poor, and decent canteen facilities had to await the war. Those men

increasingly forced to stay in the confines of the depot found what little sleep they could through the rumble and clank of engine and train movement, finally ruined by the crash of naval guns, mounted in the nearby Wormwood Scrubs prison. Old Oak people were bemused when a gang of Direct Labour Irishmen arrived, apparently set on reliving every nineteenth century legend, particularly the more lurid exploits relating to drinking and fighting. The foreman was wholly up to the task however; holder of a Canadian 'Golden Gloves' title, he apparently held absolute sway over this extraordinary band of men. They busily set about excavating ground for three extra stock lines, fronting the carriage sheds. A canopy, the 'Paint Shop Extension', was put up over the new roads to stable carriages retrieved from various scrap yards and with minimal attention converted into living quarters. Conditions in this peculiar 'hostel' were quite unbelievably bad – the occupancy was relieved by unlimited dosages of beer and freedom but nevertheless the two or three lines of mouldering coaches – steam-heated in winter – were characterised by filth, damp, and vermin.

An MP was called in by ASLEF to little effect but the revolting conditions and the resulting contrition on the part of the authorities were factors in the later establishment of the Old Oak Hostel proper. The denizens of the Paint Shop Extension had at least enjoyed, from about 1943/4, excellent food, supplied by Lyons to the American General Lee's staff train, parked prior to D-Day in the carriage yard. The relative luxury of the Americans greatly influenced subsequent negotiations, though the brick hostel was held to bring about scant improvement in the youngsters' morals. It opened after the war to the rear of the roundhouses and stands today, converted by Paddington Church Housing Association to units of five single bedroom flats with central kitchens – railway staff in residence were given the choice at the time of whom they shared with and, despite problems of allowing non-BR personnel 'on railway land', the changeover was eventually achieved with relative smoothness.

Quite the most ordinary, everyday, facilities had long been basic in the extreme; ugly troughs were all that were available for washing, fed by (often scalding) water from the boiler washing out plant. One of the toilets, twelve either side, open and facing each other, more often than not accommodated the depot bookie, a 'fitter' on a sinecure, and his customers.

Goods engines occupied the two northernmost sheds, passenger engines the other two, but washouts were concentrated in one of the former, the 'north-west' part furthest from the yard and main line. The hot water plant served this 'washout table' where pipes hung down in a circular arrangement (a complete traverse, high above the locomotives, was a feat popular with one or two more eccentric individuals, and decidedly less popular as an initiation trial for various apprentice grades). The Great Western

Canteen for Old Oak Common

A canteen for the provision of food to the staff of all departments employed at the Company's Old Oak Common depot, London, was officially opened by the General Manager, Sir James Milne, on February 2. He was supported, among others, by Mr. Gilbert Matthews, Superintendent of the Line, Mr. K. W. C. Grand, Assistant General Manager, Mr. W. N. Pellow, Locomotive Running Superintendent, and Mr. R. C. Kirkpatrick, London divisional engineer. The function was presided over by Mr. H. G. Kerry, London divisional locomotive superintendent, who welcomed the General Manager and expressed regret that the Company's Chairman, Sir Charles J. Hambro, who had also intended to be present, was prevented from coming because of the loss of his mother. It was unanimously agreed to send a message of condolence to the Chairman on his bereavement.

Mr. Kerry said that the canteen, which had been provided by the Directors free of cost, would be greatly appreciated by the staff who, he felt sure, would not abuse in any way the facilities to be found there. He then invited the General Manager to open the premises.

Sir James Milne also expressed regret that Sir Charles Hambro had, at the last moment, been prevented from attending and performing the opening ceremony. He knew it was the Chairman's intention to be with them at their canteen, and also to carry out an inspection of the depot. That would now have to be deferred until another occasion. He (Sir James) could wish he knew what Sir Charles intended to say, but one thing he was sure of and that was that the Chairman would wish to pay a tribute, as *he* did, to the excellent work of the footplate and shed staffs in the present abnormal conditions. They all knew the difficulties the men had met and were meeting, and the fine spirit they had shown in face of them. The shed staff were key men in the servicing, preparation and repair of the locomotives. This was an essential part of the work at the depot and he hoped they would maintain continuous effort to ensure the quickest possible turn round of engines. This was a matter of the first importance and he was sure that the men were all of one mind in doing their best and so maintaining the high reputation of the Great Western Railway. The General Manager said there had been some talk as to the kind of canteen that should be provided. He thought the weather that morning was an indication that their decision in favour of a wet canteen was a wise one! He concluded by wishing the canteen every success and said it gave him great pleasure to hand over to Mr. Henry Holsgrove, chairman of the canteen committee, the keys of the premises.

Mr. Holsgrove, in accepting the keys, expressed on behalf of all the staff who would make use of the canteen their gratitude for what had been done. He said that the need for a canteen of this kind had been felt for a very long time, but it had needed a war to bring it into being. Of the extensive use that would be made of it there was no doubt; already 1,660 members had been enrolled. After having spoken of the hardships which the men had experienced under rationing conditions without the facilities they had now been granted, he said he felt sure the men would fully appreciate the new canteen and in no way abuse it. When he was invited about a year ago to associate himself with the enterprise, he said then that the only thing he would be interested in was a first-class canteen. He felt now that that had been provided, and

Mrs. Morris and her famous daughter ran the Old Oak hostel, holding absolute sway and providing an almost non-stop service. Hoisting beer barrels with all the assurance of any seasoned landlord, she is remembered with affection. The railway, to a considerable extent, ran on beer and tea and the wartime canteen was a blessing. 'I'll have the sugar in the lid, please miss', was the standard wartime request.

it was the duty of the members to see that it was kept a first-class canteen. Mr. Holsgrove said that he and his committee had had plenty of work to do in arranging for supplies and in other directions, and he expressed particular thanks for the hard and excellent work that had been done by the canteen secretary, a fellow driver, Mr. W. G. White.

Mr. W. N. Pellow then spoke. He said that to his knowledge everybody, from the General Manager downwards, had taken the greatest possible interest in this new venture. He was sure that the facilities provided would be both wisely and widely used. In this connection Mr. Pellow emphasised that the facilities were available to, and would be used by, staff of all departments at the depot.

As it was necessary for the General Manager to leave for another appointment a vote of thanks was then moved by Mr. Holsgrove, who again expressed thanks on behalf of his committee and all the men and women employed at the depot for the provision of the canteen. Sir James briefly responded.

Engines 'out of order' on the passenger side, due to some problem on the coal stage. On occasions such as these, the grab crane coaled from piles dumped on the ground about the approach roads and 'firepit'. *R. C. Riley*

does not seem to have bothered with numbering for its roundhouses, knowing perhaps that local usage would inevitably prove more enduring. The turntable nearest the running lines was always known as 'the bottom passenger' and inevitably the roundhouse behind was always the 'top passenger'. The goods engine roundhouse adjacent to the 'bottom passenger' was logically the 'bottom goods' but the fourth of these was, in deference to its specific function, simply 'the washout'. The 'washout' further doubled as a home for the diesel shunters and they entered from the early fuelling point, 'through the side'. Boiler sludge in 'the washout' was simply sluiced down through drains in the pits, the whole operation carried out over twenty-four hours with two sets of boiler washers to each shift.

Payment for all this came in a cashbox (top link men could do quite well with mileage payments – an hour's pay for every 15 miles beyond 140) on a light engine from the Treasurer's Office at Paddington. Men would queue at the shed office for an oval metal disc (later rectangular and in brass, no less) which further entitled them to queue for their money, contained in a tiny tin box which (after emptying, of course) was tossed into a wooden collecting chest.

The feeling of camaraderie – 'the company' might be fair game but theft from one's fellow was an absolute crime – was high at Old Oak Common and, of course, at most other British railway sheds. There was an *esprit de corps* which went with the steam job, crews staying together until one or other was promoted out of the link. Disciplinary procedures (for anything other than a minor offence) were highly developed on the railway and were generally agreed to be

No. 6026 *King John* on 12th August 1951 alongside the gaunt remains of the ash dropping shelter. The effects of several years' careless fire-iron handling are obvious; they were dreadful structures cordially disliked and used only 'because they were there'. One at least of the shelters was considered for re-use elsewhere (or at least the framework) in 1948 and in June that year plans were drawn up for a two-road 'shelter for wagon repairing', to be erected close by the east end of Llanelly Dock, alongside Embankment Road. It is unclear whether the transfer took place and difficult to believe that such an exercise could be economically worthwhile. *P. J. Kelley*

fair. They incorporated at an early date many of the best and most sensible features of latter day practice – rights to a representative, rights of appeal, etc.

Even in the terrible blackout years accidents at Old Oak were few. Men could be out for more than 24 hours, breakdowns on the road were constant, trains were strafed and bombed and a crew could spend the entire day struggling from London to Plymouth – from one air raid to another and back again next day. The Great Western

employed shelters, of doubtful efficacy, for wartime firedropping, and two, on either side of the stage, were put up at Old Oak. They were small and the brittle asbestos sheeting was very quickly holed and broken, by fire irons or whatever. In reality, of course, at Old Oak they 'took the chance', as at most other depots in the country – such work simply could not be confined to daytime and safety relied on the dull glow of spent ashes. This contrasted with the incandescent glare from an

Continued on page 104

No. 4700 alongside Old Oak Common Engine Shed Signal Box, on 10th August 1957. The Old Oak Common 'bobbies' were loathed by engine crews and blamed for all delays. This was largely irrelevant 'going out' but a wrong signal when 'coming home' provoked instant rage. If air was ever to turn blue, this would be the site; a system generally regarded as absurd was introduced whereby a driver had to shout his name to the luckless 'bobby'. The capacity of such a system to intensify the time-honoured practice of baiting signalmen was utilised to the very fullest. Some of the names announced were scarcely believable, let alone repeatable.

R. C. Riley

Right: No. 1505 with the stock of the 'Royal Duchy' on 2nd April 1960. The '15s', 'outside cylinder tankies', were an expression of post-war concern with accessibility and ease of maintenance, owing much to the 'USA' tanks of the Southern, put ashore at Newport and evidently got into working order at Ebbw Junction shed.

Merchant Navy Preservation Society

Below: No. 1507 on 11th June 1961. The '15s' 'bounced a bit' at anything approaching speed but were enormously powerful and dragged almost any load along with little trouble. They were characteristic of the London Division, like the '35s' and other tanks before that, though one or two were employed in South Wales. Some at Old Oak were lined out, in deference to their duties at Paddington, along with other panniers, 8773 for instance, and 5409 at Slough, in the Windsor jobs. Southall and Oxford had a '15XX' on goods but they are remembered chiefly for their work out of Old Oak. Their great size and bouncing gait were startling to behold, an impression of width and girth and power greatly beyond that of any 'coffee pot' image of an 0–6–0T. Beyond is what remains of the post-war oil fuelling plant. Two 176,000 gallon tanks had been planned in October 1946, accompanied by a 'Temporary Coal Bunker', pump house and boiler house. 'Three fuelling stations on six inch headers' were planned on a concrete apron, the northernmost road past the 'Factory', into the 'top goods' roundhouse to become the loco fuelling road, 'renewed where necessary'. On 27th March 1947 the contract was approved 'for pumps and pipework for oil

fuelling depot, Old Oak Common, at £2392, from Messrs. Simmons & Hawkes'. The small tanks were for 'light oil' and were adapted for the first diesel shunters, ahead of the main dieselisation of 1964-5. The second tall 176,000 gallon tank was not built, though a horizontal light oil tank was provided in its place, ordered 'retained' in early Western Region days 'for gas turbine locos'.

Merchant Navy Locomotive Preservation Society

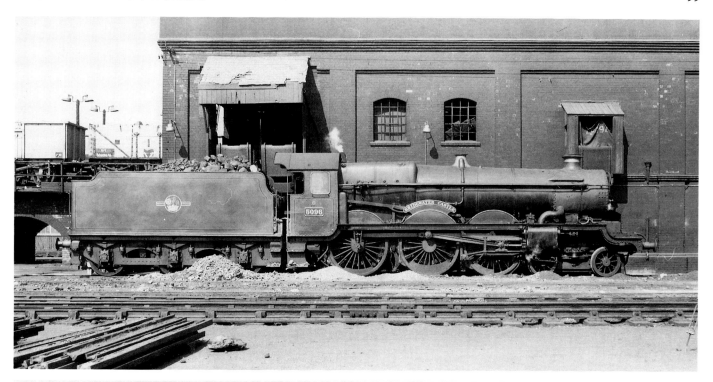

No. 5096 *Bridgwater Castle* (top) and (above) 6873 *Caradoc Grange.* The 'Granges', in particular were well liked and considered by many superior to the 'Halls'. A couple of the first batch had come new to Old Oak and they were particularly in evidence on summer Saturdays. Despite the problems deemed to derive from the mechanical handling of Welsh coal, a number of schemes were examined for the replacement of the vast Old Oak stage, worked almost entirely by hand power. The usual range of alternatives was drawn up and evaluated (in early Western Region days); the simplest envisaged a reduction of the coaling ramp, from two roads to one, regraded at 1 in 40 and served each side by diesel hydraulic coaling cranes, with power-operated 10 cwt grabs. This parallelled the ash crane arrangement and was the sort of 'stop gap' measure employed at many places in the 1950s. Another idea was to erect a series of overhead bunkers across the west end of the coal stage, retaining the tank, six 30-ton bunkers, two on the goods side and four on the passenger, to be served by a travelling overhead crane. After this came two 200-ton skip hoist mechanical plants, one each side, followed by an idea for a gigantic 600-ton coaler, on the east end of the existing tank, with two bunkers, 400 tons for the passenger side and 200 tons the goods. Whether for reasons of politics or economy, none of these ideas came to fruition and the Western Region remained firmly devoted to hand coaling.

P. H. Groom and R. C. Riley

'County' No. 1017 on 3rd July 1949. The Hawksworth 4−6−0s were unpopular engines; they were regarded as unsatisfactory steamers, 'rotten for firemen'. The foreman's office lay at one time beyond the engine, callers ignored unless in possession of the knocking code. This was regularly broken by the LDC, and prompt revision ordered.   *R. S. Carpenter*

Left: Formidable front ends at Old Oak. Despite the spacious nature of the roundhouses, great care had to be exercised on many roads, to leave sufficient room at the turntable end for men to pass between locomotives. Stabling was always tricky, for engines were often low in steam and braking unpredictable; a crashing jolt meant an engine had jumped the stops provided at the end of each road. Turntables were prone to wear, distortion and settling, and all four at Old Oak were subject to exhaustive tests in the 1930s. Profiles drawn up showed them all out of true to various degrees, but remedial work was expensive and difficult; it was necessary to largely make do with minor repairs and there was a quite definite 'jump' on leaving the 'tables, violent enough to break and splinter the rails on occasion. New works authorised early in 1925 included: 'Extensive repairs be carried out to the locomotive turntables Nos. 1, 3 and 4 at Old Oak Common, and No. 10 at Didcot.' On 23rd January 1930 repairs to all four 'tables were ordered, totalling £4,600 and turntable No. 4 was ordered replaced on 24th October 1946, at £6,000 – 'to be supplied and erected under the supervision of Cowans Sheldon'. There was a fifth turntable at Old Oak, a 55 ft example in the carriage yards, intended for turning coaching stock but very occasionally used for locos. It had been there from the beginning, part of the 1900 contract and was subsequently replaced, a 70 ft Cowans Sheldon turntable being ordered on 28th March 1935, at £1,295.
R. C. Riley

The Great Western roundhouses were designed with a single approach/entrance. This was an obvious inconvenience but extra access roads were only provided after some years of complaint from the LDC. With over 800 enginemen at Old Oak, the links were large and varied, and changed at intervals. There were some 15-20, from the cripples and shedmen at the bottom end, through the various 'locals' – shunting, goods and passenger in ascending order and thence to the 'main line' jobs. The goods were mostly 'Double Homes', unpopular on almost all counts. Even the best lodges were seldom better than grim and there was little to do other than go on the beer. "Years on the 'Double Homes' meant never seeing your kids grow up", but there were some compensations in the senior passenger links, carefully negotiated to include as much work as possible 'in daylight'.
R. C. Riley

Bryngwyn Hall on 12th September 1964. Engines stabled at Old Oak had a secure, safely berthed look about them, their serenity perhaps in part a contrast to the sometimes hectic negotiation of the turntable. Engines in low steam would rattle across the table(s) and it was advisable to screw the brake firmly on when turning — the rotational impulses thus engendered on more than one occasion set the engine off, with alarming consequences. Unfamiliar engines were particularly susceptible to movement errors and USA S160 2–8–0s, with water in the cylinders and brakes poor, were seen to hustle across the turntables with unnerving, but happily harmless, results.

R. C. Riley

Tanks at Old Oak.   *Photomatic*

No. 1500 at rest.   *K. C. H. Fairey*

open firebox door and GW locos with their wide open cabs required to be covered by tarpaulins. This was in general loathed by the crews who were used to the draughty GW layout. Stopped (often for hour upon hour) on a warm night, conditions in the cab could become unbearable and it was risking much to open up the sheeting. Old Oak men got diesel shunters just prior to the war, for the Acton jobs and went with them on their subsequent transfer to Barry Docks. They had both the American and British (Stanier and Riddles) 2–8–0s and had acquired a wide experience of wholly new types before the BR standard engines arrived in the 1950s. Despite this, the Britannias, for instance, were not liked, the objections centring mainly on the design and layout of the cabs.

Old Oak, of course, saw its share of experiments or whatever and after the war was selected as an oil fuel point, as Swindon began turning out (renumbered) atomiser-fitted engines. Crews at Old Oak coped well with this though there were, naturally

The Old Oak 'Firepit', the labour eased only by grab cranes. One was provided each side of the stage, four having been ordered as far back as 1939. On 14th December that year four two-ton travelling steam coaling cranes were ordered from Taylor and Hubbard at a cost of £6,740, 'for Old Oak Common, Wolverhampton, Oswestry and Carmarthen'.   *Photomatic*

No. 5054 *Earl of Ducie* on 12th September 1964. The smoke troughs decayed over the years and some were taken out; bomb blast in the war further damaged the roof and the ties holding the chutes. In late 1947, in suitably ecclesiastical terms, a contract was let for 'the restoration of the glazing and restitution of the roof'. At one time each stall had its number prominently displayed on the smoke duct above, odd numbers, for some reason, on one side and even on the other.   *R. C. Riley*

Three 'Castles', Nos. 4082 *Windsor Castle*, 7032 *Denbigh Castle* and 7036 *Taunton Castle* at Old Oak on 11th April 1964 lined up out of the way, ready to substitute for failed diesels. Pilots customarily stood on the siding by the south-east corner of the shed, their blowing off appropriately interrupting diesel instruction in 'Room 13' but the chaos of dieselisation and the unreliability of the new units required up to half a dozen 'spare' engines.
R. C. Riley

No. 4701 out of use (it can also be seen in the view above) on 11th April 1964. Beyond lie 'Hymeks' and 'Westerns' outside 'The Factory', destined for conversion to a diesel maintenance shed. The changeover was rapid and by December 1965 *The Railway Magazine* in a dismal item entitled 'Steam Out and Diesels In', could comment on two years of conversion work. 'The opening of the new diesel servicing and maintenance depot at Old Oak Common on October 20th virtually coincides with the completion of the changeover from steam to diesel traction which will be effective throughout the Western Region by the end of the year'. Three of the four types in the main illustration have since been scrapped and the fourth largely eliminated from express passenger working. 'Hymeks' were generally popular with crews but the North British engines less so. It was a highly charged period, and contemporary political figures linger persistently in the demonology — Macmillan, for instance, was reckoned to be the toast of the North British shareholders. The old oil fuel tank, 176,000 gallons, was utilised for diesel fuel and even before the onset of diesel-isation, the traverser had been removed. This was unpopular, for a change of road could involve light engine movement over a considerable distance. No. 4701 stands close by the weighbridge (not labelled but clearly shown on the plan overleaf), a device remarkable for the 5 ft spanners necessary for its operation.
R. C. Riley

enough, problems of familiarisation. It all ended as we know rather embarrasingly, particularly so for the punctilious GWR. Announcing the new system with customary panache, it fell victim to its own publicity machine, when the whole endeavour collapsed in ignominy. At Old Oak the fuel oil, a revolting viscous material, arrived in black stinking wagons; it was best to avoid all contact with these noxious vehicles and no mere overalls were protection while a string of them were successively connected up to fill the main tank. The oil had to be passed through a separate heater before it could be pumped into loco tenders and it cannot be said that the sudden demise of the whole operation provided for any real regret. The gas turbine locos Nos. 18000 and 18100 were a different matter – considered the apple of Swindon's eye and cosseted accordingly, they were used on the main line only and great care taken with their fuelling and lubrication. Employed mostly on the Plymouth run, they were exclusively in the charge of a handful of specially selected drivers and the term 'blue-eyed boys', little used these days, was invariably applied to them.

Diesels proper, once the modernisation programme got under way, were accepted with alacrity, despite the endless wrangling over payments etc. 'Warships' in the D600 and D800 series initially, they were allocated at first to individual jobs, a 'tutor driver' giving instruction on an individual basis. This was 'on the job' training, giving way to five-day schools held at Swindon, at Emlyn Square adjacent to the present GWR museum. This proved inadequate before the full pace of dieselisation in the early 1960s and classes were conducted 'locally', in the notorious 'Room 13'. This lay high up in the block by the south-east corner of the shed, where the modern amenity block was later put up. Room 13 had long been empty, with good reason, for classes held in winter were often interrupted by snow, wafting in under the roof. In these days 'the pilot road' lay outside, with a pair of 'Castles' invariably stabled, 'right way round' for any emergencies. Regular blowing off, of course, meant an enforced suspension of any teaching.

The modern and open layout at Old Oak enabled a relatively straightforward conversion for diesel traction, with demolition and rebuilding proceeding amidst a still active steam allocation. The 'top passenger' turntable was retained and a three-road servicing shed erected on the approaches, that is, on the site of the 'bottom passenger'. The traverser, long in poor condition, was taken out and 'The Factory' of steam days (it is still known thus) converted with neat simplicity into repair premises. The original fuel point had

Tanks on the 'top goods' approach on 26th May 1954. Rounding the northern curve took one into a wholly different part of the depot. This road was normally considered an exit only, engines entering from the coal stage and leaving the rear roundhouses, the 'washout' or the 'top passenger' via these loops, well away from the concentration of engines 'at the front'. The tanks have been lined up here by the shedmen, preparatory to passing off for their pilot work but standing, unattended, they only enhance the peculiarly deserted air of this corner of Old Oak.   *T. Wright*

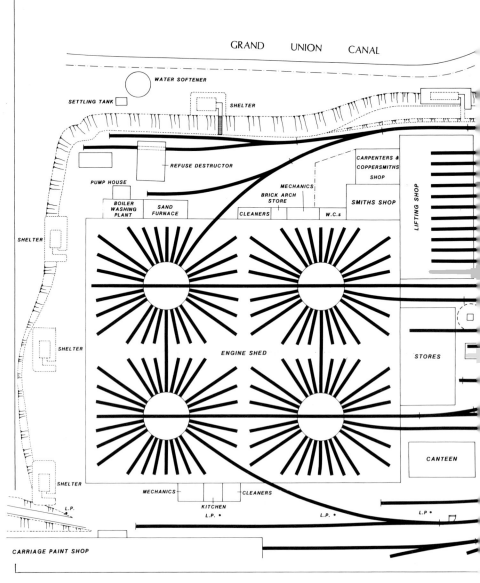

stood next to the loco coal roads, by the canal, and the shunters, which preceded the main line diesels by some years, were long parked there, as a matter of convenience. The new servicing shed and its 'service sequence' layout required new fuelling arrangements and the earlier plant went out of use. 'Blue Pullman' multiple units could not be satisfactorally dealt with and were kept in the former carriage lifting shop, inevitably rechristened 'The Pullman Shed'. A separate fuel point was established outside, so that Pullman sets could be refuelled as they entered. The unit would halt outside for the first power car and then proceed into the shed for the second power unit to be attended to. The 'Blue Pullman', introduced in 1960 and abandoned partly through poor suspension characteristics, was in its principles no different from present day HST sets. These today are responsible for most Old Oak jobs and are housed in purpose-built premises on the south side of the main carriage sheds. In the shop alongside the 'Pullman Shed' the two Old Oak independent snow ploughs are still housed (taken out once a year round the Greenford Loop, to check for hot running) and it was here that 6018 *King Henry VI* was long stored. Rumours persist at Old Oak of the cloak and dagger substitution of this engine for 6000 *King George V*.

Ranelagh Bridge

Ranelagh Bridge was an Old Oak booked job, a single crew to turn the engine, liven the fire a little (they were not dropped at Ranelagh Bridge), whilst a labourer trimmed the tender. While this was going on, the 'foreign' crew (from Bristol or Wolverhampton perhaps, but not as far as Plymouth for instance – this required a much longer stop over) took a breather. Old Oak supplied, in addition to an engine crew and labourer, a fitter and his mate, and a chargehand (the latter not a 'front line' man, as it were); day and afternoon shifts were worked but no night turns, Ranelagh Bridge seeing little use at night. The crew virtually lived at Ranelagh Bridge and would jump on the pilot and take it at once to Paddington in the event of a failure. The engine could be turned in minutes and sent out if an incoming failure occurred at say, Acton.

The pilot, for many years a 'Castle', was withdrawn before the end of steam, and a diesel, wherever possible a Brush Type 4

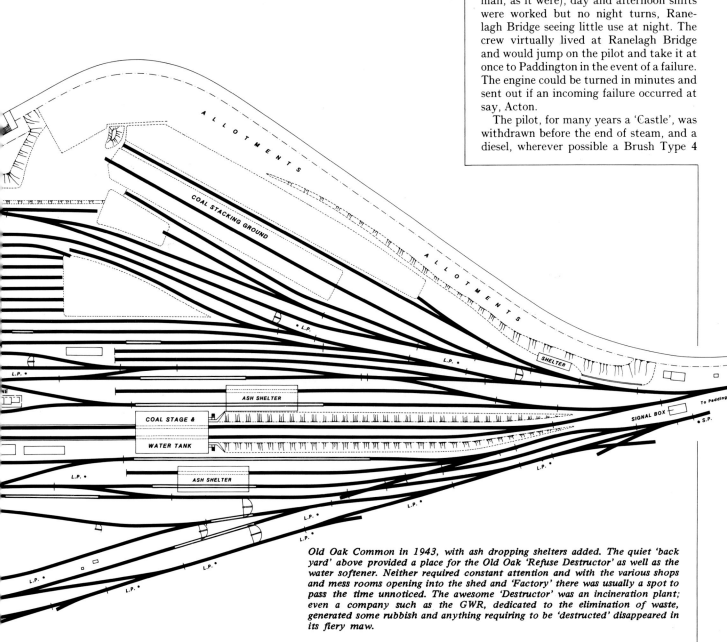

Old Oak Common in 1943, with ash dropping shelters added. The quiet 'back yard' above provided a place for the Old Oak 'Refuse Destructor' as well as the water softener. Neither required constant attention and with the various shops and mess rooms opening into the shed and 'Factory' there was usually a spot to pass the time unnoticed. The awesome 'Destructor' was an incineration plant; even a company such as the GWR, dedicated to the elimination of waste, generated some rubbish and anything requiring to be 'destructed' disappeared in its fiery maw.

Ranelagh yard on 29th January 1957, with 7026 *Tenbury Castle*, 70016 *Ariel* and two more 4–6–0s, a 'King' and a 'Castle'. The place was truly appalling for the residents (the site had originally been occupied by an elegant villa, in its own parkland) and conditions worsened with the diesels. A 22,500 gallon water tank with 'cabin' beneath was provided at the corner of the depot, off to the right in the photograph. Proposals were drawn up late in 1907 and the tank was completed at some date after this. Engines did not coal at Ranelagh Bridge but it was not originally envisaged that this should be so. A coal stage and water tank was designed in July 1908 to serve the approach road nearest the main line, followed in 1913 by a similar proposal, with a tank 40 ft by 20 ft. This concern with a tank for the several years up to 1913 suggests that the proposal of 1907 (i.e. the tank house demolished only a year or so ago) might not have appeared until this time after all. Ranelagh Bridge was notable for, among other things, a 1930s film of an engineman going mad and attempting to murder his fireman. The director, with great atmospheric sense, had the madman live in the adjoining terrace, an irony 'Ginger' and her long-suffering neighbours would have understood too well.

P. J. Kelley

(class 47), substituted. This in its turn was withdrawn for economy reasons, a development welcomed, as one less engine at least, by the long-suffering nearby residents. It was impossible not to cause gross disturbance with the otherwise elegant terrace so close, and some occupants, driven to distraction, kept up a barrage of complaints to Paddington, Old Oak Common, Swindon, MPs, Councillors or whoever else they could think of. One unfortunate woman, nicknamed with scant sympathy 'Ginger' (she had red hair obviously), was reduced to hurling empty milk bottles (and abuse) from her kitchen window. Diesels were noisier than steam, with 'Hymeks' the most unpleasant of all, and Westminster City Council even installed noise recorders. Worse, the landlord of the local pub claimed that vibration from the diesels upset his beer, preventing it from settling.

Manorbier Castle, much improved by a reversion to traditional form.
C. C. B. Herbert, courtesy A. Swain

'King' 4–6–0 alongside a local '61', No. 6115. There was a small incident in 1919, requiring turntable repairs to the value of £950 and conversion of the depot for diesel working meant a relatively simple alteration, removing the 'table and extending the sidings. There was plenty of money about for this and the yard was dressed up with paving and renewed pits, apparently in the period 1964-1965. Ranelagh Bridge then became principally a refuelling point and an even more miserable period began for the local residents. The 'fill to spill' principles employed, with tank indicators so unreliable, left the whole yard awash with diesel fuel. Pumped under pressure, the innocuous term 'spill' in reality meant a fountain of fuel gushing six feet or more across the yard. Perhaps only Paddington and King's Cross, with no whiff of electrification, maintained a system of working at least vaguely recognisable from steam days. Both had a busy locomotive servicing area and their own depots further out. 'High Speed Trains' and electrics have now largely severed these tenuous links and Ranelagh Bridge lies now trackless and deserted. Even at Old Oak a Sunday morning can boast less than a dozen locos, and apart from HSTs, the days seem numbered of the 'last and vital London link in a chain of major servicing and maintenance centres established at strategic points throughout the Western Region'.
Courtesy A. Swain

The great iron footbridge together with the water softener, were the dominant features at Southall. The bridge was the principal point of access to the shed; it was 'the approved walking route' for purposes of payment and was for years graced by a spiral staircase on the north side, dropping down into the area of the bay. The 'viaduct' (the coal stage) was rumoured to be of great age, a belief strengthened by the near inability of BR contractors to blow it up. There were two columns at the London end of the station, one on the Relief and one on the Main, used less by the capacious '61s' but vital for their less generously appointed predecessors. Southall men, into the 1930s, worked London trains with open cab '35s' sprinting from one column to the next. One was soaked as a matter of course in the rain but could also 'catch a load' in these ancient (yet well remembered) machines if the column was less than gingerly handled.

British Railways

SOUTHALL

The Southall water softener followed Great Western practice; it relied upon a tall tower, the 'Kennicott' principle whereby untreated water enters at the top to be mixed and allowed to settle downward through a settling cone and driven upwards through baffle plates. The Great Western installed only a handful of softening plants but they were introduced early on, in the first years of this century. *L & GRP, courtesy David & Charles*

It was inevitable that a thriving goods traffic should grow up at Southall. Wholly obscure when the main line was laid across its clay farmland, a station was first opened 'to make a convenient connection' with the Grand Junction Canal. The Brentford branch, to establish a Thameside dock for the GWR, followed in 1859, and Lyons and Mountford (*An Historical Survey of Great Western Engine Sheds 1837–1947*, OPC 1979) note a single road building with turntable outside, opened in that year. As recorded in the work mentioned above, locomotives were assigned to 'the Brentford branch'. Whatever, sustained development soon demanded a more comprehensive provision; further engines were necessary, to augment the single example originally provided, moving Armstrong in 1865 to approach the Locomotive Committee. Ignoring the term 'Brentford Branch', on 1st November he opined that 'the present Coking arrangements at Southall, with sacks and baskets, should be superseded by a small Crane and Tub, Estimated Cost £91'.

Accommodation at Southall was beginning to prove awkward, and the difficulties had become extreme by the early 1880s. New buildings had been countenanced before this but a new shed, properly laid

out and occupying the site of the existing collection of sidings and shacks, was not put up until 1884. A variety of detailed alterations were discussed and drawn up during the early summer of 1883. The basic design was for some eighteen tender engines, if not miserly perhaps then an ungenerous provision, although an engine workshop contiguous with the shed itself was welcome indeed. Details of the shed forwarded to Swindon in 1901 show it originally to have been single-ended, apart from one road taken a few yards through to spare ground at the rear. This road, at 180 ft, was 30 ft longer than the remaining five. There were pits, 136 ft, on all roads and a 75 ft pit in the repair shop. This, 'roofed in saw tooth' like the shed proper, and slated on timber principals, stood some eight feet above the main part of the building, to accommodate a travelling lifting crane. The building was mainly executed in brick apart from (an allowance for future expansion) 'the South wall, wood, temporary'. All running lines in the shed were 'used for repairs as required' and as numbers at Southall grew, 'in steam' work was increasingly undertaken outside.

On 8th October 1902 various detailed alterations were first considered, beginning a slightly confused period, which ended

with a new turntable, extended roads and other modifications. £2,000 was approved in the original 1902 proposals, for: 'Repairs to Engine Shed and Coal Stage, renewal of Coal Tip, removal and erection of water crane and provision of an additional crane with the necessary mains, extension of Lines at the rear of the Engine Shed and slewing sidings'. On 12th April 1905 this work was reviewed and an outlay of £3,806 approved, 'for when the work was taken in hand it was found desirable to modify the stage, so as to permit of 20 ton coal wagons being dealt with and also to renew the permanent way fittings in the yard'. Later, at the end of June, a further £1,265 was found for a water softener, and the tender of the Pulsometer Engineering Company accepted, £965 'for supply and erection' thereof. It was originally put up immediately to the west of the coal stage, a lofty tower, but was subsequently built anew at the east end of the tank.

Around this period the Great Western was much concerned with enlargements at Southall; enormous care and planning went into the purchase of a 100 ft strip of land at the rear of the shed and a typically complex and far-sighted plan, doomed inevitably to oblivion, was got out during 1906. It was obviously influenced by developments at

Continued on page 123

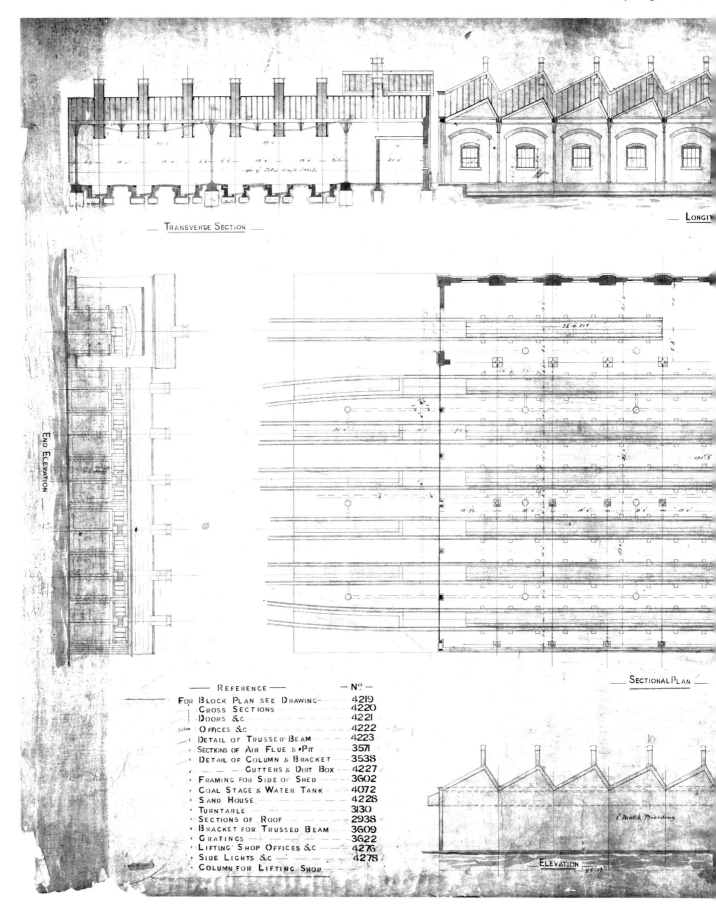

TRANSVERSE SECTION

LONGIT

END ELEVATION

SECTIONAL PLAN

ELEVATION

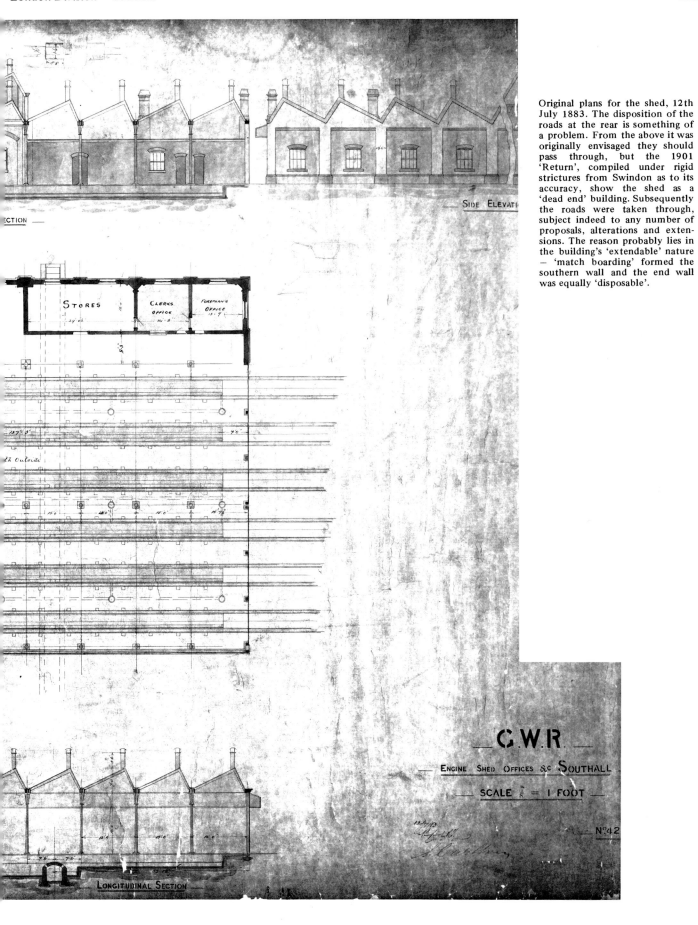

SIDE ELEVATION

STORES

CLERKS OFFICE

FOREMAN'S OFFICE

LONGITUDINAL SECTION

G.W.R.

ENGINE SHED OFFICES &c SOUTHALL

SCALE = 1 FOOT

N°42

Original plans for the shed, 12th July 1883. The disposition of the roads at the rear is something of a problem. From the above it was originally envisaged they should pass through, but the 1901 'Return', compiled under rigid strictures from Swindon as to its accuracy, show the shed as a 'dead end' building. Subsequently the roads were taken through, subject indeed to any number of proposals, alterations and extensions. The reason probably lies in the building's 'extendable' nature — 'match boarding' formed the southern wall and the end wall was equally 'disposable'.

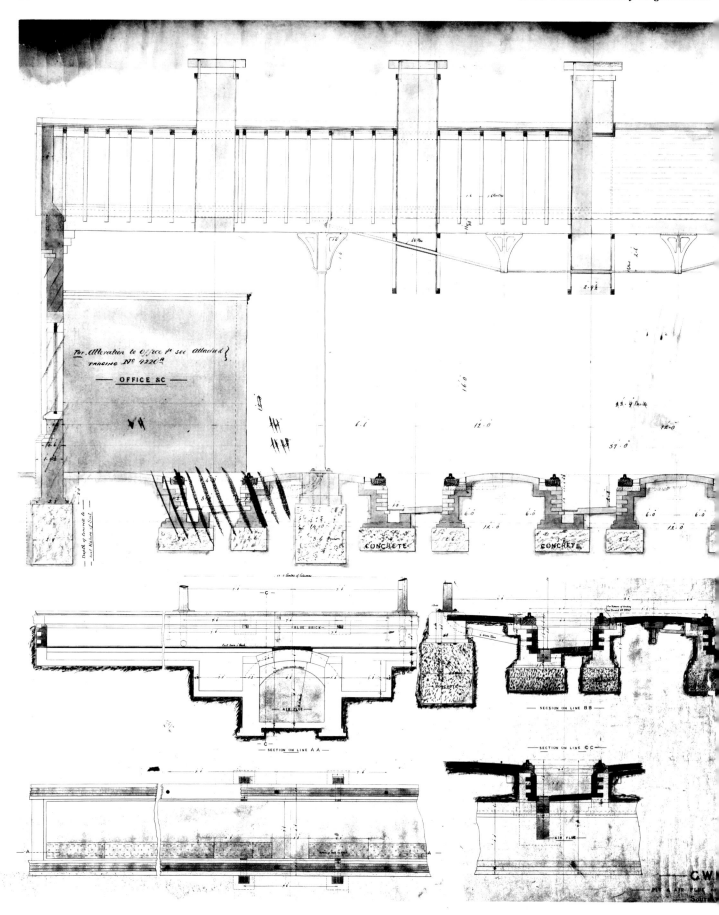

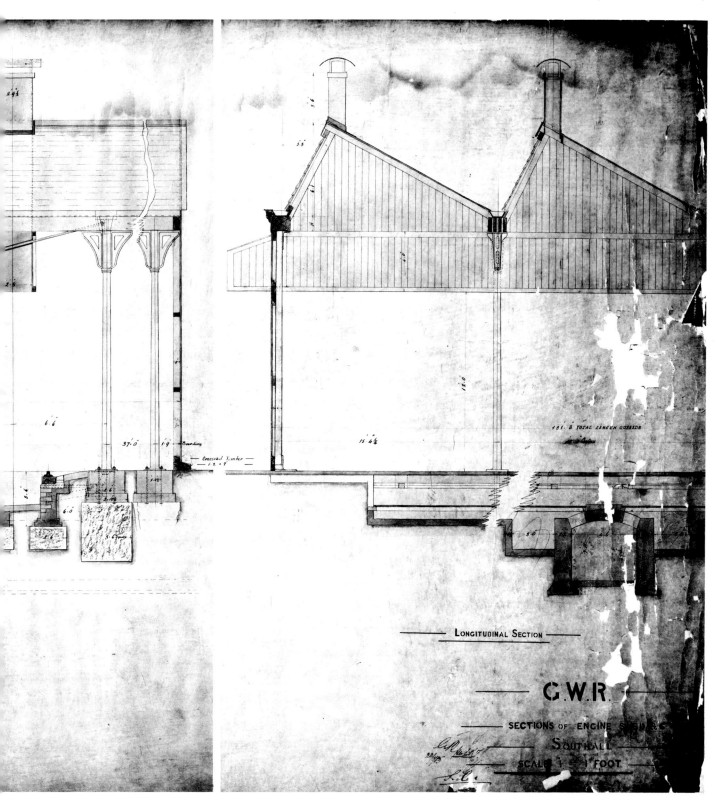

Longitudinal Section

G.W.R

Sections of Engine Shed &c

Southall

Scale ½ = 1 Foot

Detail at Southall, dated May 1883. The 'air flue' is a curious subterranean device presumably intended as an aid to draughting for engines 'lighting up'. The offices and stores are seen to be internal 'partitions' rather than an integral part of the building.

Column and pit details of June 1883.

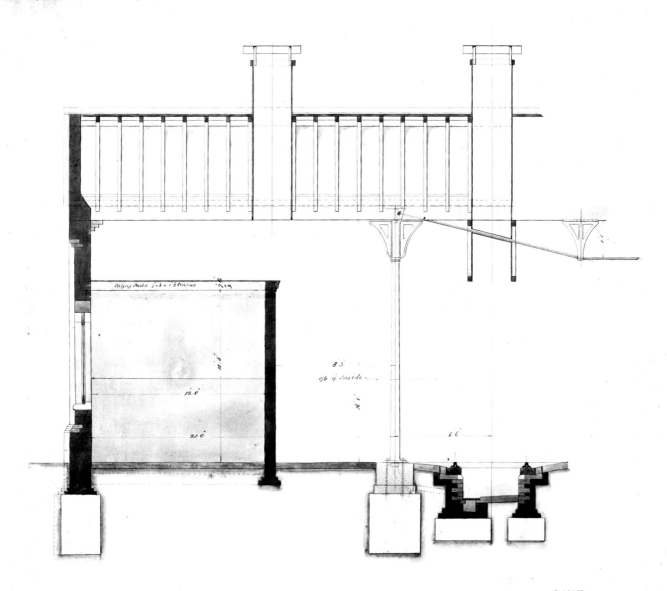

GWR
SOUTHALL ENGINE SHED
SECTION THROUGH OFFICES
SCALE ½ⁱⁿ = 1 FOOT

Nº 4220ᴬ

The raised repair section was characteristic of GWR sheds of this period, and as additions to earlier sheds — witness Weymouth and, say, Oxford.

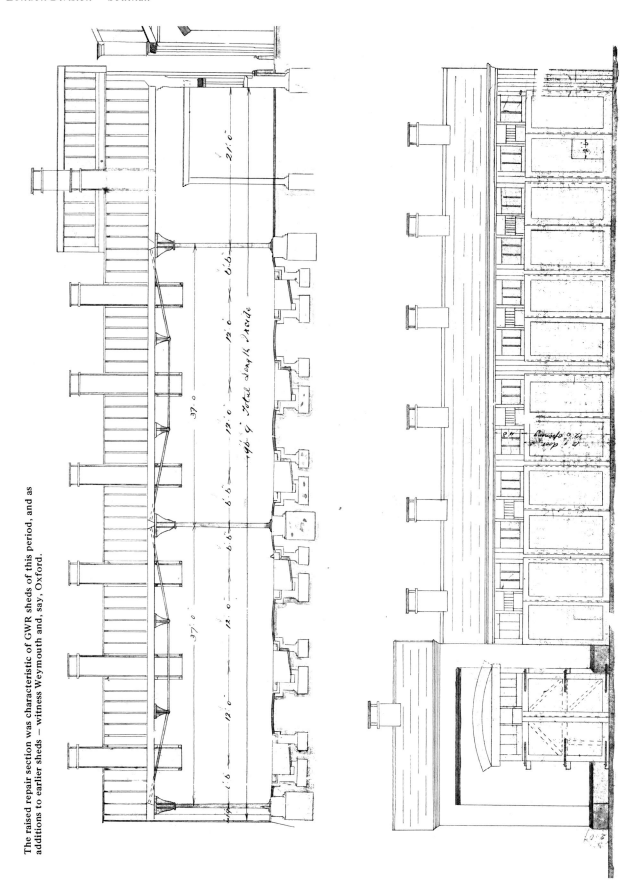

END ELEVATION

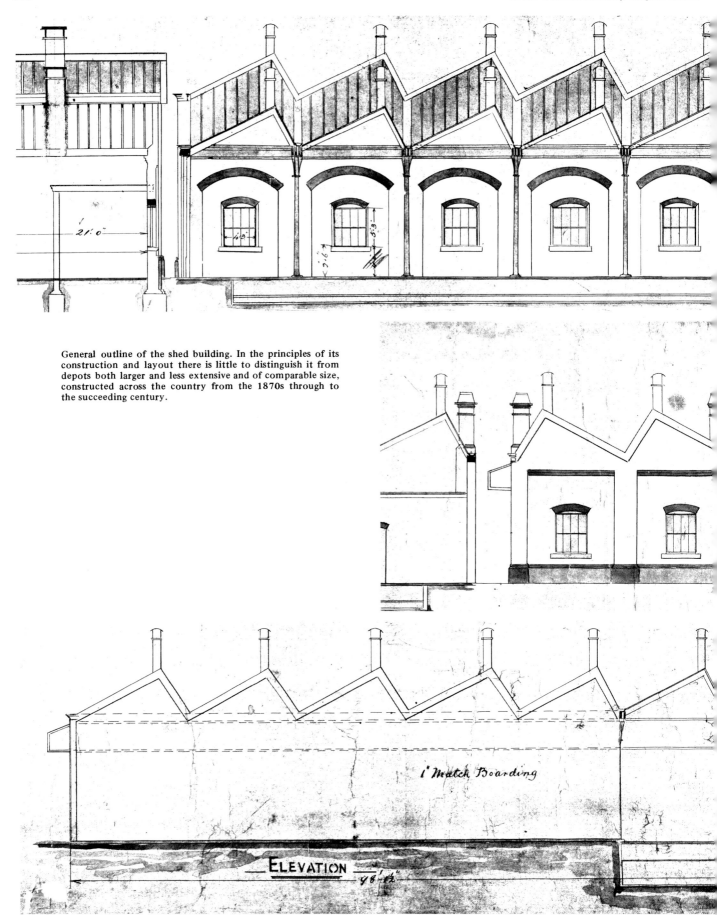

General outline of the shed building. In the principles of its construction and layout there is little to distinguish it from depots both larger and less extensive and of comparable size, constructed across the country from the 1870s through to the succeeding century.

ELEVATION

LONGITUDINAL SECTION

'There was wood everywhere at Southall'. This was true of much of the construction, the doors long surviving at the shed principally through being pegged more or less permanently open. Southall was a busy place with constant engine movements and this was the only way to avoid the inevitable splintering and alarming destruction. In the rebuilt depot, doors were dispensed with. Plans show iron supporting columns, though timber was actually made much use of.

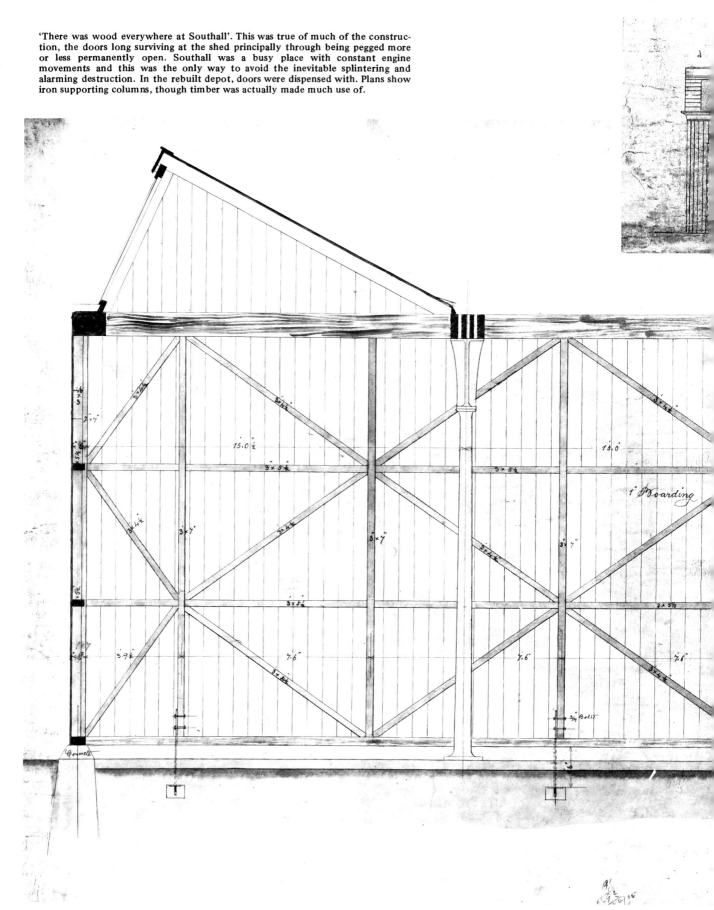

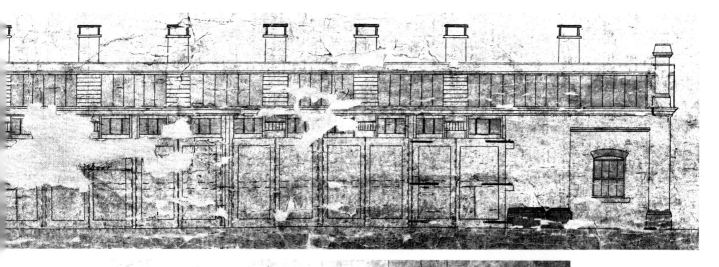

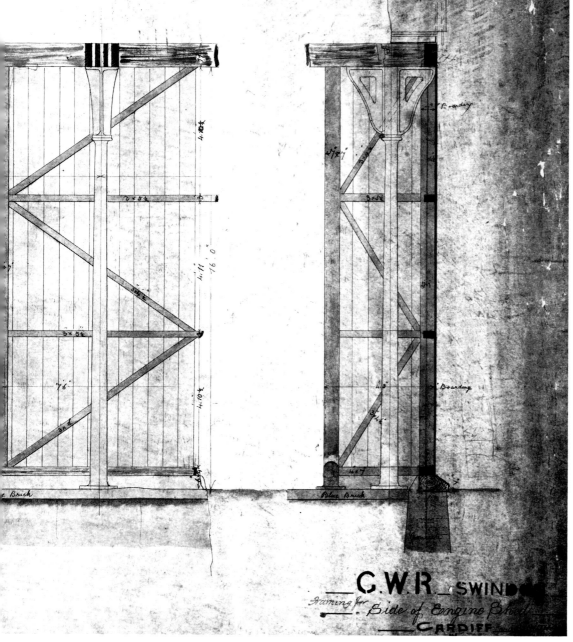

G.W.R. SWINDON

Side of Engine Shed

CARDIFF

1902 drawing with successive stamps and signatures

Old Oak and envisaged a similar four-roundhouse structure, to the east of the shed. Approach lines would be taken round either side of the straight shed and the southernmost one would cross a new, outside turntable, a 65 ft unit which eventually appeared in 1909. Extra round-houses were considered at one time or another for all the London area sheds, a further dozen or so; none of them came to anything, unfortunately, and the era of Churchward expansion and re-equipping was compressed into a relatively short time.

In contrast to the lavish provision at Old Oak, the sheds disposed around London remained underdeveloped, cramped and overcrowded. Southall continued to be ill-provided for with respect to space, and extensive coal stacks were proposed in 1921, partly in order to remedy supply difficulties then being experienced. Again little was accomplished beyond the planning stage and variations were still being tried in the 1940s. The 'proposed coal stacking ground' would have occupied all the land purchased for the abandoned new

roundhouses, eight roads to the rear of the old shed, 10,500 tons, and a further eight roads alongside the Brentford line to hold 11,100 tons.

It is not entirely clear how all the various alterations were related chronologically; on 8th April 1908, for instance, a further £1,883 is set aside for 'extension of roads at the back of the Engine Shed', though this was presumably only a minor adjustment – much of the sum was for the 'fixing' of a new turntable. The original 45 ft 'table of 1884' was still in place, a wrought iron hand-

Outside-framed 0–6–0 No. 2370. The tall softening column contrasted in a way with the much 'less progressive' coal stage. The Southall softener was rebuilt (probably post-Grouping, the new filter system dated from March 1938), and the tank itself was renewed with a roof. Softening on the GWR in the period 1904/1905 concerned the 'incrustation of locomotive boilers'. C. T. Cuss to the GWR Mechanics Institution, Swindon, on Tuesday 10th January 1905:
"1.– WATERS AND INCRUSTATION. – The following table shewed the analyses of (a) good and (b) bad water for locomotive use.

LOCOMOTIVE WATERS

	(1) GOOD	(2) BAD	
Total solid matter in solution	15.8	51.2	Grains per gallon.
Chlorine in chlorides	1.4	1.2	,, ,, ,,
Alkalinity, expressed as chalk	6.7	12.5	,, ,, ,,
Hardness, temporary	4.2	10.0	Degrees
,, permanent	3.2	25.8	,,
,, total	7.4	35.8	,,
Suspended matter, small quantity			Trace
Reaction, very slightly alkaline			Slightly alkaline

(1) This sample is of good quality for locomotive use.
(2) Cost of materials for softening 1,000 gallons, 2d.

(c) The future of the locomotive is dependent on the efficiency of the boiler, and to shew the importance of treating boiler feed water generally, the Author had obtained thirty-one samples of incrustation taken from boilers in the GWR Swindon Division, stationed at Reading, Bridport, Gloucester, Lydney, and Swindon, and from the specimens

exhibited, it could be seen that the average thickness was about 3/16″, the thickest being 5/8″, except one, which was 2″ thick. Most of them were hard and dense, for only four could be called soft, and of these one was honey-combed. In one case, the quantity removed by one weekly wash-out of a goods' locomotive boiler weighed 18 lbs., the thickness being 1/8″. An average 1/8″ scale would not reduce the efficiency of a boiler very materially, but the maximum plate tempera-ture would rise from about 400° F. to 700° F., causing excessive expan-sion and contraction each time the fire-hole door was opened or closed, and it was hardly surprising that under these circumstances steel fire-boxes were not a success. In some cases a boiler got badly choked with scale in one district, whereas on removing it to another district the scale entirely disappeared. A water highly charged with salts was even more dangerous than lime-scale-forming properties, due to corrosion of the plates, for unless the boiler were frequently washed out the scale concentrated and caused priming. A very thin scale was regarded as a desirable protective coating, and to some very alkaline waters lime was added to give this effect. A most interesting account of 'An enquiry into the working of various Water Softeners' by Messrs. Stromeyer & Baron, appeared in the *Engineer*, between December, 1903, and January, 1904. Seventeen different types of softeners were dealt with, most of them using lime water and soda-ash for re-agents to remove the scale-forming solids, the principal difference being in the mechanical method of regulating the proportions and mixing. However perfect a method may be for a certain water, intelligent control was necessary, particularly where a variable water was dealt with, as was often the case when a supply came from more than one source."

Collection R. S. Carpenter

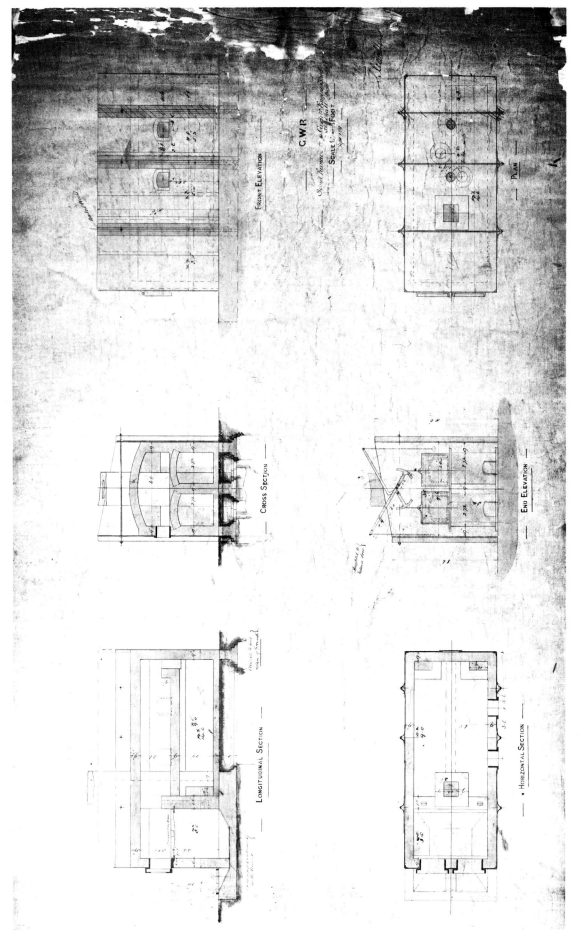

Sand furnace for Cardiff Canton 1881, the same model to be provided at Southall.

No. 3599 on 20th October 1923. The 'Metro' 2–4–0Ts were long characteristic of the London Division and were still at Southall when the Second World War started. They remained on passenger work out of Paddington though increasingly turned over to pilot work and 'put on the passenger only if in a bit of a spot'. The open cab examples presented a curious sight, lower than the coaches and bouncing perceptibly on their springs, the driver and fireman going up and down in unison. *Collection R. S. Carpenter*

No. 3592 on 2nd August 1936. The 2–4–0Ts are generally regarded now with some affection, though with such constricted cabs they were awkward to work. There wasn't really enough room to turn round properly and it was advisable to find a short shovel, one with the blade cut back. Skinned knuckles and burns were common and bunker-first running in rain required fiddling with a company-issue sheet. Coal was taken from a peculiar little well at the base of the bunker and the water feed operated by pulling up a rod from the floor. These were frequently worn and could drop down, unless propped up with a gauge glass spanner, a tool of just the correct height. The description 'they fair rattled along' accurately recalls their 'seasick' mode of progress. *G. H. Daventry*

The steam railmotors were parked at the south side of the station, near to the bridge. They were customarily shunted to and fro when low in steam, for instance, or if in need of attention at the shed.
                                                                                                                                                                                B. Y. Williams

operated machine largely fabricated at Swindon works. New foundations were put down, a little beyond the old installation, in the winter of 1909, a new 65 ft unit, again built at Swindon, coming into use during March. What was left of the 1884 turntable was taken up, and on 2nd April consigned to Swindon and an unknown end. Power for the shed services had long been provided by two vertical boiler engines, but by 1911 these had become less and less reliable. At the end of June they were deemed 'beyond repair' and a 'locomotive-type boiler' ordered 'in lieu thereof'. A lean-to was erected for it at the south-west corner of the shed, the whole costing nearly £400. The tall chimney survived, patched up and altered as each mischance befell it over the years, until a new oil-fired boiler house appeared in the 1950s, when the Western Region remodelled the whole depot.

Numerous alterations were made to the water supply over the years – a new 11,250 gallon tank and water column, to replace a conventional 3,000 gallon pillar tank in 1918 and a new pump house and wells on the south side of the Brentford branch. These were proposed in 1928 and lay halfway between the shed and the Grand Union Canal. There was a 'travelling gas tank' based on Southall; first set up about

1908, it resided on a short stub siding immediately at the country end of the goods shed. It fed mains to the sidings and the motor shed, and was presumably for the replenishment of carriage stock and steam railmotors. From about 1920 its removal was arranged to the north side, close by the road overbridge between the fan table and the horse platform.

Around 'Brentford Junction' a bewildering array of manufacturing endeavours had grown up, and even before the First World War, sidings leading off north by Hayes and Harlington station served such disparate concerns as a gramophone factory and marble and slate works. An extensive gas works had appeared by Southall station, whilst further sidings in early and planned 'estate' fashion led on the south side to factories devoted to engineering, emulsions, wallpaper, jam and more besides. Opposite the shed a vast margarine factory had grown up, the various food smells proving a lasting, slightly pained memory for any driver who knew the area in wartime. These were all precursors, harbingers of the light industry destined to dominate whole swathes of the area west of London. Innovatory developments continued in the Western Avenue project of the 'thirties, a momentum sustained through to

the 'fifties; its descendants in a sense can be discerned in the lamentably christened 'sunrise' activities now stretching out through Maidenhead, Reading and elsewhere. Southall engines thus came to deal with a variety of goods and shunting work, as well as having a part in the interminable coal traffic into London. Old Oak Common was responsible for much of this; Southall, laying conveniently on the edge of the metropolitan area, could prove a most useful refuge. Crowded traffic could become most inconvenient around here and Southall was ideally sited. Light goods, incessant transfers and commuter work ensured a considerable stud of tank engines. By the summer of 1933 the complement was made up as follows:

457, 1152, 1494, 1548, 1765/7/93,
1848/50/77/80, 1994, 2081, 2376, 2417/89,
2626, 2765/74/87, 2843/54, 3047,
3562/4/5/6/9/83/5/8/96/9, 4589, 5400/8–19,
5500, 5744, 6112/42/7/50, 6391, 7779.

(Railway Observer)

Southall had steam railmotors for its several branches, followed by motor trailers and diesel railcars. Early on a special railmotor shed was built; on 11th May 1904 the 'Erection of a corrugated Iron shed for the accommodation of Railway Motor Cars' was approved at a cost of £660, 'subject

The shed at Southall was dominated by, of all things, margarine, a product as redolent of the period to the 1950s as the 'Metro' tanks were of the 1920s. There were food factories all about, useful to an extent during the war but more often in a frustrating proximity. *J. E. Kite*

No. 1453, the 'Steam Carriage Shed' beyond. *J. E. Kite*

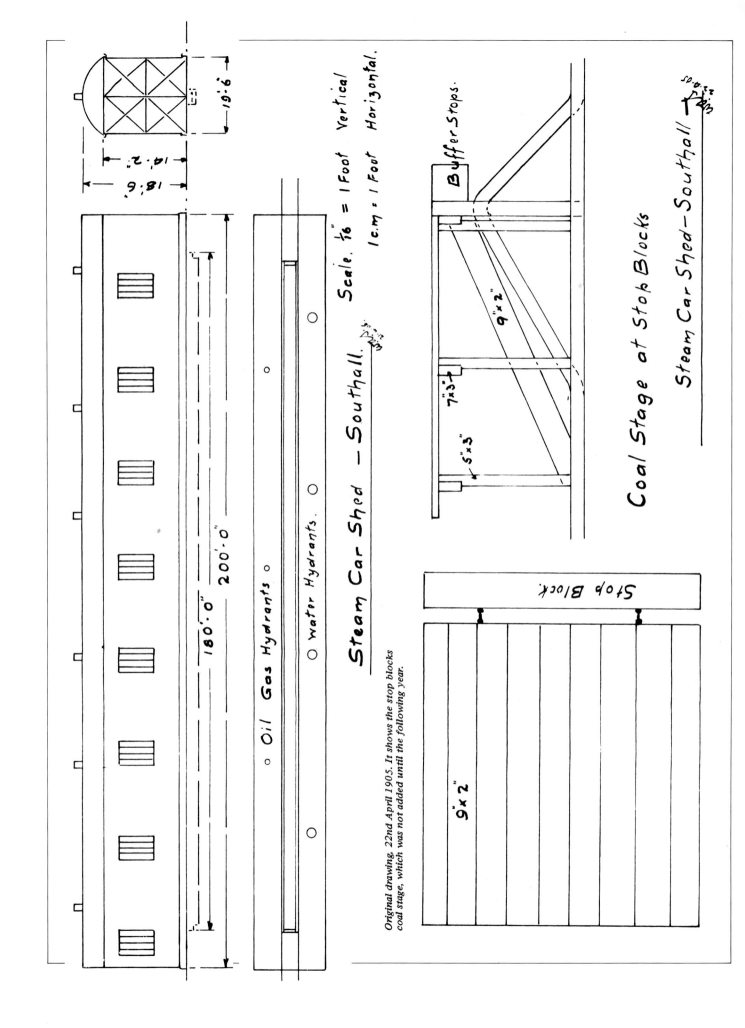

9'.6"

14'.2"

18'.9"

180'.0"

200'.0"

o Oil Gas Hydrants o

o Water Hydrants o

Steam Car Shed — Southall.

Scale. $\frac{1}{16}$" = 1 Foot Vertical

1 c.m = 1 Foot Horizontal.

Buffer Stops.

9" × 2"

7" × 3"

5" × 3"

Coal Stage at Stop Blocks

Steam Car Shed—Southall

Stop Block.

9" × 2"

Original drawing, 22nd April 1905. It shows the stop blocks coal stage, which was not added until the following year.

to the Engineers' approval'. This was not formally given until April 1905, though a certification of the facilities at Southall on behalf of Armstrong gives the opening date as 28th September 1904. In corrugated iron on a steel frame, this shed was 200 ft in length with a pit of 180 ft. Traffic was never heavy on the Brentford branch and it closed to passengers in 1942, but at first, at least, business was fairly brisk. On 2nd May 1906 the Traffic Committee approved 'a half hourly instead of hourly motor service on the Brentford branch between 9 a.m. and 2 p.m. on Sundays, an extra 35 miles per Sunday'. From October a simple wooden coal stage was established at one end of the shed, above the buffer stops, but it is not clear to what extent it was used. The shed was poorly ventilated and the stock suffered from dirt and smoke and, although the steam rail motors may have used it at first, for years it housed only railmotor trailers. The steam units were stabled on the down side of the station and the shed used for trailers. The steam railmotors entered the main engine shed only for essential maintenance where there were again problems of contamination by dirt and smoke. It was usually known as the 'Car Shed' or 'Trailer Shed' and a 1957 *Railway Magazine* item describes its use for trailer car cleaning.... 'As far as be

No. 98 again, both views following the movement initiated on the previous page. *Lens of Sutton*

No. 5419 on 20th May 1933. Southall men were quite familiar with 'the pull and push'. 14XX tanks were considered a bit cramped, like the 'Metros' (customarily called '35s') but the '54s' were most popular. The links at Southall were varied and frequently changing but 'the cars' were worked generally by men in the higher links, around 3 or 4, with 12 sets in each. High Street might be something of a branch line ramble but 12-14 Vine Street trips was a formidable shift. The 'Trailer Shed' had a fine blue brick floor, bought up on its demolition by a Southall driver who had just acquired a new house.

                                                                                                                                              A. W. Croughton

ascertained it has always been used for this purpose'. Railmotors ran to Brentford, on the Ealing Broadway–Greenford and the Westbourne Park–Northolt services some of the latter terminating at Old Oak Lane halt – 'surely the only Halt to have a bay platform'. The Uxbridge branches, Vine Street and High Street, were also Southall jobs. All eventually were given over to engines and trailers, the last steam rail-motor working being on the Brentford branch, No. 88 a regular unit around 1928/29 and in 1931. A railmotor working from Slough to Windsor was also at one time part of the Southall allocation, the shed at Slough in some respects partly dependent upon the larger establishment at Southall.

Southall took its part in the lively Pad-dington passenger traffic, relieved by push-pull work on backwaters such as the Uxbridge High Street line, and night work (unsettling and lonely, with hooting owls and stranger noises) at Staines. Branch work, 54XX panniers sandwiched between two trailers, contrasted with fast and

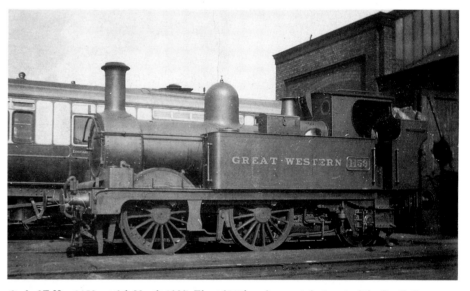

0–4–2T No. 1159 on 6th March 1927. These '517' engines were but part of the Southall passen-ger tank engine complement. They were presumably for branch work, whilst 2–4–0Ts and 0–6–0Ts worked the Paddington services. A postcard message of 8th February 1919: 'I had a journey today from Windsor to Southall behind 634, 0–6–0 side tank which together with 641 has been working Paddington-Slough stopping trains during the past few days, instead of the 2–4–0 tanks.'

                                                                                                                                    Collection Peter Winding

The '61s' characterised the Division more than any other type, almost perfectly judged for the work. As at Slough they were operated as 'tandem engines', each with two crews which prompted a pride and interest in their running and mechanical condition. There was a vast coal stack at the rear of the shed — 'The Stockpile'. It had long been religiously whitewashed at the front though it had been untouched for years — grass grew on the top and the coal was in very poor condition, dust, dirt and iron deposits running through it. It was finally taken up during the war when coal trains were infrequent and unreliable, a job for the cleaners with the wagonloads taken away through the shed. *National Railway Museum*

No. 5500 in September 1932. The small Prairie tanks were apparently sent more or less new to the London area, in the years before the First World War. That they soon gravitated away to become characteristic of the country districts is well known, though the precise reason is not clear — they presumably represented a marked improvement upon 2—4—0Ts on passenger work and could presumably cope with empty stock handled by 0—6—0 tanks. For long years they remained only odd visitors to the London Division though Oxford had a couple through to Nationalisation. Remarkably, several examples returned to Southall in the last years, to work out mileage before withdrawal. *V. R. Webster*

Pilot turns abounded in the shunts, yards, factories and depots about Southall. The 'tanks' on these jobs could be found anywhere in the yard where repairs often had to be carried out through lack of room in the shed. Coupling rods and superheater elements litter the ground by No. 1969 on 20th April 1938.   *Collection Peter Winding*

20th April 1938, with 2725 and 6835 *Eastham Grange* stowed out of the way amongst the customary dump of empty barrels.
Collection Peter Winding

0–6–0 No. 2547 on 20th April 1938, the 'Standard Goods' (the 'Dean Goods' of enthusiasts) made legend by, amongst others, the *Great Western Magazine:*

The 2301s in Peace and War

'Not least among those who are lining up to do their bit in the present war are the veterans of 1914 to 1918; and notable among these are the Great Western engines which saw service abroad during the last war and are again included among the Company's engines selected to go overseas. Some of these locomotive veterans are already working with the vanguard in France, and when present schemes mature, 26 of the 100 Great Western engines to go overseas will be going for the second time.

' . . . . When the standard goods were introduced they were among the crack engines in the service. Especially in their early days they were employed on a wide variety of work and, particularly before the arrival of the 'Bulldogs' and other larger engines, frequently worked passenger trains and vacuum goods. From Neath to Birmingham on Onion Fair day, and from Wolverhampton to Weymouth on seaside excursions; between Chester and Barmouth, and from Newport and Cardiff to Aberystwyth — were typical of their passenger work. . . .

'In the heyday of the 2301s, railway practice was very different from that of to-day. Every driver had his own engine — and regarded it just as jealously as a mother does her first baby. This was encouraged by the fact that the driver did much more for their engines than they do to-day when shed work is more highly organised. Every week there was a shed day when the engines were washed out and cleaned and polished until, to quote the words of one old driver, "they shone like palaces". Not content with this, many of the old brigade who handled the 2301s and their sister engines would regularly walk down to the shed on Sunday mornings on the excuse of doing, perhaps, a little gland packing — but actually, it is said on good authority, to see how their engines were! . . . .

'The war of 1914 to 1918 wrote an entirely unexpected chapter in the history of these engines. Their construction and capabilities were peculiarly suited to certain classes of war work and 62 were taken from the proprietorial care of their drivers to undergo the perils of war service overseas. . . . .

'That the 2301s did their full share in the winning of the last war — and that they will do so again in this — is shown by the mileage they covered. Of the five engines listed in our December issue as going overseas for the second time, No. 2403 covered over 40,000 miles on its first expedition, No. 2461 covered over 53,000, No. 2480 over 27,300 and No. 2518 over 35,500, all in France. No. 2533, whose photograph in its new livery was reproduced in the December *Magazine*, worked in France from March, 1917, to July, 1918, when she was taken to Greece. She returned to Swindon in March, 1921, after covering 27,500 miles.

' . . . . To every right-thinking man an engine is something to be regarded at least with respect. To a driver it becomes a living personality and its welfare a matter for real concern. Great Western men who have been associated with the 2301s in their peacetime work will be interested to know that some, at any rate, of those already overseas are in the hands of men who thoroughly understand them. They are working in France with the Great Western Railway Companies of the Royal Engineers. — F. G. RICHENS.' *Collection Peter Winding*

The Brentford branch motor train propelling out of Southall between the coal stage, 'the viaduct' and the 'steam car shed'.

B. Y. Williams

Engines at Southall, left to right 2–8–0 No. 2843 and tanks Nos. 3565, 5409 and 3564, representing the enormous variety in the shed's duties. The 'tankies' of different sorts were occupied with anything from Paddington trains, branch push and pulls and any amount of shunting whilst 'the big stuff', which included 47XX 2–8–0s off Old Oak, were used on heavy goods to Westbury, Severn Tunnel, Tyseley and elsewhere – 'the Double Home Link'. *Pendon Museum*

'Tankie' 3564 on 22nd June 1932. The last '35s' seem to have left Southall about 1942. *A. W. Croughton*

No. 2875 at Southall. The '28s' were considered capable of almost anything, powering the 'Pool Trains' (100 empty wagons, like the 1.10 Acton), the Paddington goods and the 100-wagon '2 p.m. Slough'. These trains were handled by the senior goods links, approximating to Nos. 5 and 6, the 'Double Home Link' and the 'Spare Goods Link', the latter in particular being hard work.   *H. F. Wheeller*

heavily laden trains such as the 'Oxley Goods', an 'accelerated C' which used troughs, the crews swopping footplates in a brief changeover at Banbury. 28XX 2-8-0s were always to be found at Southall ('in and out all the time'), and the 47XX engines, often Old Oak examples, were frequently put to use. They were not allocated to the shed, but Southall men gave them the warm approval familiar at Reading and other sheds in the London area. They were considered very heavy on water but nevertheless 'lovely' engines. The 'D. home' link at Southall was responsible for much of the principal goods work, lodging to Tyseley, Severn Tunnel Junction and Westbury. There was beer to Woodford in BR days, whilst the nearby Southall gas works demanded something like 400 tons of coal a day, from 'up north, beyond Woodford'. Southall worked 100-wagon coal trains, collecting empties from the district and using 28XX engines. There were numerous pilot turns, 0-6-0 tanks in the main, and probably at their busiest during the Second World War. There were two 57XX panniers, 'one each side' at Brentford dock, coping with a minimum of five trains a day. There was also a lot of shunting at the Firestone factory and in order to relieve, men travelled down by bus, the Brentford passenger service having been withdrawn 'to great local fuss'. At night one pannier tank came up to shunt the shed coal stage and one of these attended to Brentford's heavily publicised 'First Export Train to Russia', the first load of Monsanto chemicals in the post-war period. The Mayor of Southall was a Southall driver, and had a

regular job on the Brentford branch. Further pilots were required at West Drayton and Southall, and other places (the 'Hayes pilot', for instance, often worked by the 'Cripple Link'), and Southall engines also shunted Acton yard, the 'east end pilots', 'Masons Lane' (the 'middle pilot') and the 'back road'. The tanks stayed out, the crews spending an entire shift until relieved, taking meals on the engine and the odd forty winks when appropriate.

Southall was in the heart of the London wartime work and its crews endured much

hardship. The Hayes Loop, by the Gas Works, frequently held three big freights and it would commonly require more than one shift to clear it. Fires went out and Southall pilots had to be sent to haul the affected engines in. There was a material dump at Taplow, from which a train of tanks on flats for Southampton might be cleared in a night, whilst the area Ambulance Train, which 'might be worked by anybody', was kept at Reading. USA 2-8-0s (regarded with some suspicion) came in the war, followed by WD 'Austerities' which could be found at Southall through-

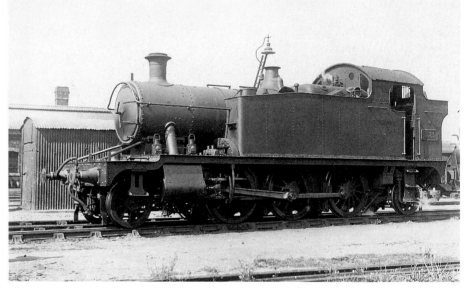

No. 4589 on 20th May 1933. Southall men rarely saw these engines but they did appear from time to time and were regarded as goods locos, comparable to a good pannier.   *A. W. Croughton*

Southall shed was a busy place, though with much of the work being night goods, there was something of a lull from about 9.00 in the morning to about 3.00 in the afternoon. Doors were accordingly open for most of the time and in winter great 'devils', vast iron cauldrons punched through with holes and mounted on legs, were set up. These 'frostfires' kept the shed's plumbing in order in icy weather and made examination work a trifle more bearable.

Lens of Sutton

Nos. 1152, 1850, 2393 and 1164 at Southall.

J. E. Kite

Southall on 4th June 1939. Present that day were 46 locomotives, 1969, 2264, 2381, 2547, 2835, 2855, 2858, 3585, 3592, 3620, 3704, 3750, 3799, 4825, 4826, 5400, 5401, 5408, 5410, 5413, 5414, 5415, 5416, 5420, 5961, 5727, 6110, 6112, 6118, 6125, 6128, 6139, 6147, 6148, 6156, 6842, 7710, 7730, 7731, 7732, 8755, 8764, 8774, 9301, 9731, 9755 and railcar No. 1. Despite the provision noted on page 126, there came to be two stationary boilers, principally for hot water washing out, placed in line, each with its own chimney, with access through the shed wall adjacent to Road No. 7 (they were numbered from the main line side). A man on the shed link would be booked for an eight-hour shift to look after the boiler, with two more to cover the 24 hours. The boilers were switched over for attention every week or fortnight, washing out generally taking place on Roads 6 and 7.   *W. A. Camwell*

out much of the BR period. Elderly GW
4-4-0s, 'Bulldogs' and even 'Dukes', were
on freights in the war and after, an endless
round of pick-ups. All manner of engines
worked into Acton and LNER B17s,
remembered as the 'footballers', among
numerous other types turned up. LNER
and LMS 0-6-0s (the latter including 'Scot-
chmen') came to the area in the Second
World War as replacements for Dean goods
loaned for war work, and all were poorly
regarded. (See under Didcot for the
abysmal condition of most of these
invalids.) A strategic link from the
Southern onto the GWR Staines branch
was opened during the war, bringing traffic
round the safer western margins of London,
and Southall had a hand in it, including
convoy trains from Southampton. Avon-
mouth–Acton was another principal
conduit for war work and goods trains were
'endless' when the convoys were in.

Rebuilding

Southall, despite its size, was predominantly of wooden construction –
nonetheless the building had fared well
over the years, avoiding the worst rigours of
fire and smoke. A network of blackened
beams and pillars – 'teak everywhere you

Southall in 1904. Normal procedure was for engines to arrive at the station end, often crossing over the main line in pairs or threes, coming in from the various yards. Engines approached the turntable to the right of the ash bin, where fires were thrown out, proceeded to the turntable, turned if necessary and moved forward to have the smokebox dealt with. They would then move up the yard, coal and reverse back into the shed.

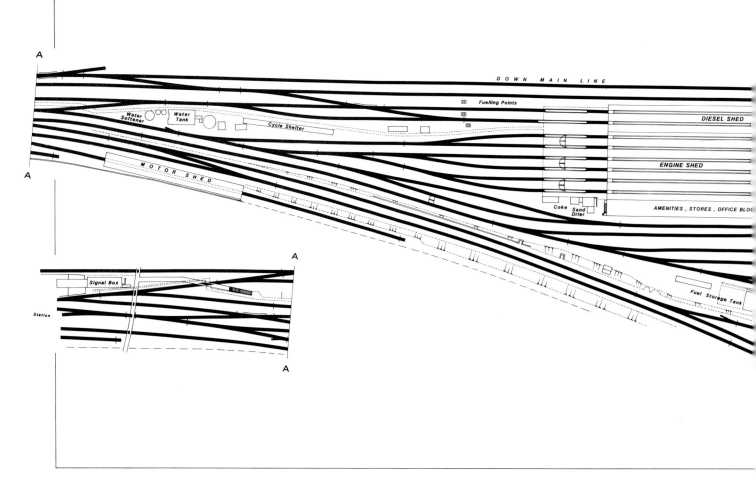

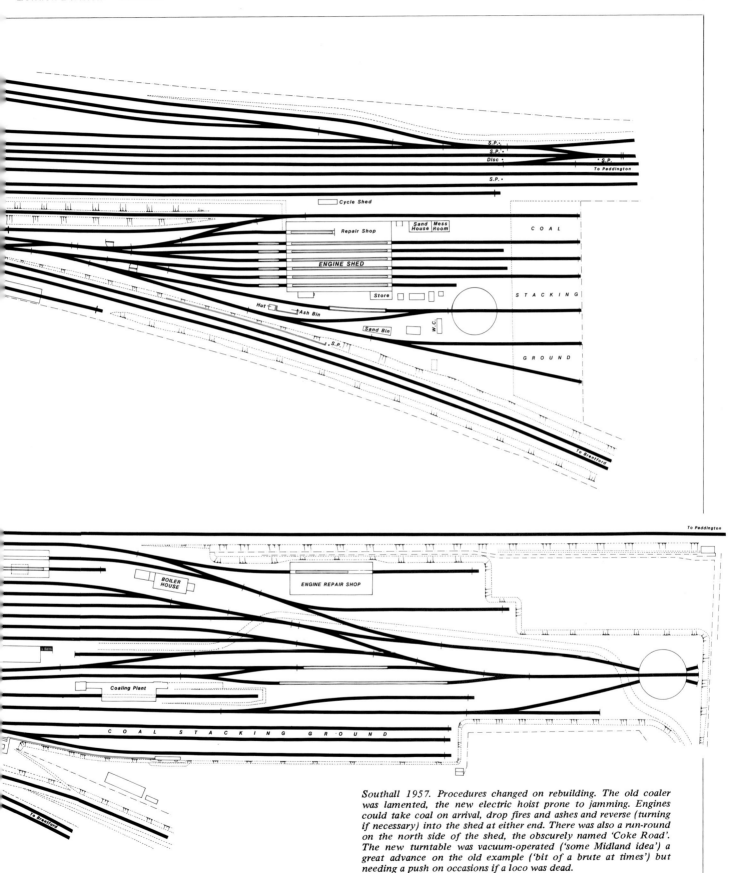

Southall 1957. Procedures changed on rebuilding. The old coaler was lamented, the new electric hoist prone to jamming. Engines could take coal on arrival, drop fires and ashes and reverse (turning if necessary) into the shed at either end. There was also a run-round on the north side of the shed, the obscurely named 'Coke Road'. The new turntable was vacuum-operated ('some Midland idea') a great advance on the old example ('bit of a brute at times') but needing a push on occasions if a loco was dead.

The area was bombed in the war, though the shed did not receive a direct hit. The roof was sufficiently shaken up, however, to require a temporary covering. The Southall tool van was invariably parked outside the fitting shop, and further vehicles, like this mess van, were provided for the staff, both those displaced by bomb damage and those extras taken on, including women. A bicycle shed was put in at this point, on the spare ground.   *British Railways*

looked' – supported a shell of planking. The low northlight pattern roof would have been vulnerable – it was still intact on the outbreak of war, but, by the early Nationalisation period, had been cut back and 'knocked about'. The original GWR slated roof had disappeared and a crude central ridge covering, of obviously temporary appearance, substituted. This covering was inadequate and the date of its application is not known. Proposals for a full scale renewal of the shed appeared first in April 1942, a wartime strategic proposal involving a comprehensive remodelling of the yard with enormous coal stacks, reflecting the depot's operational importance. Nothing came of this and the shed emerged from the Second World War battered, but more or less in its original disposition.

The GWR was much concerned with engine shed provision in the period between the end of war and Nationalisation, and in March 1947 Hawksworth appointed a

With so many yards and pilot turns, Southall engines often began and ended a trip running light for some distance. A return from Acton, having sweated hard, could be a freezing experience, or light to Park Royal tender first to pick up 'a Tyseley'. One could also work tender first for hours on a ballast train, all the way from Bicester, for instance. The coach body was put in during the war to serve as a cabin for Italian prisoners of war, put to work as firedroppers and on any other tasks that could be found.   *British Railways*

The 'Committee on the Construction of Locomotive Sheds and Layouts' issued its preliminary report on Monday, 21st April 1947, having been appointed by Hawksworth a few weeks before, on 7th March. It noted that 'type layouts and designs may not be literally applicable to any specific site' whilst 'Proposed Headings' included 'Roundhouse v. Straight Shed', 'Size in relation to Engines Allocated', 'Lighting, Ventilation and Heating', 'Smoke Abatement' and 'Clearances between Roads at Entrances'. On 5th June six designs were presented by the Chief Engineer, P. S. A. Bewidge, three in reinforced concrete, three in steel. 'The most novel features were the smoke chutes . . . Alternative D met with Approval'. On 30th October 1947 the new design for Canton, Cardiff, was approved, with Southall considered the same day, a rebuild noted as 'in mind'. A visit to the LMS shed at Aston, re-roofed in concrete, resulted in a confidential report, so appalled were the officers at the construction, Ashford on the Southern prompting a similar response. Exhaustive data were gathered, ' . . . Assuming that the distance on the periphery is equal to the chord subtended, the maximum number of tracks possible is $\frac{\pi \times 90}{11.21} = 25.2$.' Analysis of nineteen sheds built 1920-1947 found a weighted mean of 3.5 water columns per shed, whilst hundreds of frequency curves were presented. There were obscure statements — a single turntable was deemed suitable for up to 81 locos, but 82 required two. Construction was got underway, possibly in late 1951, certainly in 1952. It proceeded with all the haste post-war piece rates could bring about and little is remembered of the Great Western's endless computing. Enginemen were bemused at the almost frantic pace of the work, with scant regard for the operation of the shed. Engines were restricted to two or at most three roads, moving across as the work proceeded. The 'navvies' gave little thought to red lights or warnings, and rails were simply taken up as the job moved on. Now this could happen while the unsuspecting shed man was at breakfast, the engine innocently taken forward (in darkness) only for its front wheels to crunch into the now rail-less surface. The engine had to be dragged back by a '28' conveniently stabled behind, the problem then to get them both out . . .   *British Railways*

'Committee on the Construction of Locomotive sheds and Layouts'. The Civil Engineers' Research Section was called and an exhaustive programme of testing and theorising took place, employing a wholly mystifying programme of statistical, mathematical and ergonomic techniques. Other sites were visited, from Avignon in France to Aston and Leicester on the LMS, Darlington on the LNER, and Ashford on the Southern, and plans were examined for the new LNER roofs at Stratford and King's Cross. All were rejected as more or less inadequate. Experimental chutes and Robertson ventilators were installed at Old Oak and it was decided 'to keep these under observation'. All this had the crucial advantage that the company need make little capital investment while National-

isation approached: 'the complete rebuild of Southall' was 'in mind' in 1947 and on 30th October it was decided that the company 'should just reclad the roof, with 3 Robertson ventilators on the main shed and 2 smaller Robertson vents over the repair shop'. This was not carried out and only in the last independent days, on 18th December 1947, was a plan submitted for 'the new shed at Southall .... elimination of all supports in the shed is achieved by spanning the area in a single span ...... Agreed, subject to doors being omitted ...... doors for the diesel engine portion of this shed, however, should be omitted'.

Work did not finally begin on the new depot until the 1950s, a complex task carried out as all the shed's everyday activi-

ties took place round about. Most of the new depot came into use during 1953.

Steam came to an end at Southall about December 1965, row upon row of blackened, smoke-wreathed engines, with numerous LMS and BR types, and diesels, proving a lasting memory. In the late 'fifties and early 'sixties the overwhelming impression when confronted with a group of *Great* Western engines was bright brasswork in a sea of green. Undoubtedly engine cleanliness on the Western was ordered to a high standard; to the end morale owed much to being GWR, but much of it (amongst enginemen) was tongue in cheek, it being essential to establish superiority over any 'foreigners' and little good was acknowledged in the products and practice of others.

The new Southall taking shape in September 1952. The parcels car was crewed by the 'Diesel Link' — it included multiple units of Great Western design and was the second passenger link, but with only six or seven turns. The 57XX tank is likely to be the West Ealing pilot, sent out at about 4.00 p.m. with a (necessarily) full bunker. It would shunt most of the night, both sides, at the coal depot, coming back around 1.00 a.m. with an empty bunker.   *British Railways*

The six 'steam roads' and the two for diesels. Shed practice at Southall, as elsewhere, was, put simply, 'first in, last out'. The last engine off, say at 10.00 a.m., would be placed at the back of the line, followed by one off at say, 8.00 a.m., getting a row of up to ten, with the first off at 1.00 a.m. It was seldom possible to avoid hauling out a few to insert one in the line, but the new shed with its access at both ends, made work easier in this regard. *British Railways*

Southall remained a cold, draughty place, for whatever new design of shed was arrived at, engines would always run through doors. *British Railways*

On completion, the diesel portion of the shed had still to await its multiple units. Later there were to be all sorts of problems — both DMUs and locomotives often had to run all night to avoid non-starting in the mornings, and the heavy exhaust defeated the Robertson ventilators and hung in the shed. Without wind, conditions inside became worse than anything experienced in steam days. There was no proper disposal of spilt oil and for years a 'fill to spill' practice meant the whole area was soaked in fuel oil. It finally found its way out along the Brentford branch and an expensive separator, dug in a pit, was only put in when closure was in sight.   *British Railways*

0−6−2T No. 6654 and 4−6−0 No. 5952 *Logan Hall.* 'Halls' were popular at Southall with No. 7910 *Hown Hall* considered to possess a distinct superiority over the rest. The 0−6−2T had been put to work on Southall-Reading freights, returning the same night (there had, in the old days, been Southall lodging turns to Reading, of all places) and despite the usual association with South Wales, Southall men were familiar with the other big tanks, 2−8−0 and 2−8−2.

      British Railways

'Austerities' were common at Southall from their introduction. 'They used to rattle and bang a lot' and the mechanical lubricators were considered a bit odd. The new boilerhouse was relatively palatial and straightforward to operate and the new repair shop (below) a luxurious provision, highly regarded. A grab crane was provided for ash and clinker and the whole site was open and easy to work.   *British Railways*

The changeover steam to diesel was a long drawn-out, messy affair, blighted by deteriorating relations between enginemen and BR, but lightened, as ever, by humour. Diesel shunters came early, based at Old Oak and stopping at Southall for a week or so at a time, and Southall men had long been familiar with the AEC railcars and parcels cars of local origin. They were never popular, cold (an oil stove had to be provided for the driver!) and prone to breakdown. Diesel railcar sets on the London commuter work brought un-dreamed-of *green* uniforms; when asked to take out a steam engine, a 61XX perhaps, if a DMU was unavailable (a frequent event), these men would insist on returning home to change. Inevitably, they were christened the 'Untouchables'.

The rebuilt Southall was well equipped for diesel work and serviced much of the considerable Western Region London fleet of railcars through the '60s and '70s and Southall men worked 'Hymeks' on freights and had a 'Warship' for Thame oil trains.

Interior, Repair Shop.   *British Railways*

It was customary (as far as circumstance allowed) to stable the pilots (i.e. tanks) principally on one side and the '61s' on the other, with goods locos generally in between. It was not rigidly adhered to and engines were frequently mixed up (see opposite for instance). As elsewhere in London, the '61s' were worked as 'Tandem' engines with just two crews apiece, beautifully attended to with locks on each burnished lamp. Twelve sets of men, the Top Passenger Link, drove them exclusively, taking great pride in their charges, arriving early to warm the driver's oil in cold weather and packing their own glands. There were over 400 men at Southall, something like 180 sets of enginemen, and promotion was swift in the 1950s as all the top men were put onto DMU work, formed into four links.   *British Railways*

Southall in 1958 with (left to right) 1446, 6148, 5753, W21W, 3812, 90188, 6125 and 2890. Closure to steam came at the end of 1965 and the long run down and decline was underway. They were bitter years, punctuated by strife. The LDC voted on this motion on Wednesday, 13th April 1960: 'We are of the opinion that the present shortage of staff is due entirely to low wages in the industry and to general mismanagement of nationalisation. The policy of the management especially since the introduction of Dieselisation, has caused general dissatisfaction and frustration. We consider there is insufficient consultation with the men. No definite statement of policy and far too little notice of intended alterations of workings. The Operating Dept know weeks and sometimes months ahead of intended alterations, yet we whose lives have to be altered owing to changes in the link workings, are given only a few days notice. In consequence of this firemen have lost all sense of security, while drivers, particularly the older men, are dissatisfied and frustrated. This has been added to at this depot by the exceptionally low category of work on Diesel turns and the taking away of freight work from the depot. Until this is rectified, there will continue to be resignations. We feel that the working of rest days would worsen this position. – The mover and seconder agreed to an addendum that this resolution be sent to the management the E.C. and Sectional Council. Carried by 55 for, 1 against.'
A. E. Bennett

The railcars remain in use across much of the suburban and local network of the WR, an extraordinarily long-lived fleet which, despite signs of age (the bodies can distort at high loadings, making it difficult to shut the doors), looks set for use for some years to come. DMU work was run down at Southall in the 1980s leaving at the last only a few men, booking on and off. There was an element of farce about the whole thing – closure had been delayed again and again and the last fourteen met for their farewell dinner on Friday, 7th November 1986. The previous day BR had suddenly asked everyone to *stay on* and indeed, a number did. Reading, incensed, threatened a strike for the Monday . . .

Southall had proved a secure haven for various preserved engines over the years and curiously one of these proved to be the depot's 'last loco'. Back in the 1960s few could have foreseen Bulleid 4-6-2 *Clan Line* in this role; used on the Stratford steam specials, it spent much of the summer at Southall, initially for attention to worn horn plates, then bogie and boiler repairs. The opportunity to run it about the yard proved irresistible.

DMUs ousted the '61s' on the 'Paddingtons', the 'untouchables' understandably loath to transfer at short notice to the tanks. Eight hours on a rundown '61' would soon put paid to the new green uniforms.
Merchant Navy Locomotive Preservation Society

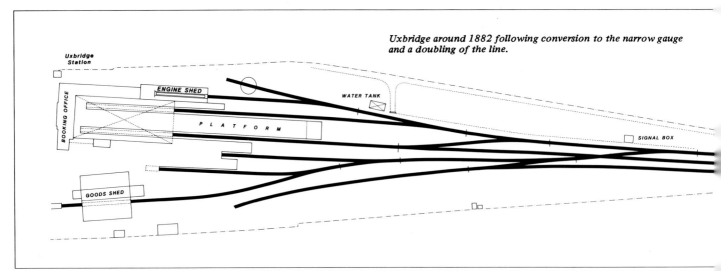

Uxbridge around 1882 following conversion to the narrow gauge and a doubling of the line.

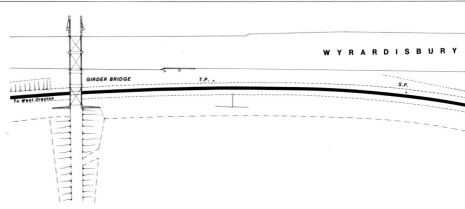

UXBRIDGE

The shed at Uxbridge opened with the broad gauge line in 1856. It was arranged, as noted elsewhere, in comparable disposition to the Henley building, and enjoyed a similarly murky history. It survived conversion of the branch to standard gauge but, with Southall so close, it was put out of use by 1897:

> The engine shed at Uxbridge, which has been unoccupied for Loco Dept purposes since Dec. '97 was pulled down in the latter part of 1899 (precise date not ascertained) by the Engineering Dept. The pit has been filled up, and the engine shed line is now a goods siding.
>
> The branch engine now stables at Southall and runs light to and from West Drayton daily.
>
> No Loco Dept work is now done at Uxbridge except coaling engine from a truck direct, which is done in one of the goods sidings. No coal stage. No staff is kept, the work being done by the West Drayton pumper who goes to Uxbridge for a short time daily.

Some consideration at least was subsequently given to engine work at Uxbridge and in October 1920 the Locomotive Carriage and Stores Committee approved the extraordinary sum of £200 for 'an engine pit'. In the event, this lavish facility does not seem to have been provided.

Uxbridge station had the architectural elegance of Henley, its close contemporary, but lacked the social advantages. The demolished shed and its filled in pit lay on the east side of the station. Motor trains, principally worked by Southall engines, typified the everyday branch service though through trains brought some variation and Slough men were familiar with the branch. Engine work ended at Uxbridge with demolition of the shed — the branch was too short, the service too intensive and engine depots too close for the retention of a single road shed (like at, say, Staines).
L & GRP, courtesy David & Charles

Four sets of men at Staines looked after the basic service. 'Nights' involved fire dropping and cleaning and the coaling of the engine, a miserable job and thus frequently, as 'relieving sick', given over to Southall men. The place was an overgrown, untidy corner, the shed a flimsy and insecure structure, remembered principally for the nocturnal unsettling rustle of vegetation and the hooting of owls. A wartime loop put in to the ex-LSWR line brought goods trains up into Acton. It was used largely during periods of bombing or when convoys had landed in the west. It was a booked Southall turn, the crews travelling down by train and awaiting arrival of the goods at Staines Moors box. They would 'read the road' for the Southern crews and come back with them, sometimes more than a shift later, with the return working. *J. W. Sparrowe*

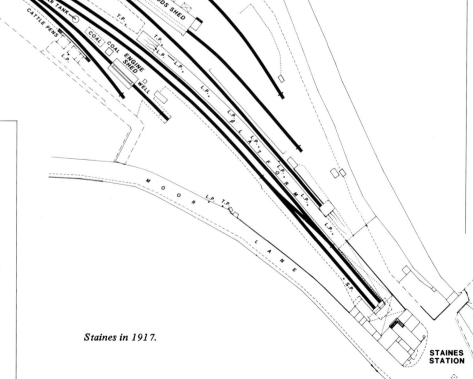

Staines in 1917.

STAINES

The line to Staines from West Drayton opened throughout in 1885 with a wooden shed put up for the branch engine. A couple of crews were based there over many years with an overnight job for a cleaner to attend the fire and other minor duties. Staff shortages, through the particularly unpopular nature of this turn, meant Southall men were frequently sent down to deputise. The shed closed in 1952 and seems to have been demolished by about 1954.

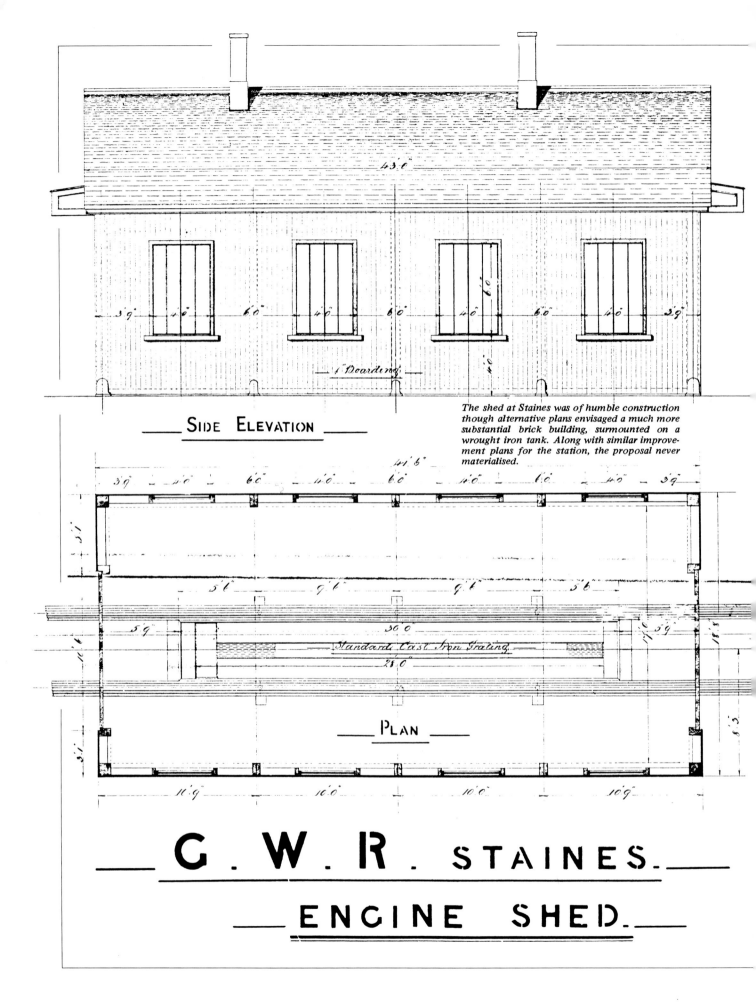

SIDE ELEVATION

The shed at Staines was of humble construction though alternative plans envisaged a much more substantial brick building, surmounted on a wrought iron tank. Along with similar improvement plans for the station, the proposal never materialised.

PLAN

G.W.R. STAINES.

ENGINE SHED.

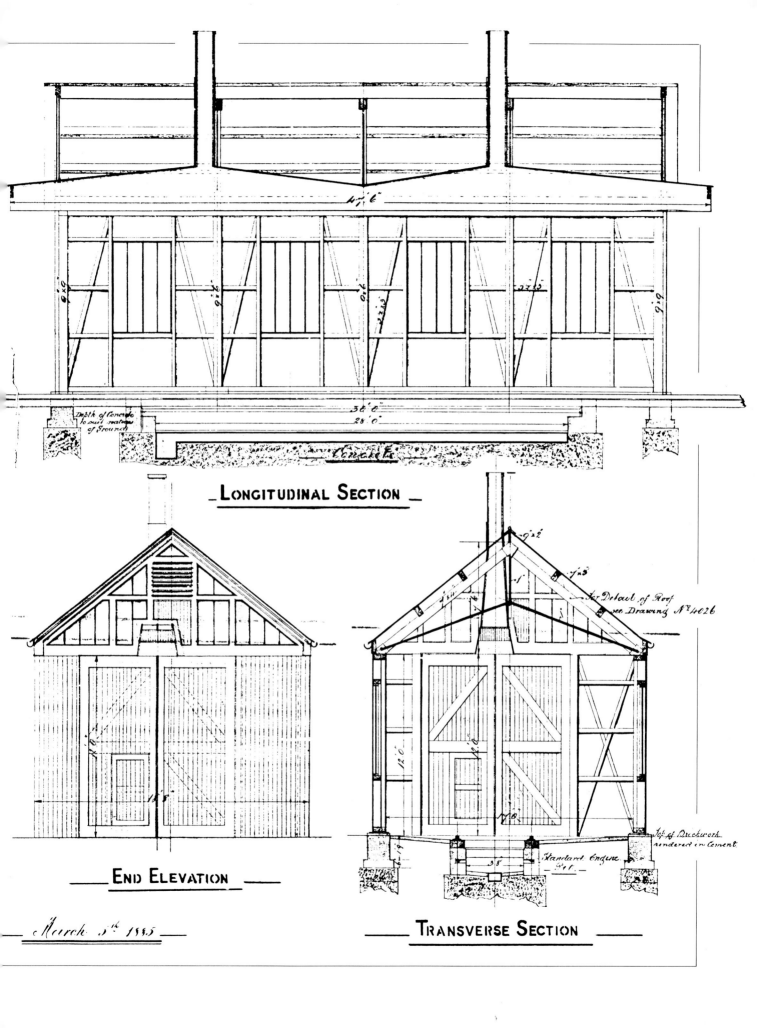

LONGITUDINAL SECTION

Depth of Concrete
to suit nature
of Ground

38'0"
28'0"

Concrete

END ELEVATION

March 5th 1885

For Detail of Roof
see Drawing Nº 4026

Standard Engine
Pit

Top of Brickwork
rendered in Cement

TRANSVERSE SECTION

SLOUGH

Slough was one of the first sheds to open on the rudimentary Great Western main line; it was well established when detailed plans of the proposed Windsor branch were submitted to the Buckinghamshire Clerk of the Peace at Aylesbury, on the 9th November 1847 'at half past one of the clock in the afternoon'. These ancient documents show the first broad gauge shed, a timber building (it is believed) reached through a separate arch in the Stoke Poges road bridge. A new shed came into being only in halting fashion, if contemporary notes made by the Superintendent, Armstrong, are accurate; it had four roads and opened, according to further brief notes made many years later in 1901, in at least two parts. The first section, the two roads nearest the running lines, 'came into use ... about 1868'. This unfortunately is difficult to reconcile with other records – 'part previously existed as a goods shed' – it is difficult to imagine a goods shed having being established here for a few years only, though the arrangement of the building, with its offset through road, does lend some weight to this version. The explanation may lie in the materials used – perhaps the Slough shed was built with bricks or structural parts salvaged from elsewhere. The second portion of the shed, and again this is odd, is said to have been added in 1872, 'together with the boiler house'. This date again is not entirely trustworthy, the Ordnance Survey (dated 1875) showing the main building without the boiler house. In place at this time moreover are the wooden lean-tos forming the workshop and stores, said by Armstrong to date from 1889. The 1875 O.S. map shows only three roads entering the shed at the west end, though this is most probably a drawing omission. Only the road nearest the running line is shown passing through the building, past the foreman's office ('part of the original goods shed') and onto a very early coal stage.

Early records and references contained within the Great Western Locomotive Carriage and Permanent Way Committee Minutes hint at Gooch's thinking on the Slough engine shed, but unfortunately do not satisfactorily illumine the construction stages, their precise dates nor the question of the 'goods shed'. On 28th October 1863 Gooch had sought approval 'for a new Engine House to be built at Slough Station, of sufficient dimensions to contain eight Engines, the present structure which affords accommodation for three Engines only being in so dilapidated a state that it must be taken down ...' [The planned east curve of the Windsor branch (dated 1847) took the new line *through* the building; it

was not constructed precisely on this course for the shed survived. Its subsequent demise owed much to a generally ruinous condition, though bridge renewal and widening would have demanded its eventual removal.]

The Committee recognised the desirability of providing accommodation but 'as a considerable outlay was involved therein', deemed it advisable 'that the Board of Directors should determine whether it is expedient to incur this outlay'. Expedience inevitably counselled delay and over two years later, at the end of 1865, Armstrong was still wrestling with the Committee in a report 'relative to the additional shed accommodation which with a view to the efficient working of Engines ... should be provided at various places on the Line'. An estimate of £1,800 for a 'New Shed to accommodate 6 Engines, the present one being in dilapidated condition' was 'referred to the Expenditure Committee'. This last proposal confirms that a two road shed, whether or not incorporating some earlier goods shed component, was now in prospect.

The origins of the second Slough shed lie then in the latter part of the 1860s; there had been a broad gauge 'turnplate' at the

'Slough for Windsor'. Commuter working out of London varied greatly amongst the companies and was both a part and a reflection of the widely different social groupings they served. From the west there was to be little of the workmen's services so characteristic of other parts of the capital and the Great Western stations, it can almost be imagined, seemed to proclaim this, with an elegance and spaciousness of style.   *Lens of Sutton*

original shed but this disappeared along with what was left of the building. After the new depot opened, this old site, long marked as a patch of rough ground, was given over to a coal stage of eccentric layout, with track behind. It was subsequently replaced by a stage of more conventional GWR pattern, less than perfectly sited for the operation of the shed, the peculiarities of which are described later. Along with a 45 ft turntable, it was put in place 'about 1885' with a new turntable following

some four years later. The main and Windsor lines were long in mixed gauge, the new shed and its yard having standard 4 ft 8½ inch track only.

The Slough district prospered; the whole belt of southern England of which it is part still does, and even before the end of the century the lines about the depot were cluttered with sidings and stock sheds. A greatly expanded station, yards and sidings dealt with a varied traffic – commuter trains, goods and shunting. This prosperity

Slough on 23rd August 1919.   *L & GRP, courtesy David & Charles*

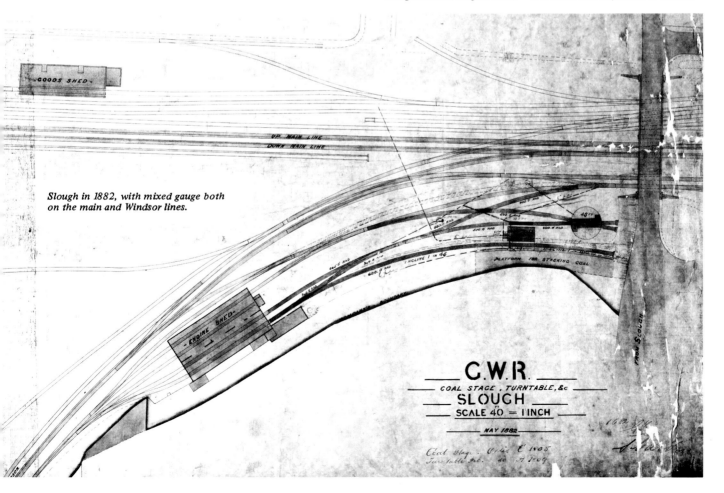

Slough in 1882, with mixed gauge both on the main and Windsor lines.

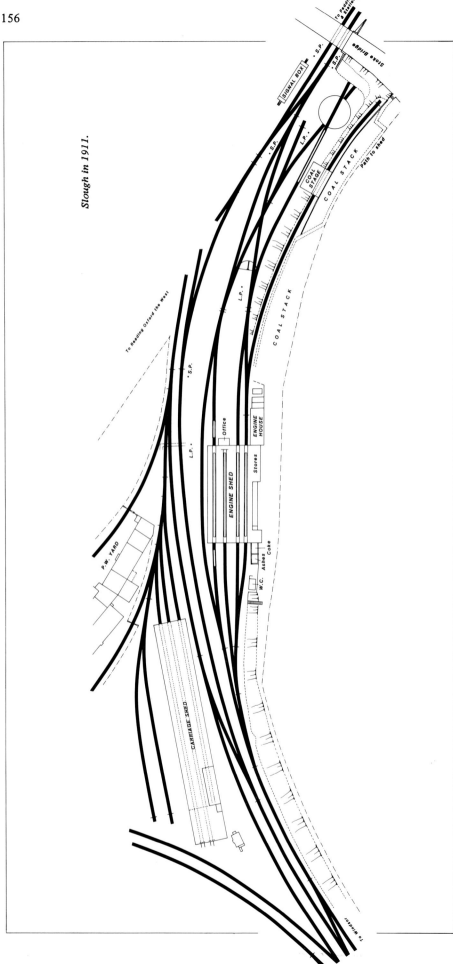

Slough in 1911.

now has largely side-stepped the railway which remains at Slough little more than a commuter channel, an inconsequential routing through post-war development of almost breathtaking crassitude; the Brunel *Bus Garage* lies within hailing distance of the shed site. From an early period Slough engines were chiefly concerned with passenger work, the town serving as railhead for a wide district, particularly that sweep of country to the north and west. By stages it was drawn into the Great Western upmarket London commuter system; there was also a lot of goods and shunting work and the engine complement was characterised by tanks. The turntable was never enlarged and served principally to switch engines around the various roads. Only one or two tender locos could be found at Slough over the years – 2–4–0 No. 810 was there in 1920 and during the war 0–6–0 No. 3696 was working out of the shed, on loan from the LMS. Mainstay of the passenger work, certainly as the 'twenties drew on, were the 'County' 4–4–2Ts, working the best London trains including the fast Windsor services. The 6100 2–6–2Ts of 1931 were very quickly put to work at Slough; they enabled withdrawal of the older types and the *en bloc* allocation improved life for all concerned. The class was concentrated in London, and Slough retained the largest single complement. By July 1933 they had brought about a transformation:

'517' 0–4–2T	574, 1486
'Metro' 2–4–0T	1404, 3500. 3563, 3589, 3598
'2021' 0–6–0T	2046, 2069, 2072, 2087, 2112
'County Tank' 4–4–0T	2221, 2224, 2225, 2226, 2239, 2242, 2244, 2247
'2721' 0–6–0T	2752
'3901' 2–6–2T	3919
'6100' 2–6–2T	6102, 6104, 6106, 6110, 6113, 6114, 6115, 6116, 6121, 6123, 6125, 6126, 6128, 6129, 6130, 6136, 6139, 6143, 6145, 6149, 6151, 6153. 6156
'5600' 0–6–2T	6623, 6634
'5700' 0–6–0PT	7798

The entire class of '61s' would have visited Slough in their thirty years of London working and most were based there at one time or another. In addition to the above 6100, 6101, 6105, 6107, 6108, 6117, 6119, 6124, 6127, 6131, 6133, 6140, 6146, 6150, 6152, 6154, 6157, 6160, 6161, 6164 and 6167 (and doubtless others) all spent periods at Slough. They were worked very heavily, on the regular basis of two crews per engine.

Continued on page 172

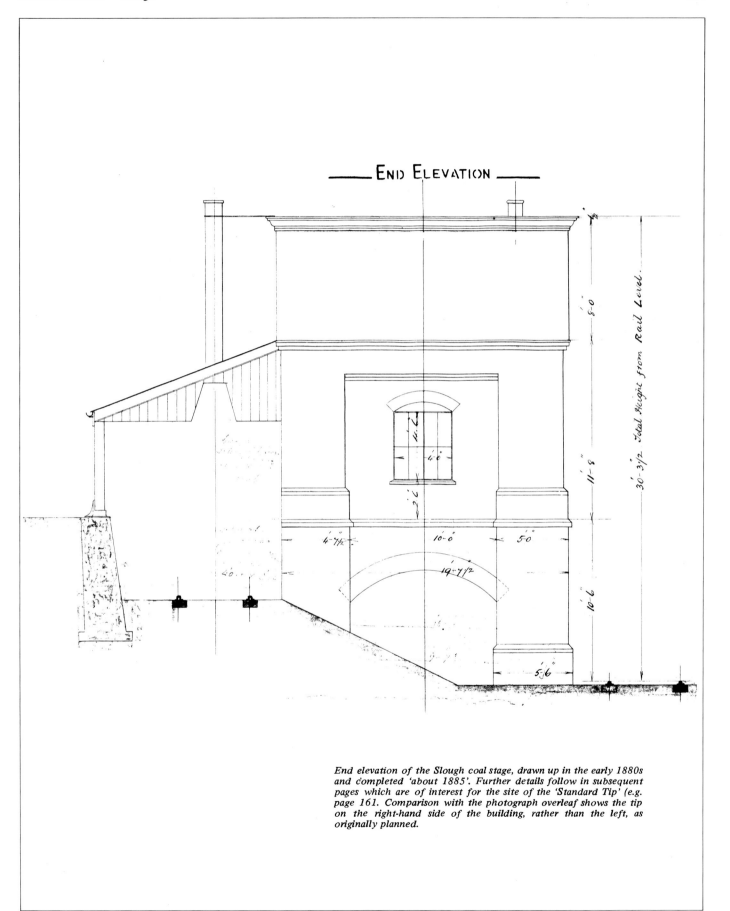

END ELEVATION

End elevation of the Slough coal stage, drawn up in the early 1880s
and completed 'about 1885'. Further details follow in subsequent
pages which are of interest for the site of the 'Standard Tip' (e.g.
page 161. Comparison with the photograph overleaf shows the tip
on the right-hand side of the building, rather than the left, as
originally planned.

No. 3596 with large cab on 1st November 1919. The tankhouse may have been built so, or the tip repositioned subsequently. The evidence of new brickwork on the left possibly indicates the latter, though whether it took place for operational reasons or as a result of some accident, is not known.

L & GRP, courtesy David & Charles

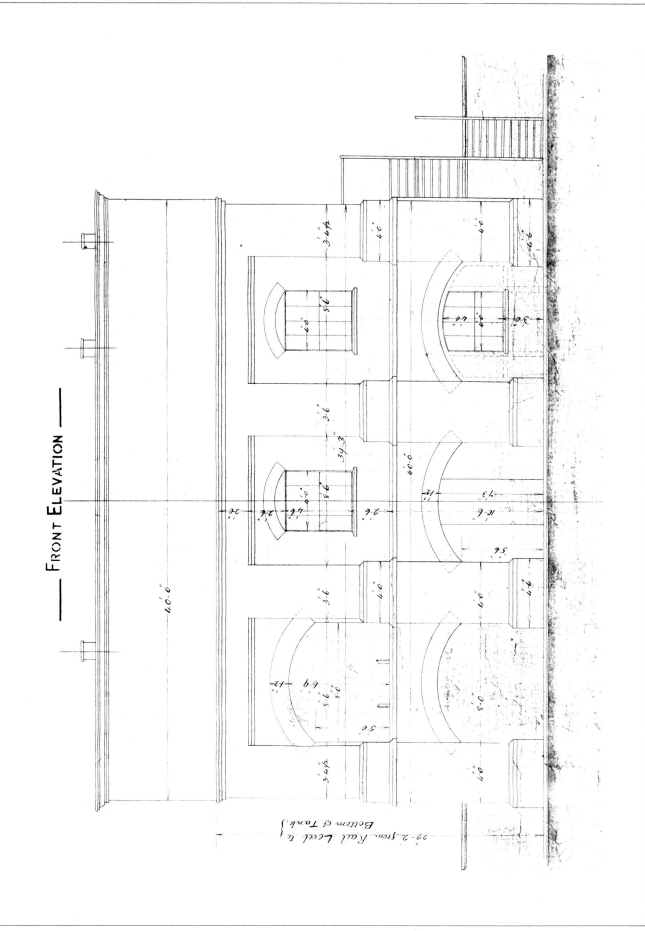

— Front Elevation —

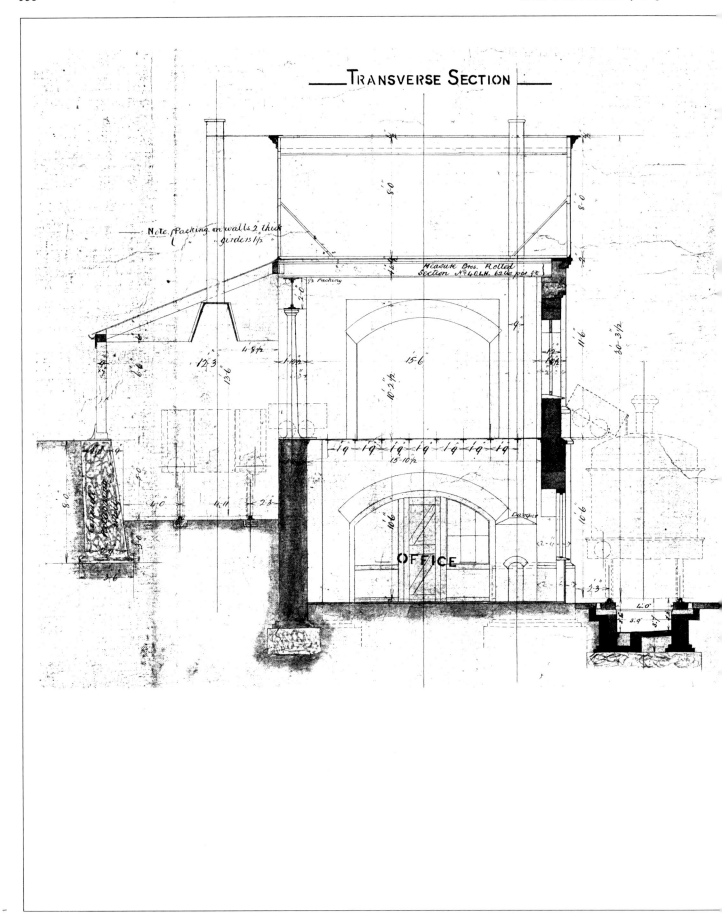

TRANSVERSE SECTION

SECTIONAL PLAN

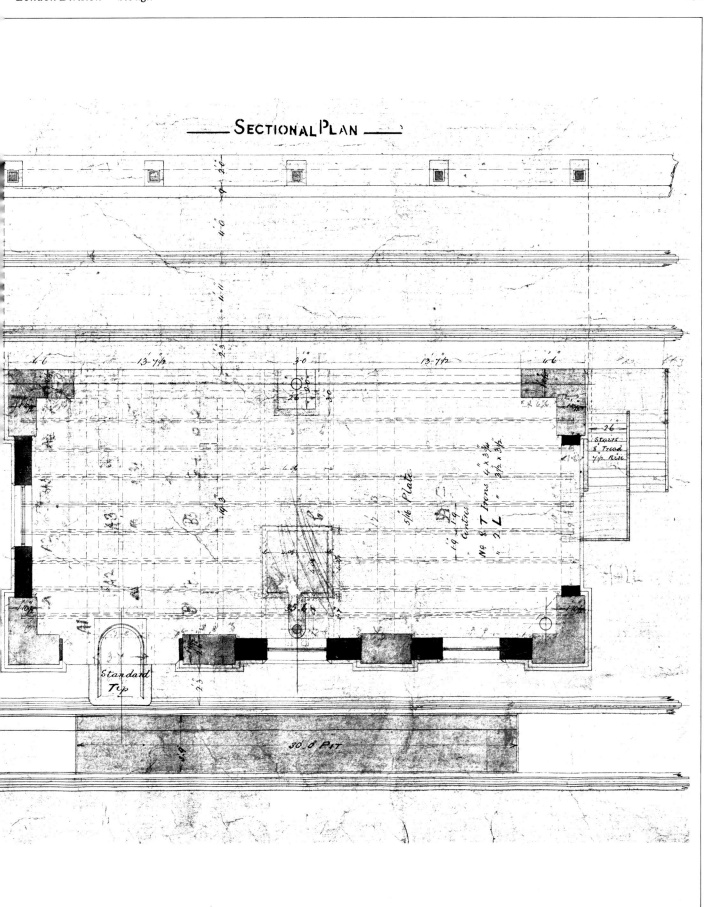

End Elevation

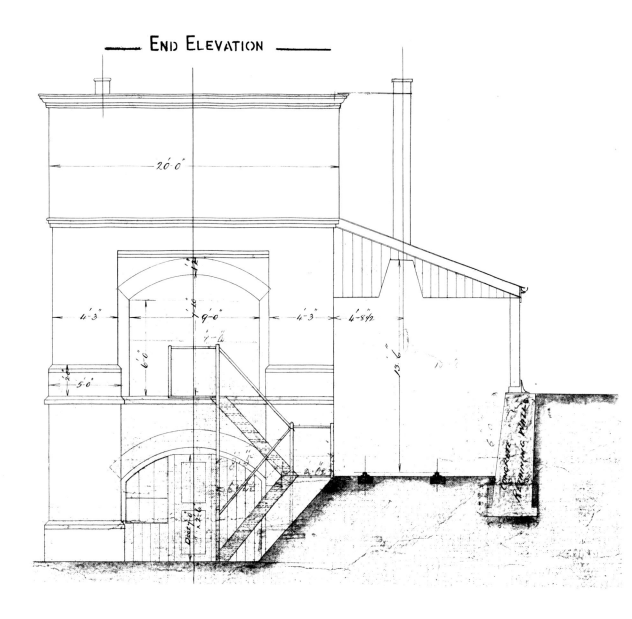

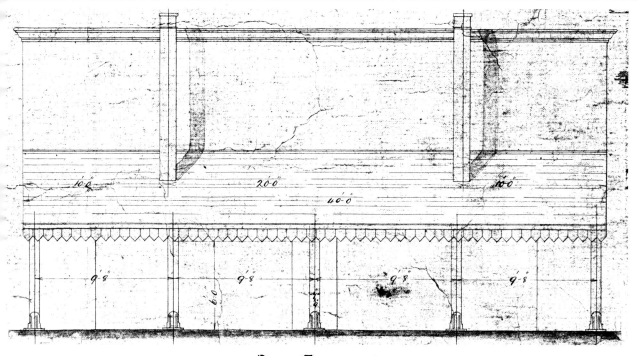

BACK ELEVATION

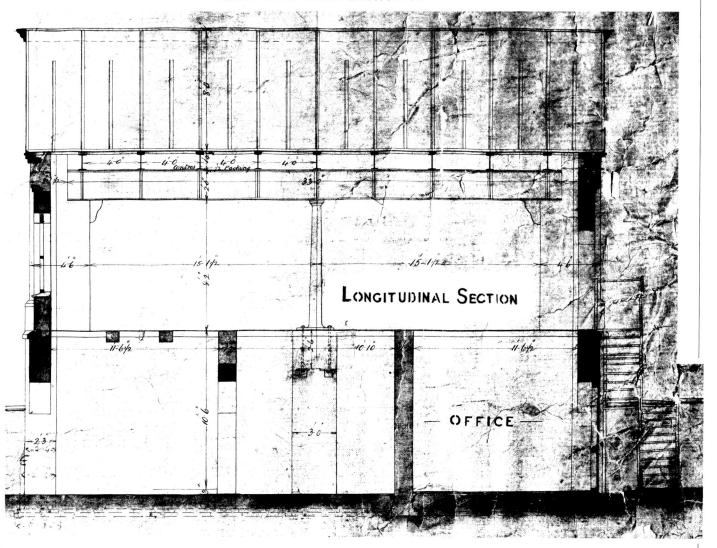

LONGITUDINAL SECTION

OFFICE

The shed at Slough was a curiously hybrid structure, such to make a sensible description, for the information of William Dean at Swindon, somewhat difficult. It was described as built in 'brick and slate' with roof principals in both wood (the earlier portion of the shed — 'part of which existed previously as a goods shed') and iron. Some indication of the stabling difficulties is contained in the details relating to the pits:

Length of each Line used for running Engines — 3 lines 136 ft each; 1 line 133 ft — Total = 541 ft

Length of each Line used for repairs — Part of running line No. 2 (about 60 ft) customarily used

Engine Pits — length of each used for running Engines — 3 lines 115 ft each, 1 line 73 ft

Engine Pits — length of each used for repairs — Part of running line No. 2, about 60 ft. *British Railways*

Slough from the Windsor end, with 'the stopblocks' off to the right.

L & GRP, courtesy David & Charles

No. 2343 at Slough in February 1920.

Collection R. S. Carpenter

No. 3226 in 1921. Tender engines were rarely allocated to Slough but 2—4—0s and 0—6—0s, in considerable numbers throughout the Division, turned up on a daily basis. Beyond is the brick stationary engine house; as at Southall, there were two boilers, side by side, one constantly in use for hot water washing out whilst the second was itself washed out or underwent maintenance. The building also housed an ancient and exquisitely crafted steam engine, like the two boilers, in the care of a fireman, driving through belts the contents of the machine shop alongside. This Victorian belt-driven shop remained in use until the end of steam, the half dozen or so Slough fitters and their mates occupied chiefly with the re-metalling of bearings, fitting new rings — jobs which did not require the lifting of an engine. Southall dealt with this sort of work whilst valves were sent to Swindon, in special, beautifully made valve boxes. The 'Slough Engine Shed Machinery' on 6th June 1930 amounted to: 'Drilling Machine, Shaping Machine, Lathe, Fan for Coppersmiths' Hearth, Compressor for Signals Department, 3-throw pump, Tangye pump, 2 Boilers'.

J. N. Maskelyne, Collection J. E. Kite

No. 2229 on 14th August 1920. The 'County' tanks, about eight of them, were on the main Slough jobs (principally the through Windsor trains) into the 1920s, replaced as the 'top link' type only by the '61XX' Prairies. 'The Windsors' were often non-stop from Slough and also ran to High Wycombe over the line from Maidenhead. They invariably worked chimney first to London.

Collection R. S. Carpenter

From the 1930s there was less and less variety in engine types to be found at Slough. The '61s' took charge of all the best Paddington turns, though some 2−4−0Ts remained and '57XX' panniers increasingly replaced the old collection of 'side tanks, saddle tanks and all sorts'.

W. H. Whitworth

For some decades prior to the 'thirties, 'Metro' 2−4−0Ts had taken a great part in the work of the London Division. They remained a characteristic feature and could still be seen on Paddington trains, an ever more peculiar sight amongst the 2−6−2Ts, until the outbreak of the Second World War. No. 1418 in November 1919.

J. E. Kite

Dean Goods No. 2512 and a Slough '35', No. 3563, on 9th May 1931.

A. W. Croughton

Nos. 3568 and 3592, condensing engines used on the Smithfield meat trains (see Old Oak) after arrival at Slough. They were displaced by the '97XX' pannier tanks and, after a period put aside out of use, went to Slough where they seem to have been designated as 'spare' engines. In February 1935 they were apparently disused but the condensers were removed, and 3592, for instance, on 18th July 1936 was at West Ealing on the 1.33 p.m. non-stop from Paddington.

V. R. Webster

No. 3568 minus its condensing gear on 4th October 1936.

Collection Peter Winding

Slough on 17th May 1930.

H. C. Casserley

No. 6133 of the new tanks, at Slough on 4th October 1936. The official unveiling of July 1931 read thus: 'By the courtesy of Mr. C. B. Collett, O.B.E., we are enabled to reproduce a photograph and outline dimension drawing of the first of a new series of 2−6−2 type tank engines, 60 of which are now being built in the Swindon shops for working Metropolitan suburban traffic. In this class the cabs are built low to suit the Metropolitan gauge and the engine has a tractive effort of 27,340 lb. as compared with 24,300 lb. of the 51XX class, giving an increased acceleration which will be very useful to meet the special conditions of the suburban services. The boiler barrels are made of special high-tensile steel to allow the working pressure to be increased to 225 lb. per sq. in. without increasing the weight on the axles. The plates are of nickel steel (36-40 tons tensile), supplied by Guest, Keen & Nettlefolds Limited. As the engines will have to work trains over the Great Western main lines and also the Metropolitan lines, they are being fitted with special automatic train control shoe apparatus on the pony trucks for the Great Western lines and trip-cock gear to suit the train control on the electrified lines. In working order the engine weighs 78 tons 9 cwt., and empty, 66 tons, the weight distribution being as shown on the drawing. The tanks provide accommodation for 2,000 gallons of water and the bunker 4 tons of coal.

Collection Peter Winding

The 'Old Boys' were a perennial institution at every shed and one or two could be found most Sundays cleaning and checking 'their' particular engine. They would be most put out if the object of these devotions was unavailable; it might happen that an engine suffered a minor derailment during shed movements and the first available '61' would have to be taken out. This upset everybody and the innocent shedman luckless enough to have been moving the loco went almost in fear of his life. The work included the Paddington–Henley 'fasts'; the posh 'bowler hat lot', the '61s' working chimney-first down and bunker-first back. Chimney-first working was preferred if it were possible – crews didn't bother with the Henley turntable but would, if time allowed on the Henley jobs, run out to Ranelagh Bridge and turn after arrival at Paddington. The everyday commuter work did not usually allow for this, timings were different and trains normally ran into the commuter side at Paddington remote from the Ranelagh Bridge pathways. Apart from the convenience of controls, bunker-first working could be made unpleasant through coal dust blowing in as the fireman opened the bunker for coal. The big 2–6–2Ts were enormously popular at Slough, they were extremely reliable machines and prompted a strong sense of loyalty. Over a period of ten years a crew might have as 'regulars' four or five different '61s'. Douglas Quar-

The shed approach on 13th March 1938.

R. F. Roberts

terman, between 1952 and 1957 (when he moved to Southall as driver), had 6106, 6113, 6164, 6150 and 6131, the latter a 'beauty' very strong and free-steaming. A friendly rivalry existed and Mr. Quarterman's father, also at Slough, swore his 6167 could out perform anything 'with practically no steam at all'. The cab brass-work was usually highly polished, the copper pipes burnished, the paintwork oiled down and the driver would have *lino* on his footboard.

The '61s', out all day demanded a generous helping of coal carefully piled up to the level of the cab roof. The windows protected by bars were seldom damaged, and in warm weather (with coal low) the bunker doors between the windows could be opened for ventilation, excessive draught prevented by the 'wind plate'.

The commuter lines radiating out of London and the series of north-west connections made for superlatives of time-tabling; the 2–6–2Ts were suitable both for heavy fast work and the lightest of branch traffic, and their abilities in this regard were thoroughly exercised. There was enormous scope for intricacies of the working day,

No. 6129 on Sunday 13th March 1938 with the 2.35 p.m. Paddington-Aylesbury train via Maidenhead, High Wycombe and Princes Risborough. The big Prairies rattled off duties such as this, and were popular partly because of it. They had to be handled with some care under particular conditions, however, and some Old Oak men at least experienced blow-backs unless suitable precautions were taken.   *R. F. Roberts*

No. 6148 with driver alongside. There was something like eighty sets of men at Slough, plus fitters, smiths, clerks and cleaners. Pay came from 'the office' at Paddington every Thursday at 2.30 p.m. and it was the solemn duty of the Chief Clerk to walk past the shed yard down to the station to meet the train. He was accompanied by a slightly nervous youth, a cleaner of perhaps sixteen years, whose job it was to carry the precious bag. Any attempt on the Slough wages would have evidently required the theft of a cleaner too, the bag being locked to his wrist through a chain passing up both sleeves and around the boy's back. Men queued in a corridor at the shed, a weekly ritual unusually productive of caustic humour. Money was only paid during that Thursday afternoon and anyone out on a shift or not due on until the evening either made arrangements for the next day or came in early.   *R. F. Roberts*

Tanks on 'The Smokebox' (above) on a crowded Sunday, 13th March 1938 and (below) No. 6133, long a Slough engine, on Road No. 1.   *R. F. Roberts*

illustrated by the regular Slough Christmas Day job, a '61' with perhaps six coaches on a trip to Paddington, thence to Aylesbury, two return trains to Princes Risborough, an Aylesbury–Paddington service, finishing up with a Paddington–Slough working. It required a full bunker of coal, regarded as a waste 'when you were lucky to see more than four passengers all day'.

The other tanks at Slough were occupied with a host of shunting, pilot and branch turns, complicated by the interwoven nature of traffic working around London. There was an enormous amount of relieving, with Slough and Southall men working tender engines from elsewhere, principally on goods. The limits of Slough working lay at Paddington, Aylesbury, Oxford (Yarnton on Goods), Swindon and Basingstoke, using Southall, Old Oak and other locos as well as their own. Pannier tanks worked one or two passenger trains like the 6.22 a.m. Slough–Wycombe. Slough shed covered Aylesbury for sickness and holidays, the '61' provided by Old Oak. Watlington had its own crews but again Slough men would be sent to cover. Disdainful of the ex-horsebox provided for their comfort, they very sensibly lodged in a pub in the town. Men and engines were provided from Slough for the High Wycombe pilot duties and the shed also 'stood relief' for Marlow. The branch 0–4–2T was changed weekly, a Slough engine taken out on a Sunday morning and the 'old' one brought back. The Marlow branch, belying its present denuded 'basic railway' status, was a very busy part of Slough working, particularly post-war when Thames excursions were extremely popular. Many came from the Midlands and

Pannier tank No. 3769 on 18th July 1938. Slough, as we have seen, was a tank engine depot but the crews did a considerable amount of relieving on Old Oak, Southall and Reading engines, moguls, 0−6−0s and 2−8−0s, 'Halls', 'Castles', 'Granges', and even '9F' 2−10−0s and Britannia Pacifics in BR days. The BR standard engines were inevitably disliked, though on grounds of comfort rather than performance. The coal slakers were a fine idea but the footplates were inadequately drained, the water running through the shovelplates. Various guards had been thoughtfully provided around hot pipes but proved to be receptacles for ash and detritus, impossible to clear. As the engine bounced along, the stuff blew up in a disconcerting fashion.

L. W. Perkins

No. 2087 on 13th March 1938.

R. F. Roberts

Windsor end of the shed, on the right the unlovely toilets, in front of the sand furnace, to the left the evil 'Smokebox'.   *Lens of Sutton*

the north, and Slough men (it was a favourite driving opportunity for passed firemen) travelling by train would relieve at High Wycombe, working the train to Marlow. This brought 4–6–0s to the little terminus where a 'Castle' could run round only by placing it against the buffers, clearing the points by a few inches. While the excursionists took a river trip to Windsor, engines (perhaps three or four in a day) and stock would proceed to Slough, where they could be coaled and any necessary adjustments made. The shed would be entirely overloaded on such an occasion and engines, once coaled, were stabled outside the wooden carriage shed or 'anywhere out the way'.

All manner of problems were encountered; the tip for the 10 cwt coal tubs was too low for 4,000 gallon tenders, and the fireman was required to shovel the two or three tons required. A number of requests went in for improvements at the coal stage and eventually the drop guides were motorised so the full coal tubs could be raised electrically. It was an imperfect solution and still involved fiddling and awkward positioning of the tenders.

The boat trippers were picked up from Windsor for their return journeys; this left several hours for disposal at Slough, time enough for familiar engines, but problems sometimes arose when the shedman was

confronted with something out of the ordinary. There was little about the servicing of a steam engine which by any stretch of the imagination could be described as sophisticated; on the Great Western it remained the most basic activity, with most of the firebox debris going out via the firebox door. The excursion traffic brought an LNER B17 'footballer' to Slough on one occasion, an engine fitted with a rudimentary drop grate. It promptly jammed in the 'open' position and with its train of sightseers sailing ever nearer Windsor, panic began to manifest itself with a phone call to Neasden shed. Neasden could make little of the foreigner's explanations and sent a man over to remedy the fault, crushingly, in minutes. The culprit was merely a piece of clinker jammed and out of sight, a daily occurrence where these engines were serviced but inexplicable to the uninitiated.

There were many other excursions, from the west and South Wales, fortunately bringing engines with none of the absurd foreign frills. These trains were destined for Windsor, and Slough men often relieved at Reading. Some passengers would look round the castle and take a short river trip, and Slough men would return them around 6 o'clock in the evening. Others went on to Paddington, for an evening at the theatre. This would also be a Slough job, but the return at night would be handled by Old

Oak Common or if possible men from the theatre-goers' home town or district – Exeter, Cardiff, or wherever.

There were yards, sidings and loops all the way into London, together with the estates and factories, making for a most complex series of workings. Slough lay at the extremity of this belt, working a considerable goods traffic, including esparto grass (for banknotes) and coal for paper mills, up the Bourne End line. Whole logs, teak and mahogany were worked to the Marlow timber yard and Slough also provided a number of local pilots. There were two at Slough, pannier tanks for years (successors in all probability to saddle tanks) and a Taplow pilot. The latter was important during the war (it was afterwards done away with and the engine put to work at Slough yard); Shermans from the Canadian Army tank depot at Farnham Road, Slough, were driven to Taplow and loaded onto trains in the down main sidings. There were two pilots at the height of the work (the down side looked after the tanks), the trains destined for Southampton and worked as far as Basingstoke by the inevitable Slough '61'. There was no balance working to return in the disruption of war and the 2–6–2T came back light immediately (having watered at Reading) without the Southern (or anybody else) getting their hands on it. There was also an 'Iver Pilot' during the war; a 'change yard' was established there for splitting 'Old Oaks' and 'Actons' etc., and Slough's wartime LMS 0–6–0 No. 3696 was regularly in charge. There was no water at Iver and only a tender engine could stay out all day. The engine was loathed but no amount of ill treatment could persuade it to do the right thing and fail.

Slough men worked other locos during the war including Southern 'Remembrance' 4–6–0s and the suspect USA 2–8–0s. Slough had wartime experience closely akin to those of other London sheds – interminable delays, relieving trains that hadn't moved in an entire shift, and sheltering under a '61' bunker during air raids. Direct hits on Paddington are vividly recalled. Precautions were taken to protect the Slough Trading Estate (rail-

served but worked internally by its own engines) by the simple device of a smoke-screen. This was precisely the sort of insane scheme relished by the British in 1940, its complications and side effects causing as much damage and dislocation as the average raid. The plan involved oil drums of some noxious substance dotted about the town like pillar boxes, to be fired on moonlit nights in whatever sequence suited the prevailing winds. Thus the vital industries of Slough ground to a halt in a choking yellow cloud of smoke, workers and others all but asphyxiated. The yellow haze lingered for days in people's houses and the vile drums were a hazard to anybody in the blackout, Slough shed call boys not the least.

One peculiar wartime institution at Slough was the 'Bomb Pilot', a sombre duty demanding an engine in steam at the shed

from about 9 p.m. Its train was stabled in the P.W. yard, 10-ton trucks of rubble and debris and a team of men ready to attend any crater damage, to fill the holes with a minimum delay to traffic. It was called upon several times, particularly near to Paddington, and its existence is an illustration in part of just how difficult it could be to destroy a railway. Some sort of service could usually be restored in days if not hours, a feature both the Germans and later the Allies failed to appreciate.

The last Slough lodging turn, a Taplow – Oxford goods (booking on at 2.15 a.m., off shed about 3.00 a.m., back up the next night), had been done away with on the outbreak of war. Such an arrangement was anomalous in any event and wartime imperatives allowed its swift demise. Perhaps the major phenomenon of the war

From the *GW Magazine* of January 1944 – 'Preparing for a clean start. Eton boys, who have volunteered to clean GWR engines, make a shine at Slough'. The real Slough cleaners had either been upgraded to fill vacancies or were engaged in other work. There had been thirty in 1940, organised roughly into seven gangs of four each. Within each gang the senior cleaner claimed those parts which had been cleaned most recently and thus represented the lightest work. The other three in order of seniority took boilers and tanks, with the most junior left with the motion and wheels. The smokebox was always cleaned with cylinder oil, and brasswork with brickdust, mixed with oil in the cleaners' stores. The shed owed its dismal interior, until electricity arrived, much to the antics of the cleaners, who promptly flicked to destruction with cleaning rags any working gas mantle, on the principle that the poorer the illumination, the less the foremen could see. The reality of cleaning life at Slough, with its 'Smokebox', was so far removed from that at Eton as to be almost grotesque. Given the anarchic tendencies of the Old Oak and Willesden boys, it is hard to believe this experiment lasted long without violence.

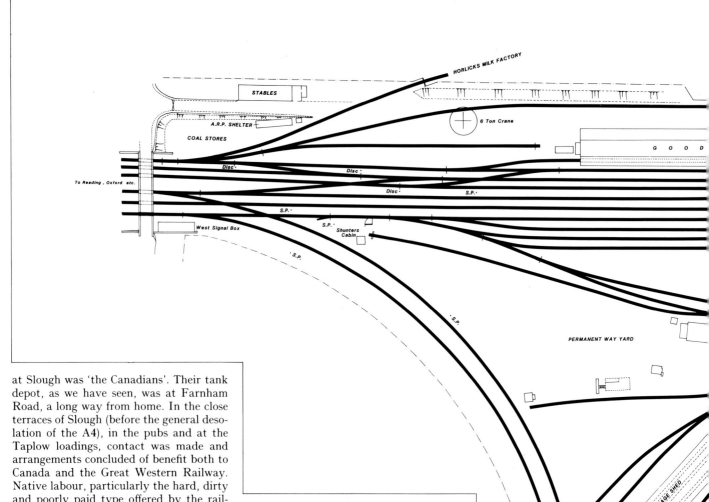

at Slough was 'the Canadians'. Their tank depot, as we have seen, was at Farnham Road, a long way from home. In the close terraces of Slough (before the general desolation of the A4), in the pubs and at the Taplow loadings, contact was made and arrangements concluded of benefit both to Canada and the Great Western Railway. Native labour, particularly the hard, dirty and poorly paid type offered by the railways, became scarce in the Second World War. The two coalmen at Slough were expected to shift $14\frac{1}{2}$ tons *before* piece rates began but were 'past it' in the 1940s. With the operation of the depot dependent upon the proper coaling of engines, an elaborate and entirely unofficial system of working was instituted. Canadians from the Farnham Road depot worked nights shovelling coal on a strictly 'cash on the nail' basis, the sleep made up in daytime kips (by rota) inside Shermans at the depot. The system survived a notable 'clamp down' raid by MPs to become a local institution in its own right. GWR men in the Southall–Slough area (and others through further bartering initiatives) were for months envied for their Canadian issue cigarettes (recognisable in packs of 24), boots, and other items.

There were six links at Slough – No. 1, the 'Top Passenger', comprising 18 turns. The principal advantage of a place in this link was the 'daytime' nature of the work. You were likely to have a more settled existence with the earliest turn at 4.45 a.m. and the latest around four o'clock in the afternoon. No. 2, the '2nd Passenger Link',

started earlier at 3.25 a.m. and the 18 turns could start through to 1 a.m. the following morning. No. 3 was the 'Top Goods' Link, 24 turns over 24 hours with one or two passenger jobs. Much of the work involved relief on 2–8–0s from Southall, Reading and elsewhere, and involvement in the freight traffic from Moreton Yard to Hayes, Slough, and Acton and transfers with the SR at Reading. The link included the Oxford goods and the 'Aylesbury Petrol', the latter at 1.45 a.m. the first engine off Slough shed light to Taplow to pick up a train of petrol tanks. No. 4, the 'Iver Link', was again concerned with goods. There were 12 turns, most of them 'control' jobs, the foreman phoning for instructions as necessary. The 10 turns of No. 5 link were generally light duties – pilots and local goods, and No. 6 was the 'Pilot Link' – 12 turns including the shed and some local shunting. There were over 150 footplatemen at Slough, the cleaners, fitters and clerks bringing the total to something like 300.

Various small improvements took place at Slough over the years. Some attention was given to the coal stage in the summer

of 1907, with £403 approved for a 'renewal' of 'coal stage tip and engine pit'. There was trouble with the well in the late 'thirties, and on 23rd August 1939 it was agreed to pay Messrs Guthrie Allsebrook & Co. £313 13 s. 9d. for the 'sinking of a new supply borehole'. A steam pump sufficed for the well until the 1950s, when it was replaced by a rather less reliable electric pump. The old steam arrangement gave almost continuous service but required rather more attention; the electric replacement 'gave out every now and then' and the columns had to be served by an emergency town supply, at 10d. per 1,000 gallons.

A road ran alongside the shed to provide access to the west part of the yard and its

Continued on page 189

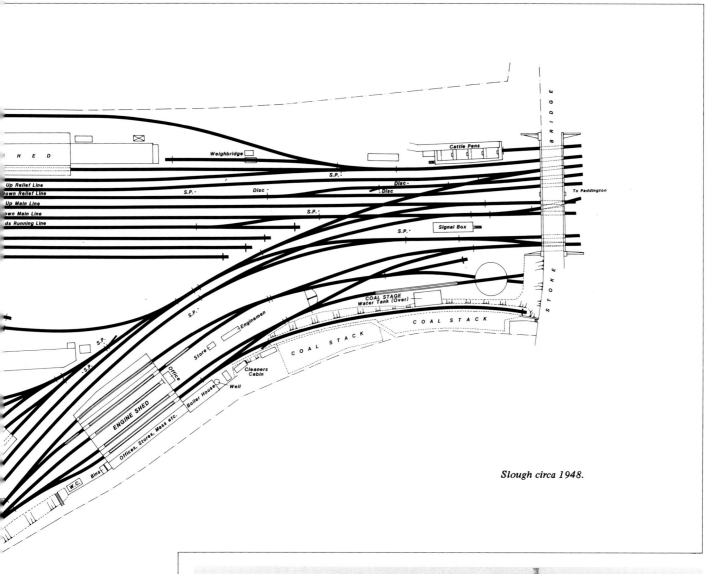

Slough circa 1948.

No. 2112, notable for its many years' service on the Watlington branch. *F. M. Gates*

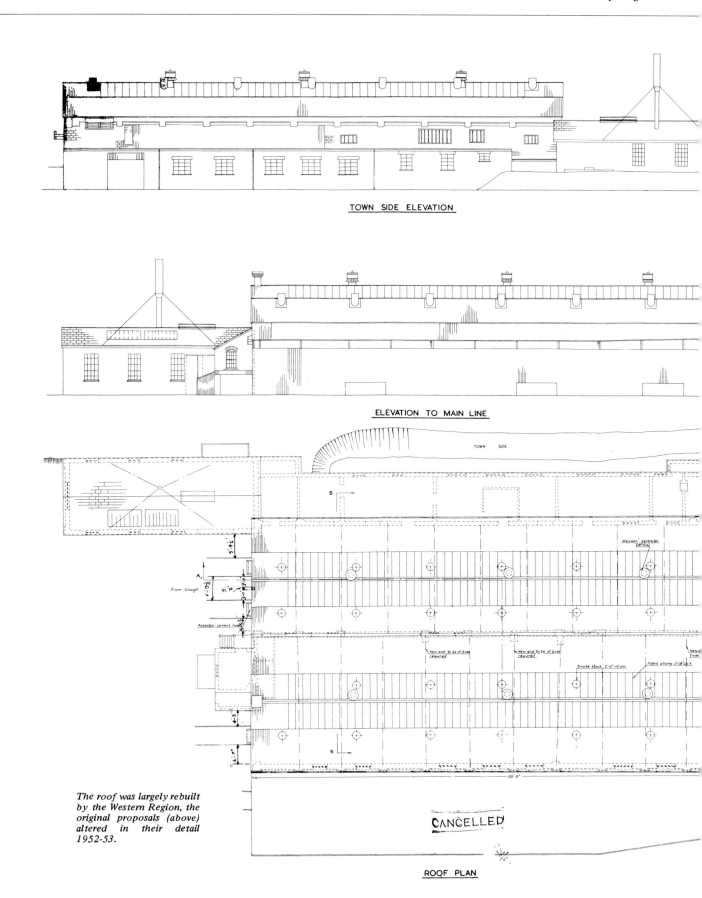

TOWN SIDE ELEVATION

ELEVATION TO MAIN LINE

The roof was largely rebuilt by the Western Region, the original proposals (above) altered in their detail 1952-53.

CANCELLED

ROOF PLAN

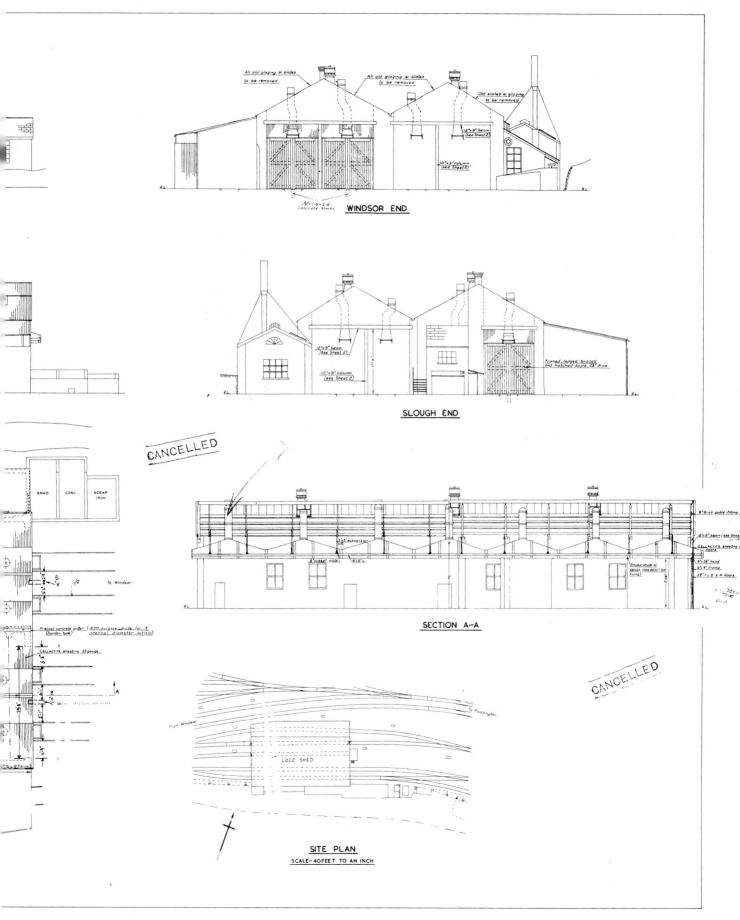

WINDSOR END

SLOUGH END

CANCELLED

SECTION A-A

CANCELLED

SITE PLAN

SCALE-40 FEET TO AN INCH

LOCO SHED

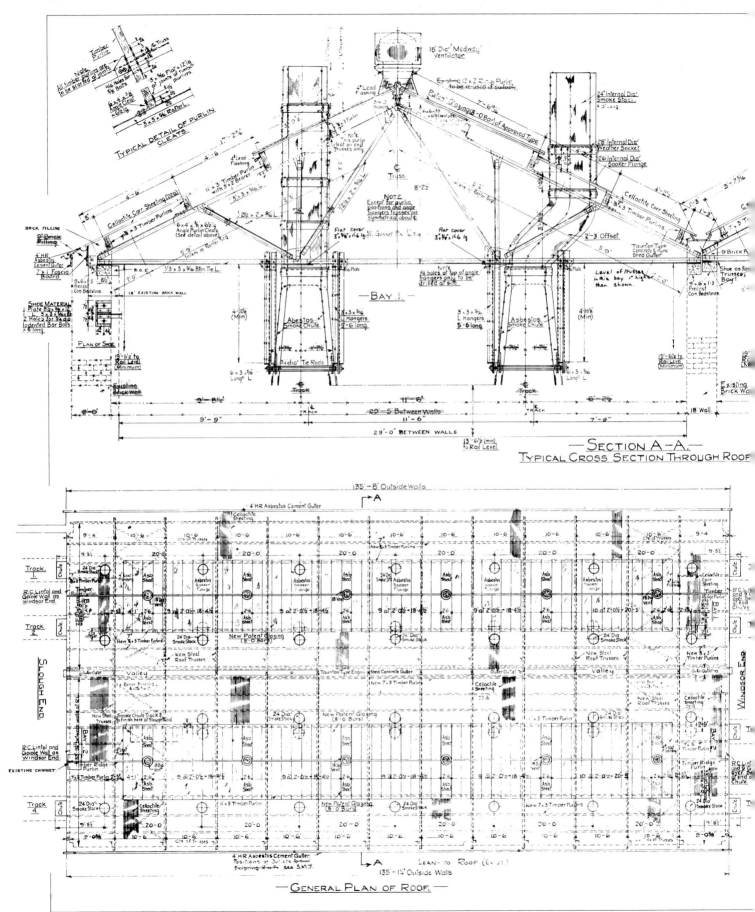

— SECTION A–A —
TYPICAL CROSS SECTION THROUGH ROOF

— GENERAL PLAN OF ROOF. —

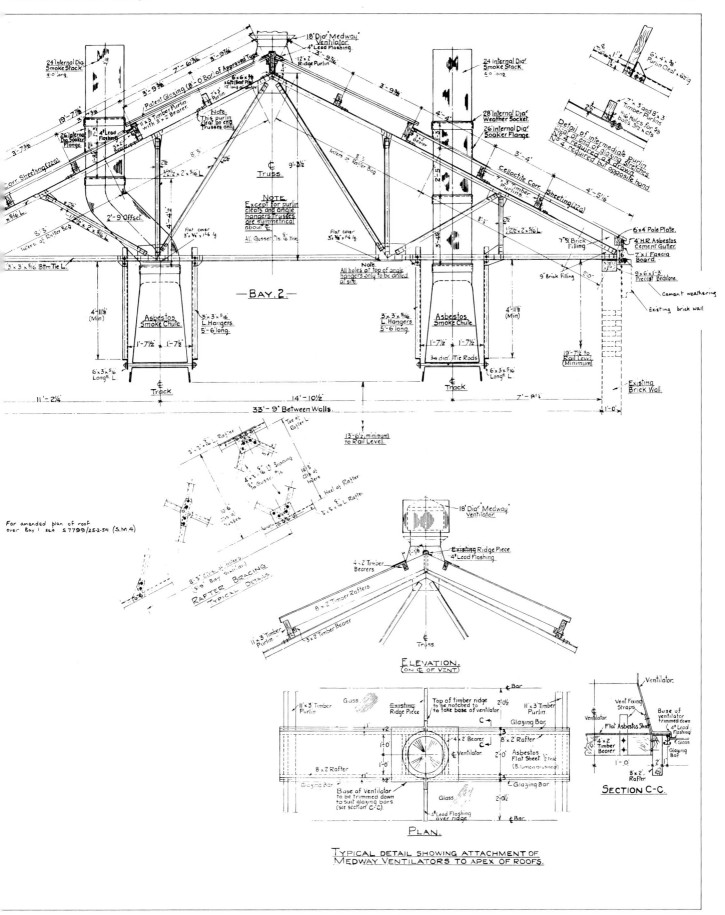

ELEVATION.
(ON ℄ OF VENT)

PLAN.

SECTION C-C.

TYPICAL DETAIL SHOWING ATTACHMENT OF
MEDWAY VENTILATORS TO APEX OF ROOFS.

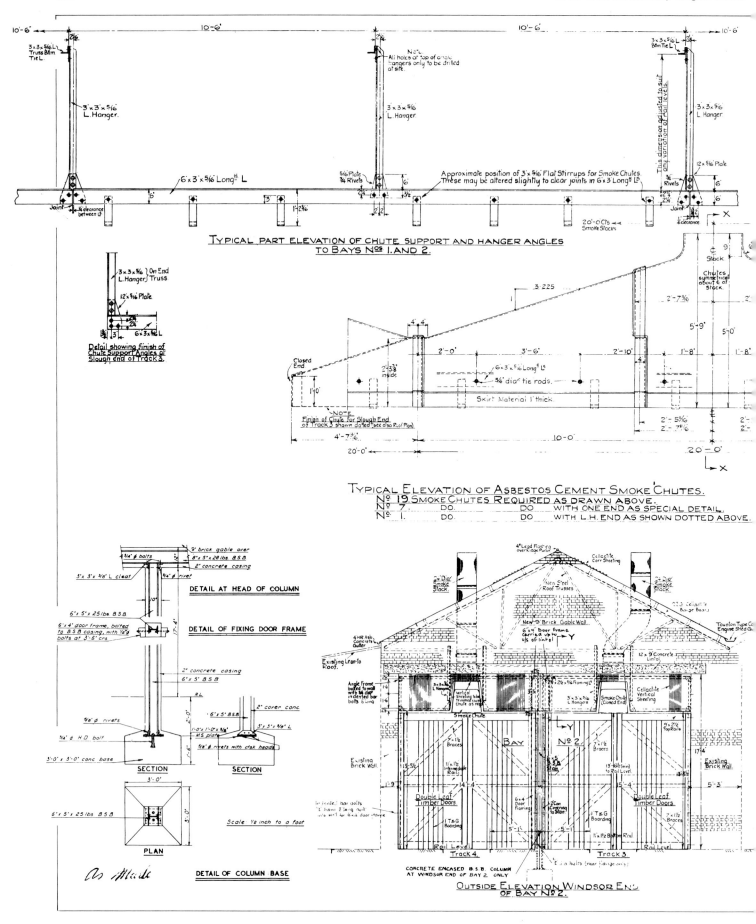

TYPICAL PART ELEVATION OF CHUTE SUPPORT AND HANGER ANGLES
TO BAYS Nos 1. AND 2.

Detail showing finish of
Chute Support Angles at
Slough end of Track 3.

TYPICAL ELEVATION OF ASBESTOS CEMENT SMOKE CHUTES.

No 19. SMOKE CHUTES REQUIRED AS DRAWN ABOVE.
No 7. DO. DO. WITH ONE END AS SPECIAL DETAIL.
No 1. DO. DO. WITH L.H. END AS SHOWN DOTTED ABOVE.

DETAIL AT HEAD OF COLUMN

DETAIL OF FIXING DOOR FRAME

SECTION

SECTION

PLAN

As Made

DETAIL OF COLUMN BASE

Scale: ½ inch to a foot

OUTSIDE ELEVATION WINDSOR END
OF BAY No 2.

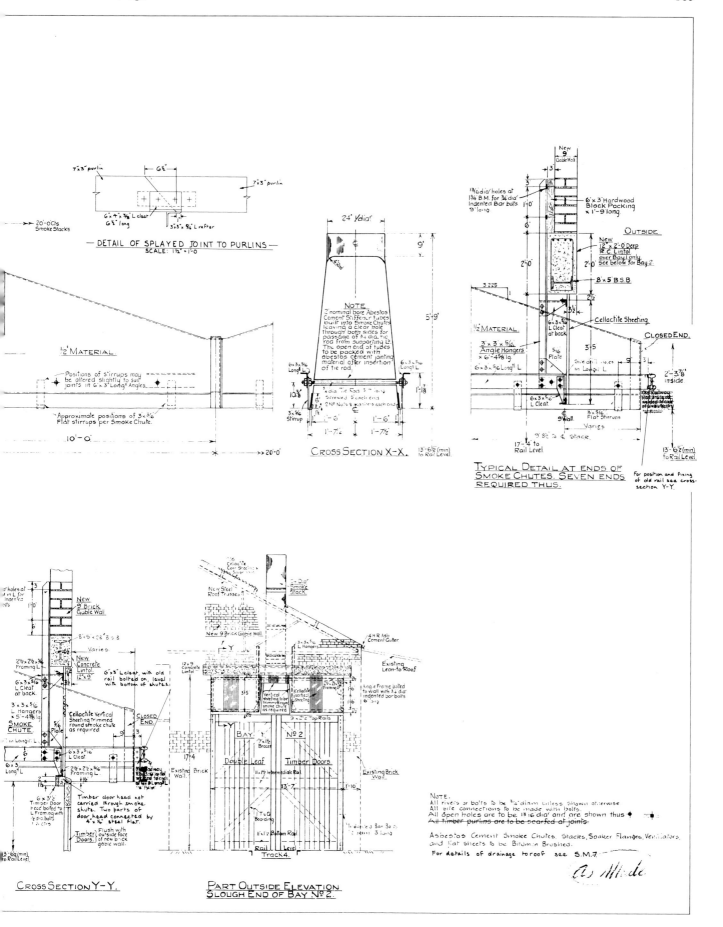

DETAIL OF SPLAYED JOINT TO PURLINS
SCALE: 1½" = 1'-0

CROSS SECTION X-X.

TYPICAL DETAIL AT ENDS OF SMOKE CHUTES. SEVEN ENDS REQUIRED THUS.

CROSS SECTION Y-Y.

PART OUTSIDE ELEVATION
SLOUGH END OF BAY Nº 2.

NOTE.
All rivets or bolts to be ¾" diam unless shown otherwise.
All site connections to be made with bolts.
All open holes are to be 13/16 dia' and are shown thus
All timber purlins are to be scarfed at joints.

Asbestos Cement Smoke Chutes, Stacks, Soaker Flanges, Ventilators
and flat sheets to be Bitumen Brushed.

For details of drainage to roof see S.M.7

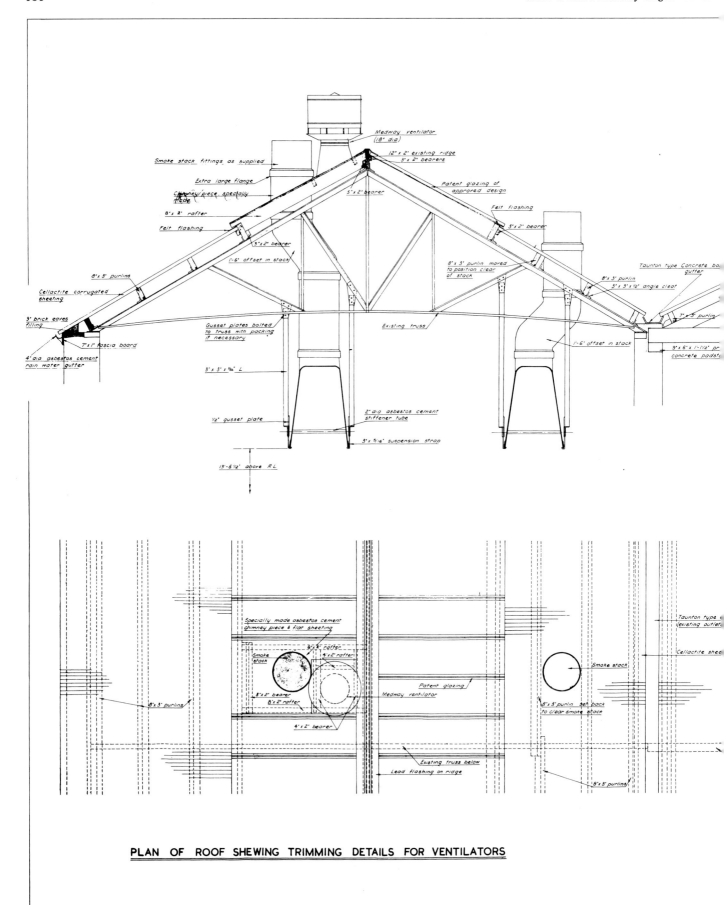

PLAN OF ROOF SHEWING TRIMMING DETAILS FOR VENTILATORS

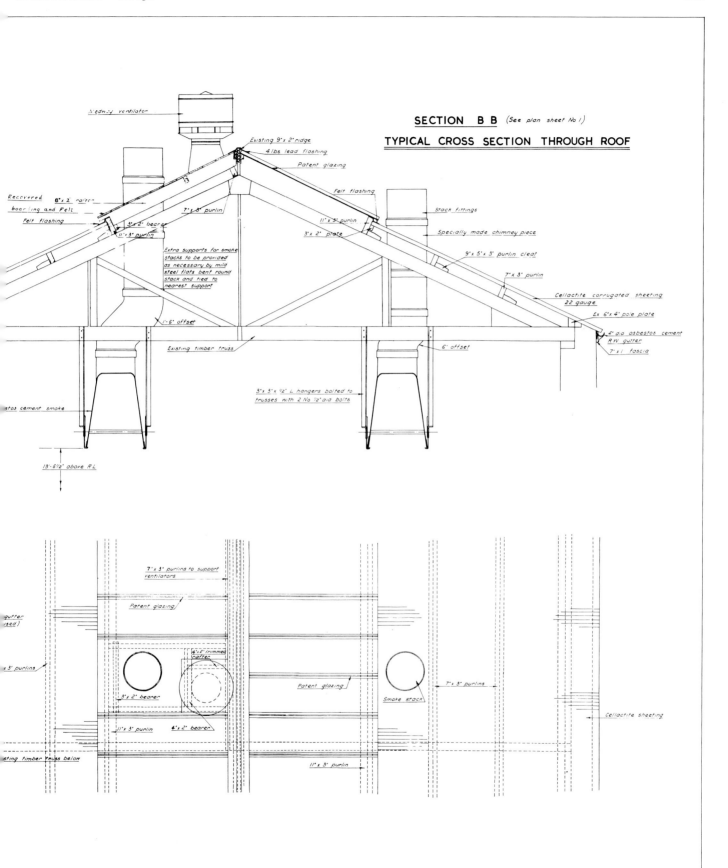

SECTION B B *(See plan sheet No 1)*
TYPICAL CROSS SECTION THROUGH ROOF

Medway ventilator

Existing 9" x 2" ridge

4 lbs lead flashing

Patent glazing

Felt flashing

Stack fittings

Recovered   8" x 2" rafter
boarding and Felt

Felt flashing

7" x 3" purlin

3" x 2" bearer

11" x 3" purlin

11" x 3" purlin

3" x 2" plate

Specially made chimney piece

9" x 5" x 3" purlin cleat

7" x 3" purlin

Extra supports for smoke
stacks to be provided
as necessary by mild
steel flats bent round
stack and tied to
nearest support

Cellactite corrugated sheeting
22 gauge

Ex 6" x 4" pole plate

1'-6" offset

4" dia asbestos cement
R.W gutter

7" x 1 fascia

Existing timber truss

6" offset

...tos cement smoke

3" x 3" x ½" L hangers bolted to
trusses with 2 No ½" dia bolts

13'-6½" above R L

7" x 3" purlins to support
ventilators

Patent glazing

gutter
...ised)

..3" purlins

4" x 2" trimmed
rafter

Patent glazing

3" x 2" bearer

Smoke stack

7" x 3" purlins

Cellactite sheeting

11" x 3" purlin

4" x 2" bearer

...ting timber truss below

11" x 3" purlin

The roof renewal amounted almost to a rebuilding of the shed. A variety of further proposals emerged later in the 1950s to adapt the depot still further for diesels, but little appeared apart from the ill-starred fuel tank. The adjacent P.W. yard and carriage shed had proved handy over the years at peak periods (engines off the Marlow excursions might be stabled here) and for whatever DMU sets required to stop for periods at Slough. Tuition on the railcar sets was rudimentary in the extreme compared to that subsequently given on the main line diesel locomotives and some bizarre incidents occurred, one set being reversed straight through the rear wall of the old carriage shed.

Lens of Sutton

termination, the 'stopblock'. Engines came on to the shed along this road and smoke-box cleaning was usually the first part of the disposal procedure. Inevitably, with the railwayman's unique economy of speech, it was referred to as 'The Smoke-box', a description made uncomfortably more appropriate with the erection of a lean-to, ugly and unventilated. It was pro-vided during the war, the Slough smoke-screen not considered sufficient to mask the less than brilliant light of flare lamps. £1,290 was approved for this work on 25th May 1944 and 'The Smokebox', essentially a covered ash shelter on the principle of those at Old Oak and elsewhere, became in most respects a worse place to work than the open air.

There were few sheds less suitably laid out than Slough. It was a hotch-potch arrangement of buildings and tracks in a disposition so perverse as to be practically unique. Engines came on to the shed from the east, from Slough station, and, after passing under the roadbridge, halted or proceeded, depending on the signal displayed. 'The Smokebox' and its road would be considered full with three or four '61s' and the shedman would change the 'signal' – actually an engine head lamp – from white to red. With tubes blown, the engine would be moved across to the turn-table area, a concrete apron known as the 'firepit' – there was no actual pit here and fires were merely thrown out on the con-crete base. With specific crews allotted each engine, it was important to stable at Slough

in the order of 'going off', and the foreman's list would be carefully scrutinised. Engines were taken onto the 'table and either turned or simply 'switched' for the coal stage road, the operation dependent on whether the engine was next required for Reading or Paddington. In either case it would be positioned chimney first. The engine would be coaled before stabling and, whilst under the stage, the ash pan was usually raked out. Water was taken only when going off shed. The shed roads (ign-oring 'The Smokebox') were numbered 1 to 4 beginning with that nearest the running lines, and, after coaling, engines would proceed to No. 4, which was always kept clear, pass through and reverse into No. 3 or No. 2. If the engine needed some fitting attention – valves pistons or something – it would be stabled on No. 2, the dead end road; if it was to go out fairly soon, that afternoon or whatever, it was placed down by the 'stops'. No. 1 was the washout road though this could sometimes take place at the back end of No. 3. It was indeed a 'hell of a jigsaw' with all engines (up to forty) to be tucked away by midnight. Sometimes the last in was first out, an instance requir-ing the engine to reverse outside No. 4 after leaving the coal stage, then reverse again to stable outside No. 1. At each end of the latter were preparation pits, a feature in extremely short supply at Slough.

Operations at Slough were complicated by a cramped and primitive nineteenth-century building and layout. This was a disadvantage many depots laboured under,

but at Slough the staff were compelled to adopt procedures that were positively arcane, if not downright bizarre. No. 4 road, as we have seen, was customarily left clear; it served indeed as a principal point of ingress-egress to the depot. This was awkward enough, in that engines pro-ceeding from the coal stage required a path through the shed – less covered accom-modation was in consequence available for stopped and stabled engines, but there were far more troublesome aspects to the eccen-tric siting of the coal stage. It was a con-ventional ramp approach and the string of loco coal wagons had to be shunted *through* the shed, via the ludicrous No. 4 road, immediately prior to a vigorous hoist up the coal stage incline. Maximum effort was required just as the shed 'tankie' was under the ancient rafters; bits of the timber smoke chutes were constantly blown off under the force of the blast and No. 4 was generally littered with debris. These antics had a less than beneficial effect upon the roof, which was subsequently rebuilt with the type of ventilators finding favour on the GWR in the late 1940s. As part of the support for the new structure, a wall, with door open-ings, was erected between Nos. 2 & 3 roads.

That Slough shed was impossibly arranged was acknowledged; there had been various plans and proposals over the years, the most comprehensive dating from the early years of the century. Two round-houses were contemplated at one time, the new coal stage and approaches taking up the old shed and its yard. In the middle part of 1952 plans were got out for the comprehensive remodelling of the primitive yard; the shed would remain the same but a considerable excavation of the embank-ment alongside was to allow space for a 150-ton mechanical coaling plant, amended to a much lighter steel-framed 'Stranraer' unit, 'according to Railway Executive Ruling'. LMS & LNER practice during the 1930s had arrived at a standard unit for secondary shed coaling – a simple hoist device ideally suited for a shed such as Slough. There was also to have been an ash handling plant, with 'hopper below firepit for receipt of ashes from tubs and elevators to overhead storage hopper to discharge into wagons'. In accord with proper 'service sequence' principles, the various new roads were to lead onto a new 65 ft. turntable. None of this ever appeared.

Diesel railcars and shunters came quite early to Slough, and although com-prehensive courses were arranged in later years, drivers at first were simply given a peremptory 'going over' and left to get on with it. Two large oil tanks and a fuelling point were also installed, various plans dating from March 1957 and the latter part of 1958. They recalled the great oil-firing programme of 1947; tanks and heaters were

Detail of renewal work at Slough. *Photographer unknown*

Slough at the last. Various alterations are seen to have been made to the coal stage, though it remained a dismal structure, hard work unrelieved by the simplest comfort. There was a 'cabin' for the coalmen in the dark basement of the building, where washing facilities amounted to two buckets. This could not be considered efficacious for men so dusty that they were recognisable only by white circles around the eyes. You peeled off your overalls, stepped hesitantly into the ridiculous buckets and splashed oneself in front of the fire beneath the tank. There was also a mess below, where coal dust trickled through the floor above onto the plates and food. There were slightly more advanced bathing facilities in the shed itself, a GW standard 'washing trough' bearing an unpleasant resemblance to a pig-feeding trough. This was a super wheeze dreamed up by the Great Western, a stone gulley, within the main part of the shed, entirely unprivate and thus prey to draughts, gusts of wind, pools of oil or whatever. They ran (Old Oak and Southall had them, among others) off the hot water washing out system and more often than not delivered a crippling burst of scalding steam, rather than the intended 'hot shower'. They were not popular.
S. J. Dickson

installed at Old Oak, Didcot and Reading, the latter two never used and elaborate plans were also made for Slough. A separate road was proposed 'for oil tank wagons and locos', a siding alongside 'The Smokebox', which indeed came into being as (the officially listed) 'Polly's Siding', the title convolutedly derived from the *persona* of shift foreman Perkins – 'Polly' Perkins in the inimitable patois of the engine shed. The abortive oil-fuelling project reflected in its scale the vital place Slough held in the London workings, but its demise scarcely evoked regret; Welsh coal was dusty and penetrated the most tightly drawn clothing but it was as nothing to the clinging, stinking mess of the oil lines.

The diesel period is remembered almost universally as a kind of ghastly accelerating decline, a disorientation as age-old practice was brutally thrown over. Staff relations sank to new lows, the management seen as calculating dissemblers, unworthy of trust whilst a sense of exasperation took hold at the precipitate pace of change and the consequent waste.

The railcars worked by Slough men were based at Reading and Southall, so prolonging the depot's long tradition of relief work. The diesel fuel tanks installed under the 1958 proposals were all that appeared of a scheme to convert the whole depot to diesel working. The malodorous 'Smokebox' was to become 'a runround and emergency fuelling road for 3 car sets' and 'the Washout' an 'examination pit for single power units'. The new tanks fed fuelling points over by 'Polly's Siding', of a petrol pump type suited to the railcars. When stabled at Slough, however, the DMUs were invariably parked in the old carriage shed and were never booked to take fuel. Slough got a couple of diesel shunters but these unfortunately were fuelled on a different system, a locking hose, and had to trundle off to Old Oak Common once a week, a signalman's nightmare as the diesel ('seasick fashion') tottered from the refuge of one loop to the next, all the way up the main line. It was usual to do this trip on a Saturday, and the engine could often return in more sedate fashion with an engineering train. The procedure was next to impossible during the week, and if fuel ran low through heavy working, the tank inspection cover, a bolted plate, would have to be removed and the loco replenished through the access hole. So it was that on closure the half-full Slough oil tanks required to be pumped out, removing the very fuel with which they had originally been filled. Apart from the irregular 'topping up' of the odd shunter, practically their only use had been to refill the heater tanks of DMUs off the Windsor branch, when snow made a trip to Southall awkward. Slough men also worked diesel locos off other depots, Type '3' Hymeks in

particular, and the ill-starred North British 6300 series Type '2's. Experience with both did little to discourage reservations regarding the conduct of the modernisation scheme, particularly the feeling of improper haste. The 6300 diesels could rarely be relied upon and, although the Hymeks were fairly well regarded, they were considered overtaxed on trains such as the 'Worcesters' – '49s put on a 'Castle' job'.

Slough closed in the early summer of 1964, the '61s' gone and the shed indeed bereft of all its steam locos in the last months. Crews not involved with DMUs worked Southall engines on what duties could be salvaged in the general decline and run-down, and were eventually removed to a signing-on point at Slough station. The shed stood empty for a while and was then knocked down.

The coal supplied to Slough was usually reasonable stuff though a conviction existed that Old Oak took the best. Coal from the Oakdale colliery was considered the finest, going beyond white heat to a greenish glow. Risca was termed 'Mackintosh Coal', so dusty that water ran off, but Blaenavon was considered to be the worst, with severe clinkering. The coal stacks long lay on the raised area adjacent to the coal stage and were lifted in latter years, the cleaners got in on a Sunday to wheelbarrow it off onto trucks on the ramp. The stacks themselves backed onto the cattle market; the *North Star* pub opened all day for the market and pints could go down well at the end of a shift, even at six o'clock in the morning. *S. J. Dickson*

No. 1421, probably the Marlow engine, on the Slough turntable. The 'mangle' at either end would catch in clothing with unfortunate results, and, although 'a hard slog', the turntable was in good condition and generally considered reliable. It was taken up on closure and the pit turned into a dump for much of the rubbish from the destruction of the coal stage. *British Railways*

MARLOW

Yet another branch engine shed, relating to the opening of the line, it was arranged in customary fashion, with coal stage and water tank sited outside. It appears to have opened with the line in 1873 and closed (with dieselisation?) in 1962. An exhaustive account of the shed and its workings is included in *The Marlow Branch* by Karau and Turner (Wild Swan).

'The Donkey' at Marlow. Loco and autocoach covered over 200 miles in a day, 97 in the morning and 115 in the afternoon, the engine returning once a week to Slough for washout.

W. A. Camwell

With the engine pounding up and down the line, Marlow shed remained largely unoccupied throughout the day. After the last run, in the last years at least, it uncoupled from the coach, which was left in the platform, was taken out of the station and reversed into the engine shed siding, to attach itself to a coal wagon, in latter days loaded with briquettes. Now the crew could cheerfully go home, leaving the overnight work to a night fireman from Slough. He drew the coal wagon to the stage, uncoupled it and took the engine forward to the shed entrance. It was then necessary to connect up the flexible hose to the whistle fitting (having removed the whistle) to supply steam to a flywheel type pump housed in the adjacent brick hut. Over two or three hours every night with the pressure falling below 100 lbs, the engine pumped water from a well into the tank, enough for the next day's work, with the fireman shovelling coal from the wagon onto the stage, again sufficient for the morrow. Removing the hose and refitting the whistle, the fireman had then to clean the fire, shovelling it out off the footplate, adding to the pile on the shed floor. Enough glowing coal was left on the firebars to get a new supply 'on the go', the firedoor partly closed and the blower left on slightly. The night fireman still had work to do, with the next job being to reverse the engine out of the shed entrance, bunker up against the coal wagon. Then the smokebox had to be cleaned out and the engine bunker filled direct from the coal wagon. Approaching the end of these labours, the night fireman propelled the wagon into the siding, leaving it roughly opposite the station, afterwards taking the engine forward out onto the line to at last reverse into the station and connect up again with its coach. If all had gone well, there would be time for an hour or two of rest before preparation work began again, building the fire and raising steam for the driver's arrival for the first train out. The engine tanks were filled from a tap and hose on the station platform. Illumination for this work, which in winter took place entirely in darkness, came in the form of a single flare lamp. *P. J. Garland*

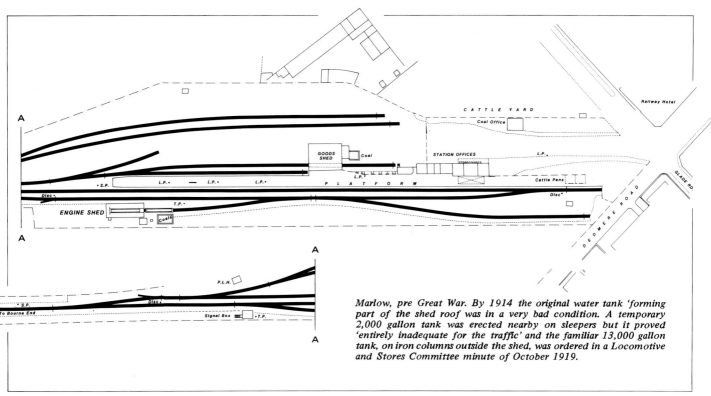

Marlow, pre Great War. By 1914 the original water tank 'forming part of the shed roof was in a very bad condition. A temporary 2,000 gallon tank was erected nearby on sleepers but it proved 'entirely inadequate for the traffic' and the familiar 13,000 gallon tank, on iron columns outside the shed, was ordered in a Locomotive and Stores Committee minute of October 1919.

There were two drivers and three firemen on the Marlow complement, with Slough covering all relief work. An exception worked by a Slough engine and crew was the Sunday afternoon train, about 2 o'clock, a '48XX' with a six-coach ECS set. This was taken to Bourne End and left for the 7.30 a.m. Monday morning train, the engine proceeding light to Marlow to stable in the shed there. The Slough crew relieved Marlow men on the auto, and worked the branch for Sunday afternoon and evening, bringing back the 'old' engine to Slough and leaving the 'new' one.

A. Attewell

Watlington around 1900.   *Collection Paul Karau*

0–4–2T passing the shed around the turn of the century. Slough pannier No. 2112 worked the line for many years (see page 179) but the locomotive history of the line is a tangled one which requires some further unravelling.   *R. E. Gilbert*

Two victims of the 1906 fire, an intriguing pairing, which raises questions as to the early operation of the line. It was officially worked on the 'one engine in steam' principle and there is as yet no explanation for the presence of two locos at Watlington. The saddle tank carries a battered 'Not to be Moved' sign and was presumably receiving attention at the time of the disaster.   *Collection Mrs. Collins*

WATLINGTON

The line opened in 1872, the Watlington and Princes Risborough Railway, and an unsettled period followed, the company suffering the calculating indifference of Paddington until it was ready to offer itself up on suitably ignominious terms in 1883.

The story of the branch was outlined in most entertaining fashion by R. K. Kirkland BA in the *Railway Magazine* and is described by Holden in *The Watlington Branch*, (OPC), and Karau *Great Western Branch Line Termini Vol 1* (OPC). All note the 'tantalising paucity of information' regarding the early locomotives. The shed presumably had opened with the line, to house (apparently) an engine on hire from the Great Western; 'No. 1', a 2–2–2WT arrived later and then 'No. 2' a better regarded 2–4–0T.

Obscurely, the branch engine was provided by Slough 'of all unlikely places' as Kirkland rightly comments. A 57XX pannier sufficed in latter years, a successor to the smaller, but stalwart '2021' class saddle and pannier tanks used almost exclusively from the early years of the century right through the Second World War. The practice continued despite the minor inconvenience of the shed burning down in September 1906, after which the engine simply stabled over the pit. The shed at Watlington, uniquely comprising a 'pit only' for half a century, 'closed' at sometime in the 'fifties. A letter to the *Railway Magazine* of September 1956 refers to the branch engine stabling on the site of the shed 'until the regular fireman was called for national service and no replacement could be found at Watlington'. The same letter (from Mr. G. E. Jones) turns to the subject of English film (see Wallingford):

> The Watlington branch has been used in the production of a film; in 1950, scenes for 'Portrait of Clare' were shot at Aston Rowant. A '2021' class 0–6–0 pannier-tank, No. 2112, was the branch engine at the time. It was replaced by '74XX' (Nos. 7441 and 7442) and later the present '57XX' pannier-tanks.

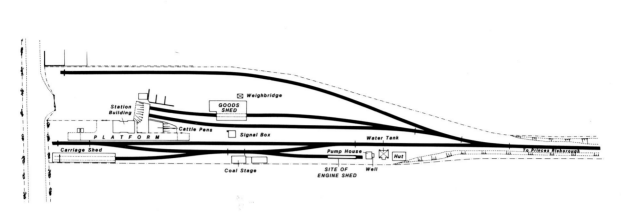

Watlington in 1912. Shortly after this, serious consideration was given to a replacement shed, a substantial scheme involving a rearrangement of the sidings and a new building nearly half as long again as the old shed, with separate coal siding and pillar tank. It would have been easier, of course, simply to re-erect the shed on the old foundations, but instead a siding was proposed, on new embankment work past the south side of the old shed site (to avoid moving the well) to a shed, 75 ft by 22 ft, on made-up ground to the east. The scheme was drawn up late in 1913 and the estimates approved in February of the following year:

£1,850 Engineer
£ 160 Locomotive Superintendent
£ 130 Signalling Engineer
£2,140 Total

The ideas were abandoned, possibly due to the war and never revived.

Watlington operated like many small Great Western engine sheds at the end of branch lines — a couple of crews to cover 'daytime' work with relief and any extras provided by the 'home' depot. There were two drivers and two firemen, and Slough covered in the event of sickness or holidays. It differed from Marlow in its remoteness and men would lodge for a week at a time, in a pub in the town. One Watlington driver of a time was noted for a certain taciturnity and the consigning of young, wide-eyed firemen to the place was a sort of institutionalised Slough joke. Sent to Watlington for a Saturday job, it would scarcely cross one's mind that the route home might pose certain difficulties — after dropping the fire about 8.30 the dismal truth would haltingly be made known, that the only course lay in the Watlington station bike, to Princes Risborough for the 8.30 a.m. *Sunday morning* train. With

no money or food, the Watlington horse-box was an appalling prospect. Ever afterwards one exacted cast iron guarantees for one's safe return, if necessary a 'chit' for a taxi. The system once mastered, could work to some advantage — claiming lodge and motor cycling home to Slough in less than an hour.

Following abandonment of the 1913-1914 proposals, locos continued to stable on the site of the old shed. A feature of the scheme had been a 3,000 gallon pillar tank and in 1919-1920 this indeed was provided, on a site opposite the 'shed'. On 1st August 1918 the 'existing wooden structure' was noted 'in need of renewal' and on 29th May 1919 the acquisition of 1r 26½p of land was reported at £592. On 4th December it was declared, a saving of £154 might be possible, on 'the use of an old tank removed from Taunton'. *J. H. Ahern*

AYLESBURY

Aylesbury station.

L & GRP, courtesy David & Charles

The Wycombe Railway and the Aylesbury and Buckinghamshire Railway evidently shared the costs of a station at Aylesbury, opened in the autumn of 1863. The former company had made its way from Maidenhead to High Wycombe in 1854 and on to Thame (through Princes Risborough) by 1862. The Wycombe Railway's line to Aylesbury ran from Princes Risborough and was at first broad gauge, conversion to 4 ft $8\frac{1}{2}$ ins (by the Great Western) coming in October of 1868 ... 'in accordance with an Agreement made with the Aylesbury and Buckingham Railway'. For long this tract of countryside had been debated land, empty of railways, the LNWR and GWR gazing sullenly across it at each other. Its geopolitics and 'the intricacies of successive outflanking manœuvres are studies rewarding principally to those delighting in the arcane'.

The Aylesbury and Buckingham Railway, from Verney Junction southwards to the jointly-financed station at Aylesbury, was spawned, in part at least, through somewhat murky LNWR connections, and was completed in October 1868, a matter of weeks before the Wycombe Railway (following the Agreement between the two) was narrowed. The LNW had withdrawn all support for the

scheme and the new line was worked through the aid of the Great Western. Now some shed accommodation had been provided by the Wycombe Railway more or less from the very first – a single road building in brick for the broad gauge engine. Alterations, it would seem, were under consideration within weeks: '25th November 1863 ... the proposal of Mr. Grierson for an Extension of the Engine shed at Aylesbury was ordered to be referred to the Board accompanied by a Recommendation that authority should be given to carry it into effect'. This minute relates to enlargement, rearwards, of the broad gauge shed, an additional section which was to very nearly double the length of the building.

With the arrival of the Aylesbury and Buckingham in prospect and the narrowing of the Wycombe's line accordingly, alterations were obviously required at the shed. Around the Autumn of 1868 its single set of rails must needs have undergone the necessary amendment. The whole of this line through Aylesbury is normally considered to have been marked by an absolute paucity of traffic, but it was not long before the GWR considered further shed accommodation desirable. The original shed, converted to standard gauge, enjoyed consequent high and lofty proportions, fea-

tures reflecting its broad gauge origins. It had three windows whilst the later portion had only one, and all were opened out to provide high arched doorways between the old building and a new extension. This took the form of an additional road on the north side and was by contrast a mean, squat lean-to. Drawings of the new arrangement date from 21st November 1870, the result thoroughly displeasing – unbalanced in its dimensions and ill-suited for the proper stabling of engines.

Remarkable in that the 'New Work' had served only to leave it a kind of contrived ruin, the now two-road narrow gauge Aylesbury shed was responsible for engines working both north and south of Aylesbury. A turntable had been put in, possibly in broad gauge days, for it lay immediately in front of the original Wycombe Railway part of the shed. It was still in place, with a stub siding (probably in connection with coaling) when plans were deposited in the 1881 session, showing the proposed route of the 'Aylesbury and Rickmansworth Railway'. Under this title, through opposition from both the LNWR and the GWR, the Metropolitan Railway finally reached Aylesbury ('at a temporary station') in September 1892. In the process it took over the Aylesbury and Buckingham 'as from July

Continued on page 203

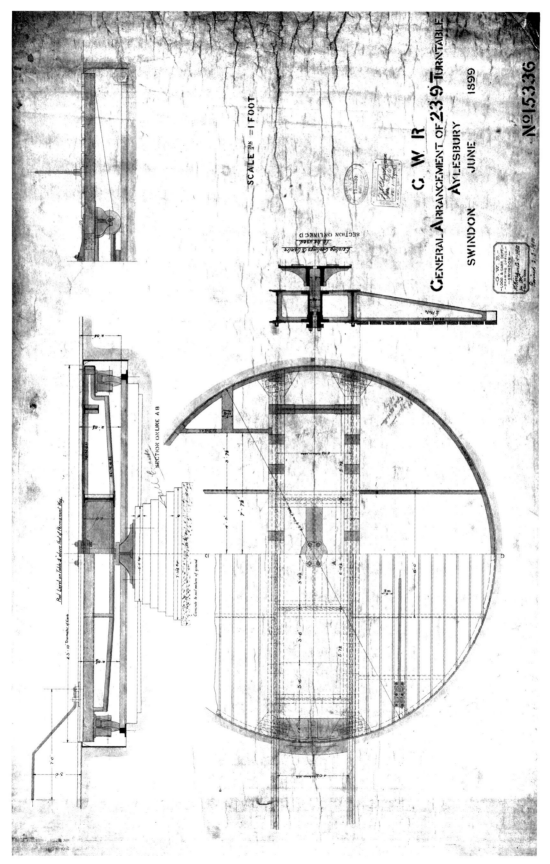

23 ft 9 in turntable of June 1899, a unit replacing a much earlier example, its precise function little understood. It is presumed to have been used to turn small tank engines, for some locally preferred direction of working. It was listed 'out of use' in 1920.

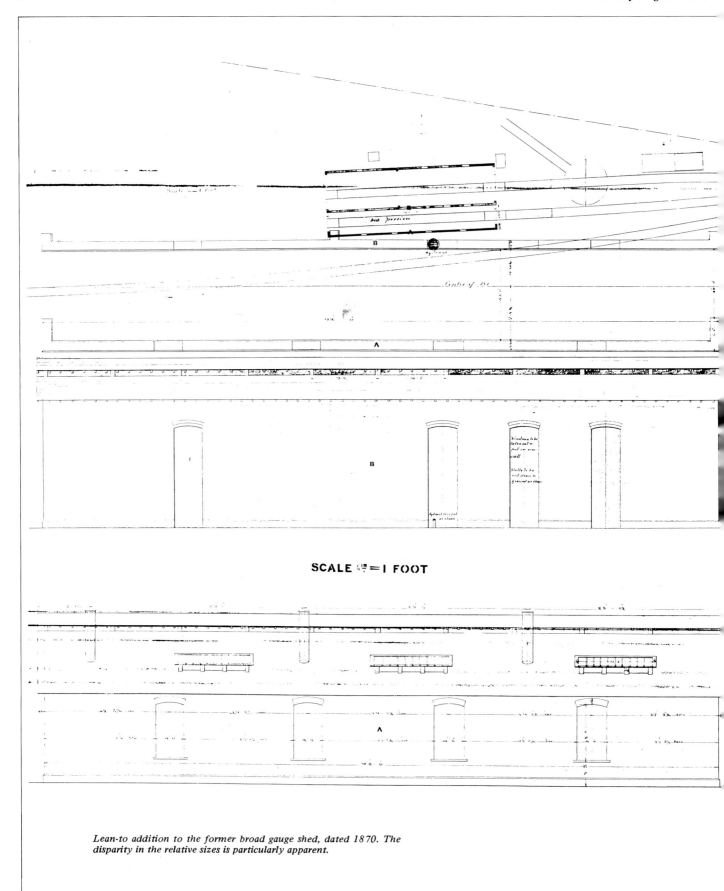

SCALE ⁴⁄₁₂=1 FOOT

*Lean-to addition to the former broad gauge shed, dated 1870. The
disparity in the relative sizes is particularly apparent.*

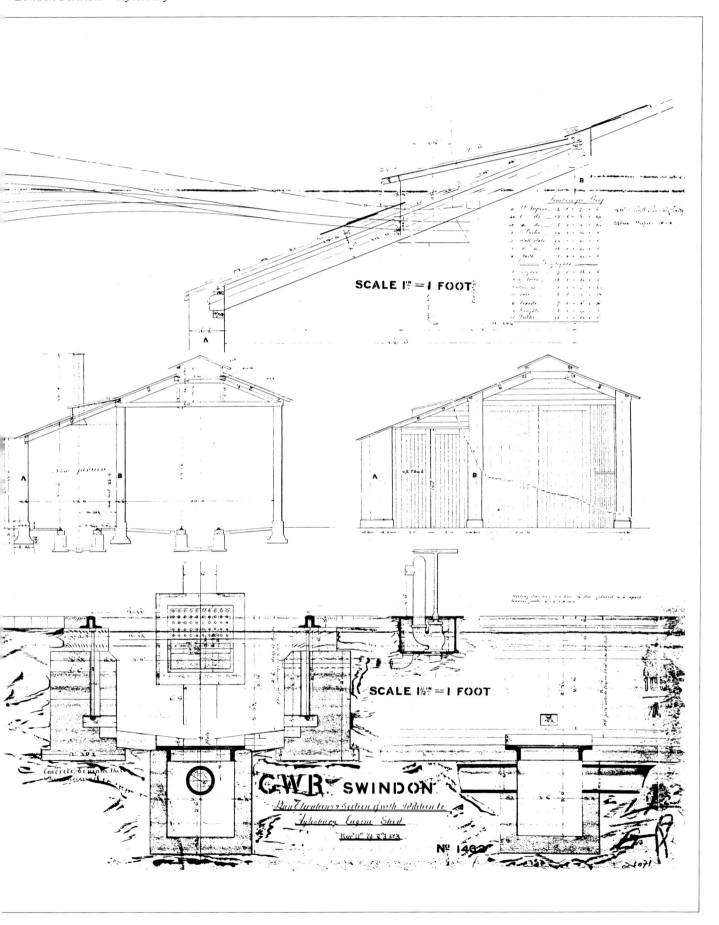

SCALE 1" = 1 FOOT

SCALE 1½" = 1 FOOT

G.W.R. SWINDON

Plan Elevations & Section of with Addition to
Aylesbury Engine Shed

Nov 70

Nº 1462

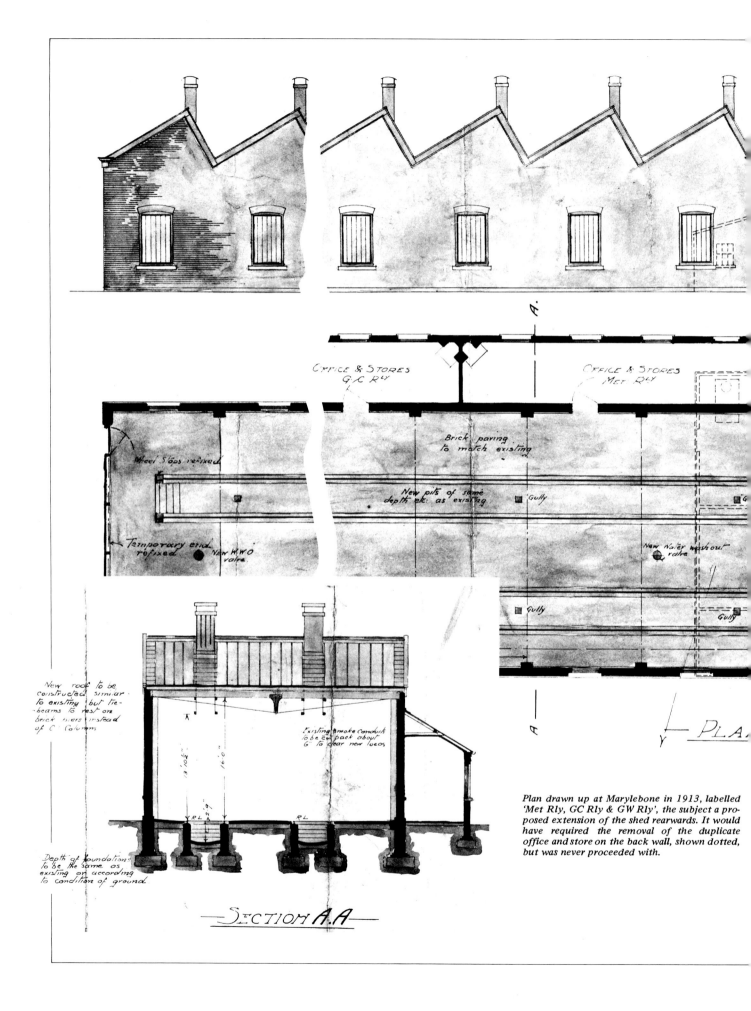

OFFICE & STORES
G.C RLY

OFFICE & STORES
MET RLY

Brick paving
to match existing

Wheel Stops refixed

New pits of same
depth etc as existing

Gully

Temporary end
refixed   New H.W.O
valve

New Water washout
valve

Gully

Gully

A

PLAN

New roof to be
constructed similar
to existing but tie-
-beams to rest on
brick piers instead
of C Columns

Existing smoke conduit
to be cut back about
6" to clear new locos

13'10½"

16'0"

R.L 2'9"

R.L

Depth of foundations
to be the same as
existing or according
to condition of ground

SECTION A.A

Plan drawn up at Marylebone in 1913, labelled
'Met Rly, GC Rly & GW Rly', the subject a proposed extension of the shed rearwards. It would
have required the removal of the duplicate
office and store on the back wall, shown dotted,
but was never proceeded with.

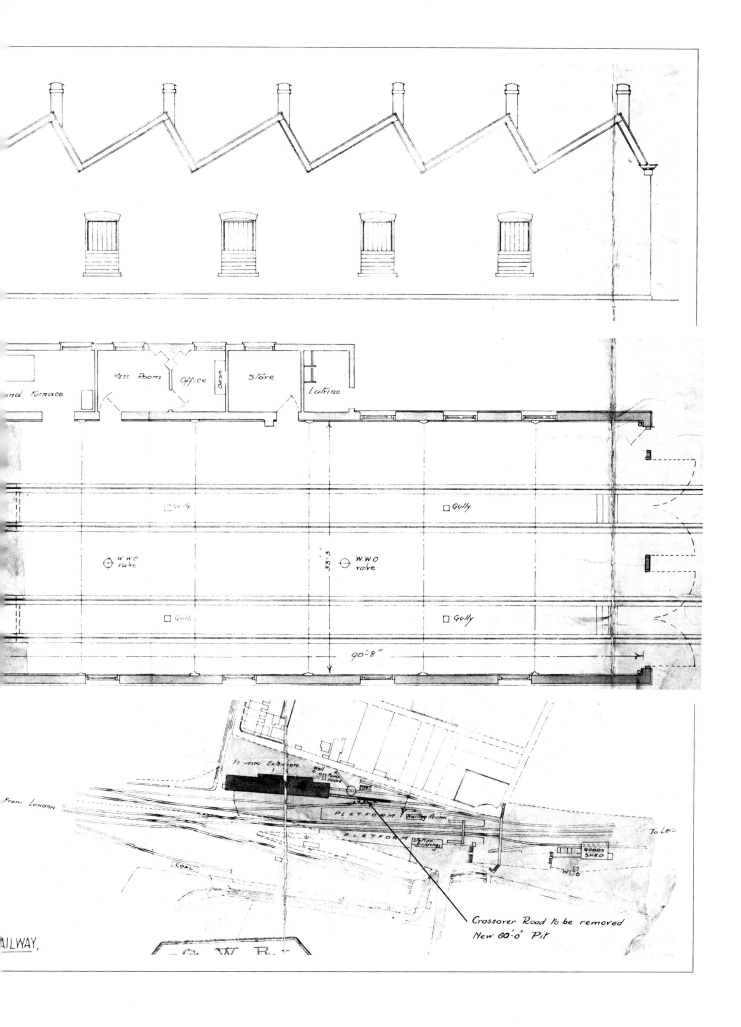

MESS ROOM   Office   Desk   Store   Latrine

nd Furnace

□ Gully   □ Gully

⊕ W W O
   valve   ⊕ W W O
                  valve

33'·3

□ Gully   □ Gully

90'·8"

From London

Proposed Extension   Wall   Pump House

PLATFORM   Waiting Room

PLATFORM

Station Buildings

COAL

GOODS SHED

W.Ho

To Leic

Crossover Road to be removed
New 60'·0" Pit

AILWAY,   G. W. R.

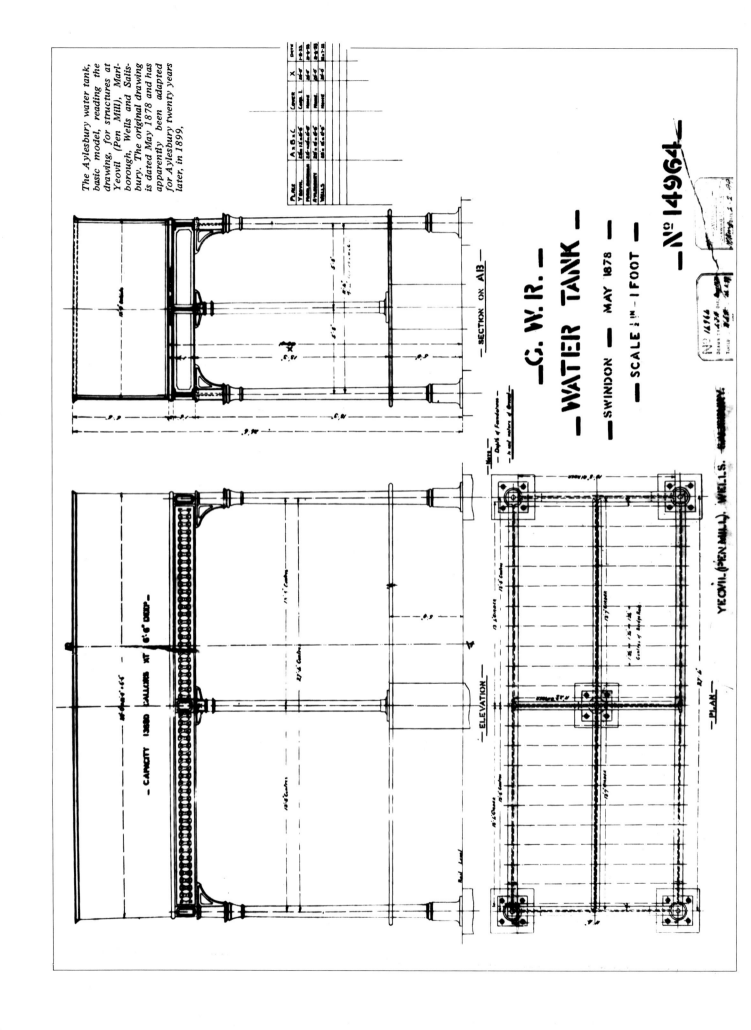

The Aylesbury water tank, basic model, reading the drawing, for structures at Yeovil (Pen Mill), Marlborough, Wells and Salisbury. The original drawing is dated May 1878 and has apparently been adapted for Aylesbury twenty years later, in 1899.

— SECTION ON A13 —

— CAPACITY 13680 GALLONS AT 6'6" DEEP —

— ELEVATION —

— PLAN —

— G. W. R. —
— WATER TANK —
— SWINDON — MAY 1878 —
— SCALE ½ IN—1 FOOT —

Nº 14964

YEOVIL (PEN MILL), WELLS.

1st 1891'. All this makes for a most complex period in the shed's history, and how the various companies were accommodated is not wholly clear. LNWR locomotives and men are even said to have worked to the place in the first part of the 1890s, loaned to the Metropolitan when the 'miffed' GWR withdrew its stock from the former Aylesbury and Buckingham Railway workings.

The engine shed was entirely rebuilt in response to these developments though the precise date is, again, not known. Despite the construction of a coal stage with water column, in the goods yard on the north side, on Metropolitan property, the 'Met' required accommodation at the shed proper. This was detailed in a list of works, much of it charged to the Metropolitan, between April 12th 1893 and August 5th the following year:

The Aylesbury shed, true to its mixed origins, was of a style difficult to immediately ascribe to any particular company. Such a building might be found widely across England or Wales.

L & GRP, courtesy David & Charles

Double Junction with Metropolitan Railway
Alterations in Sidings and Lines at the South End of Station consequent upon construction of junction
Cross-over Road to Siding at South end of Station
Catch Siding at North end of station on Metropolitan land
Additional Engine Pit and Siding at Shed and Coal Stage

Alterations in Sidings and Lines in Station consequent upon construction of new Platform
New Platform
New Station Buildings and Fencing
Footbridge
Locking and Signalling

Locking and Signalling including displaced Signal Cabin
Telegraph Department
Ditto
Footwarming Apparatus   £3,764

No. 3906, one of a succession of tanks on the GW 'Londons' out of Aylesbury, via both High Wycombe and Maidenhead. These awkward conversions were not an unqualified success.

L & GRP, courtesy David & Charles

Deduct

G.W. Coys proportion of charges included
in expenditure as above

For Superintendent	£68.18. 0	£34.2.9
For Freight	1.6.10	
	£70.4.10	£34.2.9

The shed road nearest the station
running line (called the 'western loop') was
ever afterwards known as 'the Met Road'
though it was used both by the Metropolitan and, after its arrival, the Great
Central. All this does not necessarily indicate that the shed was rebuilt in 1893–1894.
Survey records suggest this but the rebuilding may well date from slightly later, after
the arrival of the G.C. Certainly the rebuilt
shed was fully appointed and in use by
1908, for a plan of that year, dated 5th
June shows it complete and 'existing'. The
old building was partially levelled and the
new northlight pattern shed erected on the
site, making use of original foundations and
pits. The parcel of land it stood on was
owned by 'The Met. Co. and G.C., and G.W.
and G.C. Cos.' and the shed may well have
been put up by the Joint Committees. Even
Churchward was confused and he wrote to
Paddington for verification around this
time – the Chief Accountant approached
G. J. Whitelaw (of the Great Central?) and
forwarded a copy of his reply to Churchward:

Dear Sir,

Water Supply Aylesbury

In reply to your letter of the 18th inst,
the engine shed and appliances in question
became the property of the Great Western
and Great Central Railway Joint Committee,
as part and parcel of the Aylesbury Branch,
when that line was transferred under the Act
of 1907 in consideration of the payment to
the Great Western Company of the sum of
£82,000.

Yours Truly,
(signed)
G. J. Whitelaw

The shed was busy from the first and it
is clear that engines of all three companies
were serviced there. The coal stage was
extended in 1912 at a cost of £18.18.4 and
a gas engine was provided 'for pumping
water for locomotive purposes at Aylesbury'. The work in both instances was
arranged by the GW and GC Joint Committee and the costs shared between that
body and the other Aylesbury committee,
the Met and GC Joint. Plans were drawn
up at Marylebone in 1913 for the extension
of the shed (not proceeded with) quite
clearly labelled 'Met Rly, GC Rly and GW
Rly'. The turntable was replaced, inex-
plicably, by the GWR in 1898 though it is
only possible to speculate upon its use. At
24 ft the only suggestion so far relates to
0–4–2Ts, though this idea is presented with
some trepidation. It is shown 'disused' by
February 1924 but its removal was not

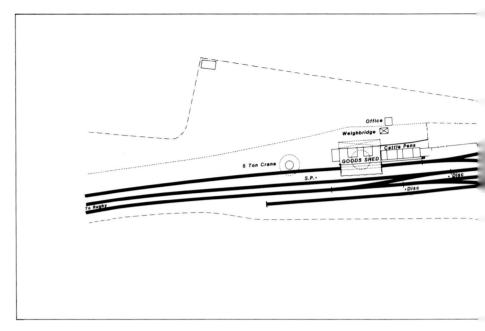

finally ordered until 25th February 1931.
At the same time, an 'electrically driven
centrifugal pump' was to be installed, cost
£177 and in the following year, on 27th
July, £18 was expended on the provision of
drinking water and lavatory accommodation. On 27th July 1938 covering was
ordered for the coal stage, £90, the cost of
this and the other work once again borne
by the Met & GC and GC & GW Joint
Committees.

True to its convoluted origins, Aylesbury
remained something of an enigmatic place –
nothing about it seemed straightforward.
The Great Central (and later the LNER)
worked it more or less conventionally but,
for the Great Western, it seems to have
served as a kind of outbase for engines off
a variety of sheds. Witness the *Railway
Observer* in 1937:

Marlow (81) is now sub to Reading (121),
not Slough (141). Aylesbury (11) is sub to Old
Oak Common (101) as well as Slough (141);
both 101 and 141 supply 61XX engines to
Aylesbury. The Aylesbury auto-engine is
maintained by Banbury (44).*

With the LNER it was simpler:

A small shed at Aylesbury – 38 miles from
Marylebone – occupied jointly with the Great
Western Railway Company, is also controlled
from Neasden. Three L. & N.E. engines only
are stabled at this place, two of the locomotives being engaged on local working
between Aylesbury and Marylebone, and the
third works a shuttle service between Aylesbury and Verney Junction.

This was the *London and North Eastern
Railway Magazine* for 1931 and concluded,
regarding Verney Junction....

The latter links up with the London,
Midland & Scottish Railway to Bletchley and
the North.

The *Great Western Railway Magazine* of
February 1940 threw further light on the
multilateral nature of operations at Aylesbury shed:

Three railway companies were represented
at Aylesbury station on Christmas Eve when
farewell gifts were handed to Mr. J. Baverstock, who was retiring from the position of
shed chargeman. The gifts – a suitcase, a
walking stick, a box of cigars, a tobacco pouch
and a purse – were presented by Mr. V. Lang-
ston (locomotive foreman, L & NER). Mr. G.
David (GWR) and Mr. J. Skeats (LPTB) were
among those who spoke of their long and
pleasant association with the recipient. Mr.
Baverstock had completed forty-seven years
of Great Western service and had been
stationed at Aylesbury as chargeman for
forty years.

It seems that 'GC' staff and engines (or
rather the GC and Met combined) out-
numbered those of the Great Western. In
the years before Grouping, around 1918–
1922, there were two GWR cleaners and a
firedropper, four sets of men for the principal turns and two sets for the 'Banbury
Car', Aylesbury men working a Princes Risborough–Banbury service. 'County' tanks
were used on 'front line' services, replaced
by '61' 2–6–2Ts. The bigger tanks also put
in time as Aylesbury and Risborough
pilots, both turns involving considerable
shunting. GC staff seem to have comprised
seven sets of enginemen, four for London
(using evidently A5 tanks) and three
engaged 'locally', this presumably including Verney Junction work. There was a
night foreman and four cleaners, who took
their turn with GW men on the gas engine.
The well was fed from a brook off the canal
and water could be raised by this engine –
it was a cumbersome procedure and put in
use only when the town supply was unavail-

*See Introduction for the vagaries of GWR coding.

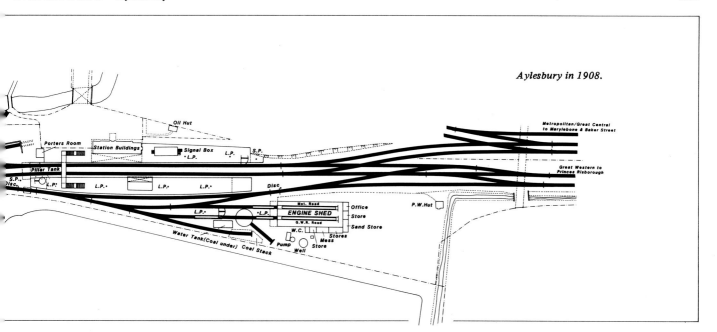

Aylesbury in 1908.

No. 6126 at Aylesbury on 30th August 1948.

J. H. Venn

Pannier No. 5420 of Banbury shed on 12th August 1961, presumably the 'Banbury Car'.   *Merchant Navy Locomotive Preservation Society*

The roof at Aylesbury had been replaced in corrugated sheeting in the period before 1948 (doubtless charged to the various joint committees) and a new tank replaced the ancient GW standard of the 1870s. The old wrought iron was utilised as a supporting framework for what passed as a new coaling shelter. Neasden was increasingly responsible for the engines; the shed had passed, of course, to the London Midland Region but the GC 'connection' ensured an unexpected variety of locos.
                                                                                                       Photomatic

Dereliction at Aylesbury.   *K. C. H. Fairey*

able. By agreement GWR men attended 9 a.m.–9 p.m., GC men 9 p.m.–9 a.m. The practice differed in latter years when the well became the sole supply, pumped through a less awkward and time-consuming arrangement. Sticklebacks and other fish from the brook found their way into the tank and spent their lives there, happily enough, apparently, over many years.

Aylesbury passed to the Eastern Region on Nationalisation, the shed being concerned principally with work on the former Metropolitan and GC lines, under the close direction of Neasden depot. The 'Met Road' and the 'Great Western Road' retained their names until the end of steam at Aylesbury but under British Railways the Great Western men were absorbed into the 'GC Link' which included work to Marylebone, the Aylesbury pilot, the 'Night Shuttle' to Quainton and even turns like the 3.00 a.m. Marylebone–Bletchley parcels. The second and junior link, 'the Met', worked Aylesbury–Rickmansworth passengers, goods and coal. The 'Banbury Car' pottered quietly through all these developments, the 14XX 0–4–2T steaming better on the

Aylesbury hard coal (which arrived every week or so in a drift 'from the north') than the South Wales Banbury supply. Banbury was responsible for the engine and any repairs, though failure at Aylesbury did, it is said, on very few occasions, bring an ex-GC 'N5' tank, No. 69257 of the 'Chesham Shuttle' onto the job. Few engines could have powered two such prosaically labelled trains.

This was a complex area for Great Western working; it was in effect 'remote' in an operational sense, on the periphery of more than one locomotive centre. Engines from several sheds would thus be outbased in the district whilst at High Wycombe a separate pilot was provided. The arrangement had been for the Great Western to provide an engine for five years, swapping over with the Great Central for an alternate five-year period. The engine was an ex-GWR one by the late 1950s; it worked the Chinnor goods and two sets of men were based on High Wycombe.

The Great Western had early on pondered the operational problems of the area and some thought was given to bringing together locomotive work, at Princes Ris-

borough. In June 1914 a three-stage plan was drawn up, for an engine shed 'close by the junction at that place', the initial part to comprise a two-road shed, 120 feet in length, to house four tender locos. The surrounding site allowed for extension to 180 ft, across no less than *eight* roads, housing 32 engines, with a coal stage and 65 ft turntable. If all this proved inadequate, space was available at the rear for a doubling of the shed; nothing came of the proposals, quite probably they were abandoned as war descended, and they do not appear to have surfaced since.

With transfer of traffic away from the GC section and the introduction of diesels, memories of Great Western working at Aylesbury began to fade from the early 1960s. With the closure of Neasden, engines for the remaining goods work came from Cricklewood, standard 2–6–0s at the end working coal from Quainton to Neasden, Willesden Green and Harrow on the Hill. Men continued to book on at the shed but, with Cricklewood 76000 moguls and Type 2 diesels, Aylesbury seems to have been finally put out of use during 1963.

READING

The first shed at Reading had opened 'about 1840', a broad gauge establishment on the north side of the station. The latter was arranged in contemporary GWR fashion, as at Slough for instance, with both up and down platforms on one side, together with a radiating pattern of sidings off a turntable, for stock movement.

This early shed had (presumably) sooner or later to accommodate engines of both gauges – on 12th October 1864 the proposed lengthening of 'the narrow gauge Engine pit at Reading' was discussed, the cost £40, and on 15th November 1865 a further proposal of some rather wider significance was under examination, that the 'Engine Shed at Reading ... should be taken down and re-erected at Weymouth'. This was 'postponed' but later in December a new sand furnace was contemplated; it is not clear when a new shed was put up, it may have been in this period or later, in the 1870s. Sited to the west of the station, the terse comment 'by 1877' remains the only official reference to its construction.

This succeeding Reading building, a roundhouse, certainly belonged firmly in the 'primitive' era of Great Western sheds – despite a rectangular habit, it was awkwardly arranged. For many years, (presumably until the end of the broad gauge) it laboured under the mixed gauge with inadequate provision for repair work, though a crude lifting shop, some 100 ft long, was carved out of the south-east corner. This meant even less space inside the already cramped shed – one of the leng-thiest corner roads was reduced by over ten feet with its neighbour left at only 32 ft. Access to the shed had developed in curious fashion, leaving nineteen radiating roads (three for entrance/exit) plus one isolated 'straight' road. The 'lifting shop' is not thought to have been original, but is believed to date from 1895, when a brick lean-to boiler house was added alongside. A pump house was added in 1901 (a wooden lean-to) and a corrugated iron messroom followed in November 1914. A replacement sandhouse, gabled and in brick, also appeared at the shed's western exit, prior to about 1898, and a 'New Sanitary Convenience' was 'completed 29th December 1916'. It is interesting to note that around 1906–7 when the more advanced ideas involved in the Old Oak Common development must have been very much in the collective mind, the Swindon Engineering Society published, in an 'Excerpt of Transactions', a paper entitled 'The Work of a Running Department'.* In this a roundhouse, of the Great Western elongate variety, was offered as the 'Ideal Shed' and much of the work at Reading which occupied the succeeding years was a less than successful attempt to adapt the place to this 'Ideal': 'All our latest sheds are designed more or less on these lines, but the Ideal Shed and Yard occupies a large piece of land, which is, unfortunately hardly ever available in practice, and the accommodation provided has, therefore, to be modified according to circumstance'.

The coal stage, a wooden shelter with platform, had long served a pair of mixed gauge tracks (the turntable too was mixed gauge but the yard was of standard gauge) in the eastern part of the yard. This ancient structure was taken down (drawings date from 27th April 1883) to be replaced by a similar construction, of doubtful advantage, sited a few yards to the east; 80 ft by 12 ft it boasted two tips. New standard gauge sidings were laid into it but it con-

*See Introduction.

Reading, the less than 'ideal shed'.   *British Railways*

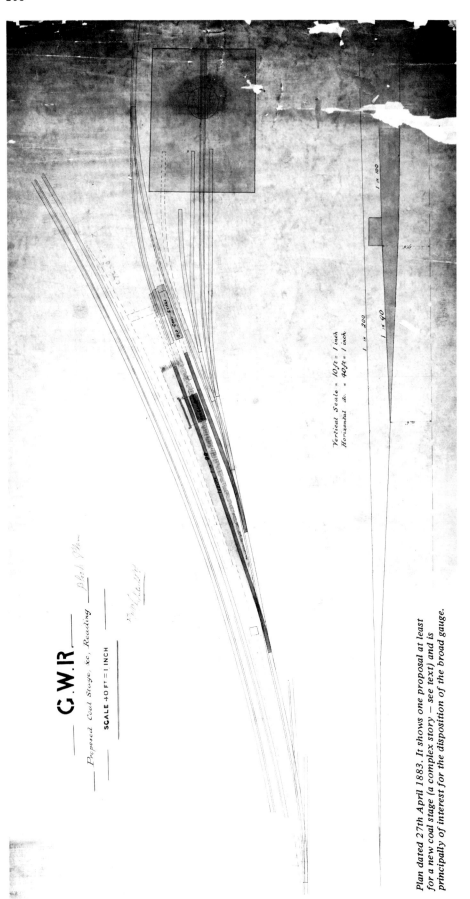

G.W.R ——

Proposed Coal Stage, &c, Reading

SCALE 40 FT = 1 INCH

Vertical Scale = 10ft = 1 inch
Horizontal do. = 40ft = 1 inch

Plan dated 27th April 1883. It shows one proposal at least for a new coal stage (a complex story – see text) and is principally of interest for the disposition of the broad gauge.

tinued to serve the old mixed gauge coal road. In answer to a late company survey – 'How Built (Stone, Brick or Wood)', the reply came – 'Iron'. This unlamented edifice was in turn removed ('Taken Down *c.* 1900') and a brick stage with earth ramp of conventional aspect put up in the west part of the yard. There was previously no yard exit to the west (the fields about were 'liable to floods') but this was remedied with the new ramp and its associated sidings. A considerable degree of raising was indeed necessary right across the yard and the whole could almost be considered 'reclaimed ground'. It demanded a new turntable (that in the roundhouse had long been inadequate, hand-operated with a rail length of 44 ft 7 ins) in conventional position beyond the ramp's end, and a new 65 ft undergirder unit, fully boarded over, eventually came into use 'from January 1914'. The whole of the work had first been authorised on 27th June 1900, £5,000 for 'new coal stage and Turntable, Sidings, etc.' Associated were new coal stacking grounds, ordered to be extended in July 1908 at a cost of £36. The GWR pondered three or four schemes before embarking on any project of import, and details of another stage had been drawn up in March 1898, roughly on the site of the existing one in the east part of the yard. It would have been the third in this position, a crude ramp about 110 feet long, placed by the Basingstoke line and standing over the old mixed gauge coal road. The approach would have been at 1:80. Now this was the logical site for the Reading coal stage but the 1900 proposals finally determined that it should be placed in the western yard. This made some considerable sense if a second roundhouse were to be built but was otherwise questionable. The new coal stage was carefully laid out with the new turntable in mind, though the latter was not to appear for well over a decade. Space had deliberately been put aside in the 1900 proposals for this turntable to serve as part of a second roundhouse, to latter day proportions and accordingly larger than the original. Various configurations occupied draughtsmen through 1912 and 1914 but no building work was proceeded with. The outbreak of war might have played a part in this, though a boiler house had appeared alongside the repair shop and a short separate siding for its coal wagon ('and a bunker') was proposed. In 1904 £700 was authorised for repairs to the shed roof, whilst further sums were spent on the water supply: '28th June 1905, Reading. The water from the River Kennet is not suitable; recommended a water softener, estimated cost £1,760, and acceptance of

Continued on page 225

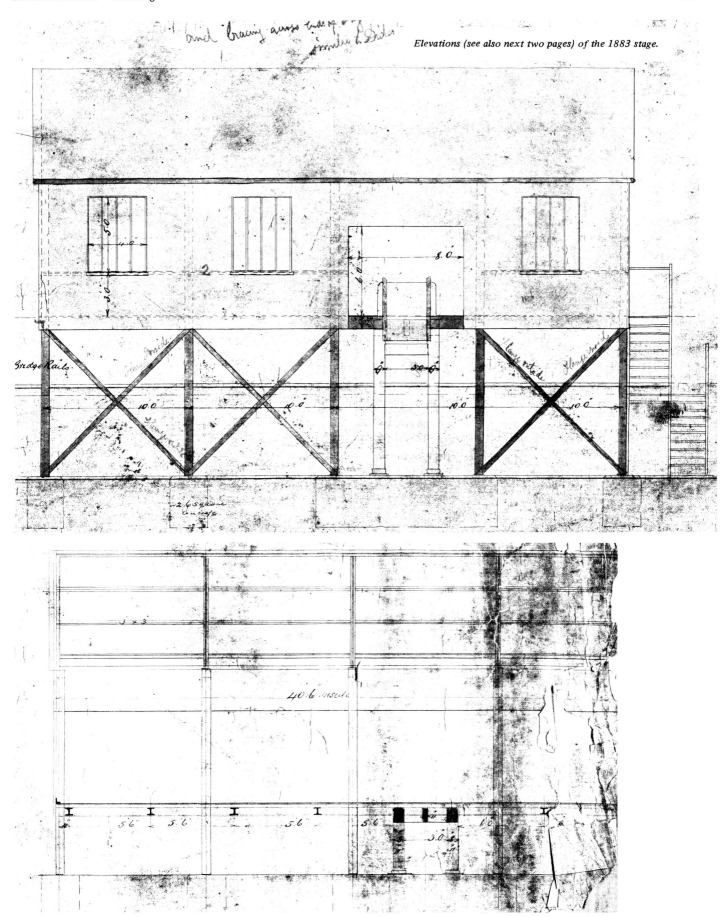

Elevations (see also next two pages) of the 1883 stage.

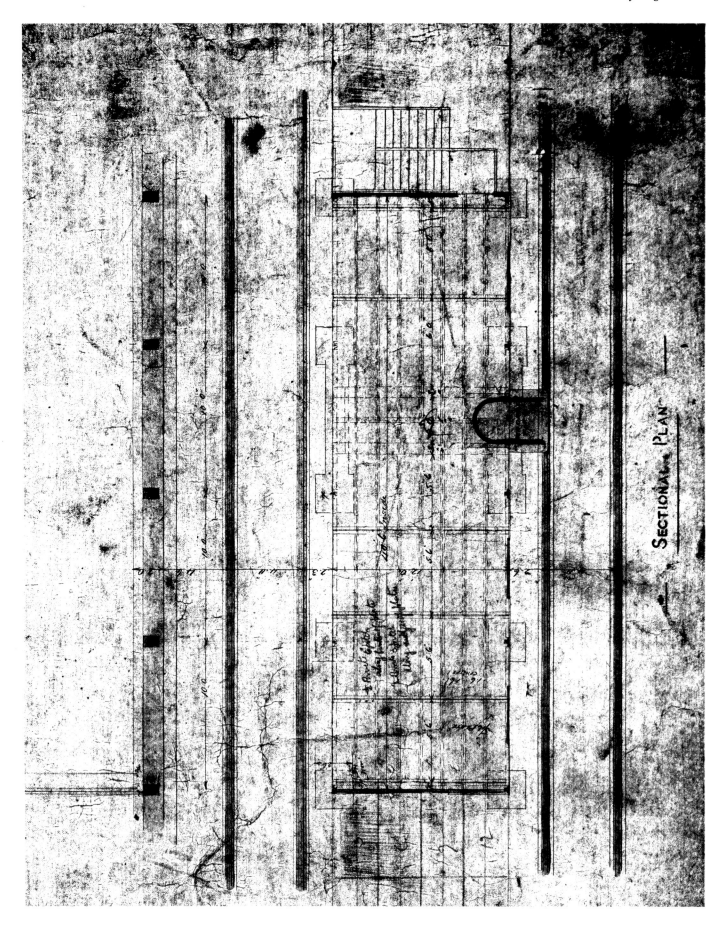

SECTIONAL PLAN

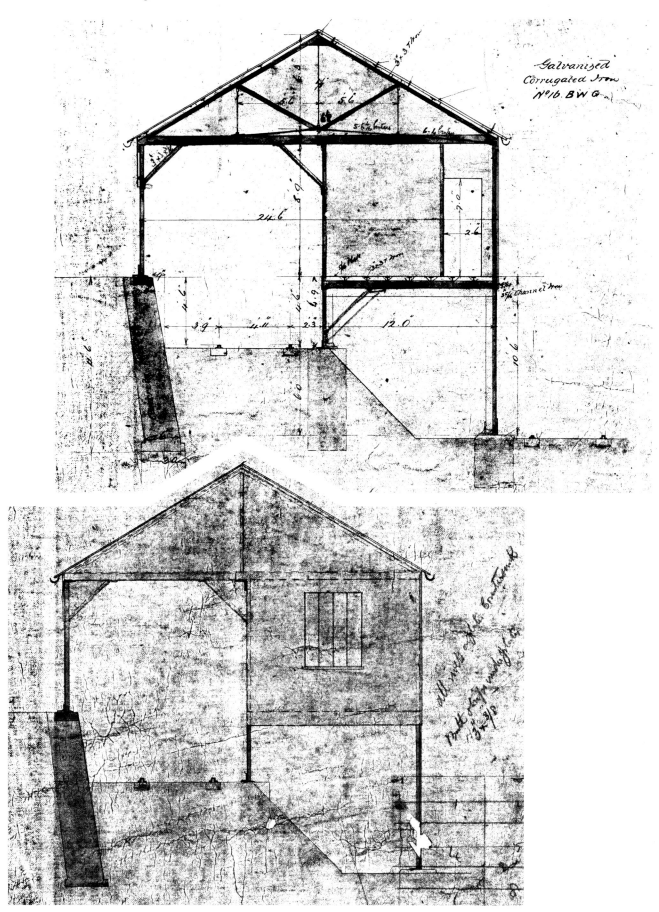

Coal stage of 1883 – 'How built – Iron'.

*Constructional detail, recording various amendments
in the early part of 1894.*

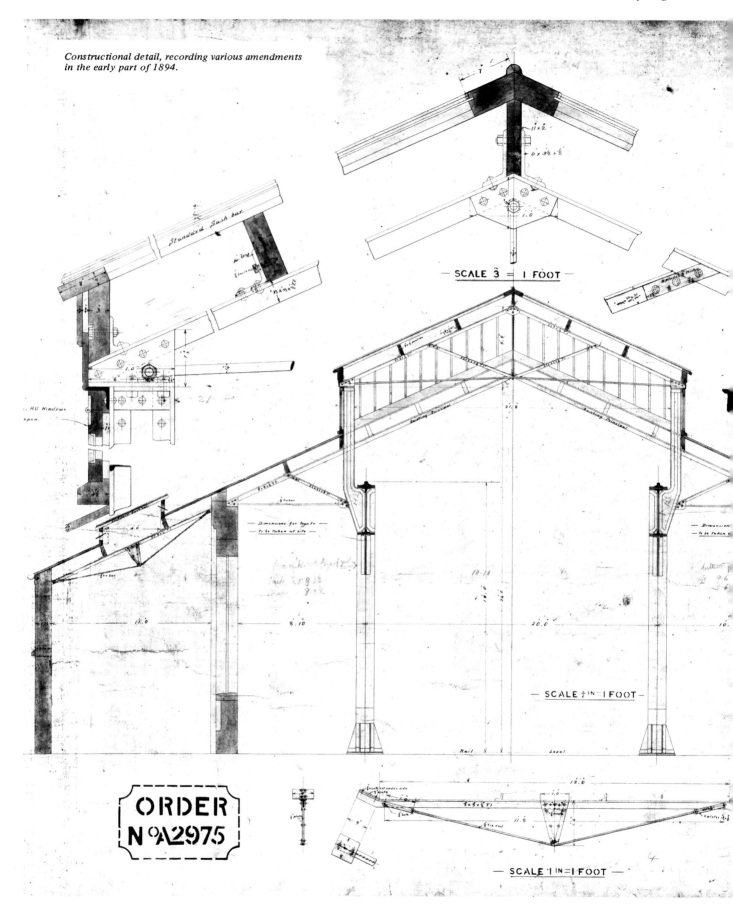

— SCALE $\frac{3}{}$ = 1 FOOT —

— SCALE $\frac{1}{}$ IN 1 FOOT —

— SCALE 1 IN 1 FOOT —

ORDER
N° A2975

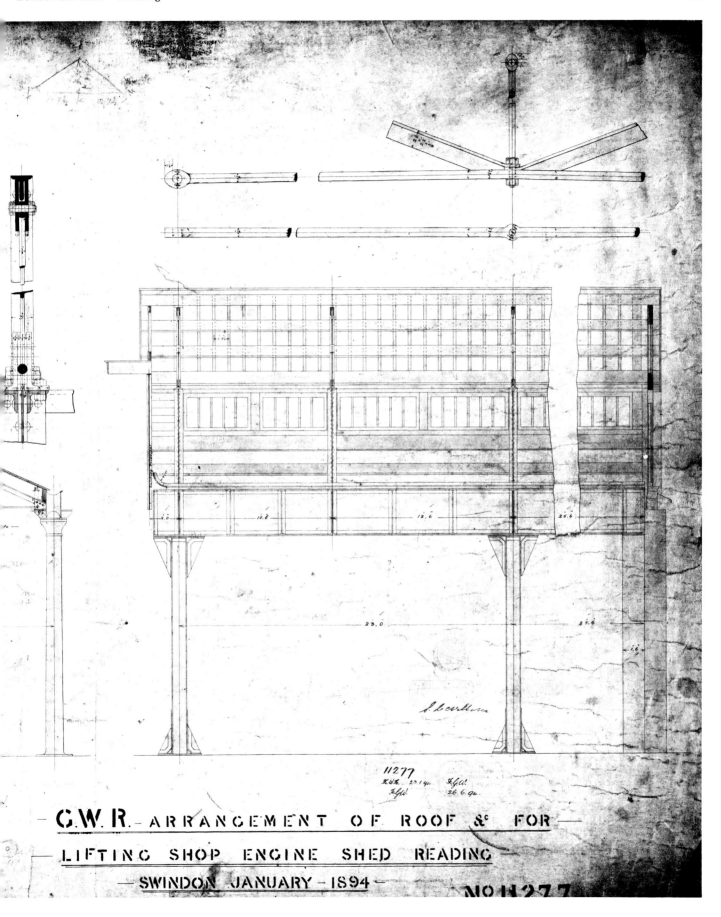

G.W.R. — ARRANGEMENT OF ROOF &c FOR —
LIFTING SHOP ENGINE SHED READING
— SWINDON JANUARY - 1894 —
Nº 11277

This drawing appears to date the water tank, a curious structure, massively built and related, it is presumed, to the requirements for 'head' throughout the yard. The text mentions the earth fill necessary about the shed and this section illustrates the uneven nature of the ground.

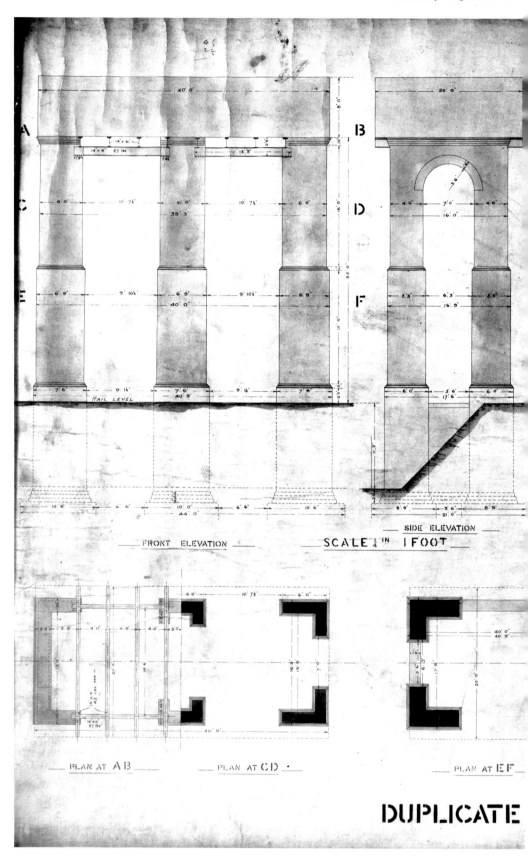

FRONT ELEVATION

SIDE ELEVATION

SCALE ¼ IN 1 FOOT

PLAN AT AB

PLAN AT CD

PLAN AT EF

DUPLICATE

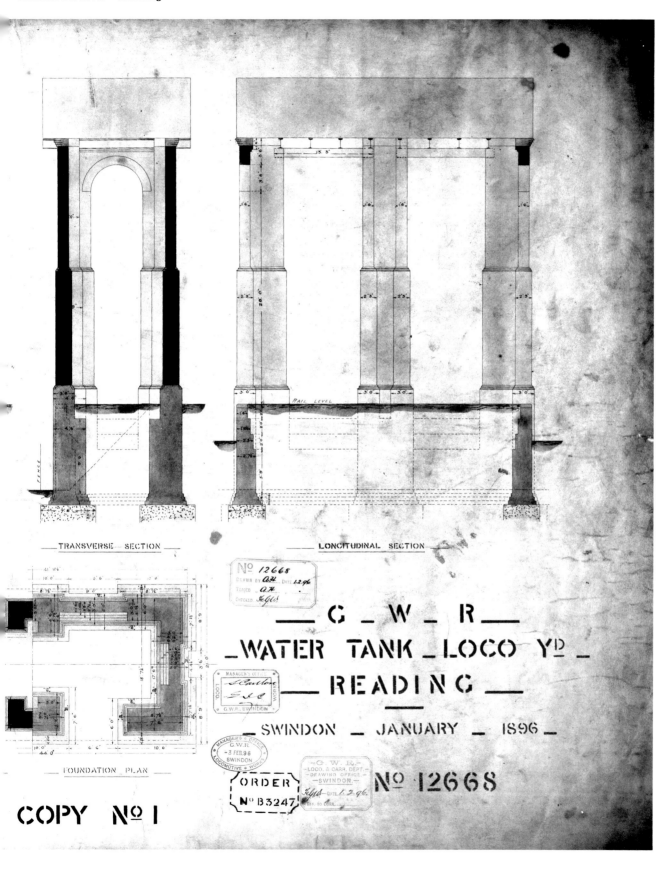

TRANSVERSE SECTION

LONGITUDINAL SECTION

RAIL LEVEL

FOUNDATION PLAN

N° 12668
DRAWN BY O.H. DATE 1.2.96
TRACED O.H.
CHECKED

_ G _ W _ R _
_ WATER TANK _ LOCO Yᴰ _
_ READING _

_ SWINDON _ JANUARY _ 1896 _

N° 12668

ORDER
N° B3247

COPY N° I

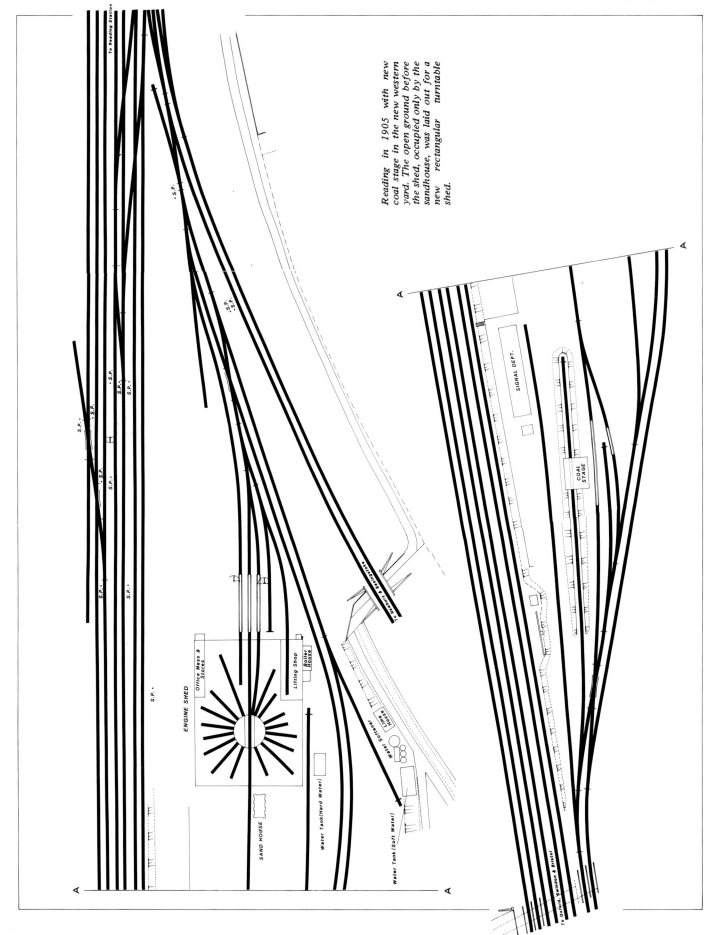

Reading in 1905 with new coal stage in the new western yard. The open ground before the shed, occupied only by the sandhouse, was laid out for a new rectangular turntable shed.

To Reading Station

S.P.

S.P.

S.P.

S.P.

S.P.

S.P.

S.P.

S.P.

S.P.

S.P.

S.P.

S.P.

ENGINE SHED

Office Mess & Stores

Lifting Shop

Boiler House

Water Softener

Lime House

SAND HOUSE

Water Tank (Hard Water)

Water Tank (Soft Water)

To Henley & Maidenhead

SIGNAL DEPT.

COAL STAGE

A

A

A

A

To Oxford, Swindon & Bristol

The Reading approaches during alterations. There was permanent way work in and around the shed more or less continuously, set as it was amidst such a notable triangle; this view is of some note in that it shows the former shed connections and, beyond the 'head stop' buffers, the beginnings of the new connection.

British Railways

The 'ideal shed' at Reading was awkwardly arranged — a roundhouse with odd roads put in and others foreshortened. The water softener was long a feature, a cleaner assigned for the more unpleasant work, whilst a boilerwasher attended to the sludge removal. It was a considerable height, of course, and a dropped rivet caused at least one unpleasant, if minor injury — on the head it could have been fatal. Water and its treatment much concerned the company, *The Thirsty Locomotive* overleaf details the subject thus in July 1940.　　　　　*British Railways*

THE THIRSTY LOCOMOTIVE
Some Facts about Water Supply

Having in earlier articles described the coaling of Great Western locomotives, a few particulars regarding the arrangements made by the Chief Mechanical Engineer's Department to ensure the supply of water for locomotive purposes may not be out of place. The importance of this phase of railway working will be appreciated when it is stated that our engines consume upwards of 2,000,000,000 gallons annually.

How the Water is Obtained

Water for locomotive purposes is purchased at about 270 stations on the Great Western system. Some idea of the quantities thus acquired in different localities may be gathered when it is stated that 220 million gallons are taken annually from the Metropolitan Water Board, and 266 million gallons from the Cardiff Corporation, and smaller quantities from other municipal authorities and water companies. Other sources of supply, subject to rental, are ponds, streams and reservoirs on private property.

In addition to these purchased supplies, an average yearly quantity of 400 million gallons is taken from canals adjacent to the railway at Devizes, Savernake, Taunton, Durston, Tiverton, Creech, Swansea, Landore, Aldermaston, Cwmbran, Panteg, Pontypool Rogerstone, Risca and Stratford-on-Avon. There are also about 180 pumping stations on the system, the sources of supply, including bore-holes and wells, being mostly situated on our own property. Lastly, at a few stations a sufficient quantity is obtained from gravitation supplies.

Making the Water suitable for Locomotive Purposes

It is not always easy to find a satisfactory supply of water just where it is needed to meet the requirements of the traffic. Even when found, natural waters are not often ideal for use in locomotive boilers, and in many cases they have to receive treatment before use. Most of the natural waters in this country are 'hard', this applying generally to supplies drawn from deep wells and bore holes, due to the fact that the water dissolves chalk and other minerals while it is percolating through the ground. The water in rivers fed by deep-seated springs is also hard, but in rivers and streams in districts with a rocky impervious sub-soil, the water is collected mainly by surface drainage and is 'soft'.

On the Great Western Railway system the majority of supplies in the Midlands and towards the East are hard, whereas those in the West of England and in Wales are soft. The chalk and other minerals in solution in the hard waters cause scale to form on the internal heating surfaces of the boiler in the same way that 'fur' accumulates in a kettle. The scale is objectionable for several reasons. It retards the transference of heat from the burning coal to the water in the boiler and thus wastes fuel, and it causes leakage and damage to boiler tubes and fireboxes, involving increased bills for repairs and causing engines to be out of service for descaling or repairs when they could be profitably employed in traffic.

This is not the whole of the trouble, as some of the substances dissolved in natural waters corrode boiler metals and, unless their action is counteracted by suitable treatment, may reduce the life of boilers and necessitate frequent and costly replacement of tubes and other parts. Fortunately, there are available comparatively simple and inexpensive means of preventing both scale and corrosion. Where large supplies are involved, the cheapest and best method is to soften the water by the addition of small proportions of lime, soda ash, sodium aluminate, etc., which throw out all the scale-forming substances as a sludge. This process is carried out in water-softening plants at the following stations, where many hundreds of millions of gallons are treated yearly:—

	Capacity *Gallons per hour*
Aldermaston	10,000
Goring	20,000
Old Oak Common	40,000
Reading	15,000
Southall	7,000
Severn Tunnel Junction	30,000
Cardiff (Crwys)	6,000

In addition to the above there are two softeners in operation for stationary boiler purposes, these being at:—

Sudbrook pumping station	15,000 gallons capacity
Swindon works	12,000 " "

The scale-forming substances settle to the bottom of the softeners, and *about 1,000 tons of sludge are removed yearly* from the water used to feed our locomotives. But for the softening process, the whole of the solids forming the sludge would be deposited as a scale inside the boilers. Tests to ensure the efficiency of the softening operations are made daily by softener attendants. A check is also carried out at frequent intervals by the Swindon laboratory staff.

With smaller supplies the erection of a softening plant is not justified, and use is made of apparatus that adds suitable chemicals to the water as it enters the locomotive tender. As the temperature of the water in the boiler is raised, the chemicals cause the substances which would otherwise form scale to be precipitated as 'mud'.

The mud, however, if allowed to accumulate, might choke the water spaces between the tubes, and the concentration of dissolved salts in the boiler water would be liable to cause 'priming', i.e. the carrying-over of water with the steam from the boiler to the cylinders, which is detrimental to the efficient working of the engine. To overcome these difficulties, locomotive boilers are fitted with a deconcentrator, or automatic blowdown valve, which enables a small quantity of water and mud to be constantly withdrawn from the boiler while the engine is in service, and thus keeps the proportions of solids in solution and in suspension within safe limits.

The deconcentrator is a steam-operated valve which opens automatically when the regulator is opened and shuts when it is closed, thus operating only when the engine is in motion. When the valve is open, water flows through it from a pipe projecting into the water space of the boiler. After passing through an orifice which controls the rate of flow, the fluid is cooled in pipes immersed in the cold water in the tender, and finally ejected on to the track.

British Railways

Evidence of the complexity of trackwork around the depot. The area close by the shed approach appears to be given over to coal stacks, removed to the western yard on rebuilding of the shed. *British Railways*

4–4–0s were the principal engine type at Reading for many years; it lay at the heart of the Division and was as V. R. Webster usefully terms it, 'essentially the first provincial shed out of London, as distinct from suburban sheds, though many of the residential trains were in effect outer suburban and had Bulldogs or County tanks.' 'County' 4–4–0s long did service on the Reading pilot jobs and were also much in evidence on the Weymouth line, working out of Reading as well as Westbury and Weymouth. A Westbury 4–4–0 would come up on, say, the 8.21 a.m. from Frome, running non-stop Newbury to Paddington, slipping at Reading and getting into London at 10.52. This returned on the 12.30 to Weymouth (arrive 4.8 p.m.). The 4.15 ex-Weymouth was also part of these services, the engine working through to London and returning to Reading on the 10.45 p.m. stopping train. The next day the 4–4–0 came off Reading shed to take the 11.45 from Weymouth at 2.50 p.m., engine and coaches then forming the 6.00 p.m. Paddington to Weymouth. This was alternately a Reading and a Weymouth engine, though it is not clear to what use (if any) it was put between its 10 p.m. arrival at Weymouth and the 4.15 p.m. the next day.   *British Railways*

County of Denbigh on 23rd June 1929.   *S. W. Baker*

An impressive attempt was made at night-time photography on the evening of the preceding view – *County Wicklow* outside the repair shop is unmoved and probably awaiting attention and a few more engines are distributed about the yard. The object of the study is presumed to have been comparative, probably a demonstration of a new lamp type. Illumination was often neglected at engine sheds and it would be entirely typical of thoroughgoing GWR methods for objective tests to be carried out. Implementation was something else: 'Normally the engine sheds and the adjoining tracks are brightly illuminated at night and staff have every facility in carrying out their tasks, so as almost to notice no inconvenience from day to night . . . '

British Railways

tender for supply and erection from the Pulsometer Engineering Company amounting to £1,260'. The Great Western softeners were nothing if not prominent and the Reading example became almost a local landmark. On 13th May 1915 a hot water boiler washing out plant was approved, cost £200.

It was necessary to return to the problem of space and accommodation at Reading after the Great War, in advance of the benefits afforded under the terms of the Loans and Guarantees Act. In the late part of 1925 consideration was given to various detailed alterations; all were designed to avoid the high cost of a new building and a number of ideas emerged. New offices and a siding for 'stores van and oil tank' were proposed for the south side of the shed and extra stub sidings (four at least) were considered for the 65 ft turntable. Towards the end of the 1920s the ancient turntable in the roundhouse was proving increasingly inconvenient. It was too small for many engines, leaving them without cover during any attention that might be required and it was ever more prone to breakdown. The cheapest remedy was to convert the building to a straight shed. Earlier notions had made more sense, a second, spacious roundhouse disposed about the 65 ft 'table; these were unfortunately finally abandoned and a largely dead end straight shed, inconveniently arranged for the western part of the yard, was wrought from the original building. The first drawings for conversion of the old roundhouse into a straight shed, labelled 'Alterations to Engine Shed, Reading', appear on 15th November 1929, with much of the work to take place the fol-

The Robinson 2–8–0s worked over most of the GWR and were familiar across the London Division on freights. They were there so long that a grudging acceptance was (almost) earned. The history of goods locos associated with the two World Wars is a fascinating one and it is a shame that so much detail of the workings is now lost. On the Great Western alone 0–6–0s were transferred away to be replaced by LNER and LMS examples (see elsewhere) and all manner of Southern engines were put to use. ROD 2–8–0s were followed by Stanier, USA and WDs, a bewildering and generally unloved succession. In the far more flexible conditions of wartime working LNER 2–8–0s – '04s' proper – worked into the Division and were put to use: 'didn't like theirs any more than ours.' *Collection Peter Winding*

lowing year; in February 1930 the *Great Western Magazine* announced:

> The existing engine shed at Reading is of the turntable type with one table and 20 radial roads. Improved accommodation is required, and it is proposed, in connection with heavy maintenance repair work now necessary, to convert the shed to the straight-road type. A new lifting shop, with a 40-ton engine hoist, is also to be provided, together with improved stores, office and messroom accommodation.

Contracts were reported placed by November, for 'Alterations to Reading Engine Shed and Lifting Shop' with Messrs.

H. B. Bowyer of Slough, and on 18th December £3,040 was authorised for six engine hoists at various sites, Laira, Landore, among others as well as Reading, not the 40-ton equipment originally envisaged but lifts suitable for up to 50 tons. These were to become standard provision, and the Reading example, housed in its own separate repair shop, was ordered from Messrs. Royce of Manchester in February 1931.

The coal stage, since its construction, served only a single road, on the south side. This connected with the 65 ft turntable but

Continued on page 242

The GWR naming policy ranged from the heroic (*Amazon*) to the menacing (*Dragon, Gorgon*) through to the prosaic (*Jackdaw, Hillingdon Court*) to the frankly dull (*Paddington*). This is *Reading*, neither heroic nor menacing, at Reading on 26th September 1925. Having coaled, the engine has turned (or reversed) to take water alongside the 'ash road', a characteristic siding provided by most GW coal stages. The *GWR Magazine* looked back to this period in June 1937: 'Of the total cost of locomotive running last year, approximately one third, viz. £1,693,254, was in respect of fuel. It therefore behoves all concerned to do their utmost to ensure the most economical use of this commodity. Coal consumption is affected by a variety of factors, such as the steaming qualities of the coal used; the type of engine; the speed and load of trains; weather conditions, etc., which make it difficult to ascribe particular reasons for variations in the figures from year to year. In the case of the passenger services, the index figure of 95.93 last year was .95 per cent below that of the previous year, and 4.07 per cent below that of the basis years. This means that 36,000 more tons of coal were used by the passenger engines last year than would have been the case had the lower rate of consumption of ten years ago obtained. On the other hand, the consumption by the freight engines was reduced last year to the lowest figure yet attained, resulting in an improvement in the index number of 1.08 compared with the previous year, and 7.24 compared with the basis. The total consumption of coal by these engines was therefore 73,000 tons less than it would have been had the average of the basis years applied. Thus, taking the passenger and freight services together, substantial economy in the use of coal was achieved.'   *F. J. Agar*

No. 3250 on 17th February 1923. The Division changed in character 'out into the country' and increasingly the engines grouped at Reading, Didcot and Oxford had an unmistakeable ramshackle look to them. All shared this feature, a lightly worked complement of ancient engines put on the lighter jobs, which abounded throughout the GWR. Reading still had 2−4−0s on Nationalisation. *A. W. Croughton*

No. 3600 on 23rd August 1930. *W. Potter*

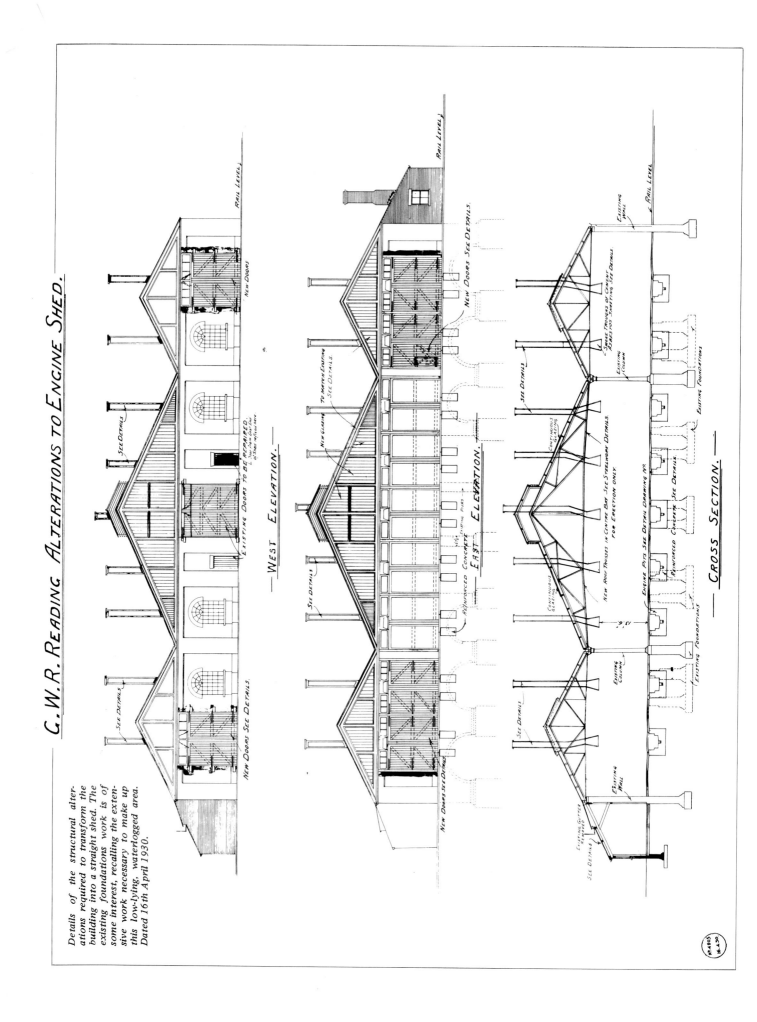

G.W.R. Reading Alterations to Engine Shed.

Details of the structural alterations required to transform the building into a straight shed. The existing foundations work is of some interest, recalling the extensive work necessary to make up this low-lying, waterlogged area. Dated 16th April 1930.

— WEST ELEVATION. —

See Details

New Doors See Details

Existing Doors to be Repaired

New Doors

Rail Level

— EAST ELEVATION. —

See Details

New Doors See Details

New Glazing to Match Existing See Details

New Doors See Details

New Existing Piers

Reinforced Concrete

Rail Level

— CROSS SECTION. —

See Details

Continuous Glazing

Continuous Glazing

New Roof Trusses in Centre Bay See Steelwork Details for Erection Only

Cement Troughs of Cement Asbestos for Sheeting See Details

Existing Wall

Existing Column

Existing Foundations

Reinforced Concrete See Details

Existing Foundations

Engine Pits See Detail Drawing No.

Existing Column

Existing Wall

Existing Gutter Removed

See Details

Rail Level

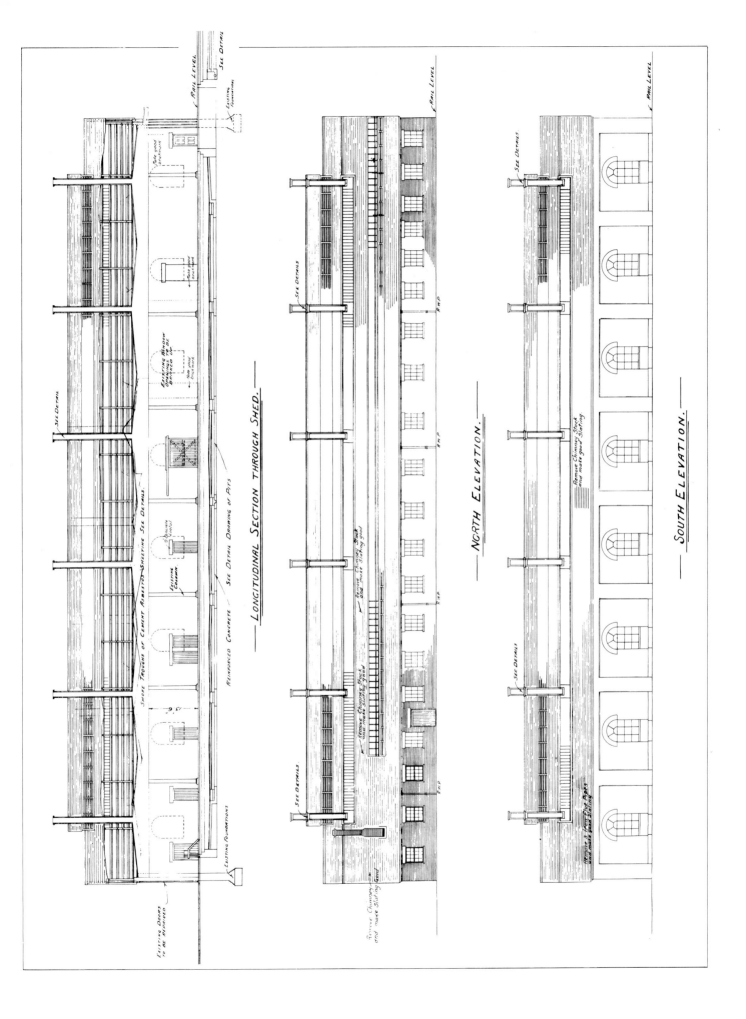

LONGITUDINAL SECTION THROUGH SHED.

NORTH ELEVATION.

SOUTH ELEVATION.

Internal arrangements, dated 28th March 1930. The new roads were renumbered from the north from the main line side 1-9 and the drawing shows No. 4 replacing a conventional turntable approach road. This originally dead end road (see earlier plan on page 218) was obviously converted prior to 1930.

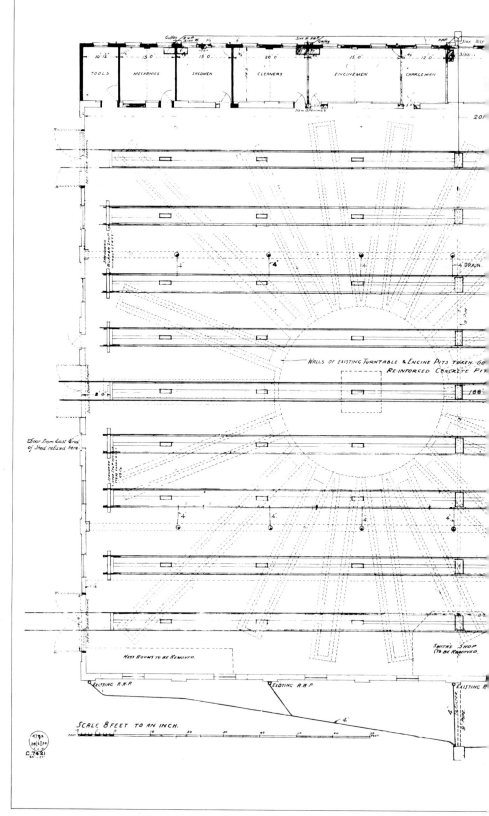

G.W.R. READING : ALTERATIONS TO ENGINE SHED.
GENERAL ARRANGEMENT.

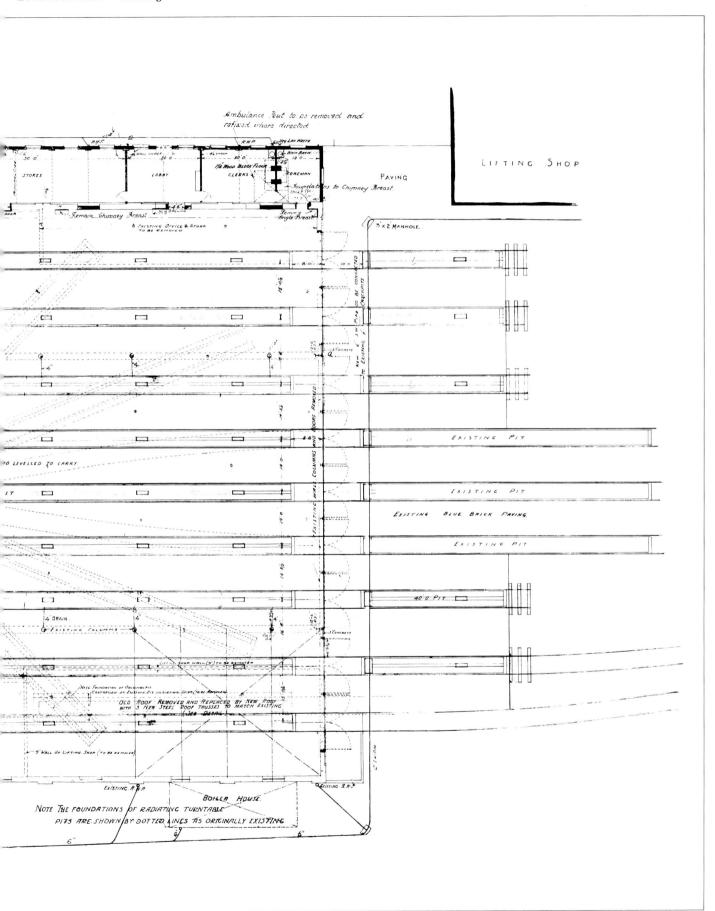

LIFTING SHOP

PAVING

Ambulance Tent to be removed and refixed where directed.

STORES

LOBBY

CLERKS

FOREMAN

Remove Chimney Breast

6 EXISTING OFFICE & STORE TO BE REMOVED

Foundations to Chimney Breast

3' x 2' MANHOLE

EXISTING PIT

EXISTING PIT

EXISTING BLUE BRICK PAVING

EXISTING PIT

40' 0" PIT

4" DRAIN

EXISTING COLUMNS

OLD ROOF REMOVED AND REPLACED BY NEW ROOF WITH 3 NEW STEEL ROOF TRUSSES TO MATCH EXISTING

EXISTING R.W.P.

BOILER HOUSE

NOTE THE FOUNDATIONS OF RADIATING TURNTABLE PITS ARE SHOWN BY DOTTED LINES AS ORIGINALLY EXISTING

New doors March 1930. They were by stages reduced to matchwood.

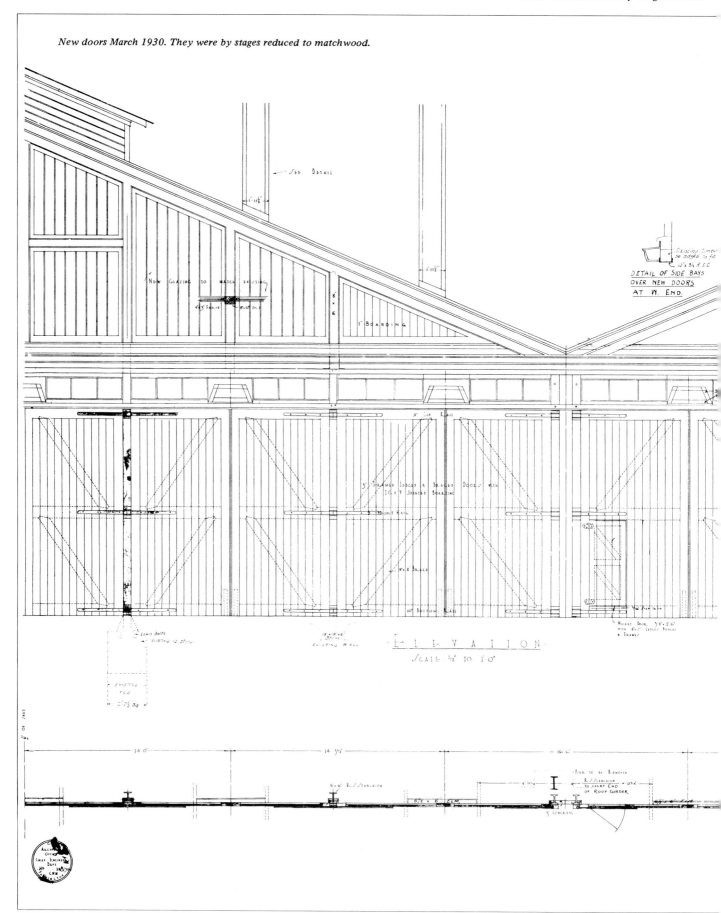

G.W.R. · READING — NEW · ENGINE · SHED
HALF · INCH · DETAILS

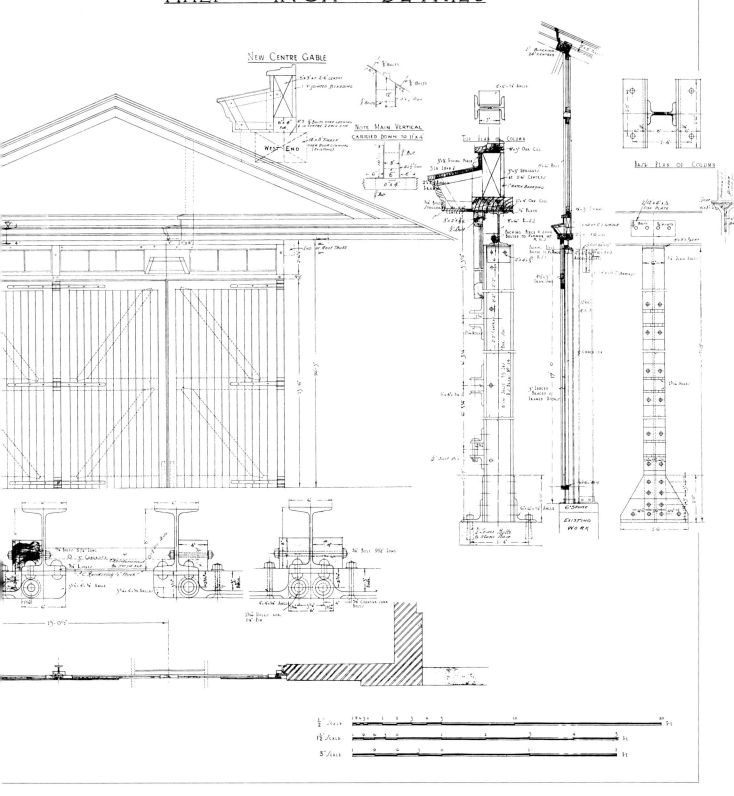

Adjoining details, drawing dated 13th May 1930. Such accommodation at most sheds was adapted and altered over the years and seldom finished up in its originally intended disposition.

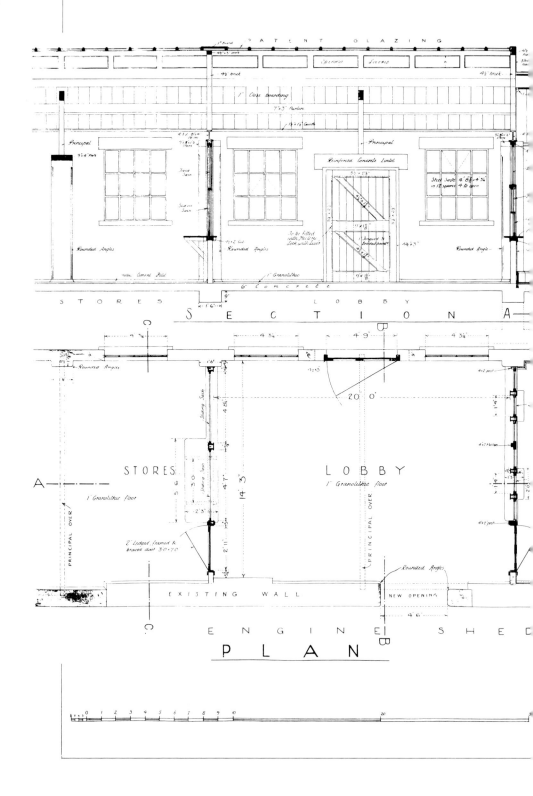

ENGINE SHED.
LOBBY &c.

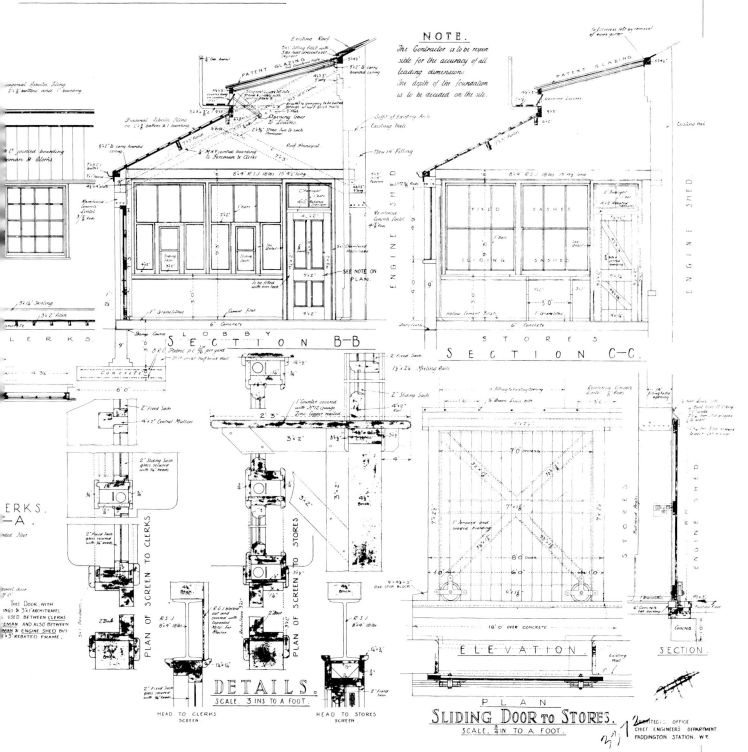

SECTION B-B

SECTION C-C.

DETAILS.
SCALE. 3 INS TO A FOOT.

HEAD TO CLERKS SCREEN

HEAD TO STORES SCREEN

NOTE.

The Contractor is to be responsible for the accuracy of all leading dimensions. The depth of the foundation is to be decided on the site.

ELEVATION.

PLAN

SLIDING DOOR TO STORES.
SCALE. ¾ IN TO A FOOT.

SECTION.

ARCHITECTS OFFICE
CHIEF ENGINEERS DEPARTMENT.
PADDINGTON STATION. W.

N° 4826
13.5.30

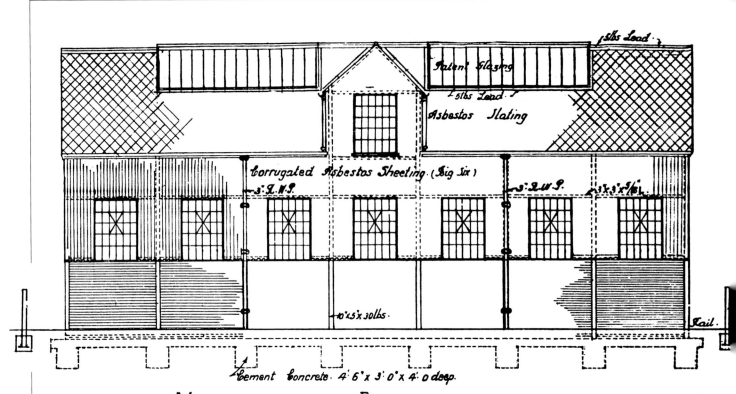

NORTH ELEVATION

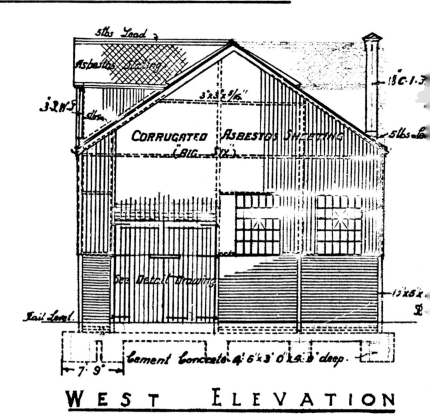

WEST ELEVATION

The Reading standard repair shed. The GWR kept repair work strictly separate – this was true of all major companies but Churchward sited the buildings physically remote from the running shed. The practice continued after his period with the 'lifting sheds', as they were usually termed, put up in 'Loan Act' style steel framing with corrugated sheeting. The drawing is dated 5th May 1930 and the work seems to have been more or less complete the following year.

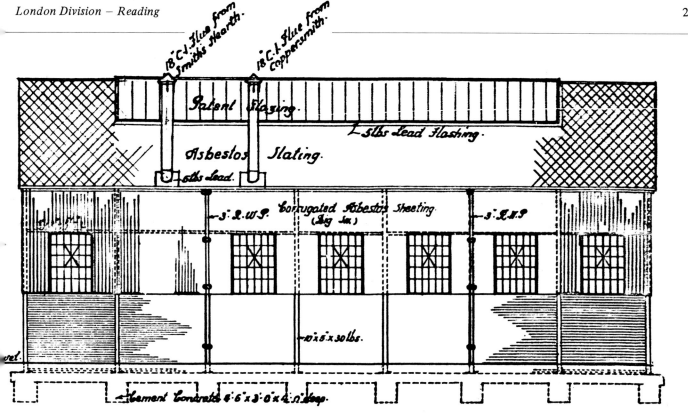

18" C.I. Flue from Smiths Hearth.

18" C.I. Flue from Coppersmith.

Patent Glazing.

5 lbs Lead Flashing.

Asbestos Slating.

6 lbs Lead.

3" R.W.P.

Corrugated Asbestos Sheeting (Big In.)

3" R.W.P.

10" x 5" x 30 lbs.

Cement Concrete 4'.6" x 3'.0" x 4'.0" deep.

SOUTH ELEVATION

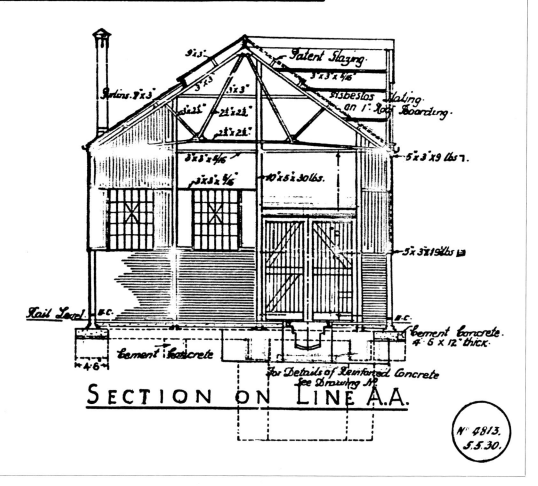

9 x 3.

Patent Glazing.

3" x 3" x 4/16"

Purlins 7 x 3

3 x 3

3" x 3"

Asbestos Slating on 1" Roof Boarding.

2½ x 2½

2½ x 2½

3" x 3" x 4/16"

5" x 3" x 9 lbs T.

3" x 3" x 4/16"

10" x 5" x 30 lbs.

5" x 3" x 19 lbs B

Rail Level.

B.C.

B.C.

Cement Concrete. 4'.6" x 12" thick.

Cement Concrete

4'.6"

For Details of Reinforced Concrete See Drawing №

SECTION ON LINE A.A.

No. 4813.
5.5.30.

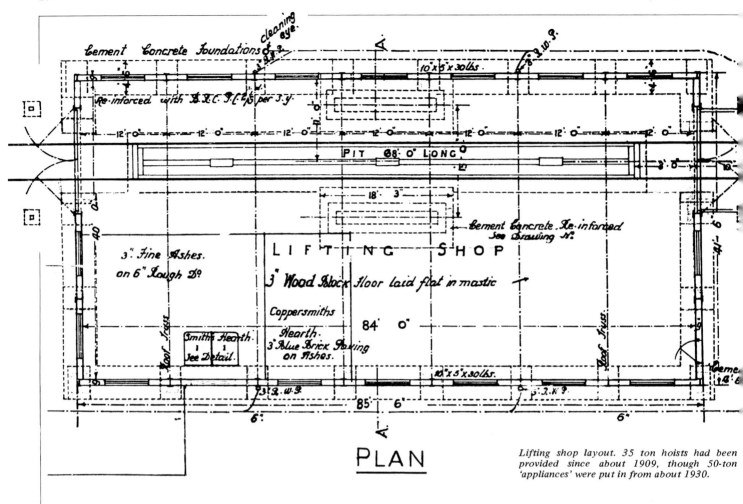

PLAN

Lifting shop layout. 35 ton hoists had been provided since about 1909, though 50-ton 'appliances' were put in from about 1930.

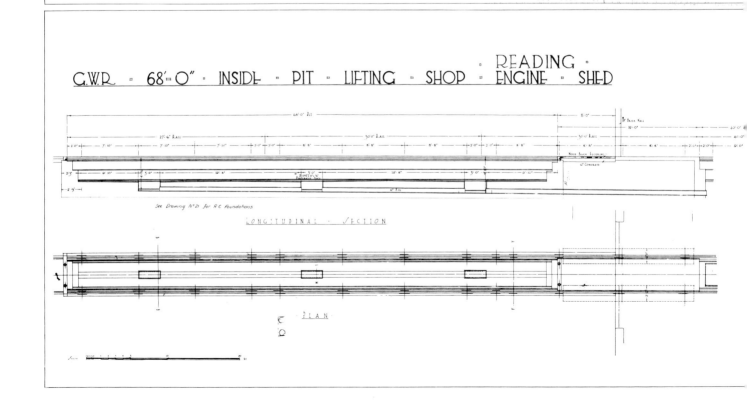

G.W.R · 68'-0" · INSIDE · PIT · LIFTING · SHOP · READING · ENGINE · SHED

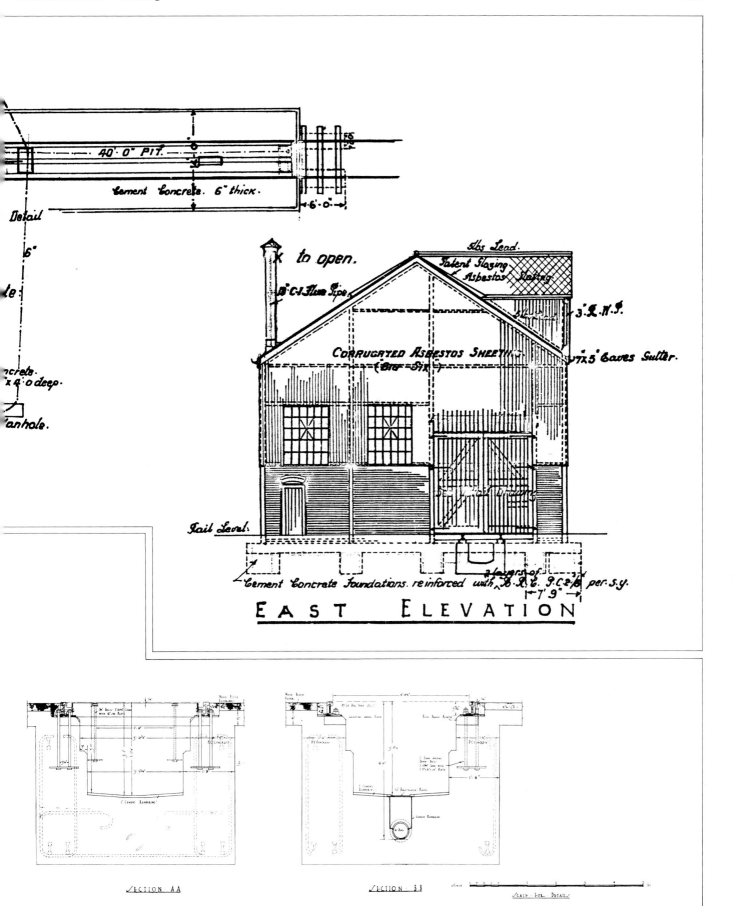

40'.0" PIT.

Cement Concrete. 6" thick.

←6'.0"→

Detail

6"

crete
x 4'.0 deep.

anhole.

to open.

9" C.I. Flue Pipe.

Abs Lead.

Patent Glazing
Asbestos Sheeting

3' L.N.S.

CORRUGATED ASBESTOS SHEETING
(B.G. Six)

7"x5" Eaves Gutter.

Rail Level.

Cement Concrete Foundations. reinforced with B.R.C. 9C2/6 per s.y.

←7'.9"→

EAST ELEVATION

SECTION AA

SECTION BB

SCALE FOR DETAILS

Ex-MSWJ 2—4—0 No. 1336 underneath what is left of the old roundhouse on 23rd August 1930. For years the three engines of the class, 1334, 1335 and 1336, were divided between Reading and Didcot.

H. C. Casserley

No. 526 at Reading on 23rd August 1930. The distinctive 'Clifton Down' stock was converted for auto working and ran for a time on the Henley service. It is not clear if the whole train went regularly into Reading shed for servicing or if the crew simply didn't bother with the tiresome exercise of uncoupling the auto-gear.

F. J. Agar

No. 570 on Saturday, 16th September 1933. Reading at this time customarily supplied such an engine for the Wallingford branch.

Collection Peter Winding

London '61' at Reading on 26th November 1938.   *Collection Peter Winding*

it was not until 1942–3 that work was put in hand to give the 'table multiple access, an elementary disposition for more convenient operation. A second coaling road (it required a corrugated iron extension to the stage, 'raised to 1:29' on the north side) was led on to the turntable, and a further road added on the south side. It all made for easier working in the conditions of wartime (it was indeed but a small part of nationally organised improvements) and included proposals for a further road on the north side of the depot, a 'spare coal wagon siding and accommodation for crippled engines'.

Reading occupied an unusual position; the town was a centre quite large enough to generate a considerable traffic in itself, a number of cross country services were routed through, whilst it also lay on the edge of the London suburban network. 'Residential' trains provided for this business, using 'Bulldog' 4–4–0s or 'County' tanks; a 'County' 4–4–0 regularly stood as down pilot ('3820 *County of Worcester*, seemingly for years') and the shed was much involved with work on the Weymouth line. 2–4–0s were common at Reading (two, Nos. 1335 and 1336, were still there at Nationalisation) working to Newbury, Westbury and Basingstoke. Nos. 3235, 3236, 3245, 3247, 3250 and 3251 were also employed in the 1920s. The hybrid 3521 class 4–4–0s were also there, with 3528 often serving as the up side pilot. Steam railmotors (diesel cars were later common at Reading) were used, on the

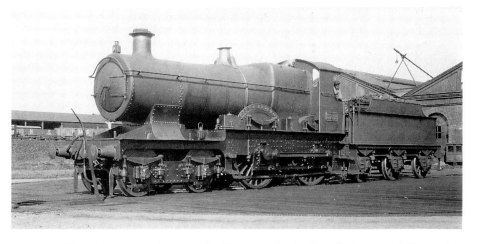

No. 3712 *City of Bristol* **on the turntable. There remained only a single approach line to the 'table passing through into the roundhouse. A number of ideas appeared over the years — the original notion of a new rectangular roundhouse turned up fairly regularly and any variation on extra radiating spurs. When the old shed was converted, the original through road remained the only direct access to the turntable. As the text relates, this left only a single coal stage road and Road No. 5 in the shed for access only, rendering it unavailable for 'stopped' work or stabling.**

Collection Peter Winding

Henley service for instance, and 'the 4.35 to Henley always pulled a trailer car as well'. No. 41 was at Reading in 1926 whilst tanks with two-coach autotrains were also on the work, No. 526 in June 1931, for example. 4–6–0s were introduced on the Weymouth services from 1927 and Reading's involvement meant that it shared the rosters. No. 2937 *Clevedon Court* thus came to be the first 4–6–0 to be stationed at Reading and eventually a 'Castle' was provided. The shed lay in the very midst of the Division and was responsible for a wide

variety of duties. Moguls and pannier tanks predominated but the allocation (which approached a hundred engines) contained a great diversity of types. In 1947 there were WD, Robinson and 2800 2–8–0s, diesel railcars, various passenger tanks, 4–4–0s and 2–4–0s. 0–6–0s were long important – No. 2573 was still there in 1950 and 2251s lasted more or less until the end. Five were there in 1959.

The numbers of 'Hall' and 'Grange' 4–6–0s increased steadily, from a dozen or so in the 1940s to nearly thirty in BR days.

Continued on page 255

Alterations, expensive and lengthy, took place during the war (unspecified improvements at Reading totalling £22,532 were ordered by the Ministry of War Transport) with the reordering of the coal stage and its approaches. Reading was part of a north-south conduit made vital by war and new construction took place wherever appropriate. Reading coaling arrangements were unsatisfactory for the greatly increased traffic and new approach roads and a rebuilt stage ('to be raised to 1 in 29') allowed engines to coal either side. *British Railways*

New pit under construction to serve the new north road and coaling shelter. It was in concrete (like the repair shop example, see page 238), which by the 1940s had superseded many traditional railway materials. All the four companies had established substantial concrete works by this time, the GWR Taunton premises dating (in a small way) from 1898. The sidings to the left were part of the plans, and appear to have been put in first to afford access to the new work, a spare coal wagon siding branching to accommodation for crippled engines. *British Railways*

The work was executed to plans dating from 12th October 1942, though the first wartime alterations had taken place very early on. Three dining coaches, Nos. 9579, 9583 and 9675, had been parked in a short siding at the south side of the station, adjoining the road, and under a 'wartime catering' order of 1st October 1939, they were to be repositioned at the shed, alongside the Lifting Shop. In the first hours of the war a siren had gone off at Reading in broad daylight — everyone had leapt under shelter, however inappropriate, in and about the station, leaving an unpleasant silence finally broken, absurdly, by a whistling kettle. Much of this was soon laughed off and there was thankfully a respite of several months before bombing began in earnest. By 1941 there had been plenty of it. The *Great Western Magazine:*

Good Work at our Locomotive Depots

One of the most notable and least publicised features of present-day transport services on the Great Western and other British Railways is the good work being done at locomotive depots, where the problems both of black-out and air raid are being tackled and overcome night after night.

Now everything is carried out under subdued lighting systems controlled by master switches, which are brought into use at a moment's notice to black-out the lights when air raids occur. Wherever possible, more work is being carried out than formerly during daytime, but there is still much that has to be done during the night hours.

The firebox has to be cleared of clinker and ashes, and at night during this operation, great care is necessary, and is, of course, taken, to prevent a glow showing from the hot clinker and ashes. A visit has then to be made to the coal stage and water column for refuelling, to the turntable, and thence to one of the lines in the engine shed where fitters and boilermakers deal with any defects reported by the engine drivers when they 'book off' their turns of duty.

Whitewashed walls and locality-marks assist the work, and, although air raid shelters are provided, things have to become pretty hot before the men cease work. Groping through the black-out is not an easy matter these nights, and the spirit of the enginemen and other members of the Locomotive Department staff is commendably resolute.

War-time brings sudden and unexpected calls to the depots, and although normally it takes three hours for a locomotive to obtain a proper 'head' of steam, means are found to meet urgent requirements, systems of distribution being now kept elastic so that engines rostered for routine trips may be changed over to other duties at short notice.

'Government traffic' is the discreet description for many of the special trains for which engine power is needed, and coal trains are also making increasing calls for locomotive energy.

In order that drivers may have their trains fully under control in the event of a sudden emergency, freight trains travel during night 'alerts' at speeds up to 10 miles an hour, and passsenger trains are operated at speeds up to 15 miles an hour. During air raids in the daylight passenger trains and braked goods trains travel at speeds up to 25 miles an hour, and other goods trains up to 15 miles an hour. Although it is impracticable to quote examples, experience is showing the value of these rules, and appreciation of that fact will help to reconcile passengers to delays which occur to their trains by reason of restricted speeds.

The local air raid is not the only cause of difficulty in making the best possible use of locomotive power. Enginemen reporting at their depots for duty on certain trains may be affected by air raids occurring in other districts, so that, where possible, alternative duties have to be arranged.

Improvement works which had been carried out at many locomotive depots before the war are, in the exceptional circumstances of today, saving very valuable time and avoiding much heavy manual labour. For instance, our water-softening plants are proving their worth, and the additional break-down trains provided are doing excellent work when calls are made upon their services.

To-day, to the disappointment of many of our readers, those enthusiasts who follow with interest and fascination the activities of our locomotives, are for the time being unable to indulge their hobby to the same extent as in peace-time. This is because, for reasons of national security, it is necessary to refrain from disclosing information which might prove useful to the enemy. But followers of locomotive practice and performance can be assured that British-built steam locomotives and their crews have accomplished feats of energy and endurance fully in keeping with their fine traditions, and that when it is possible to tell the full story of inland transport in this war, the work and adventures of our locomotives will make interesting and inspiring reading.   *British Railways*

Engines were customarily (and necessarily) lined up on the turntable approach, the scene of at least one 'incident'. A pair of 'Castles' ended up in the pit — the first having been moved forward without sufficient steam for the brake. It trundled majestically into the pit while the 'Castle' behind, without its handbrake on, moved quietly off in pursuit. This took place some time after the war and the boarding, if still in place, would certainly not have survived such an experience. The Old Oak crane came to the rescue — Reading had a tool van with jacks, etc., but could not possibly cope in these circumstances. Such basic provision had dated from Armstrong's day: '17th May 1865 — much inconvenience had been felt during the Winter months from want at the Locomotive Stations of tools and appliances requisite to meet such an exigency as an Engine breaking down. £510 for screw jacks at Paddington, Reading, Didcot, Birmingham, Newport, Pontypool.' *British Railways*

The new coal stage was completed in 1943. Coal production did not rise in the way hoped for during the Second World War and there was a constant pressure to conserve supplies. The *GWR Magazine* of January 1942 contained one such exercise — *Fuelling our Locomotives*.

Fuelling our Locomotives

Following up the remarks in our issue of November last on 'Conserving our Fuel Supplies', and bearing in mind that the coal for use in the fireboxes of locomotives forms the biggest item in the Company's annual coal bill, opportunity is here taken to consider what steps are open to enginemen and firemen to exercise footplate economy.

To get a background for the subject, and to indicate its importance, it may be mentioned that at present about 94,500,000 miles are run per annum on the Great Western Railway, and to accomplish this mileage nearly 2,000,000 tons of coal are consumed by locomotives. *Based on this huge mileage, it will be seen that a reduction or saving of only 1 lb. of coal per mile would result in an annual saving of over 42,000 tons.* And this volume of coal can perhaps be better visualised when it is stated that it represents about 4,200 wagon loads or 84 trains of 50 wagons each.

The general principles to be followed to bring about economy are well known to experienced footplate men, but the following brief notes may be of interest to all.

Economy in fuel commences with the preparation of an engine for the road by the shed staff, when, under the coal stage tips, the coal on tender or bunker is carefully stacked and trimmed *to prevent it falling off.*

The smokebox, firebox, brick arch, ashpan and tubes receive proper attention, being cleaned of dirt and clinker to ensure the proper combustion of the fuel.

When the fire is started in the box, the steam-raisers should see that it is so regulated that the engine has sufficient fire and steam pressure, when the driver and fireman arrive on duty, to enable the fireman to build up his fire, so that when the engine goes off shed it is just right to take on its train without any waste of fuel or steam pressure. Attention should be paid to all leaky joints and valves on the engine to prevent any waste of steam.

When on the road, the careful man will regulate the size of his fire to suit the grade of coal in use and the weight of the train to be hauled, as it is an obvious waste of fuel to make up a large fire when a smaller one is sufficient.

To use very large lumps of coal tends to cause voids in the fire and does not contribute to economy. The emission of smoke is in general

an indication that proper combustion is not taking place, and that fuel is being wasted instead of being burnt.

The old adage of the fireman: "little and often" is the best policy when firing a locomotive. Heavy firing is detrimental to good steaming and is avoided by the skilful fireman.

The steam blower is not used when running unless absolutely necessary, as this tends to draw ashes and partly-burnt coal into the flue tubes and choke them.

The careful man is mindful of the stage reached on his journey and so regulates matters that, as the engine nears the end of its trip, the fire is worked down, until on arrival at the shed there is the least possible amount of fire left in the box, and the engine is ready for servicing by the shed staff.

The interest and co-operation of all concerned is to be desired. If the older men pass on the knowledge gained by their experience to the younger men it will generally be appreciated, and should result in both working together to attain that economical use of fuel which is so necessary from the country's point of view in the stern war-time conditions of today.

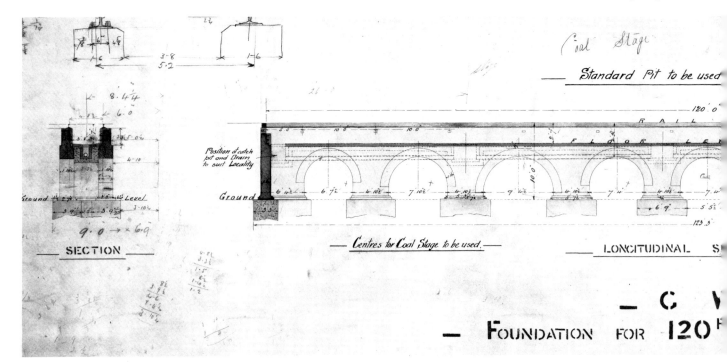

Work in progress on the southern part of the new turntable approaches.

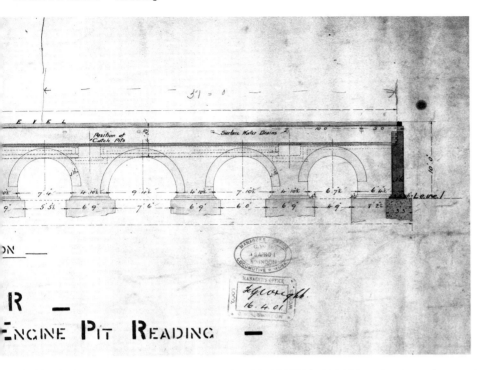

Earlier coal stage pit in conventional brickwork. Dated 16th April 1901, a working drawing suitably adorned with notes and scribble.

Southern Railway No. 933 *Kings Canterbury* at the temporary servicing area. SR engines long had a connection with the GWR shed despite the company's own engine shed in the town. 4—4—0s worked in from Fratton on through Portsmouth/Southampton-Reading trains via Basingstoke, whilst in the 1920s an engine would come up from the Southern shed to work the 8.38 p.m. to Basingstoke. This was probably a mileage 'balancing act', the engine returning with a fast mails at about midnight. Locos included 2—6—4T No. 804 (before the Sevenoaks derailment) and LSWR 4—4—0 No. E422. Reading men knew their Southern counterparts well and they were considered a 'decent bunch', if something of a law unto themselves. They were notable for a most peculiar and quite obscene joke 'matey' name ascribed to their unfortunate association with 'the Navy' (all Southern men were assumed to come from Portsmouth). *British Railways*

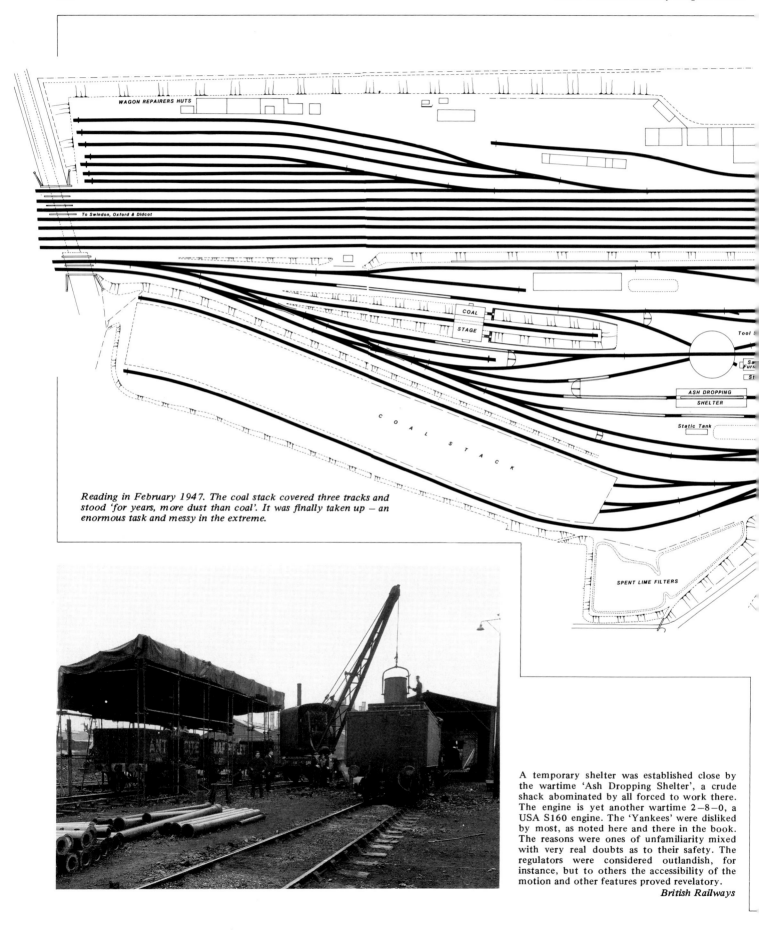

WAGON REPAIRERS HUTS

To Swindon, Oxford & Didcot

COAL STAGE

C O A L   S T A C K

ASH DROPPING SHELTER

Static Tank

Tool S

S
Furn
St

SPENT LIME FILTERS

Reading in February 1947. The coal stack covered three tracks and stood 'for years, more dust than coal'. It was finally taken up — an enormous task and messy in the extreme.

A temporary shelter was established close by the wartime 'Ash Dropping Shelter', a crude shack abominated by all forced to work there. The engine is yet another wartime 2–8–0, a USA S160 engine. The 'Yankees' were disliked by most, as noted here and there in the book. The reasons were ones of unfamiliarity mixed with very real doubts as to their safety. The regulators were considered outlandish, for instance, but to others the accessibility of the motion and other features proved revelatory.

British Railways

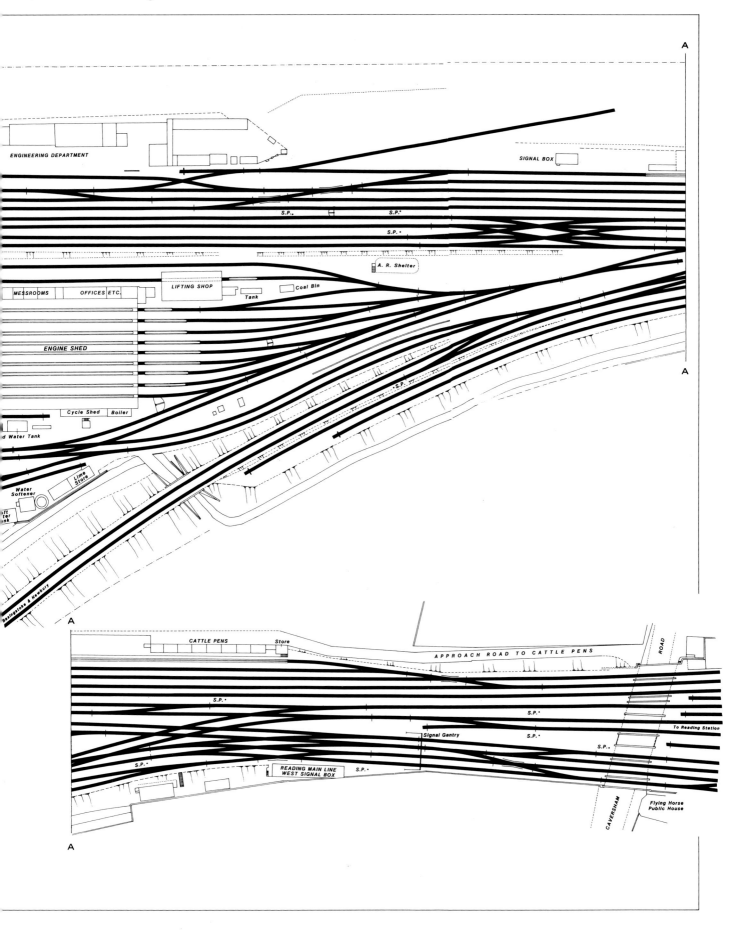

ENGINEERING DEPARTMENT

SIGNAL BOX

S.P.*

S.P.*

S.P.*

A. R. Shelter

LIFTING SHOP

MESSROOMS OFFICES ETC.

Tank Coal Bin

ENGINE SHED

S.P.*

Cycle Shed Boiler

d Water Tank

Water Softener

Lime Store

ft er nk

Basingstoke & Newbury

A

A

A

A

CATTLE PENS Store

APPROACH ROAD TO CATTLE PENS

ROAD

S.P.*

S.P.*

To Reading Station

Signal Gantry

S.P.*

S.P.*

S.P.*

READING MAIN LINE WEST SIGNAL BOX

S.P.*

S.P.*

CAVERSHAM

Flying Horse Public House

A

Reading straight shed. The engine on the left appears to be an LMS 0–6–0 which would seem to date the period 1940-c.1945. Details of the exchanges were given in March 1940 in the *Great Western Railway Magazine*: 'Engines for War Service — The following additional 2301 class, 0–6–0, engines have undergone repairs and have been despatched overseas, this making thirty-nine forwarded to date:- Nos. 2418, 2562, 2553, 2441, 2429, 2481, 2400, 2526, 2412, 2455, 2454, 2544, 2447, 2432, 2560, 2416. In all, a hundred engines are required for this purpose, and at the request of the War Office the whole of them are to be of the same Great Western pattern. To compensate the Company for the withdrawal of this stock, forty 0–6–0 engines are being transferred from the London Midland and Scottish Railway, and forty 0–6–0s from the London and North Eastern Railway. As the Great Western share of the hundred engines 'called up' twenty engines have been selected from the condemned list to go back into service after re-conditioning. Their numbers are:- 4–4–0 Nos. 3378, 3335, 2–6–0 Nos. 2640, 2652, 2657, 0–6–0 Nos. 876, 884, 885 (ex Cambrian Railway. Nos. 74, 87 and 88 respectively). 0–6–0 Nos. 2315, 2354, 2380, 2–6–2T No. 3170, 0–6–0T Nos. 1910, 1979, 2004, 2019, 1742, 1747, 1795, 1875. So far, the fifty-four London Midland and Scottish and London and North Eastern engines shown below are in the possession of this Company, and they will soon be seen in service:- L.M. & S. — 3023, 3027, 3039, 3047, 3048, 3078, 3081, 3085, 3096, 3108, 3109, 3119, 3121, 3126, 3127, 3196, 3372, 3485, 3516, 3517, 3526, 3536, 3543, 3545, 3564, 3603, 3688, 3689, 3696, 3758. L. and N.E. — 29, 257, 536, 1963, 1969, 1973, 1981, 1982, 1986, 1989, 1992, 2000, 2040, 2047, 2061, 2065, 2069, 2071, 2073, 2075, 2076, 2135, 2136, 2138. The London Midland and Scottish engines are, for the time being, allocated to the Old Oak Common and Bristol divisions, and the London and North Eastern engines to the Wolverhampton and Worcester divisions.'

British Railways

'Reading sheds GWR circa 1945'. The diesel railcars were less than enthusiastically regarded at Reading for the teething troubles were protracted. Nos. 1, 2 and 3 were all at the shed, customarily stabled on No. 1 Road. Railcar No. 1 in particular is remembered for its long sojourns here 'usually having its engine out'. Beyond the south side of the shed lay the ancient coal stack, an area called 'The Field', a favourite enginemen's term in use at both Didcot and Oxford. Engines at Reading, as elsewhere, were serviced as appropriate and stabled as far as possible in their order of 'going out', which would determine their 'way round'. Official procedure was a barely acknowledged ideal practice laid out as much else in exact detail:

Cleaning the fire grate and disposal of ashes

'Just as we rake out the fire at home and take up the ashes, so is it necessary to clean out the fire grates and smokeboxes of locomotives.

'On arrival at the shed after completing a turn of duty, the engine is left on the coal-stage road, and at a point nearby the fire and smokebox are cleaned out, as also is the ashpan — a long ashpan rake being used for the latter purpose. This work is important, as the steaming of an engine can be adversely affected by a choked ashpan, and the firebars are also liable to be burnt.

'The boiler tubes, through which the gases from the firebox pass, are generally 'blown' or cleaned on the ashpit road. This is done with what is known as a steam lance, made up of a length of flexible armoured hose, to which is attached a metal pipe about 7 feet long, tapering to a nozzle at the end. The flexible pipe is coupled to a steam valve on the front plate of the smokebox, and the nozzle of the lance inserted in turn into each tube. When the steam valve is opened a powerful jet of steam rushes through the tube, removing the soot, etc. The tube plate and brick arch at the firebox end also receive attention; all ashes thrown on to the brick arch are removed and any deposit on the tube plate is cleaned off. The cleaning of the boiler tubes and brick arch are very important items in the preparation of an engine, as the best steaming results can only be obtained from a boiler with clear tubes, and an economy in coal is also effected.

'The shed turner now moves the engine from the fire pit and stops it under the coal-stage tip. The smokebox ashes are kept separate from the rough or firebox ashes, and both are finally loaded up into separate trucks for sale. Those from the smokebox are sold as fine ashes and those from the firebox as rough, some 20,000 wagon loads being disposed of annually by sale. Until recently many thousand tons of ashes found their way to various housing sites, but latterly the bulk have been sent to camps, aerodromes and factories in course of erection.'

There were three shed turns at Reading, amongst the lowest of the links and covering 24 hours. These men would move engines from the 'fire pit' or coal stage or wherever to their desired position in the shed or yard ready for the off, whenever that might be. Occasionally dead engines had to be dealt with, for which permission was necessary. An engine lying in 'The Field' in steam was on one occasion utilised to shift a dead engine in the yard. Hand points (short lever — sudden clonk) were employed on exit from 'The Field', and the engine was taken out before it was decided another could be more conveniently used (to dire verbal consequences). Reversing back, the engine came off the tracks, smashing the ATC and deranging the points, stuck partially open through one of the innumerable coal lumps off the decaying stack. The fitters knocking off at 5 o'clock, and anyone else not sufficiently fleet of foot, were immediately press-ganged by the foreman for the necessary remedial action. This sort of event was very much everyday stuff around any fair-sized engine shed and the tool van with its jacks was designed for just such a minor incident. Familiarity, however, did little to temper the language and the general opprobrium heaped upon the hapless fellow 'responsible' for the disaster.   *M. W. Earley*

Railcar No. 12 on 27th April 1957. Reading came to be the main (DMU) depot for the London commuter stock, a three-road shed dating from at least 1957, eventually responsible for all the sets. The introduction of the GW cars was wholly unpromising, 'it was a long time before they worked properly', and they were considered something of a nuisance. Heads shook sadly as the hapless No. 1's engine came out 'again and again'.   *R. C. Riley*

Renewal work in April 1956.

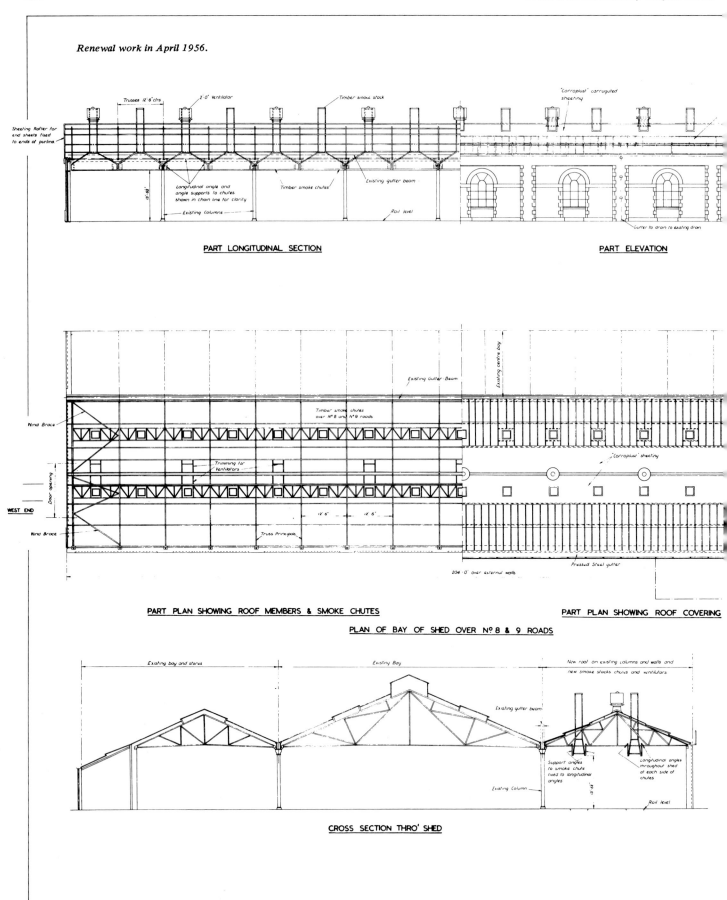

PART LONGITUDINAL SECTION   PART ELEVATION

PART PLAN SHOWING ROOF MEMBERS & SMOKE CHUTES   PART PLAN SHOWING ROOF COVERING

PLAN OF BAY OF SHED OVER Nº 8 & 9 ROADS

CROSS SECTION THRO' SHED

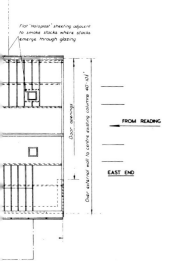

The new roof, etc., over Roads 8 and 9. The area of 'The Field', in latter years used increasingly as a dump. The redundancy of so many 0–6–0Ts was a dramatic feature on the Western Region in the 1960s. The GWR had employed 'tankies' more than any comparable company and it was precisely the work with which these engines were concerned that collapsed so dramatically. *Photomatic*

BRITISH RAILWAYS		WESTERN REGION
CIVIL ENGINEER'G DEPT STEELWORK SECTION		PADDINGTON
REVISED	LONDON DISTRICT	
	READING LOCO. DEPOT.	
	PROPOSED ROOF COVERING SMOKE CHUTES & STACKS OVER ROADS Nº 8 & 9	
	SCHEME A4.	

D.E.	CORR	C.E.	APPROVED		SCALES ⅛" TO I FOOT
22060/1EA S 4978					
C.J.B.					D.E's. No. 10697.
SHEET I OF I		CHIEF CIVIL ENGINEER			C.E's. No. S 4978

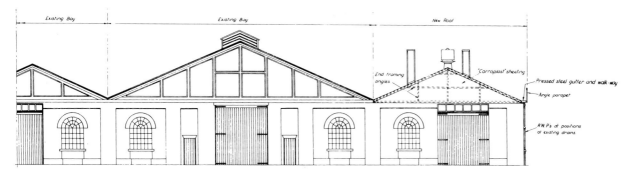

WEST ELEVATION

Reading west end on 10th August 1951 with (left to right) the tender of No. 1335, the MSWJ engine against that of mogul No. 5377, pannier tanks Nos. 5762 and 9402 and the tender of 6802 *Bampton Grange*. No. 4995 *Easton Hall* stands by the decrepit ash shelter in front of 3453 *Seagull* and 2894.

W. Potter

4085 *Berkeley Castle* was the only engine of its class in 1947 but more appeared in the 'fifties, displaced elsewhere by diesels.

Reading seems to have been rather a happier place than most (the foreman, Mr. Brown in the 1920s, was remarkable for eschewing the almost obligatory bowler hat, if that means anything) and the place was notable in latter years for a high proportion of mild eccentrics. Amongst the usual range of extroverts was a bathing enthusiast, renowned for his taking of a full dip in any weather, inside a suitable tender.

There was a lot of tank engine work at Reading, principally concerned with the London passenger trains and the '61s', 2–6–2Ts of the 6100 series, enabled some considerable changes to be made to the service from their introduction in the 1930s. They were of a (relatively) prodigious power and size and characterised the London passenger jobs until replaced by railcar sets. A 'double tripper', Reading to Paddington and back twice in a shift, was a hard day and 'you knew you'd done a day's work'. Reading men also worked a

lot to Basingstoke; the one-coach, fondly remembered, 'Basingstoke Mail', at 3.0 a.m. was customarily worked at precipitate speed and three springs were broken one night in an attempt to 'break the record'. Another opportunity for unaccustomed speed was the '6.5 special' (named after an early and unlamented *Top of the Pops* predecessor); it left in front of the down 'Red Dragon' and was required to be accordingly fleet of foot. The big 4700 2–8–0s were used by Reading men, notably on 'the Hawkeridge', the 11.45 p.m.

Coaling the Churchward way at Reading. The *Great Western Railway Magazine* of May 1940: 'The coal stage is a means of conveniently transferring locomotive coal from the wagons it arrives in to the tenders of engines. It consists of an elevated platform about 14 ft. above the rail level of a road running alongside it. On the other side of the stage and parallel with it, is an elevated road rising from rail level, on a gradient of about one in thirty, to within one foot of the platform level. Through the stage the elevated road is level, but beyond, it again rises on a gradient of one in eighty to the dead end. The loaded wagons having been pushed up into position at the top of the elevated road, this inclined road arrangement makes the further movement of the wagons independent of engine power, as in the language of the shed, it permits the loaded wagons to be 'dropped' down by gravitation, as required, to the coal stage platform, and when unloaded to be passed on down in the same way to the bottom of the incline, where they are moved by the shunting engine to the 'coal empties' road. Coal from the wagons is shovelled into trolleys holding 5 or 10 cwts., and from these it can be easily tipped from the side of the platform on to the tenders of engines on the coal stage road below. The coal arrives at the shed sidings in varying qualities, but before it is shunted on to the elevated coal stage road, the trucks are marshalled to enable the coalmen to mix the different qualities. The coal is then distributed to the various engines according to the nature and mileage of the next booked turn of duty. The largest tenders carry 6 tons of coal and are 'self-trimming', the slope to the coal plates being such that the coal automatically feeds to the front of the tender.'
M. W. Earley

No. 5075 *Wellington* on 10th August 1951, wartime camouflage still evident. The war was a sore trial, with little praise — 'all the kicks and no h'apence'. H. G. Kerry, the Divisional Locomotive Carriage & Wagon Superintendent, set out to remedy this somewhat in his lecture to the Debating Society on 30th January 1947: 'It will be remembered that at some periods during the 'blitz', 'alerts' were in operation from dusk to dawn and yet, somehow, the work was got through and the service maintained. I went round the sheds during the war at night-time and saw for myself what was being done, and I speak with some feeling when I say that the efforts of the C.M.E.'s Department in general, and the individuals in the locomotive sheds in particular, were never properly understood or appreciated. . . . I say without fear of contradiction that the Railway Company owes a big debt of gratitude to the men in the locomotive sheds who carried on under all sorts of difficulties at night-time and I repeat here and now my thanks to all those men who were under my supervision during the war.'   *N. E. Preedy*

No. 6101 on 16th February 1958. The '61s' were by this time already in retreat before the railcar sets or the planning thereof, and the complex diagrams across the division were scrapped, to leave those tanks in reasonable condition for whatever goods or odd jobs might be available. The ending of 'tandem' work on these engines was one source of dissatisfaction with the new working practices.   *Alec Swain*

Reading to Hawkeridge Junction, Westbury, 'firing like hell' to Savernake, then taking a nap on the bucket. Nos. **4708** and **4709** (and doubtless others) were used on this during the 'fifties and, apart from the crudities inherent in the construction of the steam locomotive, were considered excellent engines.

This is a recurring theme, primitive machines, responding in great part to the judicious use of various heavy and peculiarly named tools. Those who enjoyed life on locomotives look back with affection to the camaraderie, the sense of shared difficulty and the humorous incidents. The 'Splendour of Steam' and other such stuff understandably figures less than highly in all this. Night goods to Acton held little romance but were the 'bread and butter' jobs of sheds like Reading. There was time for a couple of hours sleep on the engine before returning, propped up on a shovel (a coat wrapped around the handle) in the midst of Acton Yard. Roused suddenly, one famous fireman, in the confusion of sleep, leapt automatically into action. Grasping up his shovel and making a swift firing movement he recalled his boots, carefully placed on the coaling implement, only too late, as they sailed irrevocably into the infinite depths of the Churchward firebox. This sort of thing one was never allowed to forget.

Reading turns took men regularly to Southall (where the new messroom was upstairs and considered palatial) and less often to Old Oak Common, where the 'cabin', befitting the depot's premier status, was remarkable for a *piano*. It seems to have had something of a frontier atmosphere, with everything going on, from singing and card-playing to sermons. The Oxford mess was 'a bit of a state' and certain of the coal stage staff, were at one time regarded with some considerable circumspection. There was also a 'Fratton job, right into Pompey docks', usually with a '49' Hall. Reading's 'top train' was for years the 7.48 a.m. Henley and it was felt that the influential commuters it served demanded an extra clean engine. A three-road railcar shed had been constructed in the late 1950s and these sets rapidly displaced the 'big Prairies'. In the 'sixties Reading was largely reduced to a freight engine depot, involved towards the end with such workings as the Banbury coal and empties, hauled by Stanier 2–8–0s until finally replaced by diesels. A 2251 0–6–0 remained until late, employed on the Coley branch and the Henley pick-up. The 'Manor', **7808**, was also notable seeing out its mileage, but on the end of steam, around December 1965, the remaining staff simply shuffled over to the diesel depot.

Reading in 1962. WD 2–8–0s were much in evidence in latter years along with 'Castles' displaced by diesels.
W. Turner

The old Reading tank with water softener and secondary tank beyond. The noisome 'sludge pit' lies to the right.
M. Romans

Despite rebuilding and dereliction much of the ancient lineage of the Reading building remained apparent.

M. Romans

The Reading 'table acquired a guard rail at some point, a useful safety practice employed particularly on the Southern. It would not have proved an obstacle to errant 'Castles'.
M. Light

Redundant instructions at Reading.
M. Romans

HENLEY

Brunel had fixed notions regarding 'the Disposition of the Branches' and two early broad gauge termini at the London end of the railway were closely similar, Henley and Uxbridge. It is quite likely that the original sheds at both places were akin in their construction but no real evidence exists. The Uxbridge building is wholly obscure, put out of use in 1897 and demolished two years later, and the early Henley shed (if there was another) is hardly better known. Karau (*The Henley on Thames Branch*, Wild Swan 1982) notes the lack of evidence and refers to a hipped roof structure (perhaps in timber) shown on the original plans. The shed opened with the branch in 1857, conversion to standard gauge taking place (overnight) in 1876.

Despite a complex timetable, the branch engine was wholly confined to branch passenger services plying between Henley and Twyford, classes involved being largely Metro 2–4–0Ts and later 57XX/8750 0–6–0PTs. The shed appears to have officially closed at the end of 1958 following dieselisation of the branch services though through trains and goods remained steam-hauled. The *Railway Magazine* of April 1959 reported it 'now closed ... since October last'.

No. 5932 *Haydon Hall* at the terminus and (below) pannier tank No. 9763 at the shed, on 18th June 1949. The branch saw two sorts of service, smartly timed direct trains to Paddington, using 4–6–0s (including 'Castles'), and a sort of shuttle service from Reading. This was often a steam railcar though in later years auto-trailers with 0–4–2Ts were used. The steam railcars provided a particularly rough ride (Car No. 41 was at Reading in 1926) and the 4.45 p.m. to Henley from Reading pulled a trailer car as well – two-coach auto-trains were also used, 0–4–2T No. 526 being on this work 'with a round firebox' until June of 1931. Specials were also frequent at Henley and the goods service brought Reading pannier tanks and 0–6–0s.   *J. H. Meredith*

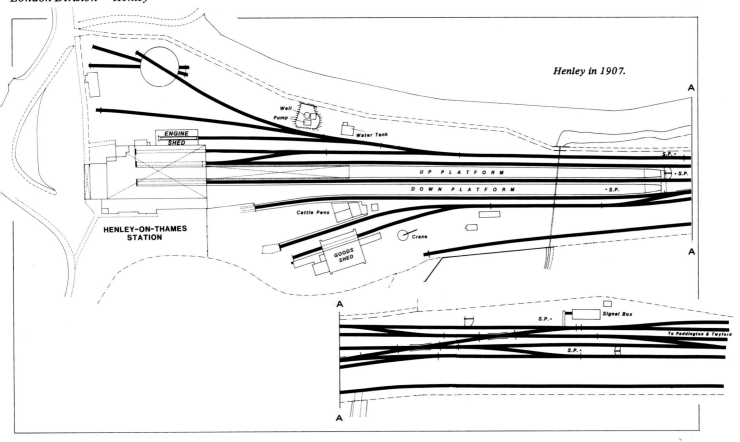

Henley in 1907.

The tank at Henley was originally flat-topped and
open, and a roof was only provided around 1933,
a drawing of 9th September showing the 'roof . . .
to be extended'. 'Done' is appended in pencil. The
tank was in cast iron with the dimensions given as
'17 ft 9 ins x 13 ft 9 ins x 4 ft 9 ins. Capacity at
4 ft 6 ins deep = 6862 gallons'. It is considered to
be amongst the most ancient of the buildings at
Henley; Karau (*The Henley on Thames Branch*,
Wild Swan 1982) provides a comprehensive description of everything within the area of the station
and its operation so that it is necessary only to
make some simple references to the notes therein.
The water tower originally incorporated a coaling
platform, out of use by 1897. Locos afterwards
took coal from open wagons and from about 1904
boarding was put up within the arches of the tower
to form the Henley 'cabin', 'where the overnight
shedman slept on the floor'(!). The 'room' became
a cleaners' store after the Second World War when
a modern 'cabin' was provided close to the shed.
Water was pumped by an engine via the usual
arrangement of connections to the whistle.

P. J. Garland

Henley on Thames. The Great Western 'commuter' system from Henley, Marlow and Windsor and the rest was sharply distinct in its character from that of other companies, serving affluent riverside dormitories.   *Aerofilms*

The shed at Henley opened as a broad gauge building and was subsequently considerably altered. It operated in conventional fashion, the crews based there for the branch service relieved by Reading men in the event of sickness or holidays. It was in a less isolated position than other similar sheds, 'more in the land of the living' and accordingly less unsettling at night. The shed building itself was out of use for some years at the end and provided a home principally for a stores van. *A. Attewell*

The 55 ft Henley turntable was approved on 25th February 1903 at a cost of £2,800, replacing an early 45 ft example. The 'table was long rumoured to have suffered a 'crack' and thus 'broke', and crews ever eschewed its use. Tenders required to be full to balance the thing and on Regatta days a team effort of several crews was advisable. It does not seem to have been used much, if at all, since the end of the Second World War. *J. H. Russell*

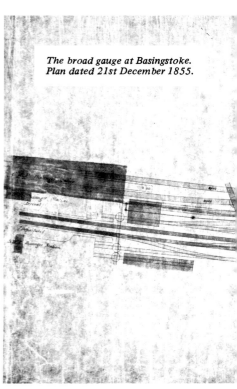

The broad gauge at Basingstoke.
Plan dated 21st December 1855.

The wooden engine shed at Basingstoke. The sign on the water tank reads: 'Men should be careful when passing engines standing in the loco sidings to see that hot ashes and clinkers are not being thrown off the engine'. The tank supplied a crane in the yard and two hydrants in the shed and, with a capacity of 4,299 gallons, measured 12 ft 2 ins x 9 ft 10 ins x 6 ft.   *British Railways*

BASINGSTOKE

Basingstoke was a timber-built barn of a building, of 'primitive' aspect akin to its less long-lived contemporaries of the 1840s and 1850s. It was built to the broad gauge though the turntable was mixed, for the convenience of the London & South Western Railway (the year of opening is presumed to be 1850). The co-operation was as close as may be, neither company was disposed to do other than what was strictly agreed, and the LSWR were less than wholly co-operative when the Great Western made enquiry of the former's water supply. Beattie of the South Western felt that the GW should 'erect their own tank for their own engines'. It is not clear throughout the various correspondence quite whether the station(s) or the engine shed is being referred to; the LSWR removed themselves to their own shed in about 1858, but continued for some time to make use of the GWR turntable. This lay in front of the shed at its western end, but was taken out and repositioned in the early 1880s (the LSWR put their own 'table down sometime before 1872) and rent was still paid to the GWR for 'use of the shed' – the turntable – into the 1860s.

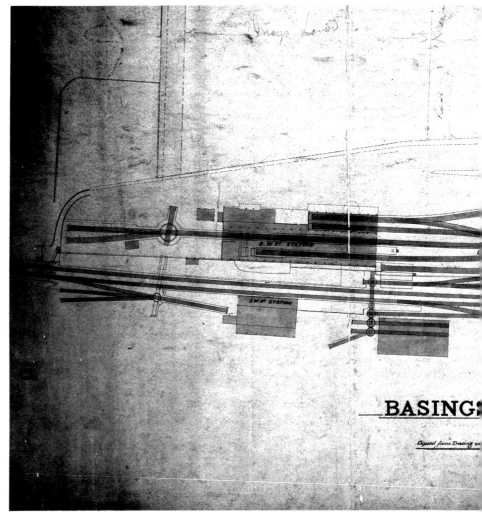

BASING:

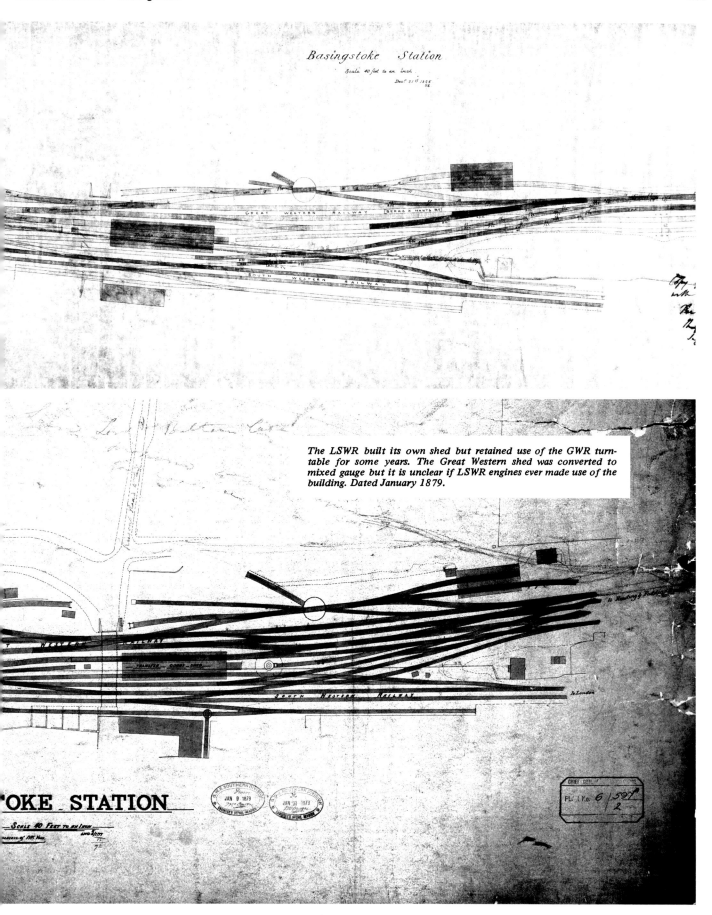

The LSWR built its own shed but retained use of the GWR turntable for some years. The Great Western shed was converted to mixed gauge but it is unclear if LSWR engines ever made use of the building. Dated January 1879.

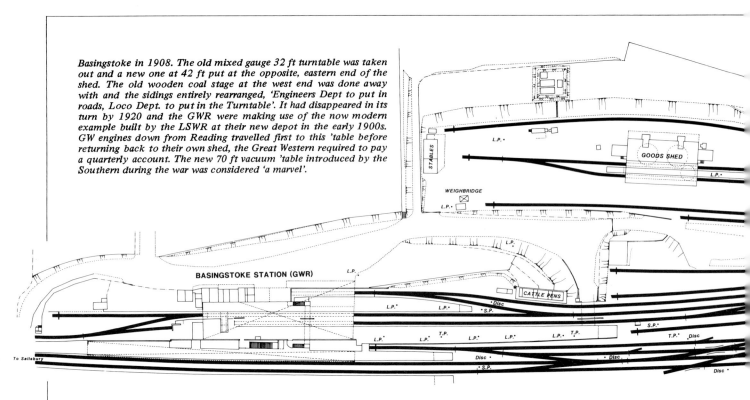

Basingstoke in 1908. The old mixed gauge 32 ft turntable was taken out and a new one at 42 ft put at the opposite, eastern end of the shed. The old wooden coal stage at the west end was done away with and the sidings entirely rearranged, 'Engineers Dept to put in roads, Loco Dept. to put in the Turntable'. It had disappeared in its turn by 1920 and the GWR were making use of the now modern example built by the LSWR at their new depot in the early 1900s. GW engines down from Reading travelled first to this 'table before returning back to their own shed, the Great Western required to pay a quarterly account. The new 70 ft vacuum 'table introduced by the Southern during the war was considered 'a marvel'.

LSWR train passing Basingstoke in 1920.

Lens of Sutton

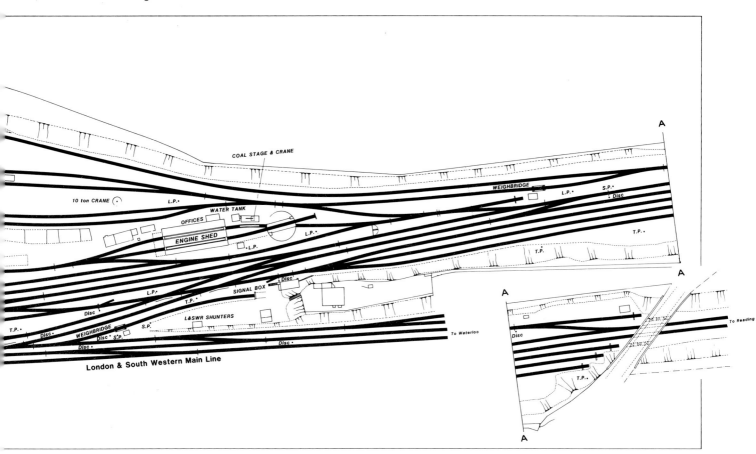

Basingstoke on 25th April 1937 with mogul No. 5380 and, inside, Nos. 6140 and 9306. The shed closed in 1950 and Western Region engines were afterwards dealt with at the Southern shed.

W. A. Camwell

DIDCOT

Oxford was a prize the Great Western could not long ignore; the main line swept northwards, tantalisingly close, and 'Didcot' proved a convenient junction for the university town. The branch opened in 1844 to a basic terminus at Oxford and Didcot's long years as a junction had begun. (The first part of the Didcot Newbury and Southampton Railway opened southward, to no strikingly effective end, in 1882.) Didcot continued a slow growth, a secondary junction relative to Reading, where extensive mileage yards grew up. As traffic needs grew, only sporadic and belated alterations with the layout were required – £1,705 was authorised in December 1872, for instance, 'for the broad to narrow gauge conversion . . . of certain lines . . . at Didcot . . . and the mixing of gauges at a junction at that place'.

A shed was provided, apparently in the late 1850s, a building which came to have 'three roads in peculiar disposition'.

The brickwork had a certain ornateness of style, marred by a low squat roof, whilst the lack of proper ventilation made for smoky and claustrophobic working. The third road, on the east side, was formed of a dull lean-to, a later addition it is said, tacked on to the original design. Internal details and the crude imbalance imparted to the building substantiate this, together with such early drawings as exist. Though later marked by an obsessive tidiness, the Great Western could in its early years display a healthy reliance on the age old principles of improvisation. The lean-to was considerably altered after about 1904 to little obvious visual benefit.

The Didcot shed was accompanied by a ramshackle coal stage, a shelter in lightweight material sitting uneasily upon an ironwork frame. There were eventually forty or so engines at Didcot, increasingly attended to in the open. The sand furnace dated from 1865 and, with the junction at Didcot taking on a strategic significance, a

new 65 ft turntable was approved on 13th October 1910, 'the old one being of smaller capacity and requiring renewal', £3,607 was set aside, with an 'additional expenditure' of £385 authorised on 23rd February 1911. This would have constituted almost the only up-to-date item, though £490 was authorised on 12th October 1916 for an engine pit of 160 feet.

An extensive ordnance depot, rail served, was established at Didcot. Its origins were in local tradition ascribed to the First World War – a munitions dump of vast scale containing every artifice of war, from horse-shoes and horse-shoe nails (the latter 'in their billions') to sixteen-inch naval guns. Everything was meticulously catalogued and stored, to be opened, resealed and repacked, regreased or whatever, at set intervals. Nothing escaped this single-minded military apparatus, grinding its course slowly through the camp. The naval

The old Didcot station and engine shed, long inadequate for the 'great wealth of traffic now worked through that place'.
L & GRP, courtesy David & Charles

guns, engineered at such cost, were stored largely in the open, greased and capped with wood and periodically opened up for cleaning and examination and resecured against corrosion. Many carried Great War dates, 1916, etc. and some, it would appear, were still in place at the end of World War II. A quite remarkable build-up of material had taken place from 1914 and the 'Didcot Ordnance Depot' occupies much of the GW War Report of 1914–1919. It is punctuated with 'improvements and additions', the sums involved rising from fairly modest amounts (the war would be over by Christmas), until it is peppered by expenditure in the tens of thousands. By February 1915 £37,000 could be approved, almost in

passing, increasing to over £60,000 before the year was out.

No matter of chance had brought this vast munitions store to Didcot. A junction on the GWR main Bristol line, the military planners also saw the possibilities of the sleepy DNS connection southwards to the great port of Southampton. Didcot was ideal for the work in many senses, a reception point for traffic from the Midlands, North and West, and an open site in the heart of England, well placed for the classic British strategy of the continental 'Expeditionary Force'. Doubtless the Great Western did not neglect this aspect when (successfully) petitioning for Government

Continued on page 278

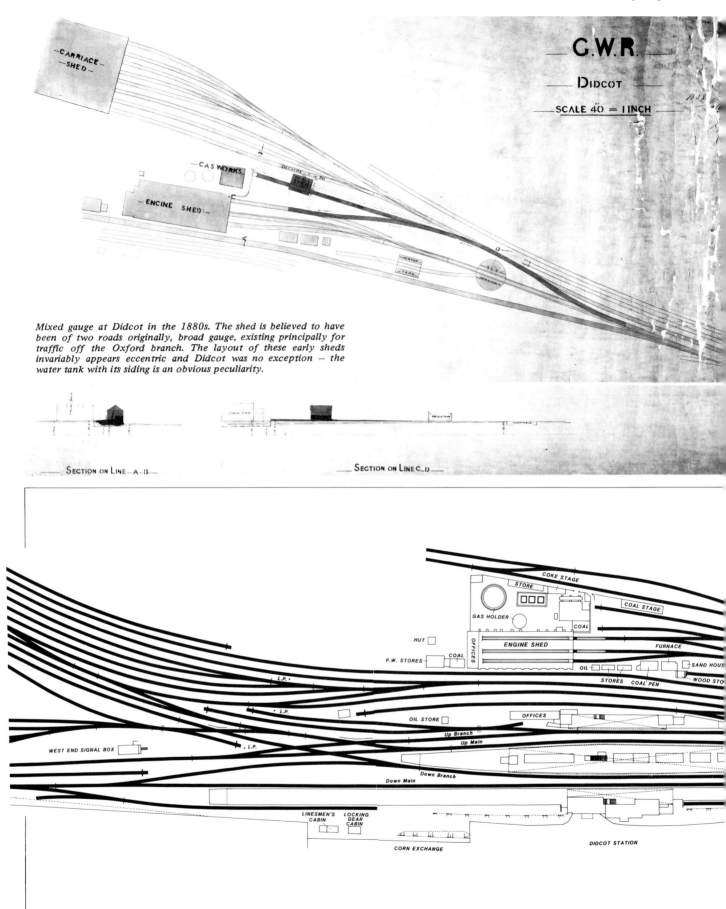

Mixed gauge at Didcot in the 1880s. The shed is believed to have been of two roads originally, broad gauge, existing principally for traffic off the Oxford branch. The layout of these early sheds invariably appears eccentric and Didcot was no exception — the water tank with its siding is an obvious peculiarity.

At the rear of the old shed, around 1929. *E. Eggleton*

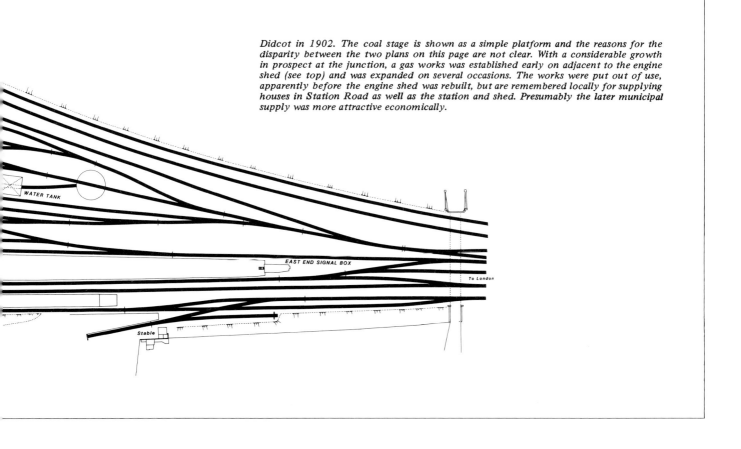

Didcot in 1902. The coal stage is shown as a simple platform and the reasons for the disparity between the two plans on this page are not clear. With a considerable growth in prospect at the junction, a gas works was established early on adjacent to the engine shed (see top) and was expanded on several occasions. The works were put out of use, apparently before the engine shed was rebuilt, but are remembered locally for supplying houses in Station Road as well as the station and shed. Presumably the later municipal supply was more attractive economically.

WATER TANK

EAST END SIGNAL BOX

To London

Stable

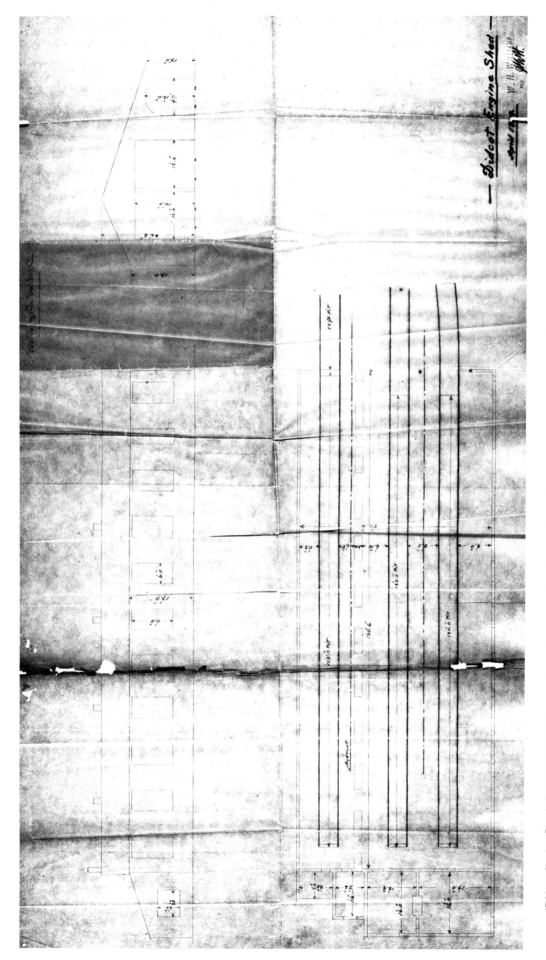

'Didcot Engine Shed'. These blackened fragments provide almost the only definite guide to the general arrangement of the building. Of the rooms at the rear ('lean to, brick, wood principals') the largest, 19 ft x 16 ft, formed the stores, with foreman's office next door. The two remaining rooms housed the enginemen and the chargeman.

2—4—0 No. 3230 inside the old shed, in December 1919. The great fascination of the engine shed lies in considerable part in its peculiar quality of timelessness. The murk, pierced by uneven, skittering shafts of sunlight, the bare pipework, the damp and the ancient brickwork, had been part of the earliest sheds and remained the most fascinating features of some of the last, in the 1960s. The principal strength of the steam locomotive, which enabled it to spread so widely throughout Britain and the world, was its essential simplicity – given time and labour, there was little that could not be accomplished with trestles, jacks, spanners and bars, and ordinary packing timber.

L & GRP, courtesy David & Charles

Didcot Junction as depicted on a Taunt postcard.   *Collection Paul Karau*

0—6—0 on what used to be the mixed gauge
road. Didcot was a 'shed' in the strictest sense
— a simple shelter, walls and a roof which
(more or less) kept the rain out.

Collection K. Bowler

The 'lean to' in October 1931.
The roofing was never adequate
and was patched up at intervals
for various small sums. A new
sand furnace was approved on
21st December 1865 and the
Didcot turntable, listed in the
division as 'No. 10', was ordered
to be repaired in March 1925.

V. R. Webster

No. 3210 ('painted black') and 4—4—0 No. 3290 *Severn*. The water tower at Didcot was an impressive structure, almost the only building of substance. The associated siding passed underneath at a pronounced oblique angle. *J. E. Kite*

No. 3610, out of use on the water tower road. The far end was used for the tool van or engines such as this, unlikely to move for a while. The remainder of the siding customarily held 'prepared' engines, coaled, serviced and 'right way' for the next duty. *J. E. Kite*

Section of the coal stage, dated 1883.

No. 519 at Didcot on 17th February 1926.

Collection Peter Winding

0–6–0 No. 27, around 1920. Didcot was ever a refuge for elderly engines and to walk up into that yard from the subway invariably brought the visitor up with a slight jolt. Outside frames and springs, rods and cranks revolving in impossibly eccentric fashion, and almost forgotten classes and wheel arrangements seemed everywhere. Even into the 'fifties 'we had every antique going'.

L & GRP, courtesy David & Charles

Saddle tank No. 307, fitted with 'busby' for the ordnance workings, occupies itself with some shunting alongside the up main line. 'The Forage Depot' or 'Provender Store', as it was more usually known, was a Didcot institution, a vast central distribution point for the hay and straw consumed by horses all over the Great Western. Horses were still used for shunting purposes, and all delivery vehicles, until lorries came increasingly available, were horse-drawn. An organisational *tour de force* kept every horse in every obscure country byway fed and stabled, a parallel to the getting of locomotive coal to the company's engine sheds. Didcot tradition long held that the Provender Store stood on the site of a mansion of the 'de Winter family', one of whom was said to have hanged with Guy Fawkes.   *Collection J. E. Kite*

assistance in 1931. A comprehensive programme of renewal and investment in traffic and engineering, in the docks and elsewhere was beyond the resources available to the GWR. Schemes were nevertheless got out for operating improvements across wide parts of the line; Didcot shed had long required complete replacement but this came only in the context of wide-ranging working alterations – witness the incidental nature of its announcement in the *Great Western Magazine* of January 1932:

> To facilitate the passage of through express trains, 'avoiding' lines are being laid in at Westbury and Frome: the former when completed will be approximately $2\frac{1}{2}$ miles long, and the latter two miles.

Alterations are in hand between Norton Fitzwarren and Newton Abbot, to improve working facilities, and these include conversion of Wellington, Sampford Peverell, Tiverton Junction, Cullompton, Stoke Canon, and Exminster into four-line stations, with provision of new station buildings, bridge reconstructions, and permanent way alterations. For similar purposes, improvements are proceeding between Didcot and Swindon; these include a new locomotive depot at Didcot, provision of up and down loops between Wantage Road and Challow, improvements at Swindon goods and passenger stations, and conversion of Wantage Road, Challow, and Shrivenham into four-line stations.

Saddle tank hoisting a line of wagons out from the sidings by the Provender Store. Wagons of hay were set back into the store itself by one of the Didcot pilot tanks, but shunting thereafter was performed by a petrol engine long in the charge of a man named Fisher, not a driver proper and firmly barred from venturing beyond the confines of the store sidings. The petrol engine driver was replaced by a Didcot man off the 'Cripple' link, with shunting at the end, as traffic sharply declined, given over to whatever pilot might be available. Beyond the store were the fields of Foxhall Farm, long taken over by the Great Western and used for rested shunting and delivery horses. 'The Company Meadows' were thus a useful source of manure for allotments.

L & GRP, courtesy David & Charles

It was but part of a vast reordering, its context fixed in a description of only a month or so earlier. November 1931:

Great Western Enterprises and Developments

Development Schemes.

Substantial progress has been made by the Great Western Railway in the extensive programme of development works undertaken in co-operation with the Government, with financial assistance under the provisions of the Development (Loan Guarantees and Grants) Act, 1929. These works, which were put in hand primarily with a view to assisting in the relief of unemployment, are being carried out in the hope and expectation that trade, industry, and travel by railway will not only revive, but expand. The financial assistance afforded by the Government takes the form of annual grants of interest on the Company's capital expenditure, at varying rates up to 5 per cent. for periods of from five to fifteen years.

There were forty Great Western schemes approved for adoption under these arrangements, involving a total expenditure of nearly

£8,500,000. Of these, eighteen have been completed, the expenditure being over £1,000,000. The completed works are the following:–

Banbury. – New marshalling yard.
Severn Tunnel Junction. – Enlargement of marshalling yard.
Scorrier to Redruth. – Doubling of line.
Rogerstone. – Enlargement of marshalling yard.
Bugle to Goonbarrow Junction. – Doubling of line.
Paignton. – New goods depot and reconstruction of passenger station.
Wolverhampton. – Reconstruction of goods depot.
Radyr. – Provision of new engine shed.

Treherbert. – New engine shed, improved coaling and watering facilities.
Cardiff (Cathays). – New carriage shop.
Swindon. – Re-arrangement of locomotive shops.
Duffryn Yard. – Improvement of coaling facilities.
Pantyffynnon. – New engine shed.
Extension of automatic train control.
Hockley. – Extension of warehouse.
Swansea (High Street). – New warehouse.
Lye. – Provision of additional mileage sidings and improved goods shed facilities.
Small Heath. – Provision of a new goods warehouse.

Good progress is being made with all the other works. These embrace extensive alter-

ations at Paddington; the re-building of Bristol, Cardiff, Taunton, and Didcot stations; quadrupling of sections of line in the neighbourhood of those places and also in the Birmingham district; and the deviations of the main line in the vicinity of Westbury and Frome.

The works which the Company had in contemplation for the construction of a new entrance lock at Swansea and an extension of the piers at Port Talbot, have been in abeyance for some months past; and in view of the present financial situation, the Directors have decided not to proceed with these works. The Directors have arrived at this decision with considerable regret, having regard to the

'Great Western Enterprises and Developments' included a reconstruction of the station at Didcot during 1930-1933, linked to improvements in the junctions and increases in the line capacity. The old shed, blackened and ancient, was a hindrance to all this and was swept away as the new depot became available for use.

British Railways

measure of financial assistance which the Government were prepared to extend in connection with the work.

New Works Authorised

The Great Western Railway Company's Directors have authorised the following works –

A halt is to be constructed at Halford Lane (between Handsworth and West Bromwich stations) for the convenience of persons attending the ground of the West Bromwich Albion Football Club. The halt will have platforms to accommodate trains from the Birmingham and Wolverhampton directions and over the Stourbridge Junction Line, and will be named 'The Hawthorns.'

At Iver, additional waiting room accommodation and platform covering are to be provided.

A siding is to be constructed at Melksham, to serve the milk factory of the Co-operative Wholesale Society at that place.

A halt is to be constructed at Celynen, between Abercarn and Newbridge stations, to serve the colliers employed at the adjacent South Celynen Colliery.

A 20-ton cart weighbridge is to be installed at Haverfordwest.

At Canons Marsh, Bristol, a portion of the Great Western Railway Company's premises is to be adapted for use by a firm of wireless manufacturers.

In connection with the installation of electric drilling equipment in the boiler shop of the locomotive works at Caerphilly, new offices and stores are to be provided.

A 55-ft engine turntable is to be installed at Radyr.

At Swindon carriage works, No. 5 electrical shop is to be extended to make provision for dealing with the increased number of electrically-lighted coaches.

The 1929 Act was intended to stimulate employment and in this regard it may or may not have been wholly effective. More than one proposal put forward by the railway companies listed as an incidental, or even principal, advantage, the possibilities of *dispensing* with labour – jobs were generated throughout the construction phase but any new development had as a corollary improved efficiency in working methods. In the changed circumstances, less labour was almost invariably required. The Didcot proposals, in operational terms, were without doubt eminently sensible, the old shed having long become quite unsuited to the work at the junction. The deleterious effects of the Depression were felt far less keenly in the Vale of Oxford, however, and traffic levels at Didcot could not be said to have suffered *drastic* reduction in the early 'thirties – the shed had probably been quite inadequate since the 1900s. The new depot, to the general 'Loans Act' pattern, a useful and accurate term employed by E. Lyons (*An Historical Survey of Great Western Engine Sheds, 1947*, OPC), opened in the

Continued on page 287

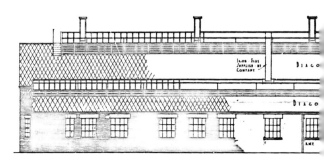

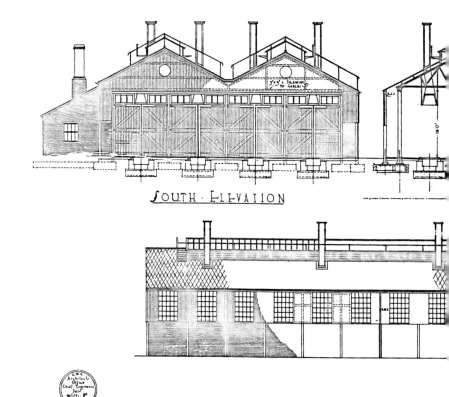

ɅOUTH · ELEVATION

· NEW · ENGINE · SHED ·

DRAWING · N° 3

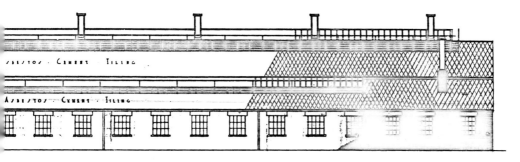

WEST · ELEVATION

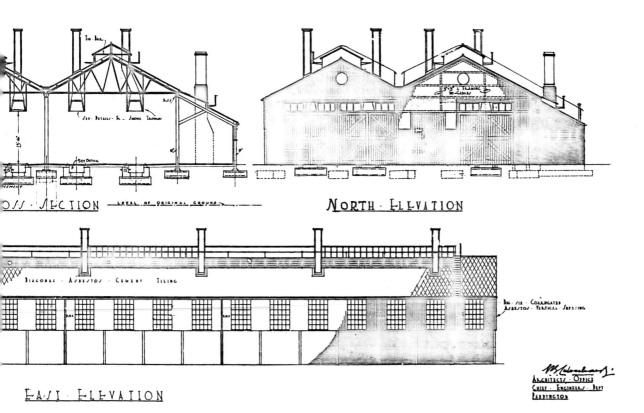

CROSS · SECTION

NORTH · ELEVATION

EAST · ELEVATION

ARCHITECTS · OFFICE
CHIEF · ENGINEERS · DEPT
PADDINGTON

The 'Loan Act' shed, its derivation from the 'factory style' of building quite apparent. The widespread use of asbestos remains the most notable and now slightly alarming feature. 'Bix Six' sheeting (the Southern Railway in particular made widespread use of this, for a variety of buildings — see, for instance, the Southern Nouveau series by Wild Swan) was employed for the upper walls and diagonal asbestos tiles for the roof. Lower walls were in brick but the general principle, straight shed of modest dimensions, with high pitched roofs, clearly recalls earlier Churchward practice. The cross sections reveal the site to be made up ground with relatively shallow foundations — the lightness of construction contributed to this, and is the origin of a long tradition at Didcot, that the shed stood on shallow 'floating' foundations, a technique said to be borrowed from America. Dated 16th January 1931.

G.W.R. · DIDCOT · NEW · ENGINE · SHE
GENERAL · ARRANGEMENT · OF · SHED

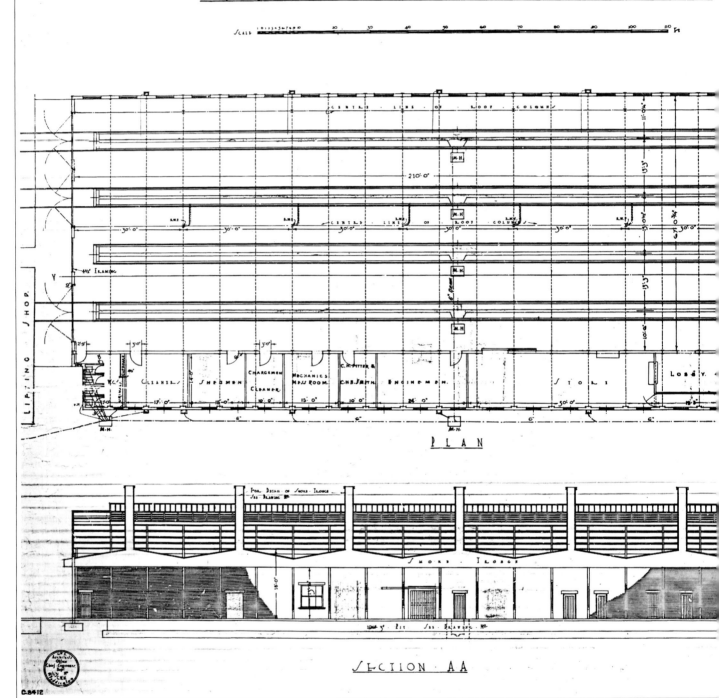

PLAN

SECTION AA

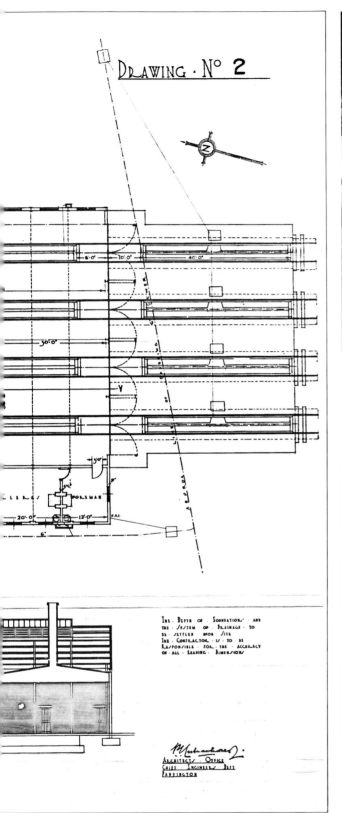

DRAWING · N° 2

The new shed had immense advantages over the old building, in lighting and ventilation, obviously, but also in the opportunity it afforded for a proper distribution of work — most fitting jobs took place in the shop, avoiding the clutter and makeshift of page 273. It made for both greater efficiency and increased safety, but the abiding features, the strange periods of quiescence, unexpectedly brilliant sunlight, and pools of shadow, remained, and echoes can still be experienced in the preserved shed today. *British Railways*

The Didcot stores. *British Railways*

Plan of 9th January 1931, with a note to the effect that final details of the foundations should (an unintentional joke) 'be settled upon site'.

The new Didcot coal stage was of completely traditional construction and layout, erected as a separate structure, the earth ramp subsequently made up to the correct level.
British Railways

Coal arrived at Didcot once or twice a week, the wagons usually broken out of a train bound for London and brought into the shed by a shunting pilot. They were hoisted up onto the stage when ready, by any engine which happened to be available about the depot. Didcot coal was never of the very highest quality but it nosedived during the war. 1930s standards were never really regained, with the various manufactured 'eggs' and 'bricks' recalled as a particular evil, dusty enough to need masks. The water tank was of an impressive height and one curious fireman 'froze', dizzy at the top of the ladder. Firmly bolted on in iron, it seemed flimsy from the top and an unnerving movement had to be made to begin the dreadful descent.

In accord with Great Western practice, the crew simply walked off once their engine had been stabled and braked by the coal stage, a habit leading to some confrontations at places like Eastleigh post-Nationalisation. The crew usually saw to it that tender and boiler were full, but subsequent movements were the responsibility of the shedmen, two on a usual turn, doubled in the war, when no less than six firedroppers (one on ashpans) were also necessary per shift. The whole depot could fill up, with mountains of ash and clinker, and engines stabled in the carriage sidings. Fire and smokebox dealt with, the shedman took the engine forward to the turntable (if required) and reversed it back to the head of the yard. 'The Firepit' was reconstructed in 1960 and fires were dropped on the turntable road — a useful opportunity for extra payments.   *British Railways*

The four shed roads were referred to as 1, 2, 3 and 4. No. 1 was 'the Shop Road', kept open as far as possible — at least the most time-consuming work was avoided — and No. 3 'The Washout'. The latter was the province of an extraordinary individual, the logically titled 'washout bloke', notable for overalls noxious through decades of grease. Tubes were blown during turn-round in the yard but pushed through on 'The Washout'. Engines having turned (or at least reversed), came back past the shed at this point preparatory to a second reversal either into the shed or onto Didcot's 'holding roads', four sidings between the shed and the main line, originally earmarked for an extension of the building.   *British Railways*

Pristine interior. For many years these 'official' views hung, framed, in the foreman's office.

First arrivals at Didcot in 1932, amid constructional leftovers of sleepers, bricks, rails and pipe. The barrels began a Didcot tradition, the area ever afterwards set aside for the storage of such items. *British Railways*

late summer of 1932, the contract having been let to Messrs F. Holcombe & Sons, Cardiff, the previous August.

Improved Locomotive Accommodation at Didcot

A new four-road engine shed, 210 feet by 67 feet, which accommodates sixteen engines, has been constructed and brought into use at Didcot station.

The scheme, which was undertaken under the Development (Loan Guarantees and Grants) Act, 1929, includes other features which greatly improve the locomotive accommodation at the depot.

A new lifting shop, complete with 50-ton engine hoist, has been provided, together with coal stage with overhead water tank, 44 feet by 36 feet, capacity 74,250 gallons. There is also a new boilerwashing apparatus and plant for calcinating sand.

GWR Magazine, Oct. 1932

In connection with the general reconstruction work at Didcot, the old locomotive depôt was swept away and an entirely new depôt provided on the triangle of line between the western main line on the left and the line to Oxford and the North on the right. The new shed is of the usual size, namely, 210 ft long by 67 ft wide, and will hold up to 24 locomotives, according to types. New offices, stores and staff accommodation, as well as a lifting shop, sand-drying plant and coaling and water facilities, have been provided. We reproduce

a site plan of this depôt as typical of the other modern locomotive depôts on the Great Western, and our illustrations are also from photographs taken at Didcot. The new lifting shop is a particularly well-lighted and equipped building. In it are installed a 50-ton engine hoist, drilling and planing machines, and a lathe; also two benches, a grindstone and blacksmith's forge. Alongside this, and separately housed, is a boiler, utilised in connection with the heating of the shed and washing out of locomotive boilers. At the south-east, or London, end of the running shed there is a small building containing a sand drier, and beyond this a new coaling stage supporting an overhead water tank measuring 44 ft by 36 ft and having a capacity of 74,250 gallons.

The offices, stores and enginemen's rooms are arranged along the south-west side of the building. They are commodious, well-lighted and warmed, and washing facilities are provided for enginemen, chargemen, fitters, mechanics, cleaners and shedmen. All the enginemen's notices, instructions and roster sheets are contained in glass cases, by which means they are kept flat, clean and easily discernible, and are posted up in a lobby between the stores and the offices.

Railway Gazette, Dec. 1933

The shed was laid out on modest lines, with four roads only. The Great Western *penchant* for separate repair premises was again in evidence, the usual lightly-built and airy shed at one extremity of the main building.

The hoist, etc., was an especially welcome addition at Didcot, there having been little proper provision for repair work in the past. Much thought was given to the construction and layout of engine sheds on British railways from the late 1920s in paticular, though activity peaked in the 'thirties. Disdainful (if even aware) of it, the Great Western found little of value in the concepts of mechanisation, planned servicing sequences, and the rest. The new Didcot shed was not a through building, neither was it built strictly on the 'dead end' principle; the turntable remained remote and no attempt was made to sort out ash disposal or sanding in accordance with new practice. The coal stage with its hand-loaded iron tubs was a design, in its essentials, at least 60 years old. Despite such deficiencies, these new sheds were light and wholesome places in welcome contrast to their often crumbling predecessors, and the yards more often than not were open and spacious. No-one seems to have complained overmuch, at least at Didcot; the old shed after all (smoke troughs were never fitted) had long been a filthy, fume-riven shell.

It was as well that the Loan and Guarantees Act improvements took place, for the Second World War, its stockpiling and movements of men and materials in the long preparations for European invasion, proved harshly testing. Work associated with the Ordnance Depot increased over and over, and traffic through the Didcot junction rose by 1944 to almost chaotic proportions. It was a problem of capacity and *ad hoc* remedies – the piecemeal increase of siding accommodation etc. did not address the main problems. It was a desperate time, when goods working Swindon–Didcot (24 miles) could be measured in days, and footplate life, as well as the lot of fitters and others, could be hard indeed. Men, already registered for the armed services but subsequently barred, could be sent to Didcot at 24 hours notice from London or wherever 'for the duration', with no option of transfer or of a place in the Forces. Crews, stuck in the

countryside on halted trains, might go 72 hours more or less without food. Forays were made to farmhouses and food bartered for. Potato fields were fair game – 'spuds' boiled in the safety valve bonnet, made a solid meal. Footplates were abandoned and relations strained with signalmen ('bobbies') seen as unsympathetic. Running men often saw the latter as unhelpful or antagonistic, based partly at least on the disproportionate opportunities for overtime. Crew 'swap-overs' were introduced in the war, to shorten the distances involved. Traffic at Didcot was often at a standstill and it was by no means uncommon for crews to work an entire shift without moving. Everybody was on 'short rest', i.e. back to work within 8 hours; ordered to

take over the 'third one at Vauxhall Junction', a crew might relieve the very men they had handed over to that morning – all without a wheel being turned. On Westbury workings it was possible to be held at a loop or siding behind at least two trains and for one or other crew member to spend the evening in the pub; at closing time the engine would still not be 'first at the signal.'

The DNS route was doubled by the U.S. Army, a typically mass-scale operation with a series of ballast engines stationed all along the line and working more or less continuously. They were re-crewed by Didcot men, travelling down by bus and making their way across fields and up embankments – whatever was necessary.

The system of repair shops on the Great Western was odd in that often no access was possible independent of the shed itself. At Didcot and elsewhere, nevertheless, this 'caused little hardship'. The shed 'was virtually empty once the morning passengers had gone off'. The Didcot shop attended to hot boxes, whitemetalling, valves and pistons, re-tubing and renewal of firebox stays. Fitting staff (along with everyone else) coped manfully with dieselisation and Didcot was lucky to have an ex-Merchant Navy man familiar with Maybach and other diesel principles. The 50-ton hoist, still used today for steam locomotive repairs, was ordered from Messrs. Royce of Manchester, the 'contract' announced in February 1931; it was a most robust piece of equipment but less impressive than the legendary Didcot fitters who disdained the normal block and tackle to raise up a side rod and present it by muscle power alone.   *British Railways*

Engines at the rear of the shed on 28th June 1936 — ancient 'tankie' No. 1925 (above), one of a gaggle characteristic of Didcot, and (below) 3266 *Amyas* and 5940 *Whitbourne Hall*. As always, engines were grouped on the principle of 'first in, last out' and those 'out the back' would be preceded off the shed by all those stabled on Nos. 3 and 4 roads. *Collection Peter Winding*

'The new shed at Didcot, 5th March 1933' with left to right: outside frame Dean 0−6−0, 'Bulldog' 4−4−0, 0−6−0 No. 2395, 2−8−0 No. 2820 and 0−6−0PT No. 1610. Having been serviced and turned, engines required to be stabled in correct order, either on the shed roads or (often more conveniently) on roads 5-8 alongside the Didcot 'Field' (to the right, behind the 'Busby' pannier tank). One of the two shedmen usually confined himself to this work though there was no strict division of the work between them; they shared the work as necessary. The chief foreman was a distant figure, the day-to-day supervision done by one of three shift foremen (Didcot ended up, like Oxford, run by an Area Manager) the precise stabling of engines in 'the holding roads' being the responsibility of (usually) 'the afternoon man'. He would be on the turn all week, would have a word with the shift foreman and chat with the fitters and the other shed man. Aware of all requirements, any necessary rearrangement over in the 'Field' he could promptly arrange using an engine in steam.

V. R. Webster

No. 3375 *Sir Watkin Wynn* on 28th June 1936.   *Collection Peter Winding*

Ancien Regime preserved at Didcot.

J. E. Kite

'Busy'-fitted pannier tank at Didcot on 5th June 1949. The spark arrestors, if not always infallible, were a certain reassurance in the Ordnance Depot workings. Including the trip engine, there could be several pilots at work in 'the Ordnance' alone – there were two parts, strictly separate, the Royal Ordnance and the RAF, a lower yard pilot and one on the 'hump', inside the complex. There were a further three, one on each of the 'gulleys' between the shed complexes and one in the 'S' shed, the largest in Europe. Soldiers based at the Depot were often pressed into service as firemen. There was a lack of enthusiasm with some, and between two bureaucratic giants, the railway and the Army, squaring the monstrous circle of paperwork in the event of an AWOL fireman, could mean procedural convulsions. There was even a passenger train from Oxford during the war, a 61XX tank with five coaches to a separate platform in the Depot, returning at night.

R. S. Carpenter

No. 3254 *Cornubia* on 9th April 1938.   *Collection Peter Winding*

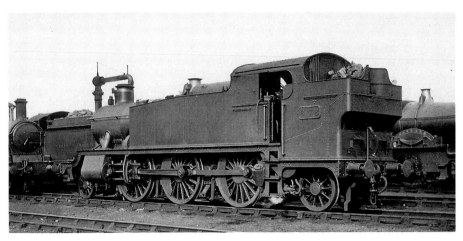

No. 6138 on 26th September 1937. The '61' tanks were less in evidence beyond the strictly commuter area though they had forays to the limits of the Division, on a daily basis. Oxford had a few and of course they were frequently seen at Didcot. There were none in 1947-1948 but half a dozen by 1950. By 1955 only 6167 was actually allocated, though as DMU sets took over in the late 1950s, a succession of displaced '61s' spread out into the country districts.
Collection Peter Winding

Didcot's Cambrian Railways 0—6—0, No. 908, on 15th April 1934.   *Collection Peter Winding*

The British Chiefs of Staff were never much renowned for their powers of imagination and a static war was expected. GWR 0–6–0s, well liked by GW men, were once again selected to serve in Europe and suitable pump alterations were effected at Eastleigh, the locos working via the DNS and crewed from Didcot. War Department depredations left the Great Western short of power in this class and both LNER and LMS engines were drafted in as replacements. They were mostly in lamentable condition and Swindon had not the time, nor the inclination, to put them in good order. This wretched collection, scoured from scrap lines across the length of England, were used wherever possible on the least demanding tasks. The 'Swindon Fly' – it settled everywhere – was a Didcot job, a passenger working to Swindon followed by a stopping goods back, shunting at stations as required, and often one of these loaned 0–6–0s would be so employed. They often had to be rescued, clacks stuck open or worse, though one made it back to Didcot, to deafening bangs and shrieks, minus half a big end brass secured with a pin cut from a convenient sleeper. Spares were almost an impossibility and Didcot shed simply had to make do – one LNER 0–6–0 which arrived without *buffers* was, with a collective shrug, put directly into traffic. The visitors spent much of their time out of use and, cannibalised to varying degrees, were dumped in a sad huddle on sidings at Didcot.

The Ordnance Depot, enlarged as the war progressed, posed special problems; it was a tempting and visible target of course, having been a well-known dump through many years of peace, and its contents, as train loads, could hardly be more unsettling in the circumstances. At its height, along with 'No. 3 Maintenance Unit' at Milton, the depot employed six or more elderly tank pilots – 0–6–0STs at first, replaced by panniers and crewed by new drivers and the youngest firemen, through 24 hours. Sparks, understandably, were to be discouraged and the pot-like arrestors, proving as they did a hindrance to steaming, could make the heavy shunting difficult. These 'busbies' were prominent at Didcot as tanks rumbled about the sidings, to and from the 'Ordnance' in endless manoeuvres. The tanks were also put to some use on branch work when there was danger of setting fields alight, though local farmers seemed to carry on with their 'regular' claims regardless. The Maintenance Unit was reached through a wooden gate, run through and destroyed at least once, and men 'on relief' making their way to a loco somewhere in the complex frequently faced a sentry's 'Hello, who goes there?'. Material came in and out all day, and there was a daily booked train through to London, 'the 10.40 a.m. Southall'. It was supposed to be a priority train, but 'you were lucky to get it past Reading'. During an air raid somewhere round Old Oak it was no comfort to shelter under a wagon of high explosive. With peace such traffic was a good deal less unsettling but security remained a necessity. A 'copper' (presumably a Ministry security man) was latterly responsible for gatekeeping, though he failed to prevent further destruction of his charge. There were seven pilots at the war's end, though traffic eased off fairly steadily. Men and equipment were 'stood down' and the more obvious piles of material gradually disappeared. The 'Ordnance' soon became an anonymous collection of huts served by a declining number of trains. It was strange work; crews took in sealed wagons and vans, knowing little of the precise loading, handed them over and took away either empties or consignments for further destinations, again only dimly aware of the contents.

In the early days of the war, everything came to a halt as a siren sounded, though very soon railway operations simply carried on. Crews were issued with tin hats and it was somewhat unnerving to be warned at Maidenhead of an air raid in West London. With a train of mines from the Morris Cowley plant, destined for Acton, capricious chance would ensure, for once, a clear road to London. The Maintenance Unit received hits on at least one occasion, when a string of bombs dropped across Milton, one very close to Didcot South Box. The threat came not entirely from the Germans:

21.7.41 04.45 DIDCOT (LOCOMOTIVE DEPT. SIDINGS). Bomb exploded in GW Loco 20-ton wagon No. 83002 blowing a hole: $13\frac{1}{2}'' \times 3\frac{1}{2}''$ in the iron side of the vehicle. Wagon worked from Partridge Jones & John Paton, Celynon Colliery, Abercarn to Didcot arriving 10 July. Police advised and took possession of bomb shell. No personal injuries. Subsequently, established that damage was caused by an RAF practice bomb.

The Great Western never really saw much reason for 'barracks' – staff hostels – which other companies had erected sporadically and more or less regularly over the years. The war proved a spur, nationally in this regard, and a substantial block was opened, principally for men on new double home workings. Didcot had its own such link, to Birmingham, but the general limits for crews lay at Westbury, Southampton, London and Wolverhampton. The *Great Western Railway Magazine for* June 1944 reported:–

New Staff Hostel and Canteen at Didcot

On May 3 a new residential hostel and canteen for the Company's staff at Didcot was formally opened by the Hon. Sir Edward C. G. Cadogan, K.B.E., C.B., M.P., Acting Chairman of the Board of Directors. Not only is it by far the largest in the long chain of establishments erected on the Company's system for the wartime welfare of the staff; its chief feature – the inclusion of full residential facilities – makes it the first of its kind.

The premises, constructed by the Ministry of Works, contain a hundred sleeping cubicles, reading, writing and recreation rooms and a large canteen served by well-planned kitchens. Another welcome feature is a room for quick-drying of wet clothing when men come in from duty. The garments are hung in a series of wardrobe bays, on racks immediately above a projecting 'grid' of steam pipes fixed at near-floor level.

The reception offices, linen and storage rooms, and the quarters for the manager, matron and domestic staff, are all planned on equally modern lines. The whole block of

'Yankee' 2−8−0 at Didcot in the war years, remembered with distrust by engine crews and some admiration by operating and fitting staff.

Mrs. S. Webb

buildings is served by two separate hot-water systems – one for domestic purposes, the other for central heating.

The hostel provides full-scale 24-hour service for residents. In addition, the canteen facilities are open to all the Company's employees at Didcot, including train crews and others working in to the depot from other stations.

Among those who attended the opening were Sir Alan G. Anderson, C.B.E., Controller of Railways and Chairman of the Railway Executive Committee; Lieut.-Col. Sir Alan Mount, C.B., C.B.E., Inspector General of Railways, Ministry of War Transport; officers of the Great Western Railway; representatives of the Ministry of Food, Ministry of Labour, Regional Welfare Office, and the Trade Unions; residents of the hostel and many other railwaymen.

At the opening ceremony Sir Alan Anderson handed Sir Edward Cadogan the key of the main entrance. Sir Edward said railway traffic at Didcot had impelled the provision of additional living-room for staff whose needs could not be met by the facilities available in the town. For some time many of the men transferred from other stations to Didcot had been accommodated in sleeping coaches and had used a dining car for meals. Those services fell far short of perfection, especially for war workers engaged on such arduous and responsible duties. The Company and other authorities concerned had fully realized the urgency of providing improved facilities; this new hostel was the outcome of their combined effort to solve the problem. Even with the opening of the new premises, extra accommodation would still be needed to house the rest of the transferred staff, and a full scheme for early construction of additional premises had already been authorised. He was pleased to see around him so many who took keen and constant interest in the comfort and welfare of the railway staff, including Government and Trade Union officials. Sir Edward then declared the hostel open. An interesting tour of the premises followed, and the many amenities were closely inspected.

Mr. Gilbert Matthews, Superintendent of the line, presided at the luncheon which followed. He said that when the Chairman of the Company, Sir Charles Hambro, left for America to undertake special work on behalf of the Government, Sir Edward Cadogan took over his Great Western duties, and from the first had seized every opportunity to gain first-hand knowledge of the working of the system. He had visited many of the main centres, and at every stage of every tour had shown the keenest interest in the welfare of the men and women who have rendered, and still are rendering, such grand service to the nation. As Superintendent of the Line, Mr. Matthews was absolutely confident that the staff, in their turn, would meet every demand that the future would make of them, cheerfully and in the true 'Great Western' style.

Sir Edward Cadogan thanked the chairman for his remarks, and said how pleased he was with the facilities he had observed in the course of his inspection of the new premises. He realised that up to now some of the staff at Didcot had had to put up with many things

Men found themselves sent to depots like Didcot 'without the option', for the war spurred on traffic almost from the first. Men came from all over, from West Drayton to Plymouth and, inevitably, South Wales; those at the beginning could find lodging in the town but later some form of accommodation had to be found and old coaches were stabled on No. 5 road for these refugees to sleep in. A canteen was provided in a restaurant car, parked in the carriage sidings, staffed by restaurant car attendants, with women drafted in to launder sheets and blankets. A '32XX' provided steam heat in winter, though damp and vermin, as at Old Oak, were awful. The station waiting room had then to be given over to staff, the whole improvised system finally replaced by the hostel of 1944.

of a 'second best' character, but he thought that in the hostel they would find the amenities most satisfactory. He hoped everyone would realise that, allowing for wartime difficulties, the hostel and its services were as complete as planning and skill could make them, and he trusted that the staff transferred from their homes to Didcot would have as comfortable and as pleasant a time as it was possible to secure, as long as their duties made it necessary for them to remain in the district.

Mr. H. W. Johns, a driver, speaking on behalf of the staff, said it gave him great pleasure to thank Sir Edward Cadogan and everyone else concerned in the provision of the building. This hostel was the result of help received through various sources. Apart from one or two minor difficulties, which he had every hope of speedily being cleared away, the residents were well satisfied with the facilities. Concluding, he said, 'I can assure you, as a

resident, I and my colleagues will do our best to ensure that the hostel will be run in a manner that will do credit to the Great Western Railway.'

In due course the extensive grounds surrounding the hostel will be developed in various ways designed to enhance the attractiveness of the block and to add still further to the amenities enjoyed by the residents. A portion of the land will be laid out for horticultural purposes and a field at the east end will be used to provide facilities for various outdoor recreations.

For purposes of control the hostel and its entire services will come under the supervision of the Chief Staff and Establishment Officer of the Company.

Didcot was always of considerable interest, both for the diversity of its engine complement and in many instances for the venerability of many of the individual members. There were perfectly good reasons for this; the depot could never be regarded as part of the 'front line' and types displaced from such duties found their way to secondary depots in the natural scheme of things. Didcot had unusual shunting turns, not considered of a particularly heavy nature (pre-war at least), in the 'Ordnance' and a motley collection of tanks served for these duties; to the end of steam 'there was a lot of tank work but not so much tank *running* as such'. Moreover, workings 'down the branch' to Newbury and beyond on the Didcot Newbury and Southampton line provided for just the kind of rambling and unhurried country trains which could be worked by almost any ancient cast-off. Again circumstances changed with the Second World War but 'The Linger and Die' quickly receded into an obscure rurality in the 1950s.

Odd locomotives were outbased from Didcot at both Newbury and Winchester on the DNS line, changed regularly and working turn and turn about with engines on the main shed roll. Karau, Parsons and Robertson have produced a fairly detailed listing for the period 1901–1923, in: *The Didcot Newbury and Southampton Railway*, reproduced below by kind permission.

'One of the ground floor corridors, and the call-board corner. Before retiring, each resident chalks on the board, opposite the number of his cubicle, the time at which he wishes to be called.'.

As a cross country route it is impossible to ascertain the numbers of all the locomotives that worked over the line at any period in time. The following list therefore only presents a few individual locos that are known to have worked on the DN & S between 1901 and 1923. The majority of those included were sub-shedded at Winchester, and in each case the years concerned are given in brackets.

'Queen' class 2–2–2
55 (1903), 1119 (1906), 1122 (1901), 1133 (1903)

'157' class 2–2–2
158 (1902), 163 (early 1900s), 166 (1902)

'River' class 2–4–0
75 (1902)

'481' class 2–4–0
489 (1917), 588 (1915–17)

'806' class 2–4–0
808 (1910), 815 (1903, 1910–11, 1914–15), 818 (1911, 1914–17), 820 (1903, 1917–19, 1921)

'2201' class 2–4–0
2208 (1917–18), 2216 (1915–18)

'Stella' class 2–4–0
3201 (1909–11, 1918–19), 3205 (1906, 1918–19), 3501 (1907, 1918), 3509 (1918), 3513 (1923), 3515 (1918, 1923)

'3226' class 2–4–0
3230 (1921–22), 3226 (1908)

'3232' class 2–4–0
3233 (1911, 1922–23), 3235 (1913–14), 3239 (1919), 3241 (1919, 1921), 3245 (1921–23), 3248 (1918, 1922–23), 3249 (1921–23), 3250 (1918), 3251 (1918)

'Sir Daniel' class 0–6–0
381 (1909), 471 (1908), 577 (1909)

'388' class 0–6–0
426 (1903), 514 (1913), 594 (1909), 795 (1911), 1084 (1907), 1101 (1907), 1102 (1908–11)

'2361' class 0–6–0
2365 (1902), 2373 (1911)

Dean 0–6–0
2323 (1913), 2357 (1907–8), 2360 (1913), 2401 (1907), 2405 (1902), 2465 (1902), 2526 (1910)

'3521' class 4–4–0
3526 (1920s), 3549 (1920s)

'517' class 0–4–2T
541 (1908), 552 (1909, 1911), 846 (1907)

'1076' class 0–6–0ST
1253 (1902–3), 1263 (1903, 1905–6), 1282 (1907), 1294 (1919), 1644 (1919), 1652 (1906–7)

'1661' class 0–6–0ST
1693 (1905)

The polyglot nature of the allocation, elderly time-servers, locomotives downgraded from other duties, and a sprinkling of 'new ones' is well illustrated in the June 1932 allocation, around the period when the shed was being rebuilt. It was first published in the *Great Western Echo* of Autumn 1969:

517 0–4–2T: 542, 1427, 1466.
0–6–0PT: 1263, 1610, 1817, 1912, 1921, 1969, 2045.
Brecon & Merthyr 0–6–0PT: 2190.

Midland & South Western Junction 2–4–0: 1334, 1335.
2251 0–6–0: 2254, 2269.
Dean Goods 0–6–0: 2303, 2395, 2397, 2405, 2430, 2450, 2463, 2512, 2532, 2547, 2549.
Duke 4–4–0: 3266 *Amyas* 3267 *Cornishman*, 3269 *Dartmoor*, 3280, 3282, 3290 *Severn*, 3291 *Thames*.
Bulldog 440: 3356 *Sir Stafford*, 3361, 3385, 3394 *Albany*, 3448 *Kingfisher*, 3454 *Skylark*.
5101 2–6–2T: 5101
43XX 2–6–0: 7306.
Hall 4–6–0: 4902 *Aldenham Hall*.

The Wallingford engine was provided by Reading but Didcot men relieved in the event of sickness, during the war and after, and therefore knew the branch. Nevertheless, on a visit on Jubilee Day, 6th May 1935 a *Great Western Echo* correspondent, Mr C. Warwick, recorded the following from the shed 'board':

Cambrian	0–6–0:	908
	0–4–2T:	1163
M&SWJR	2–4–0:	1334, 1335.
	0–6–0T:	1610, 1743, 1848, 1912, 1921, 1935, 2007, 2045, 2076.
2251	0–6–0:	2254, 2259, 2280.
Dean	0–6–0:	2430, 2450, 2463, 2512, 2532, 2533, 2547.
Duke	4–4–0:	3254, 3256, 3266, 3267, 3279, 3280, 3282.
Bulldog	4–4–0:	3324, 3375, 3380, 3434, 3448, 3454.
Hall	4–6–0:	5939.
	2–6–0:	9304, 9307.

Continued on page 304

FOXHALL FARM

Farm House

Weighbridge and Office

Water Tank

PROVENDER STORE

Water Tank

Pump House

Office

Workshop

Mess Room

Sewage Tank and Filter

UP GOODS LOOP

S.P.

Wagon Repairers C

RESERVOIR

approximate capacity 3,326,000 gallons

Weighbridge and Office

Cattle Pen

6 ton Crane

Weighbridge and Office

Goods Office

Offices

Cycles

A.R. Shelter

GOODS SHED

S.P.

S.P.

Disc

Disc

S.P.

S.P.

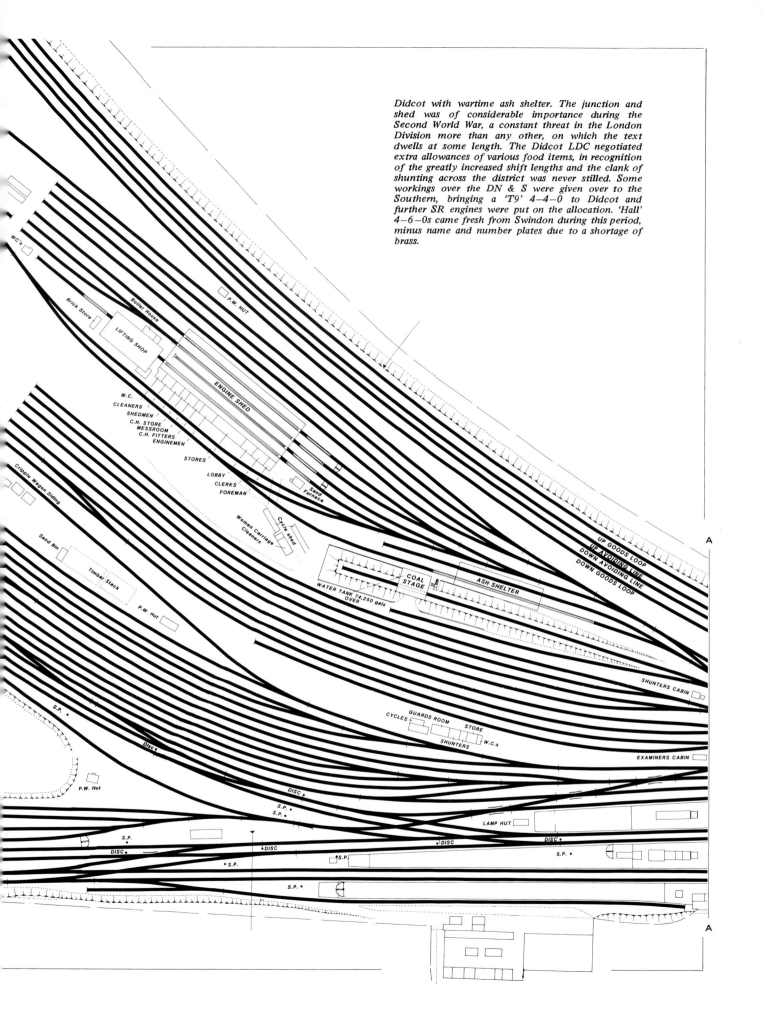

Didcot with wartime ash shelter. The junction and shed was of considerable importance during the Second World War, a constant threat in the London Division more than any other, on which the text dwells at some length. The Didcot LDC negotiated extra allowances of various food items, in recognition of the greatly increased shift lengths and the clank of shunting across the district was never stilled. Some workings over the DN & S were given over to the Southern, bringing a 'T9' 4–4–0 to Didcot and further SR engines were put on the allocation. 'Hall' 4–6–0s came fresh from Swindon during this period, minus name and number plates due to a shortage of brass.

W.C's

Brick Store

Boiler House

LIFTING SHOP

P.W. HUT

W.C.
CLEANERS
SHEDMEN
C.H. STORE
MESSROOM
C.H. FITTERS
C.H. ENGINEMEN

STORES

ENGINE SHED

Sand Furnace

LOBBY
CLERKS
FOREMAN

Cripple Wagon Siding

Women Carriage Cleaners

Cycle Shed

Sand Bin

Timber Stack

P.W. Hut

WATER TANK 74,250 gals OVER

COAL STAGE

ASH SHELTER

UP GOODS LOOP
UP AVOIDING LINE
DOWN AVOIDING LINE
DOWN GOODS LOOP

A

S.P.

Disc

P.W. Hut

SHUNTERS CABIN

CYCLES
GUARDS ROOM
STORE
SHUNTERS
W.C.s

EXAMINERS CABIN

DISC

S.P.
S.P.

LAMP HUT

S.P.

DISC

DISC

DISC

S.P.

DISC

S.P.

S.P.

A

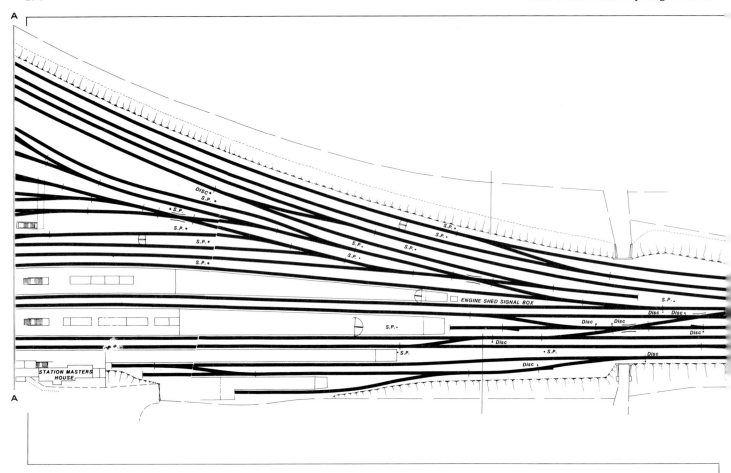

The London end at Didcot. 'Coming off' enginemen notified a ground frame — the 'engine shed signal box', manned over three shifts, and gave their destination, duty, etc. The ground frame man phoned the signal box, to tell the 'bobby' that 'the 4.15 Winchester Goods' was ready, for instance, and the signals would be arranged accordingly.

L & GRP, courtesy David & Charles

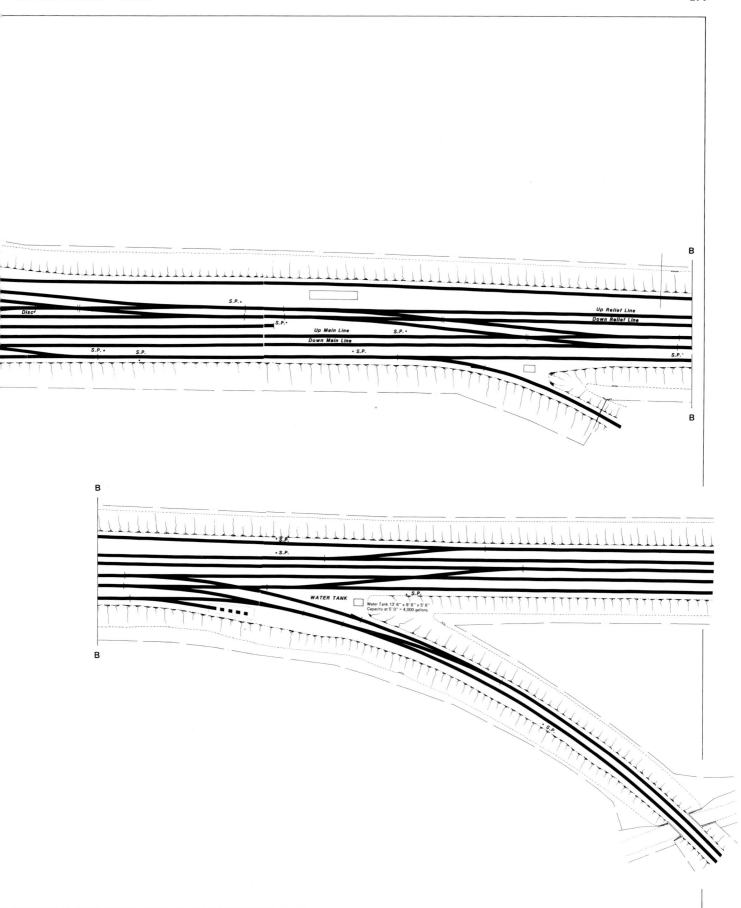

Up Relief Line

Down Relief Line

Up Main Line

Down Main Line

Disc

S.P.

WATER TANK

Water Tank 13' 6" x 9' 6" x 5' 6"
Capacity at 5' 0" = 4,000 gallons

The Great Western turntable examined in microscopic detail. The Didcot 'table was taken out before preservation, unfortunately, and after many years was replaced by a larger, undergirder unit. Various engines crashed into its shallow pit over the years including a pair of pannier tanks the shedman hoped to get 'done' at the same time. Despite the carefully equalised stresses, the massive girdering and immaculately engineered gearing and wheels, it was often a devil to turn. The Didcot joke, ritually repeated halfway through the operation, was the suggestion in order to make life easier 'to go halves on a donkey'.

Roye England and J. H. Russell

No. 6029 *King Edward VIII* around 1960,
carefully parked on one of the turntable spurs,
apparently at rest during a run-in turn.
W. Turner

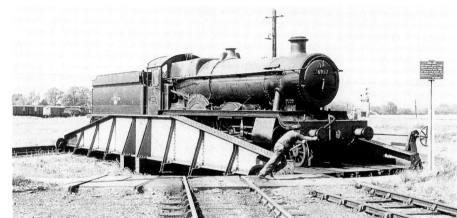

No. 6937 *Conyingham Hall* on 25th July 1964.
'Halls' were long favourites at Didcot, remem-
bered for three in particularly fine fettle —
Conyingham Hall (right), 6923 *Croxteth Hall*
and 6952 *Kimberley Hall*.
Merchant Navy Preservation Society

2—8—0 No. 2898 leaves the turntable on 25th July 1964. The 2—8—0s were enormously popular at Didcot, loading to 110 wagons in the war —
they were regarded with some circumspection, however (along with other engines), when relieved from the north. It was 'downhill all the way'
from Banbury and easy to convince oneself that foreign crews paid insufficient attention to the fires.   *Merchant Navy Preservation Society*

No. 2898 trundles off with its tender of 'eggs', back to the shed yard. This manoeuvre took it past the enginemen's cabin, scene (almost) of a bizarre railway accident. A bullet hole in the wall long bore witness to this incident — a Didcot man, unused to firearms and despairing of any glory in guarding the water tank, brought (illegally) his Lee Enfield into the cabin. It inevitably went off, with all concerned too stunned to notice their sudden deafness. The solitary .303 bullet, entrusted to this guardian of Britain's vital war transport, made a neat and lasting cavity in the bricks, for generations of cabin 'eye openers', until at least the 1970s.

Merchant Navy Preservation Society

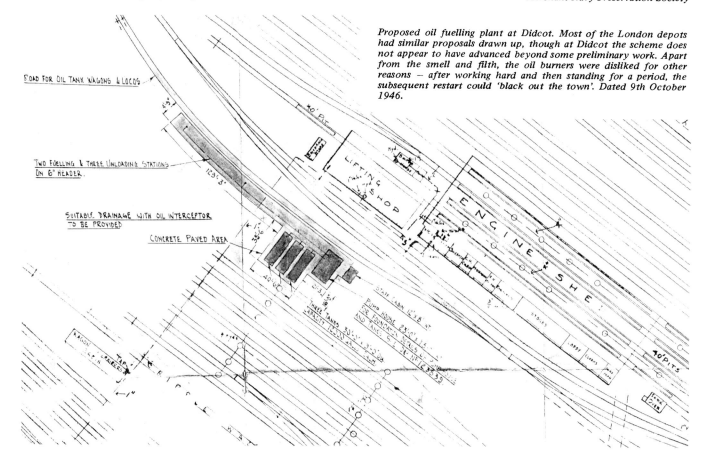

Proposed oil fuelling plant at Didcot. Most of the London depots had similar proposals drawn up, though at Didcot the scheme does not appear to have advanced beyond some preliminary work. Apart from the smell and filth, the oil burners were disliked for other reasons — after working hard and then standing for a period, the subsequent restart could 'black out the town'. Dated 9th October 1946.

Engines additionally were registered as out-based at Lambourn (0–6–0T No. 1925), Newbury (Dean 0–6–0 No. 2569), Wallingford (0–4–2T No. 1159), and Winchester (Dean 0–6–0 No. 2395).

Work at Didcot was arranged into some seven links. At the bottom were men approaching the end of their working lives and those new to the job, the unfortunately termed 'cripple link' – 'old boys and new cleaners having their first go'. The 'Ordnance' trips were available to those at the 'lower' end of the scale, and moving up through 6 and 5 links brought passenger pilot work (empty coaches to the station), the 'fly jobs', ten or so wagons to places like Uffington and back, and the 'two trippers', double workings to Reading and so on. These links included shed servicing duties which involved movement of light engines, turning and arrangement of locos for coaling, stabling or exit. No. 4 link dealt with light goods of a local nature and the next link, No. 3, dealt with goods of a more far-ranging kind, the 'Double Homes', lodging to Worcester and Kidderminster and elsewhere. No. 2 men took the highly graded freights, perishables (e.g. bananas), any fast goods and relief work. 'Any decent passenger jobs' were given over to No. 1

Didcot in 1962, with 'County' 4–6–0s Nos. 1002 *County of Bucks* and 1003 *County of Wilts*. The ash shelter absurdly still survived though it was nothing more than a nuisance. The 'County' engines were not well liked and were at Didcot really for whatever work might be found for them – 'the Friday job' to Swindon, for instance, with a five hour wait before return. 'Granges' were preferred above all, with 'Manors' regarded as weak and prone to rough running very soon after shopping.

L. Waters

No. 8720 (4959 *Purley Hall* behind) on 25th July 1963.   *K. C. H. Fairey*

The Didcot pilot turns were drastically reduced as the Ordnance Depot closed and freight traffic declined. Some diesel shunters were provided and Didcot men also worked DMUs, 3-car sets, stabled between turns on No. 1 Road. 'Warships', 'Hymeks' and 'Westerns' all followed, variously disliked for their unpleasant conditions, unreliability and an alarming tendency to catch fire. There was no fuelling at Didcot and the diesels brought an increase in relieving work, the locos maintained and fuelled at Old Oak, Ranelagh Bridge, Reading and elsewhere. Perhaps the most remarkable train worked with diesels was the 'Long Tom', 'the longest train in Britain', with 54 petrol tanks from Fawley-Bromford Bridge, using a pair of Southern Region D6500 Type 2s.
E. Wilmshurst

link which included a lot of passed drivers awaiting final elevation. Movement through the links brought Didcot men to London with increasing frequency and the Old Oak 'Cabin' – the universal term for mess room – was a familiar place. The 'top train', post war at least, was considered to be the '7.10 a.m. London', a turn of hardly any note at somewhere like Old Oak but a duty of some status at Didcot, still in many of its essentials a 'country junction'. There were compensations – a trip to Newbury racecourse could hold interest – the joyous occasion when local Hunt hounds found themselves on the course is memorable, the dogs circling with the increasingly anxious horses before a bemused Didcot crew. And there were more sombre times, relieved by humour – black, certainly, but dignified by an (necessary) acceptance of the daily perils all faced. The 'doodlebug', No. 70026 *Polar Star*, derailed at Milton in November 1955, was towed to Didcot 'much bashed about'; evidence of the violent derailment and its effects on the crew were only too apparent. At least two Didcot men were believed to have committed suicide in the nearby reservoir (a fire-fighting reserve supply); one was a driver said to have borne 'a bit of a shock' (usually taken to mean witnessing a fatal accident); a sad figure, comment centred on his taking a haircut only half an hour before. A second tragedy occurred when a man from the stores threw himself

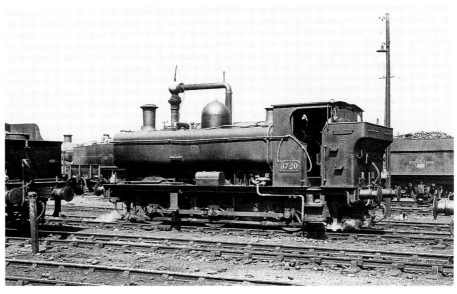

No. 8720 on 25th July 1964.   *Merchant Navy Preservation Society*

in, loaded down with nuts and bolts and bits from the dump alongside the shed.

Didcot owed much to its country origins, and the tradition of lengthy travel lasted long; for years some drivers and firemen thought nothing of walking from Steventon or Ilsley. This was no mean feat in daylight and good weather, and almost heroic during nights. Shifts varied at the convenience of the railway not the men, and it was

common to have to book on at something like 11.55 p.m., thus losing night rate payment over the succeeding eight hours. These were harsher aspects, softened by the passing of time and relieved in some part by cleaning memories, the award of half a crown for spotting a broken spring. Cleaners in the 'fifties experienced a degree of promotion unknown before; this did not meet with the approval of older hands who

'The Field' in 1961, the 'holding' Roads 5-8 with engines lined up for 'going off' by the shedman. The roof was thoroughly refurbished in the last years, the old 'diagonal tiles' were replaced by conventional sheeting, and within months of closure the pits and chutes were completely overhauled.

W. Turner

were reluctant to accept the 'new boys' as enginemen at all. The 1955 ASLEF strike caused lasting bitterness and for years afterwards certain crews would not speak throughout days of work together. The gratuities, impromptu payments by passengers to non-strikers, at Paddington and elsewhere, was a stinging memory. Much of this ill-will was never fully resolved and some remained incommunicado for years. Much of all this only served to bolster the anarchic humour which many found so sustaining; enginemen at Didcot were keen as any on nicknames and the deprecation of almost everybody else. 'Dickles and Cockles' abounded, and an unfortunate who dared to wear a shirt other than plain white was forever christened 'Technicolour'. 'Pongo' (ears) and 'Lofty' were fairly familiar, but 'Hot Socks' (he ran around a lot) was slightly more obscure. Almost every London shed had a fair quota of Welshmen who received the usual appellations, but the best were awarded (and were more permanent) for particular events both spectacular and mundane. Oxford driver Hitchcock was involved in an incident at

Leftover accommodation at Didcot, in June 1959. This old body, or something similar, was used for classes, examinations and suchlike.

J. H. Russell

Didcot with a petrol train, his fireman received both a registered caution and a commendation for the somewhat tangled events – wagons were uncoupled but unfortunately the conflagration melted a footbridge. 'Fireball' Hitchock subsequently bore comparison with Johnny 'Eager', a Reading man, who it was perceived stopped less quickly than others. Neither could surpass Didcot's Tommy 'The Bat', who always worked nights and was rumoured to 'hate the daylight'.

Steam working collapsed at Didcot in the 1960s and many men left, transferring away after briefly working main line diesels from the shed. Diesel shunters had arrived early but later main line units were not liked, the *Warship* D800s were 'horrible', and it was often difficult to see across the cab for smoke and fumes. At the end Great Western Society locomotives were sharing the shed and BR engines seem to have stopped running in 1965.

MSWJ 2−4−0. As engines made available elsewhere came to Didcot, the place lost its clanking veterans and the complement took on a much more conventional look, 'Halls', 2−8−0s, '61' tanks, '57XX' panniers and BR standard locos. *J. H. Russell*

Didcot had ever been a railway town, of the sort based not on some mighty works, but on the running of trains, a community thus out of character with its surrounds. These origins could almost be overlooked today but they really began to blur only in the 1960s. The steam locomotive still dominated the town, even then, ever present and the noises curiously sharpened at night. Enginemen tramped early morning streets and the Didcot call-boys, one for engine crews and one for guards, were familiar if lonely figures, pausing now and then for a chat with the local 'copper' and recognising enginemen by their footfalls. To enter the station subway now is to experience something of those days, the distant and muffled noise of engines and the unchanging night sounds, the echo of boots and the steady *plink, plink-plonk* of water. *L. Waters*

Opening day of the Lambourn Valley Railway in April of 1898. The shed was in corrugated iron and was later extended. *The Lambourn Branch:* 'Two extra sidings were added in 1902-3 and the purchase of a third locomotive at this time prompted the extension of the engine shed. This was carried out by a local man, W. J. Adams, whose estimate of £107 12s. 6d. was exceeded by a further £19 5s 9d. This matching extension of corrugated iron on timber framing was added to the front of the shed, increasing its size to 80 ft x 16 ft.'

LAMBOURN

A number of branch lines had emerged in the country west of London and in 1898 the Lambourn Valley Railway joined their ranks, a 12 mile line from the existing station at Newbury. Robertson & Simmonds in *The Lambourn Branch* (Wild Swan 1984) explore in great depth the line's progress from the simple tramway proposal of 1873 to its opening in 1898. A small shed, corrugated sheeting on a timber frame, was erected at the terminus, accompanied by a crude wooden coal stage and water tank. '850' class 0–6–0Ts came to monopolise the branch service from very early on, although steam railcars Nos. 1, 2, 10, 19 and 21 were used extensively in 1904/5. The odd incursion by ex MSWJ 2–4–0s and 'Stella' class 2–4–0s added some variety to the allocation over the years. The shed had originally been an outstation of Didcot, passing to Reading in 1917 – normally 'two sets of crews' covering the service with 'an overnight shed man' employed on cleaning and preparation.

No. 2007, an engine which appeared on the branch over many years. It was one of the last to survive as a saddle tank, withdrawn in 1949.
C. L. Turner

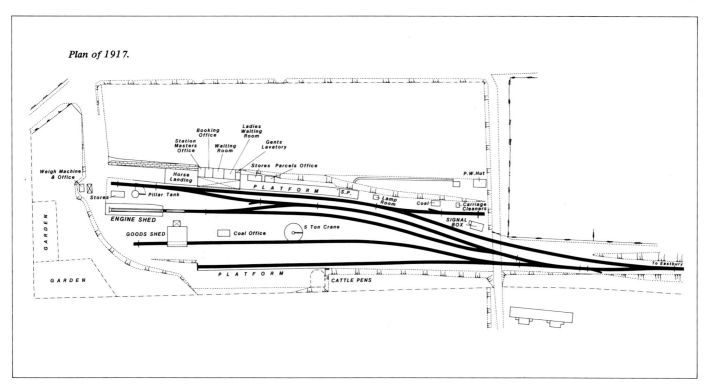

Plan of 1917.

With the introduction of a diesel service in 1937, the engine shed was closed and subsequently demolished, leaving only a rudimentary pit.

P. J. Garland

WALLINGFORD

More tiny Great Western branch line engine sheds, it seems could be found across a couple of counties in southern England then within the entire networks (any two perhaps) of its giant rivals. This was but another element in the inordinate fascination exerted by the GWR. Every slumbering Thames Valley terminus looked as if it had sprung from the pages of a modelling magazine rather than vice versa. Inevitably an 0–4–2T stood outside, untended, next to an empty platform. British filmmakers (most of them it seemed lived between Maidenhead and Ealing) inevitably picked Marlow, Wallingford or one of the many contemporaries thereof when the heroine arrived to take her first anxious appointment as governess, housekeeper, nurse, or whatever. They were favourites for comedies though atmospherics, especially fog, usually meant an expedition (real or otherwise) to the North of England. The Great Western established (or inherited) an engine shed at the end of most of its lines; it had more than any comparable English company, probably a result of its branching evolution into the west, a dendritic pattern almost in replication (in reverse) of the Thames, the company's heartland.

A single road engine shed was provided at Wallingford from opening of the line in the summer of 1866. Karau and Turner (*The Wallingford Branch*, Wild Swan 1982 –

Wallingford on 16th August 1947. The pillar tank was 'fixed' in August 1920, under a Locomotive Carriage & Stores Committee minute of 5th February 1920: 'Erection . . . of second hand 3000 gallon tank . . . in lieu of existing tank which is of smaller capacity . . . Approved.' It was supplied from a well, 20 ft 6 ins deep and 6 ft in diameter, close by the station and the wooden pump house is visible beyond the station sign. Further consideration was given to the supply on 24th January 1921: 'At present Engine pumps half water tank in morning (after 10 pm). Using town supply as an emergency only is unsatisfactory, as probably there would be nothing for the Engine to pump in the evening. Supply is available only between 2 p.m. and 4 a.m., 1/- per 1000 gallons, 25/- per week, £65 per annum. The height of the (Water Works) Tank = 45 ft. Could use our meter'.
H. C. Casserley

this short summary is based largely upon the various descriptions contained therein) speculate that the building was provided principally at the behest of the GWR, who were to work the line on behalf of the 'Wall-

ingford and Watlington Railway' (Wallingford was as far as it got). 'The [water] tank pumps crane &c' were provided by Stothert & Pitt.

The line was vested in the GWR from December 1872 following the customary show of solicitude bolstered by indifference and predatory guile. Sometime later the shed was rebuilt; the reason is not clear, but it seems to have taken place in 1890 – a Locomotive Department return of 1897 notes 'Date built or date Shed was first used . . . 1890'. The new shed, in brick, was erected to the rear of the old building, which at least suggests a planned replacement, presumably if some disaster had befallen the first shed – fire or tempest – the original foundations would have been used. The change of site, in whatever circumstances, might have depended upon the need to improve access to the gas works.

Reading provided the branch engine for many years, exchanged weekly at Cholsey; two crews were sufficient with a shedman for overnight attention. 517 0–4–2Ts, with occasional panniers or saddle tanks, were in charge of the workings over many years, until 48XX 0–4–2Ts took over in the mid-1930s.

Didcot men frequently worked to Wallingford on relief, considered a 'lovely little job' with the autos but unmentionable if a tender engine had to be put on, with constant uncoupling of the trailer. Both Didcot and Reading seem to have been involved with the branch — Reading is normally considered to have provided the engine, exchanged weekly at Cholsey but it now seems clear that Didcot engines were also put on the job at times. Certainly by 1933 Didcot officially provided the engine. 'An old chap' did the fires at Wallingford, the trailer remaining in the station when the engine was away.
R. H. G. Simpson

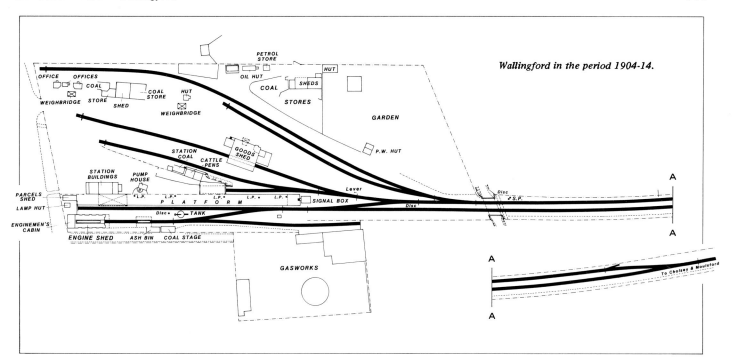

Wallingford in the period 1904-14.

'The old blokes', the Wallingford regulars, it was considered, 'crept about a bit' and Didcot men sometimes allowed a sense of fun to get slightly out of hand. One auto train thereby ended up in the main road, some yards beyond the buffers, to be dragged back by the Didcot breakdown gang. Suggestions from a District Inspector for a pair of cranes to be called up were brushed aside as unhelpful, in the light of the weight restrictions in force on the branch.

I. D. Beale

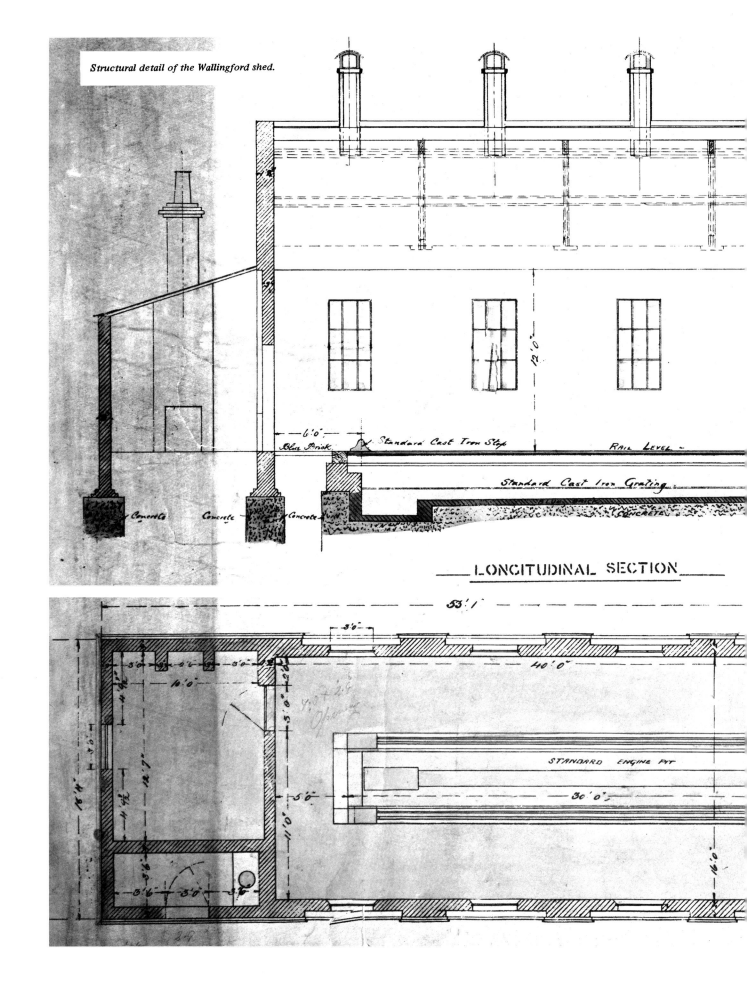

Structural detail of the Wallingford shed.

6'0" — Blue Brick — Standard Cast Iron Step — RAIL LEVEL

Concrete — Concrete — Concrete — Standard Cast Iron Grating — CONCRETE

12'0"

LONGITUDINAL SECTION

53'1"

40'0"

3'0"

STANDARD ENGINE PIT

30'0"

16'0"

10'0"

3'0"

5'0"

1'0"

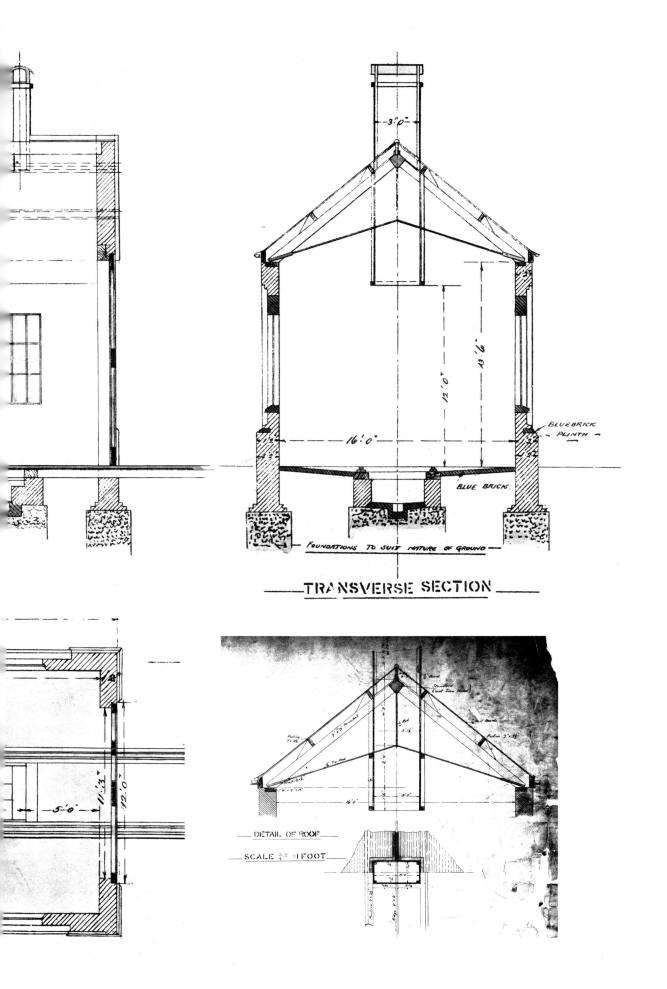

3'0"

13'6"

12'0"

16'0"

BLUEBRICK
PLINTH

BLUE BRICK.

FOUNDATIONS TO SUIT NATURE OF GROUND

TRANSVERSE SECTION

11'3"

12'0"

5'0"

16'0"

3'0"

DETAIL OF ROOF

SCALE ¾" = 1 FOOT

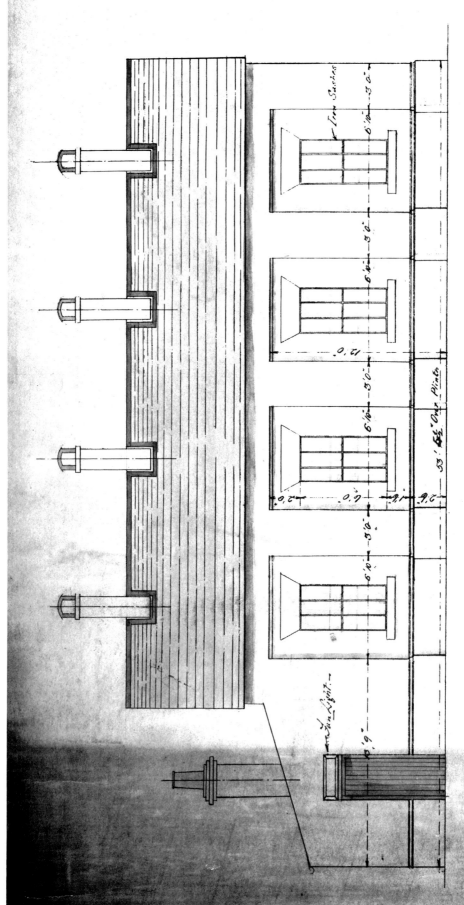

SIDE ELEVATION

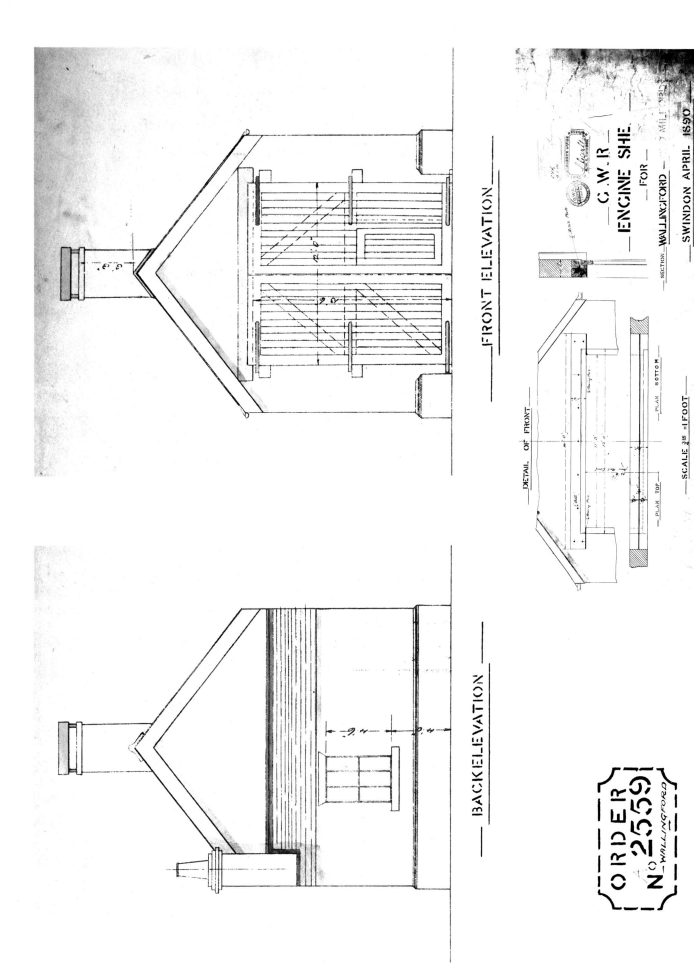

FRONT ELEVATION

BACK ELEVATION

DETAIL OF FRONT

PLAN BOTTOM

PLAN TOP

SCALE ½ = 1 FOOT

SECTION

G.W.R

ENGINE SHE

FOR

WALLINGFORD

SWINDON APRIL 1890

ORDER
No 2559
WALLINGFORD

NEWBURY

Much of the work at Didcot took men to Newbury. There was a Sundays only train, often with one of the MSWJ 2–4–0s, turning at the Racecourse to work tender first to Lambourn, and thus 'right way round' all the way back to Didcot. Four sets of men were based at Newbury and, although a shed was proposed, none was ever built. *J. H. Russell*

A Didcot 0–6–0 was at one time outbased here and a turntable was provided at least until about 1890 (see plan page 112, *The Didcot Newbury* and *Southampton Railway*, Karau Parsons and Robertson, Wild Swan), and Lyons (*An Historical Survey of Great Western Engine Sheds* OPC) makes reference to a pit adjacent to the Lambourne bay, on the north side of the station. Its exact location is not clear, for various 40ft plans unfortunately fail to reveal a pit of any description; consideration, however, was certainly given to a proper engine shed, for in July 1907 'negotiations' were recommended for an acquisition of more than six acres of land at Newbury … 'in connection with the erection of an Engine Shed at that place'. A 'Survey for new Engine Shed' had taken place in June and later plans were got out for a single road shed, some yards to the west on the north side of the line. Space was not readily available and the building, with coal siding, was to be carved out of an existing cutting, and a new retaining wall was necessary. Nothing came of these proposals.

WINCHESTER

Didcot shed was responsible for the working of the Didcot Newbury and Southampton line, latterly the 'Rural Crumb Catcher',* and one or two locos were customarily stabled overnight at Bar End, Winchester. 0–6–0s sufficed for years on both goods and passenger work, but 2–4–0s and then 4–4–0s were frequent enough visitors. The shed presumably opened with the line and remained an obscure backwater until war cast it in a role of some considerable strategic import. Once America had entered the conflict and the possibility of an invasion of Europe was made real, the line found itself a vital north-south route. This had enormous implications for Didcot shed (see, for instance, p. 288) and the sleepy DN & S was progressively transformed into a major conduit for the great docks at Southampton. As a consequence traffic increased enormously on the DN & S with Winchester 'Chesil' a haven that might take many hours to reach. There was an abrupt decline from the late 'forties; responsibility for the shed transferred to Eastleigh (Southern Region, ex LSWR) in 1950 and it was put out of use in the summer of 1953.

*See *The Didcot Newbury & Southampton Railway* by Karau, Parsons and Robertson which includes an exhaustive description of the engine shed.

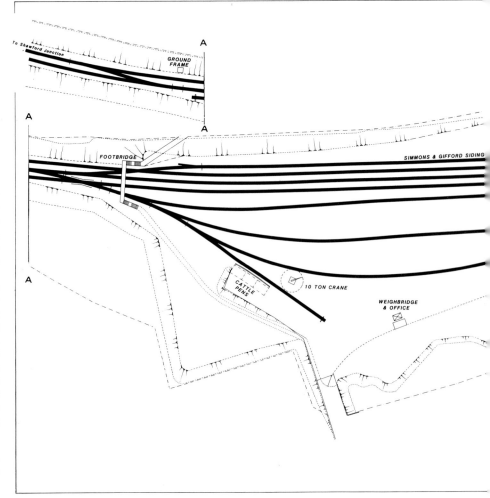

Didcot 0–6–0 stabled at Winchester. There was even at one time a lodging turn here for Didcot men.

E. Branch

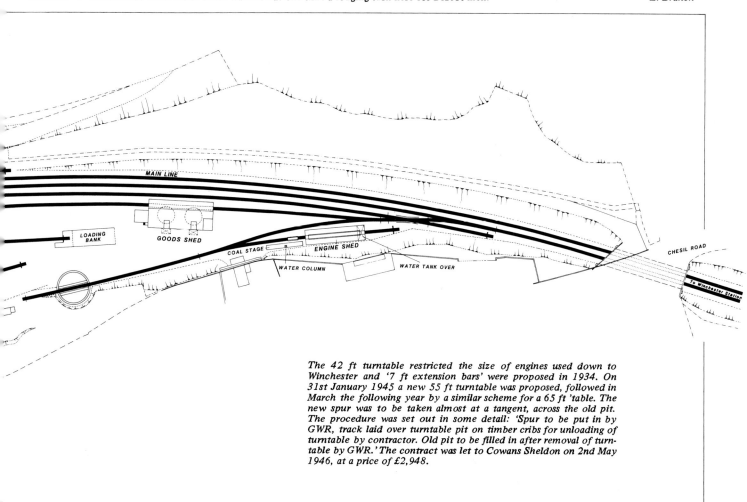

The 42 ft turntable restricted the size of engines used down to Winchester and '7 ft extension bars' were proposed in 1934. On 31st January 1945 a new 55 ft turntable was proposed, followed in March the following year by a similar scheme for a 65 ft 'table. The new spur was to be taken almost at a tangent, across the old pit. The procedure was set out in some detail: 'Spur to be put in by GWR, track laid over turntable pit on timber cribs for unloading of turntable by contractor. Old pit to be filled in after removal of turntable by GWR.' The contract was let to Cowans Sheldon on 2nd May 1946, at a price of £2,948.

OXFORD

Oxford shed was possessed of a long and venerable history, befitting the ancient and stately nature of the city itself. As at Cambridge, there was opposition from the colleges and the Oxford 'branch' did not open until the early summer of 1844. A broad gauge shed (two roads with turntable outside, north of the station on the up side) did not apparently open until about 1850. The Oxford Worcester and Wolverhampton Railway opened a standard gauge shed to the north (on the later Oxford site) around 1854 and, with broad gauge services on the wane, the Great Western transferred itself here in the early 1860s. The broad gauge shed 'closed in the 1870s with the end of broad gauge services'. The original Oxford Worcester and Wolverhampton building had probably been of one road only, inadequate even for the GWR. Work took place throughout this period (in stages, in all likelihood) for the shed had a mismatched look it was never quite to lose (in fact this effect was probably enhanced as the years passed). In 1866 William Armstrong furnished the Company with 'A report' – on the 2nd May that year

the Locomotive Carriage and Permanent Way Committee pondered this document, a survey 'relative to the additional shed accommodation which with a view to the efficient working of Engines he considers should be provided at various places on the Line'. Accommodation for '8 additional Engines' was required at Oxford, the estimated cost £1,800. The whole received further confirmation on 18th April 1866 when £1,820 was approved for 'Extension to the Engine Shed, Oxford'.

A fitting shop had been provided at an early date, enlarged incrementally to form, by the 1870s, a collection of shops, stores and offices. The main part came to be grouped around the turntable, north of the shed and close to the original primitive coal stage. A number of spur roads were laid off this 'table, space was at a premium early on in Oxford's history, and two led directly into the shop premises. This arrangement had been largely done away with by the end of the century, the old quarters set in order as a conventional single road repair shop containing hoist, bench and machinery. Despite latter day enlargements and

improvements, it possessed to the end (along with the great part of the depot itself) something of a ramshackle, improvised air.

The whole establishment was thoroughly refurbished in the early part of the 1930s, restoring in some measure the shed's capacity for repair work. The equipment as well as the premises were by now quite ancient and some substantial improvement was necessary. 'The supply of a running shed lathe' was authorised from Messrs Dean Smith & Grace Ltd on 12th February 1931 at £480 and on 26th March 'Royce Ltd' were approved as suppliers of a 50 ton engine hoist at £496. The latter was to replace a truly primordial set of equipment, but, before it could be accommodated, some enlargement of the building itself was necessary. Within a few weeks, on 21st May 1931, no less than £1,400 was approved for 'Extension of Lifting Shop and Rearrangement of Siding'. Thus equipped, the repair shop (always known as the Top Shop) continued in use until the end. The 50 ton 'chain hoist' remained its principal feature, attended to by a pair of time-served fitters

The gentle eye of the company photographer effectively masked the grime, smoke and decrepitude of Oxford shed. The 0–4–2T No. 1473 is *Fair Rosamund*, Oxford's Woodstock branch engine and reputedly named after the daughter of one Clifford of Clifford Castle. She was supposed to have been a favourite of Henry II who kept her secreted in 'a tower', actually the royal residence Woodstock Manor. Beyond the buffer stops is the foreman's (later shedmaster's) office.
British Railways

and their mates. The Dean Smith etc. lathe was not improved upon and there was no wheel lathe at Oxford – wheels were consigned in open wagons to Swindon and returned in similar fashion. The 1931 running shed lathe was housed in the fitters' shop 'next door', accompanied by a drilling machine and the usual bench vices and anvil. There was some extraordinary difficulty at Oxford in relinquishing the past; belt-driven machinery, described with some understatement as 'very ancient', survived in the repair shop more or less until the end.

The great age of the depot meant that the complement long exceeded the available accommodation, a problem overcome by the simple expedient of laying further sidings in the yard. Eventually the great part of the day to day servicing, examinations and attention took place in the 'Field', open sidings between the shed, and a new turntable/coal stage. The lack of pits at Oxford remained a problem until the end; two new ones 'near the turntable' had been ordered as early as the summer of 1906

Continued on page 334

Oxford station.
Lens of Sutton

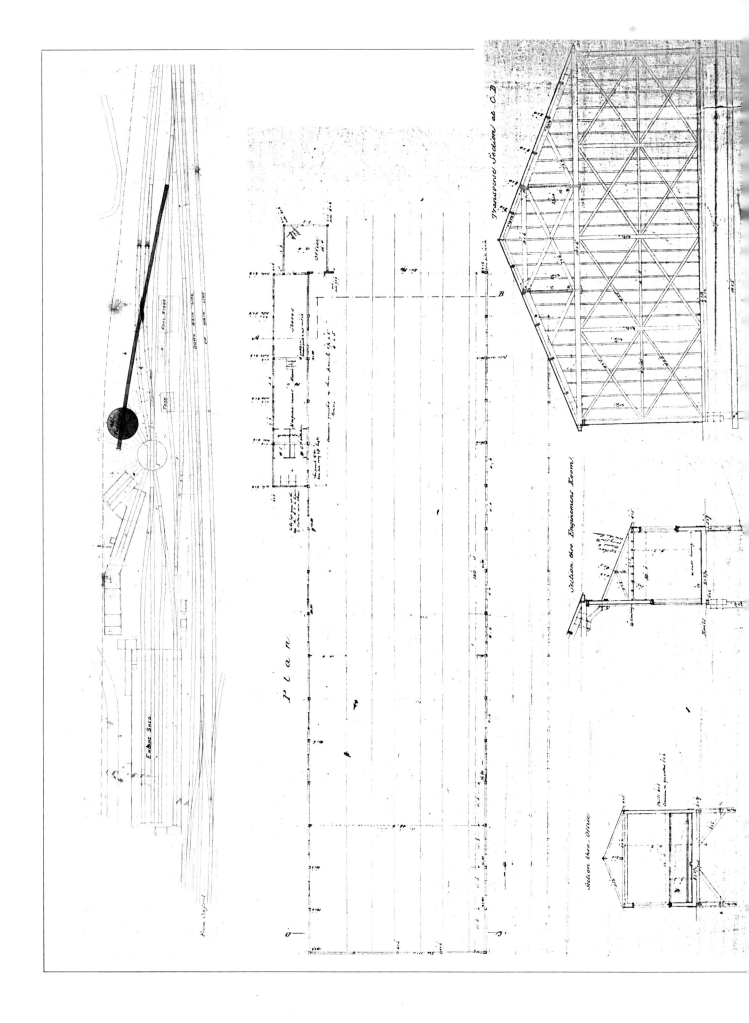

Transverse Section at C.D.

Section thro Engagement Room

Section thro Office

Engine Shed

Plan

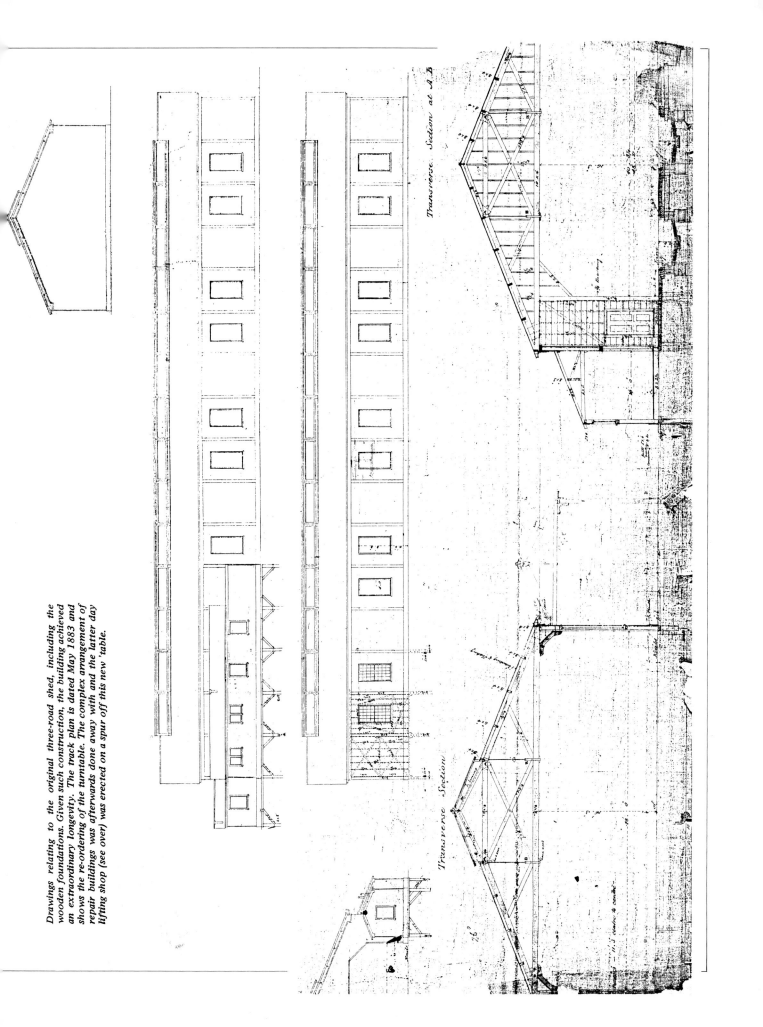

Drawings relating to the original three-road shed, including the wooden foundations. Given such construction, the building achieved an extraordinary longevity. The track plan is dated May 1883 and shows the re-ordering of the turntable. The complex arrangement of repair buildings was afterwards done away with and the latter day lifting shop (see over) was erected on a spur off this new table.

Transverse Section at A.B

Transverse Section

Enlargement of the picture on page 318, to show some further details of the timber construction.

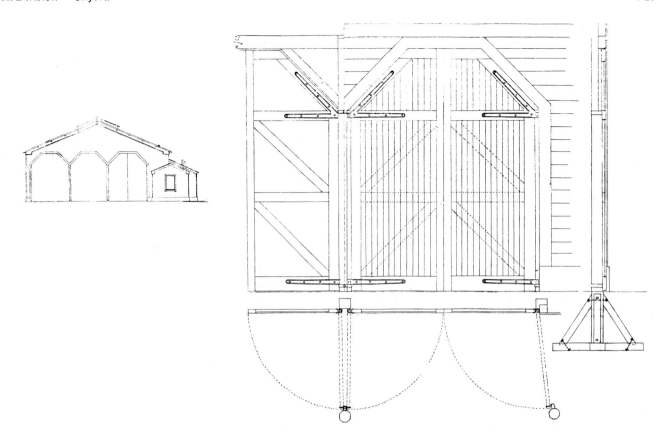

The last of the 2–2–2s, like the 'Metros', clung to life at Oxford, nurtured on the rambling duties out of the city. No. 1128 pictured here was unique amongst the type in that it was fitted with ATC gear for working on the Fairford line. It was withdrawn in 1914 (the last 2–2–2 on the GWR) but was working cross-country expresses up until its last few weeks.

Kenn Nunn Collection

The new lifting shop.

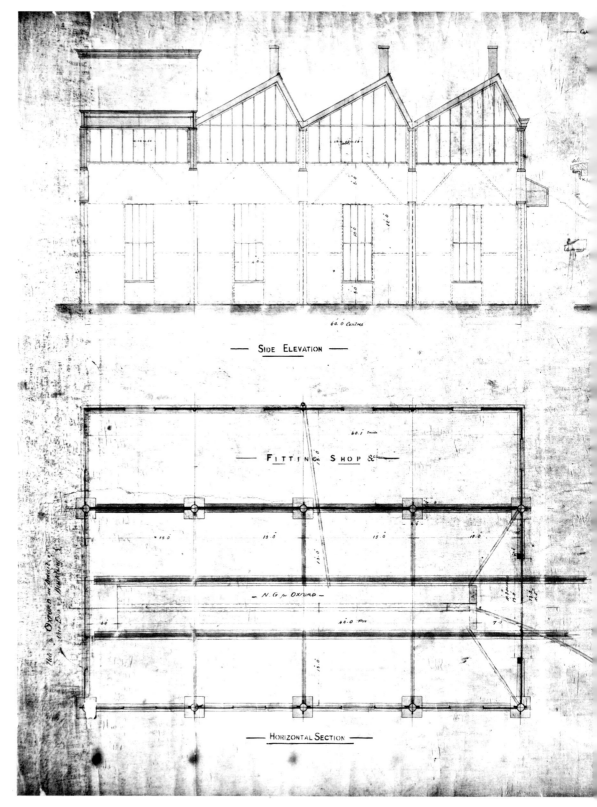

— SIDE ELEVATION —

— HORIZONTAL SECTION —

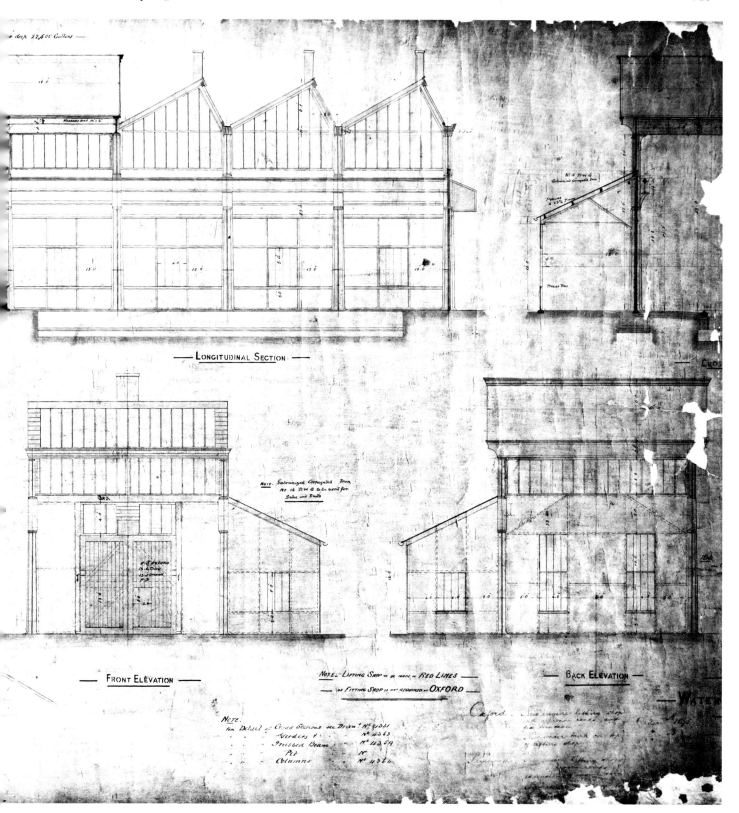

deep 22,500 Gallons

LONGITUDINAL SECTION

NOTE. Galvanized Corrugated Iron
Nº 16 BWG to be used for
Sides and Ends

FRONT ELEVATION

NOTE. LIFTING SHOP to be made in RED LINES
as FITTING SHOP is not required at OXFORD

BACK ELEVATION

NOTE.
For Detail of Cross Sections see Drawing Nº 4051
Girders & Nº 4053
Trussed Beam Nº 4059
Pit
Columns Nº 4084

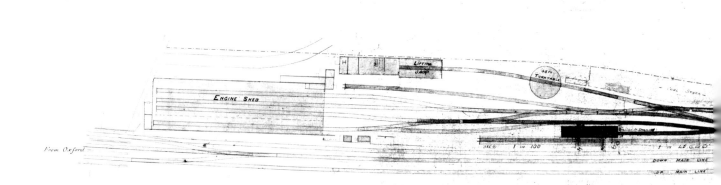

Location of new lifting shop,
May 1883.

Coal stage details (see also succeeding pages) from 1883-1884.
The drawings served also for a closely similar construction at
Weymouth, variation limited to such details as 'office and steps
. . . to be placed at the opposite end . . . for Weymouth'.

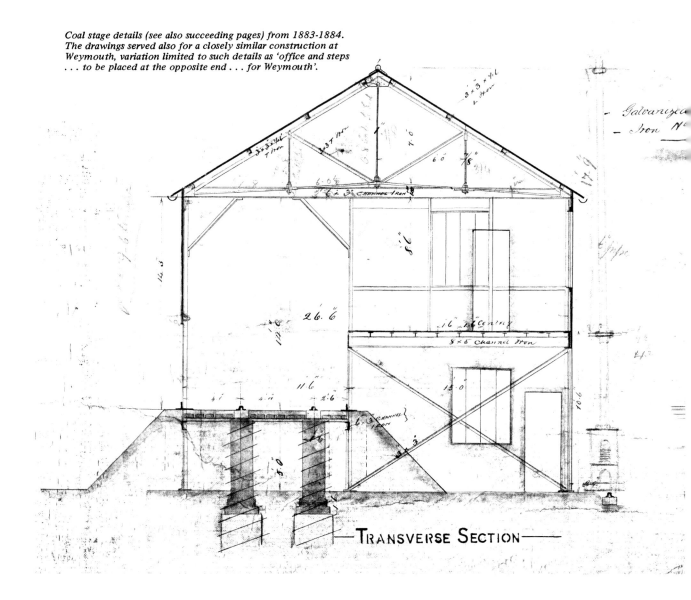

TRANSVERSE SECTION

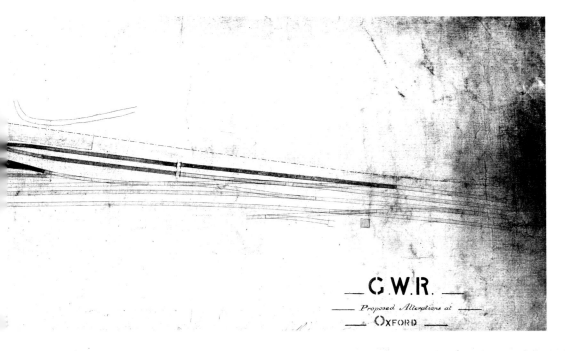

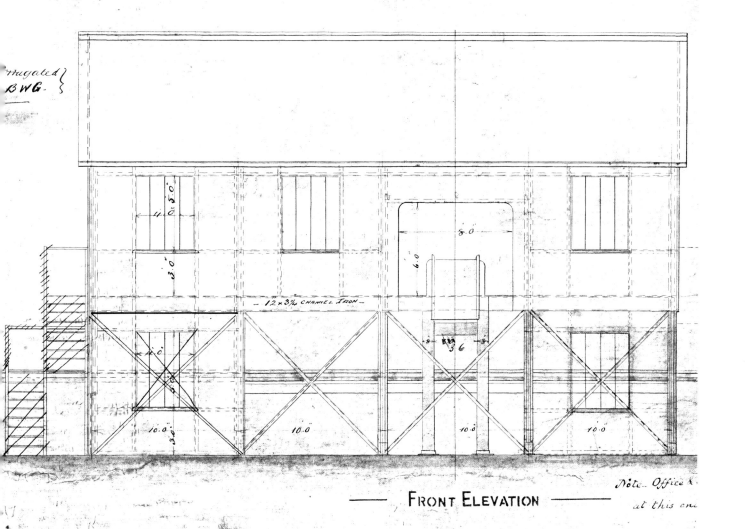

FRONT ELEVATION

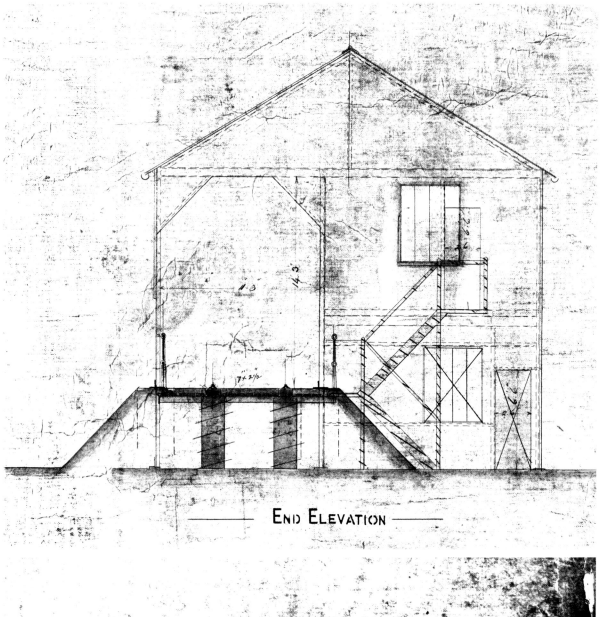

— END ELEVATION —

G.W.R.

COAL STAGE&C FOR OXFORD & WEYMOUTH

SCALE 1/4 IN = 1 FOOT

NOVR 1883

Note Alterations in Red
are for Weymouth

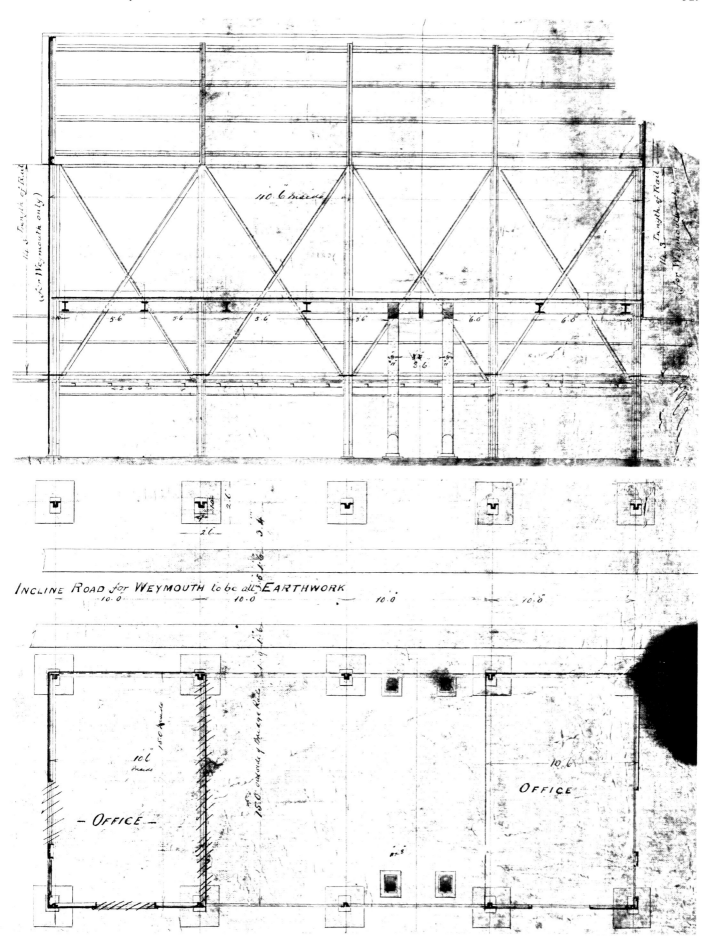

INCLINE ROAD *for* WEYMOUTH *to be all* EARTHWORK

– OFFICE –

OFFICE

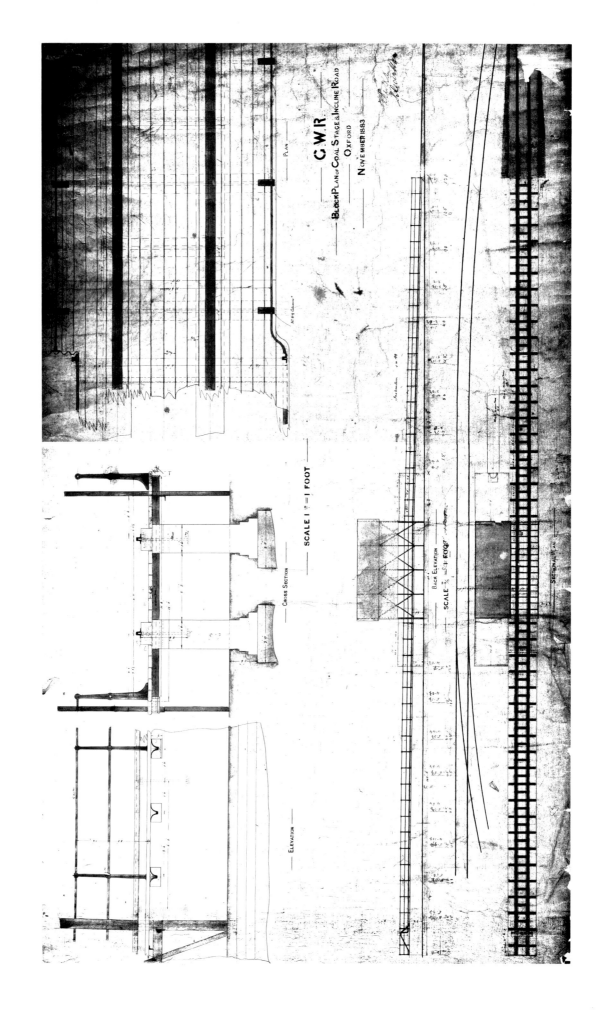

PLAN

G.W.R.

Block Plan of Coal Stage & Incline Road

Oxford

November 1883

SCALE 1 IN = 1 FOOT

Cross Section

Elevation

Back Elevation

Sectional Plan

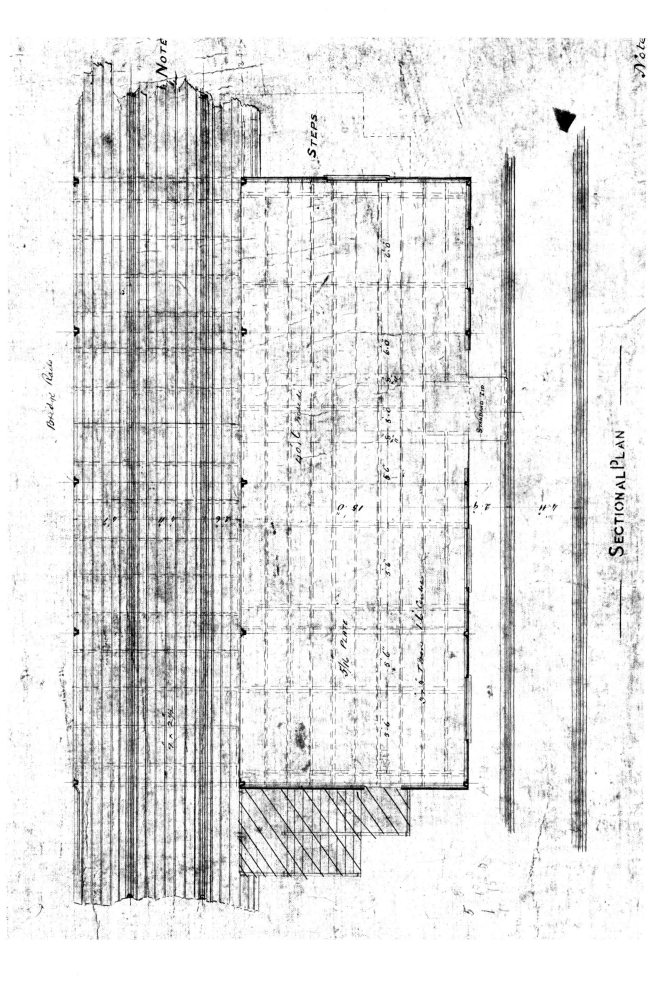

SECTIONAL PLAN

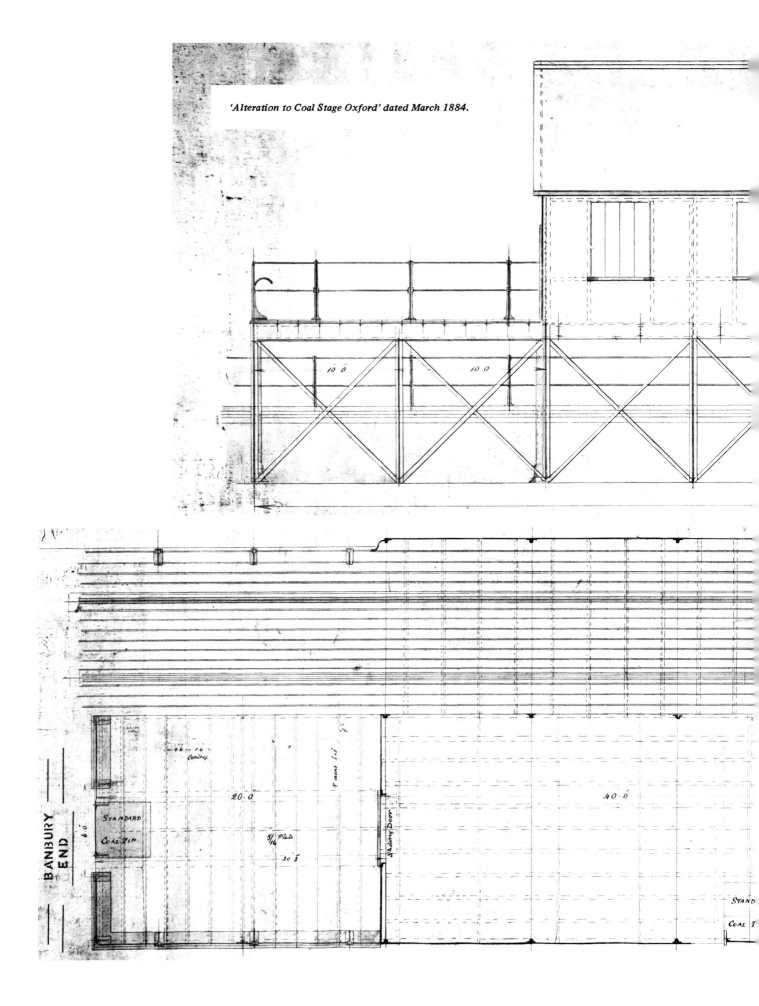

'Alteration to Coal Stage Oxford' dated March 1884.

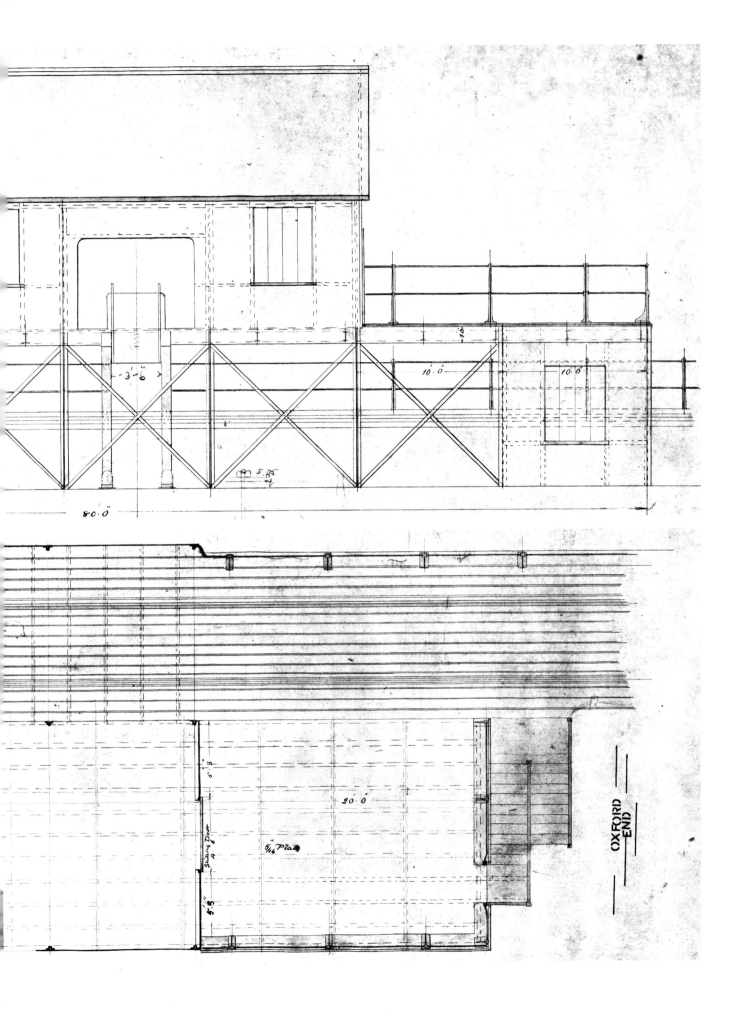

80.0"

3'-6"

10.0"

10.0"

5.3"

5/16" Plate

20.0"

Sliding Door

5.3"

5.3"

OXFORD
END

at a cost of £350, and in September 1925 'alterations' were carried out elsewhere in the shed 'so that (two pits) may be more effectively drained'. With the internal valve motion common to most GWR engines, a pit was *de rigeur* for almost any simple task – some engines at Oxford, lined up of a morning 'in order of going out', might have to await the departure of the preceding loco before moving over to the vacant pit for 'oiling up'. Relatively few engines could be accommodated in the shed itself, where one road at least was reserved for 'cripples', engines receiving prolonged attention. There were further outside roads

of note as the configuration of the 'Field' altered over the years. It seems to have originated with the new turntable in 1905 and had at first five roads, more or less equal in length. By late GW/BR times it comprised four straight roads, two long and two short, with three more tracks by the repair shop. There was for years a short 'stub' siding, its precise position changing with the new coal stage. This was always called the 'Dock' and usually held a 4–6–0 or 2–8–0. A further road provided along with the new stage lay on the west boundary of the yard and played host in the main to the LMR locomotives using Oxford after

1950. A firedropper by the name of Tommy Attwood had laboured here of a time and the siding, often known simply as 'Attwoods', was his memorial.

Coaling arrangements at Oxford, in contrast to the shed itself, saw all manner of change. The original coal shelter, a wooden canopy of sorts, was replaced from about 1883 by a more conventional timber stage with ramp, approximately on the same site. This small and flimsy structure was in poor condition by the end of the century and its replacement was proposed in 1905 along with a new turntable. On 18th January that year a 65 ft Ransomes Rapier turntable was

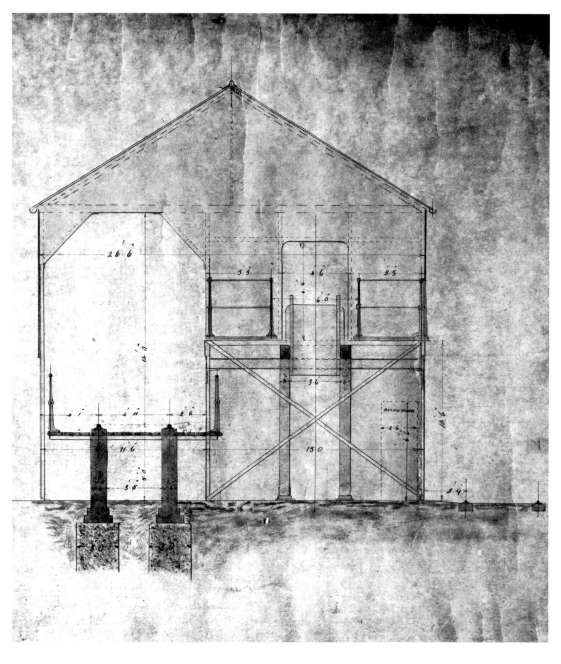

sanctioned, the cost 'approved in the Traffic Committee vote of £10,584, 8th July 1903'. The shed 'table had already been re-sited once within the confines of the original yard, but the final unit was put in on new ground to the west near to the river and beyond what was to become the 'Field'. It was extensively repaired in 1930 at a cost of £770 and further work was necessary in 1957, when an 8F 2–8–0 ran off and fell into the pit. Improvement came only in halting fashion at Oxford, the familiar sequence of projects and proposals abandoned and forgotten. The 65 ft turntable was linked within a few months, in 1906, to one of the earliest and most comprehensive schemes, for a single roundhouse with repair shop partly on the site of the old wooden shed. This would have been demolished and a new coal stage of contemporary dimensions was to be placed alongside the turntable, but nothing materialized. Space was put aside for a coal ramp on the turntable approaches, and other schemes followed in the period to Grouping, most notably plans for another roundhouse to the north. It would have occupied the Oxford North yard, the approaches to cut across the old shed yard. This idea was in its turn aban-doned and Oxford escaped demolition once again.

The roundhouse proposal emerged again in 1930, and in June 1939 an insubstantial coaling shelter with a new 1 : 30 ramp was proposed, adjacent to the existing stage on the east side of the yard close by the running lines. A proper coal stage of more generous proportions appeared belatedly, but only through the pressures of wartime, in 1944 (a variety of ideas had surfaced since 1942). Oxford could then enjoy a coal stage at least roughly commensurate with its size, though in truth the operational principles belonged firmly in the past, beyond even the days of Churchward. Else-

The *Great Western Railway Magazine* for 1906 reported under 'Departmental Doings': 'We have pleasure in illustrating a 65 ft. turntable recently installed at Oxford. Readers will remember that in the November issue we mentioned that during the last few months the Directors had authorised the installation of tables of this dimension at no less than fifteen depots. They are to G.W. standard drawings, and are known as the "Over-girder" or "surface" type. The principal advantage attaching to them is that there is no necessity for a deep pit. Moreover, the working parts are easy of access, and there is the further advantage of immunity from risk of accident, as the pit is so shallow that even should anyone come to difficulties in it, injury would probably not result. We may say that at various stations, thirty tables of this type, 55 ft. in diameter, have already been provided by the Company.'

County Kilkenny on the turntable in 1929.

Dr. I. C. Allen

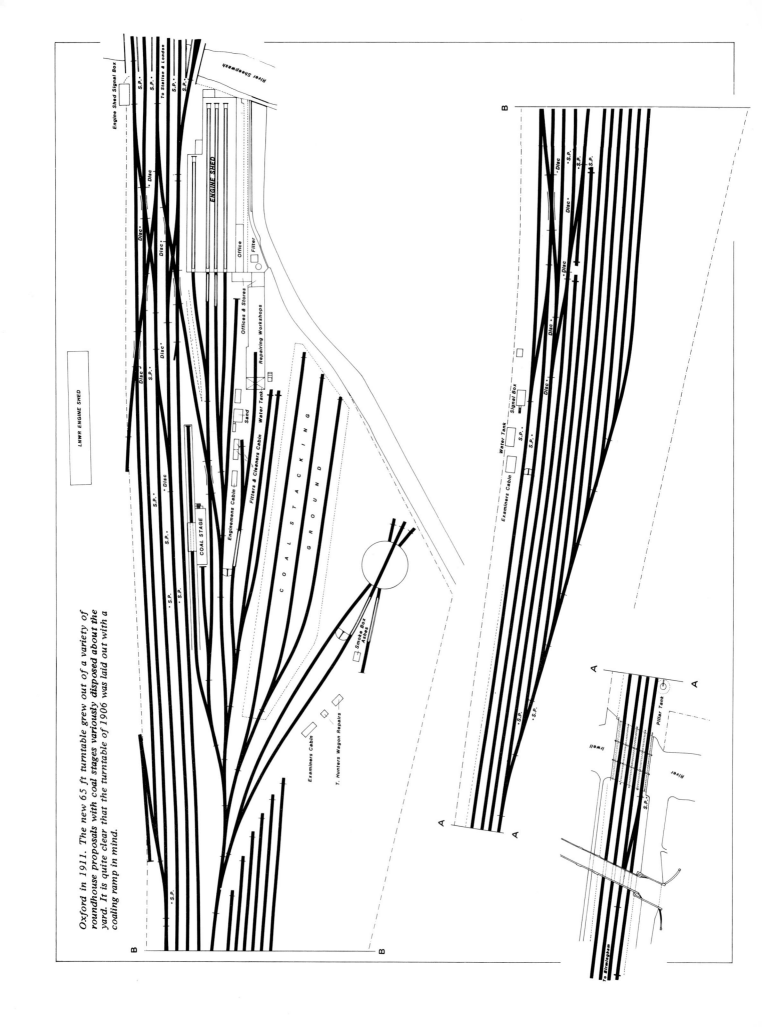

LNWR ENGINE SHED

Oxford in 1911. The new 65 ft turntable grew out of a variety of roundhouse proposals with coal stages variously disposed about the yard. It is quite clear that the turntable of 1906 was laid out with a coaling ramp in mind.

ENGINE SHED

Office

Filter

Offices & Stores

Repairing Workshops

Sand

Water Tank

Fitters & Cleaners Cabin

Enginemens Cabin

COAL STAGE

COAL STACKING GROUND

Smoke Box Ashes

Examiners Cabin

T. Hunters Wagon Repairs

Engine Shed Signal Box

To Station & London

River Sheepwash

S.P.

Disc

Water Tank

Signal Box

Examiners Cabin

Disc

S.P.

Pillar Tank

Irwell

River

To Birmingham

The shed on 9th April 1927 with one of the 'French jobs' outside. All three were at Oxford around this time, as the text relates, employed on workings to Basingstoke and Paddington and also to Wolverhampton, leaving Oxford at 12.55 p.m. The French engines also worked the 4.30 p.m. train to London, fast from Reading at 5.08, arriving at Paddington at 5.50 and returning with the 6.55. This got to Reading at 7.52 and it was from this train that the last four coaches were shed to form an 'all stations' to Oxford. Thus one could see two of the compounds in Reading at the same time.
H. C. Casserley

The GWR Mechanics Institute were naturally much concerned with the performance of the compound engines: 'The principle, as applicable to a locomotive, has also been extensively experimented upon and developed, and there is no doubt the De Glehn four-cylinder compound is the best of its kind yet produced. Theoretically, the advantages of compounds over non-compounds should be considerable, but, in actual practice, this has not been the case, in fact, under certain conditions, the effect was lost altogether.'
L & GRP, courtesy David & Charles

'Metro' tank No. 1497 at Oxford, their famous 'last redoubt' in 1932. They had arrived before 1900 and, while others on the GWR were discarded on the introduction of 2—6—2Ts, those at Oxford lingered, principally on the Fairford line, displaced eventually by '74XX' panniers, the first to arrive being 7404 in 1945. The last 'Metro' went in 1949, the story of their long years at Oxford related in most entertaining fashion by the Rev. D. A. Tipper in the *British Railway Journal* of October 1983.

J. E. Kite

where in the country such a stage with hand-wheeled iron tubs to serve a complement of over 50 main line engines would have been almost unthinkable. The last and most radical proposals for Oxford came at the war's end, doubtless with the disadvantages of the depot and its layout very much in mind. The station was itself to be rebuilt, whilst the wooden engine shed would be demolished and a two road diesel depot erected with fuel tanks placed (slightly unnervingly) inside. Between here and the coal stage, and obliterating all of the ancient yard and sidings, a six-road through shed was to be erected, open with a substantial yard at both ends and a further two roads available on the east side for future expansion. Amongst the most fascinating of the Oxford proposals, this straight shed is not the least intriguing for the insight it may have given to final GWR shed practice. In layout it resembled closely the new Southall depot, contemporary in a planning sense but not built until early BR times. Given the ventilation experiments of the 'Committee on Construction of Locomotive Sheds and layouts', Robertson vents and a high roof would have been prominent features.

Life at Oxford went on in ignorance of this and the depot languished, quietly mouldering. Nevertheless, in an operating sense it became almost uniquely cosmo-

politan and after 1950 would play regular host to engines of all four pre-Grouping companies. This was a natural outcome of its position astride a web of cross-country routes and over many years the shed was responsible for a wealth of varied duties. Apart from London expresses, there were many other workings of interest, notably Newcastle–Bournemouth trains. All three of the French compound locos were at Oxford in the late 1920s and one was gen-

erally employed on this turn, down to Basingstoke and returning as far as Reading tender first with a stopping train. The 'Frenchie' then proceeded to Oxford with the last four coaches of the 6.55 p.m. from London (fast to Oxford and semi-fast onto Worcester). The whole of this train would also be worked down from London by a French engine which had arrived in the capital on the 4.30 p.m. Oxford–Paddington. Yet another 'French' turn of note

Outside-framed trio at Oxford in 1930, a gathering that is forcefully remindful of the elderly nature of much of the complement. There were branches and a 'fly' (stopping everywhere) to suit a considerable stud of ageing locos. *E. Eggleton*

Begonia (the GWR naming was never anything but a joy) – see for instance *Reading* at Reading) and 0–6–0 No. 2344. There were also a number of 'City' 4–4–0s at Oxford in the 1920s, one often working the 7.40 p.m. ex-Paddington, a Birmingham and Wolverhampton train running via Oxford. *E. Eggleton*

Goods into Oxford from the north.   *R. H. G. Simpson*

was the 7.30 a.m. from Oxford picking up Sir Felix Pole at Reading and hence invariably away from there with a great show of punctuality. Such cross-country workings of considerable intricacy inter-linked with the Paddington trains, and a variety of goods work characterised Oxford to the end. From pre-war days to the 'sixties, working bounds for Oxford crews were customarily fixed at several points, with Paddington, of course, the best known, reached both on the up main line and up the Thame branch via Princes Risborough and Greenford. There were numerous jobs to Swindon, mainly goods but including the 9.00 p.m. night parcels, return with the morning Taunton parcels, relieved at Oxford by Wolverhampton men. There were many turns to Worcester, passenger and goods e.g. iron ore down and coal return, supplemented in season by beet trains which could load to considerable proportions. Wolverhampton was destination on several jobs, mainly goods or car trains; Oxford men were also familiar with the road to Basingstoke, a notable example in recent times an 11.00 p.m. goods using a Southern Region 'West Country' Pacific. In the later days of steam, Oxford men also worked regularly to Cheltenham and Gloucester, two routes, via Honeybourne and Toddington and Evesham–Ashchurch, the old LMS route. A final route of note was the North Warwick Line, again via Honeybourne and Stratford to Tyseley.

The LNWR engine shed was a close neighbour, rebuilt in more solid fashion than the GWR example.   *L. Ward*

Oxford was in addition responsible for three 'outstations', Woodstock, Fairford and Abingdon, and a wealth of shunting turns. The 'pilots' for these jobs were much in evidence on a Monday morning when most proceeded 'off shed' within minutes of each other. After the war Oxford was the last haunt of 'Large Metros' and these or pannier tanks were used for branch and pilot work. There were two for Hinksey (up and down yards) and also a Morris Cowley pilot which worked trips from the Cowley

plant to Hinksey. A Hinksey engine was replaced by another tank leaving the shed about 3.30 in the afternoon and would work a trip in turn to Cowley and back before returning to the shed for servicing. The Cowley pilot, after it left on a Monday, stayed there more or less until the coal ran out, with relief crews making their way by bus, 'the office' at Oxford supplying a written ticket for each journey. The new Yarnton yard, laid down in the war, accommodated all the goods and coal traffic for the Bletchley line and also required the attentions of a pilot. The station engine (two in earlier days, one up and one down) of necessity had to be capable of main line work, and for a long time came from among the ranks of Oxford's substantial 'Hall' complement. The **4–6–0** stayed out day and night more or less until the coal was exhausted, to be changed whenever the foreman could arrange a crew to prepare and bring out a fresh engine. Men from the junior of the twelve or so links at Oxford crewed these varied pilots, cleaners often entering around No 11 at least post-war when labour was in short supply. The basic 'Cripple Link', concerned with jobs within the confines of the depot, might thus be avoided. 'The Deaf and Blind' of all ages were employed on this shed link, though the system should not be thought of as rigidly defined. It may have been the case pre-war, but by the early 'fifties it was quite possible for a fireman in, say, **3** or **4** link, returning from Wolverhampton 'on the cushions', hopefully to put in a few hours overtime on disposal work, 'prepping a few engines'. A link or two up on No 10, one could expect a few Didcot trips but there was still shed work – 'prepping a few Southerns'; No 9

Continued on page 348

No. 3025 with a down goods on 9th April 1938 demonstrating the unnerving proximity of the coal stage to the running line. The 'RODs' were regarded as somewhat rough riders, the joke being that there was no need to get the coal forward, the engine shook it down for you.
Collection Peter Winding

No. 3568, 30th July 1939. The '74XX' panniers were less popular than these venerable engines, which, despite the cramped cabs, were reckoned to require less effort in firing.
Collection Peter Winding

Improvements in locomotive servicing, as we have seen elsewhere, were put in hand during the Second World War under government direction, 'thereby bringing about a proper working of the greatly increased traffic (brought about by the war)'. Before work began at Oxford, the water tank enabled a fine uninterrupted view across 'The Field' to the little Oxford North sidings, and beyond to allotments tended in wartime with especial care. The coaling crane is presumably one indication of the increased number of locos using the shed. This and the next three pictures were taken on 11th May 1944.   *British Railways*

The old stage was quite inadequate for the new traffic, it suffered from eccentric siting, making for endless movements across the yard between the shed, stage and turntable. Worse, it was unsuited to the new high tenders, the tip falling only halfway before being fouled by the tender top (see also Slough). The coal boxes in this unpopular event were lowered as far as possible and the contents shovelled in by hand — the coalman did not consider this his job and two cleaners were usually sent up to do it.

British Railways

The old stage was low, claustrophobic and ramshackle − 'a terrible rackety old thing'. The flaps of coal wagons could not even be dropped properly, so that two coalmen would have to dig down into the wagon. The worst part came as the final excavations were made, for the planks of wooden coal wagons often stood proud of each other an inch or more; shovelling against this, coalmen earned their eight shillings a day.

British Railways

The detested high tenders, with cleaners in attendance. The coaling crane supplied by 'The Field' would presumably have dealt principally with these engines.

British Railways

With a tank already provided, the new coal stage of 1944 was simply roofed in slate. The usual darksome cabin lay below for the coalmen, fire-droppers and suchlike, a group of staff which changed frequently as Oxford enjoyed the post-war boom. The task, as at Old Oak and elsewhere, fell to newcomers, traditionally Irish but increasingly Commonwealth immigrants in the 1950s. Up to forty at a time busied themselves in Oxford yard in that period. The Oxford coal stack, up to 1000 tons, was ordered to be taken up towards the end of steam, and normal deliveries were interrupted. Much of this bonanza was flogged off to staff, with the residue handed out to local pensioners. In its heyday, Oxford could get through 150-160 tons of coal a day, the 'Coal Clerk' checking the supplies and ordering new stuff as appropriate. Ash and clinker, strictly graded, was also disposed of commercially, if through more official channels, and Oxford ash is believed to underlie several bowling greens in the Oxford area, along with a variety of roads, fills, and housing developments. The first empty wagon was led carefully 'down the bank' and the brakes set firmly on. Successive wagons were coupled against it, and several slowly developing runaways, due to less than perfect brakes, were halted by frantic remedial action. The catchpoints at the base of the coal stage caught those wagons that eluded the coal stage men.   *J. H. Russell*

No. 6962 *Soughton Hall* at the coal stage. Mixed traffic engines came increasingly to dominate at Oxford — 'Halls', 'Granges', LMS 4—6—0s and BR standards. There were *forty-five* 'Halls', dead and working at one time, the former much vandalised and plundered for copper. One set of name-plates disappeared in the time it took to fetch the right spanners to remove it for safekeeping.   *R. H. G. Simpson*

Pannier tank No. 3608. *R. H. G. Simpson*

Oxford '61' No. 6111. Coal in the 'fifties frequently came in the form of the loathed 'nuggets' though the usual description was obscenely anatomical. The dust off the stuff was impossible to control and dangerous to eyes and lungs. The '61s' did hard work at Oxford, to Bicester, Kingham and back, locals to Didcot and even 'a stopper' (all stations) to Paddington at night, via Princes Risborough. *R. H. G. Simpson*

No. 2935 *Caynham Court* alongside the 'Top Shop' — water was pumped direct from the river, the pump-house sited right next to the foreman's office. The water was notoriously hard and 'the LMS men' were seen to put blocks of some substance — 'small brown cylinder shaped things' — into their tenders.
R. H. G. Simpson

was the Pick Up Link, trundling for miles across Oxfordshire and the surrounding counties, and necessary to impart an intimate working knowledge of the routes and byways out of Oxford.

Of great interest was No 8, 'the LMS Link', which brought a great variety of locomotives onto the shed. The London North Western Railway worked into Oxford having a separate shed opposite (see for instance *LMS Engine Sheds Volume I*, Wild Swan). This was closed by British Railways and the work assimilated by the larger ex-GWR shed. The LNWR line ran through Bletchley onto Cambridge, and in BR days a number of ex-LNER types could work in via this route. The LMS Link could thus find itself with J39 0–6–0s and K3 moguls, B12 and B1 4–6–0s as well as LMS locos on 'the East and West'. The idea of Great Western superiority was employed amongst (Western) enginemen more as a humorous device than through any great sense of loyalty, devotion, love, etc, and Oxford men went to great lengths to affect an attitude of pity towards those hapless individuals not provided with Swindon products. It was leg-pulling cultivated to an art, the classic mingling of pity and disbelief at the antics of others. It was all a

2–8–0 No. 3042. Oxford had a complement of freight engines, of the '28' and '38' series, but the men did a lot of relieving on goods engines on long distance work, the trains originating from one end of the country to the other.
R. H. G. Simpson

The Fairford 'Metros' (top) Nos. 3585 and 3583 and (above) No. 3589. No. 3583 was notable in the Rev. Tipper's article for its alarming condition, the boiler moving perceptively between the frames. In 1947 it had become so rough that the driver had been hurled off . . . Oxford was distinctive for its little clusters of ancient engines and in earlier years a number of 2–2–2s were similarly serving out their time at the shed, including one on the Fairford branch.

J. H. Russell

matter of what one was used to and much was made of the differences in the various tools required on an engine; LMS shovels (dismissed as teaspoons or some less polite epithet) and irons were unceremoniously hurled from the cab when a crew came on board at Oxford shed; the LMS men were said to be envious of the more robust GWR versions and Oxford men kept their tools with them when taking a break at Bletchley. This could mean hauling your shovel and lamp and irons around Woolworths at lunchtime.

Every now and then Bletchley would send an engine and van down to collect up (dumped) tools whilst Oxford would send one for a similar (pinched) supply. Anywhere non-GWR could expect to be treated with derision (ignoring the wooden, smoke-swirled poverty of Oxford itself for instance) and at Bletchley the 'frontier' arrangements were considered primitive in the extreme. The yard was very awkward and, although it could almost be conceded in an unguarded moment that the new shed building there might have one or two worthy features, the place stood con-demned for its nineteenth-century paydays – in the street outside the station from temporary trestles. This was rightly regarded as outlandish and justified the

No. 3588 and the Oxford tool van 'out the back' by 'Top Shop'. The van was frequently in action, attending to any number of minor derailments to stock and locos. The gang would take on almost any task, however, and in favourable circumstances could get an engine up off its side, using 50-ton jacks.   *R. H. G. Simpson*

most outrageous 'academic' viewpoints, accents and tall stories in the Bletchley 'cabin' – all designed to baffle and intimi-date the simple locals. A poor view was taken of most of the Bletchley line locos of both LMS and LNER origin, though of

course most would be of less than main line standard. Cambridge or Bletchley would hardly send its best down the line and the engines would frequently be approaching shopping. The GWR types were too wide for the line, and whilst at a place like

No. 1442, doubtless the Abingdon engine (the shed there had closed a few years before, the engine afterwards working light from Oxford in the morning).
                                                                                   Merchant Navy Locomotive Preservation Society

'Top Shop' near the last in 1965. It was really not much more than a covered hoist, an elderly structure of girdering and corrugated sheeting. The tank, shorn of its flimsy 'Top Shop' and converted from river to mains water, remains in use for diesels. *L. Waters*

Oxford a certain proportion of engines would be in this state, the Bletchley line workings would include a much higher percentage of such locos. This is borne out by the frequent recollection of 'rough riding'; *Eland* is remembered along with *Battle of Hastings* No (6)1066, which got so bad it received the unofficial nameplate 'Shake Rattle 'n Roll'. Bletchley put ex-LNWR 0–8–0s on the Oxford jobs, a suitable retaliation for those mess room jibes, as well as 4F 0–6–0s. Both were regarded with some disbelief and the appearance of the occasional tender cab instantly classified the engine as 'a sports version'.

In the next links up, 4 and 3 and 2, came the goods and contract merchandise, most notably in later years the Bathgate car trains, and an increasing involvement in passenger work. The car trains were impressive examples of how the railway could run smartly timed freight to regular and precise schedules, a sensible and profitable system of working that has somehow increasingly eluded transport in Britain. 9F 2–10–0s (including *Evening Star*) were used on the Bathgate car trains; 2–10–0s were based at Oxford and might be used on these jobs but Britannia Pacifics and other engines were used. The work took Oxford men to Wolverhampton; the Pacifics were considered in a sense to be 'outbased' from Crewe and were almost regarded as 'Western' engines. They were often, after all, part of the original Western Region 'batch' latterly at Canton ('or one of them Welsh places'), but internal WR designations left in cabs were pointedly sent back from Crewe *through the post*. The standard locos were however generally disliked, as across most of the Western Region,

No. 9654 wreathed in chains and girdering, 25th June 1964. Engines were attended to on a mileage basis, rather like cars, at set intervals of 6,000, 12,000, 18,000, 24,000 miles. Axleboxes, pistons, valves, rods, tubes, were repaired, replaced, reground or whatever, and with a 50-ton hoist it was a relatively straightforward matter to change wheels. 'A lovely little workshop, but old, old'. Even in the 1960s there were no less than seventeen sets of fitters/mates, many employed in the shed and about the yard, together with boilersmiths and coppersmiths. This workforce was reduced by stages ('amicably and proper') to three sets only on diesels, covering 24 hours – then the night shift went, followed by the afternoon men, to finish with a single set of men, this an undreamed-of eventuality, when 97-100 engines could be found at Oxford on a Sunday. Accidents were dealt with and the 4–6–0, worsted in a collision with an '8F' at Morris Cowley, was dragged (wholly illegally) using chains, minus its bogie, back to the shed. A new bogie was fitted in the 'Top Shop' together with the necessary 'straightening out'.

K. C. H. Fairey

a reaction which owed much to a dislike of the new. Events had proceeded on the GWR untroubled by Grouping and other tiresome annoyances, a period of great change and upheaval on the other main companies. The Great Western had contrived to remain aloof from Grouping (and even Nationalisation for years) and the almost convulsive effects to be found on, say, the LMS were absent. Oxford had a wide experience of the standard engines, and several of the light 4–6–0s in the 75000 series spent most of their days at the shed. They were designed precisely for this sort of location – highly varied traffic and poor provision of repair machinery.

No 1, the most senior link at Oxford, was responsible for all the most important passenger work, 'Paddington in an hour' and suchlike. A typical day towards the end of steam might mean booking on about 10 a.m. to take the 9.15 Paddington train on to Worcester. The Oxford crew would then take the 1.10 p.m. Worcester–Paddington, returning home with the 5.15 p.m. Paddington–Worcester, first stop Oxford.

No. 1024 *County of Pembroke* on the Oxford 'table. These engines were particularly awkward to turn and required a full tender and careful positioning. The balancing with SR Pacifics (West Country and Merchant Navy) was even more critical. The 'catchwheel' locked the 'table in position and care was necessary to avoid jamming the thing in one's overalls.

R. H. G. Simpson

Shunting of engines about the yard and 'The Field' at these medium-sized depots was done not by a designated pilot but any loco that was both in steam and conveniently sited. The arrangements at the coal stage and beyond were almost exactly similar to those at Reading. The movements engaged in by 6864 *Dymock Grange* required the turntable to be set correctly and incidents were not unknown, usually through insufficient steam for the brakes – a '38' went in tender-first one night, but it was generally a simple matter to drag engines out of the shallow pit – except when they overturned.

Merchant Navy Locomotive Preservation Society

'The Dock' occupied by 6921 *Borwich Hall*. The 'V' of the two turntable approach lines was a convenient site for a siding and pit. It was a convenient length and a handy place for a tender engine, the Oxford 'failure' loco, usually a 'common user' '49'. This was a spare engine, allowed for in the official allocation and when available 'stood in the Dock' ready for the off in any direction.　　　　　*R. H. G. Simpson*

'Clauds' off Cambridge line workings were familiar at Oxford though their visits were usually limited to a brief servicing. The 4—4—0 was relieved in the station, on arrival at 1.15 p.m., taken to the shed for turning for the 2.30 p.m. to Cambridge, relieved at Bletchley by Cambridge men. Principal 'foreign' types at Oxford, however, were ex-LMS engines, descended from the old LNWR shed merged with the GW depot on National-isation. Six sets of men and three labourers were absorbed into the GW establishment, the drivers given the option of merging into the links or remaining 'non progressive' on jobs of their own. Half opted for the former, the remainder continuing on their Bletchley jobs, together with some Oxford pilot turns. Eyebrows were raised at the age of two of the LMS firemen, 40-plus, and they were promoted almost immediately. *Photomatic*

Railcars at Oxford. They were customarily stabled on this road, outside 'Top Shop' and handy for oil and whatever peculiar (and guarded) tools they required. DMUs from the 1950s, except the Abingdon single car, stabled not at the shed but in sidings nearby. Diesel shunters arrived around 1963, with main line units not long after. A mobile twin fuel tank, of about 800 gallons, was provided, with its own pump. Fuel oil arrived as required by wagon load and an Esso petrol tank inadvertently delivered was soon serving a string of cars and household containers. 'Hymeks' were amongst the first main line diesels introduced, in 1963, the top link men 'picking it up easy as anything', after a fortnight at Old Oak. 'Learning turns' were the 9.00 p.m. Swindon parcels and the 7.35 Paddington.

R. H. G. Simpson

Oxford on 16th November 1958. The shed, though the working atmosphere was marvellous, was 'a mess'. Mr. J. Trethewey was frankly appalled at the shedmaster's office provided for him on his appointment to that position in 1960, an impression hardly tempered when the electric pump started up next door. This came on automatically as water levels fell and was an impressive beast, providing for the shed tanks and station hydrants, and tanks as far as Hinksey. The malodorous office lay in the very corner, behind the right-hand pannier tank (see also page 322).   *K. C. H. Fairey*

No. 1420 on 5th May 1957.   *P. J. Kelley*

The shed lay close to the station, though separated by the girder bridge over the canal. The windows did little to relieve the grim interior and were if anything a hazard to those walking by. Hopes were raised when a fire broke out but the brigade unfortunately arrived before it could take hold. WD 2−8−0 No. 90066.

L. Waters

LMS engines were perhaps the most familiar 'foreigners' and despite their 'teaspoon' fire-irons the more modern Stanier examples were popular enough. Great Western men were expected to 'jump up on any engine they gave us', whilst SR and LMR men, it was said, demanded days of familiarisation.

L. Waters

The shed was re-roofed in asbestos sheet in its latter days though this did little to improve the awful ventilation problems, the primitive lights were simply a waste of time in the murk, and conditions were such that it was often preferable to work outside. There was a homespun, makeshift air about the shed; the fencing and gate at the man 'Porky' (inevitably) Parsons kept pigs on an island, and various items and persons ended up in the water, intentionally or otherwise. At least one blackleg was tossed in, and a line of engines nearly ended up in there too, demolishing most of the shed rear wall at the same time. As prices rose, rumours grew of nameplates and whistles were often provided; their manufacture involved the addition of oil, which in turn imparted a water-repellant quality. It was thus impossible to 'slake' the stuff to cut down dust, any water spray immediately running off to negligible effect.

The stores was another job to go for, it meant more money and was remarkable

2−6−2T No. 5127 arriving at Oxford with the 11.05 a.m. train ex-Banbury on 27th July 1961.   *P. J. Kelley*

southern end was formed of old boiler tubing and the stationary boiler (an old Dean example) was simply placed in the shed to one side, something to be walked around. An eye was kept on time courtesy of 'Barney's Clock', the church tower of St Barnabus visible from most points around the depot. The ecclesiastical authorities were obviously aware of this, and bemused enginemen 'did their bit' when the vicar sent the plate around for contributions to its repair. Although working conditions were often hard, there is still a humour and affection for the place – a cleaner could be suspended four days for refusing to clean an engine yet be treated with understanding over a truly sackable offence – an incident put down to the exhuberance of youth and quietly forgotten. Failure of an eyesight examination was a terrible time, of awful finality.

The 'cut', the water alongside the depot, played its part in the life of the shed – one scattered about the bed. The 'long hot summer' of 1976 provided an opportunity to test this when the 'cut' dried out for the first time in memory. Needless to say, a search revealed no brass but any number of shovels, buckets, irons and lamps, and dozens of milkbottles, the haul a reminder both of enginemen's devotion to tea and the almost legendary shortage of footplate tools at Oxford. They were supposed to be provided as part of the engine 'prepping' procedure, but there was often little choice but to ignore such niceties. Someone might certainly tramp around the depot with a set, but was unlikely to actually leave them on a footplate. A cleaner could volunteer for additional jobs around the depot – the coal stage was favourite for an 'extra few bob', and firemen would frequently go up to break up their own coal, particularly if the coalmen had experienced a bit of a rough night. In later years the loathed 'eggs', pulverised and reconstituted coal, both for the wealth of spares it carried and a curious arrangement of rails for the handling of oil. A shed like Oxford would get through an enormous quantity of 'lube'; drums arrived in wagonloads from Swindon, were manhandled the length of the shed, and hoisted by block and tackle onto greased rails for up-ending and emptying into main reservoir tanks. The potential for 'dirty tricks' was enormous.

Steam on the Western Region withdrew into a series of redoubts rather than suffering confinement within a single gradually shrinking enclave. Oxford survived until January 1966 as one of these retreats, the end marked by ranks of decrepit and condemned locomotives, 'Halls' in the main, their ruinous condition masked by gently eddying snowfalls.

ABINGDON

The broad gauge Abingdon line opened in
1856 and the stone-built shed appears to
date from that year. The line was converted
to narrow gauge in 1872. A description of
the shed, the locomotives and workings is
contained in *The Abingdon Branch*, Trippett
and de Courtais, Wild Swan 1985; the building measured 52 ft 6 ins by 20 ft inside, with
pits both inside and out. The coal stage was
timber-built, and behind it lay the well and
pump house. The latter was also built in
wood and the authors (above) consider the
original water tank to have stood nearby.
It was later replaced by a much larger tank
close by the running line. An electric pump
was installed in 1949 replacing an early
steam pump operated by the branch loco
... 'by means of a flexible pipe coupled in
place of one of the whistles. The whistle
valve was lodged open with a spanner and
the pump could be heard chugging into life
in the adjacent pump hose'. The shed closed
'early in 1954', the push-pull service subsequently worked entirely by Oxford men.

The Abingdon terminus.   *Lens of Sutton*

Abingdon shed. In addition to the push/pull service, Oxford men worked coal from Hinksey to the yard at Abingdon, carrying out any necessary
shunting before returning to Hinksey with a load of MG cars, stabled there until the evening when they were worked forwards, usually to London.
M. E. J. Deane

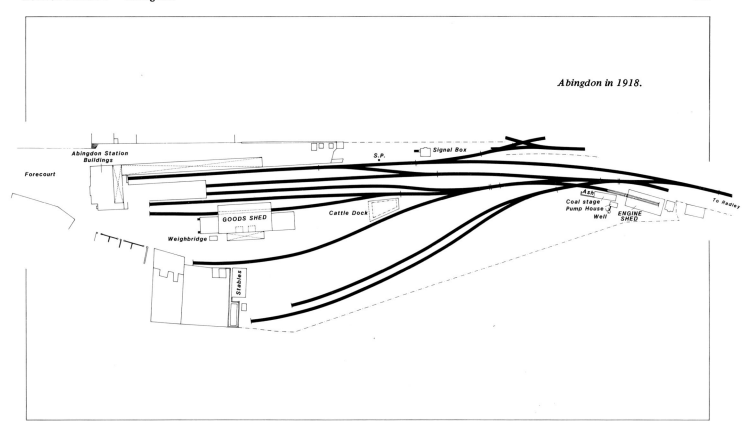

Abingdon in 1918.

The shed on 14th May 1951. A letter to the *Railway Magazine* in 1956 noted that since closure the pannier tank had not been seen, the 0–4–2T handling goods as well as passenger traffic.

R. C. Riley

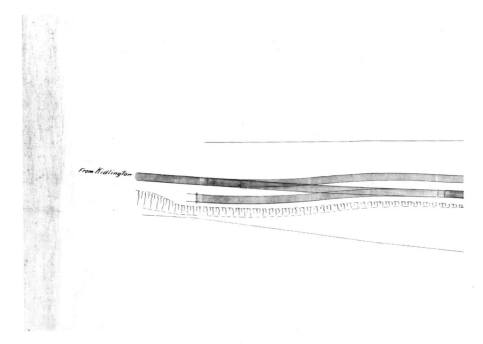

WOODSTOCK

A brief note contained within a Swindon Works 'Return' of 23rd November 1896 reads: 'Woodstock Railway opened 19th May 1890 Mr. Lambert's letter of 15.4.91. Under agreement with Woodstock Rail way to provide Engine Shed, Water Tank and Water Crane'. An engine shed was to be built under the Act of Parliament, the branch to be provided with 'proper and sufficient station fittings, furniture, sheds, cranes, water, signals, electric telegraph, and other works .... together with an engine shed, a weighbridge, a water tank and water crane' (see *The Woodstock Branch* by Stanley C. Jenkins, Wild Swan 1987). After less than ten years the corrugated iron shed was re-erected, the building shortened to 46 ft 9 ins and the original entrance from the Woodstock end 'stopped up'. The

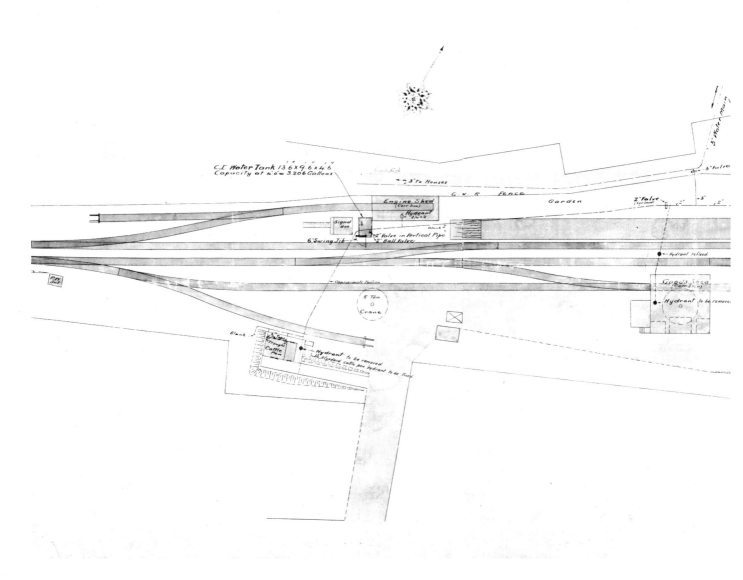

approach road was instead led in from the Kidlington end and a siding provided for a coal/ash wagon. The work took place in 1899, described thus: 'Complete re-arrangement of Yard and Shed now proceeding: shed pulled down in view of rebuilding. 20th March 1899.'

The Great Western wrote to the Board of Trade in October indicating that the remodelling was complete and requesting inspection. 0–4–2T No. 1473 *Fair Rosamund* was the branch engine at closure of the shed in 1926, the service given over to auto-trains worked out of Oxford. The line itself did not close until 1954.

Right: **Dim and distant, the 'prefabricated' engine shed at Woodstock, on 24th April 1890. The engine is Manning Wardle 0–6–0ST No. 132 with, it is believed, the Board of Trade Inspector Special.** *Bristol City Museum*

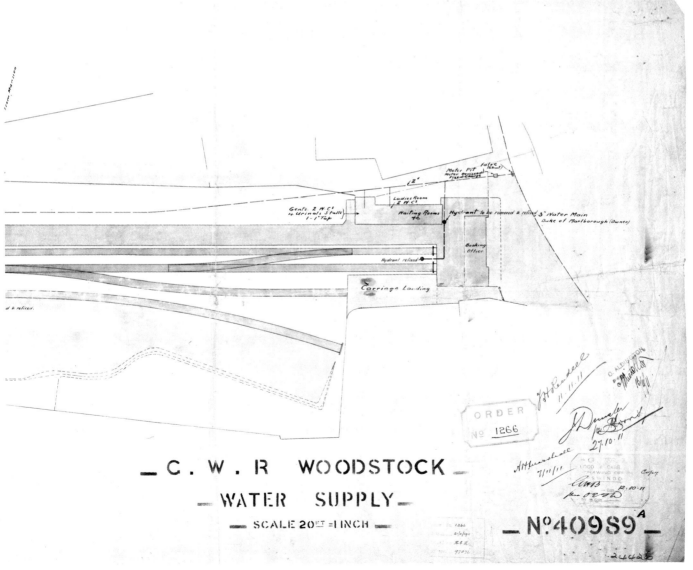

_ C . W . R WOODSTOCK _

_ WATER SUPPLY _

_ SCALE 20ᶠᵀ =1 INCH _

_ Nº 40989 ᴬ _

Plan of 1911, showing the rearrangements carried out in 1899.

FAIRFORD

The engine shed at Fairford seems to date from opening of the line. The original terminus had been at Witney, opened in 1861 under the aegis of the 'West Midland Railway' and absorbed into the GWR in 1863. A small engine shed was established. Old notions of a 'Cheltenham link' were revived in the 'East Gloucestershire Railway', a GWR–Midland battleground through much of the 1860s; reconciliation between the two left the company in financial distress, and only the Witney–Fairford portion was proceeded with. It opened in 1873 to be worked by the Great Western, who presumably made use of the shed from the first. It was timber-built with a tiled roof and stood on a dwarf brick wall; there was a pit provided inside and 'one short smoke trough' allowed for ventilation of the building. No coal stage was provided but there was a pump house, 'in wood, Length 9 ft 9 ins, Breadth 8 ft 0 ins, Height to top of roof ridge 11 ft 0 ins. Height to Wall Plate 7 ft 0 ins.'

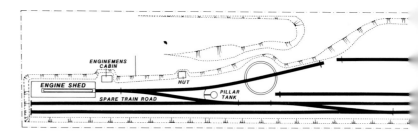

Fairford circa 1947.

Fairford shed was reminiscent of the Witney building in that it lay at the very extremity of the line, beyond the station proper. The branch was an extremely lengthy one, and a turntable, used for the branch tank engines at the end of each trip (they were also turned at Oxford) as well as 0–6–0s, on goods and other workings, was put in on a spur facing the shed. Fairford in its remoteness was little heeded, though the Locomotive Committee, nevertheless, approved an extraordinary outlay on 22nd May 1947, £5,850 for 'Replacement of 45 ft Turntable . . . by 55 ft machine'.

'Metro' tank on the branch train. Both Oxford and Fairford men worked the branch, the Oxford men frequently on goods, out of Hinksey yard. The first train of the day was the 5.55, usually with a Dean goods or 2251 0–6–0; several vans or wagons would be put off at Witney and all stations to Fairford shunted 'as required'. The engine then returned to Oxford with the 11.15 passenger train arriving Oxford at around 12.25 'engine to shed and finish'. Another goods left Hinksey at 10.15, shunting at Eynsham *en route* and finally arriving at Witney to shunt all afternoon. The engine finally left about 4 p.m. with any empties and box vans, loaded with blankets.

P. J. Garland

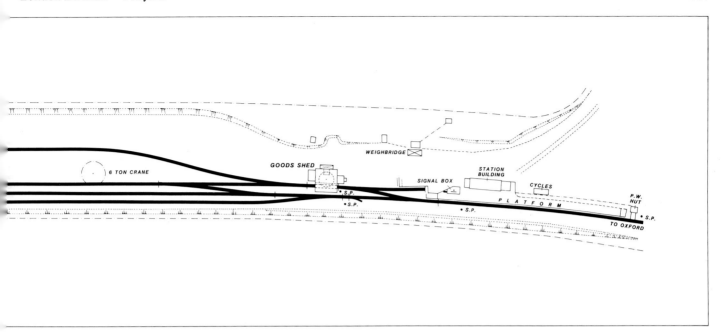

Original 45 ft turntable on 13th June 1947. On 22nd May the Locomotive Committee approved its replacement 'by a 55 ft machine' at the remarkable cost of £5,850. It has been suggested that Government money had been made available for this in connection with camps and depots, existing or proposed. The new 'table was put in beyond the original, leaving it available for use during installation work.   *P. J. Garland*

No. 7436 taking water on 14th May 1951. The last job of the day for Oxford men was the 3.35 p.m. passenger with six coaches, a heavy job for the '74XX' panniers, considered inferior to the '35s' which preceded them.   *R. C. Riley*

The new 55 ft turntable.   *R. C. Chown*

No. 7404 on 18th July 1959. There was no supply of coal at Fairford and engines always took coal at Oxford between trips, a full bunker quite sufficient for an Oxford-Fairford working and return. The last engine came to Oxford shed at about 8.00 p.m. which took coal as usual, 'and they would always take the oil and waste supplies back with them'.
J. J. Davis

The ancient van body at Fairford served as enginemen's 'cabin'; the Oxford crew down in the morning would customarily adjourn there for breakfast while the Fairford driver took the engine to pump water, using the customary swivel pipe connected to the whistle. The original pump house seems to have been a wooden 'hut' or something close, the arrangements changing when the 3,000 gallon pillar tank went in, drawings of December 1909 showing it in position. The well is shown as 8 ft 6 ins deep. There were four crews at Fairford until the end of the branch in 1962. Two drivers retired before this and were replaced and of the four at closure one transferred to Cirencester (having been at Swindon), one retired himself and the remaining pair, being very young men, came to Oxford with the firemen.
R. C. Riley

Appendix I — ALLOCATIONS

These allocations are reproduced by kind consent of John Copsey, who
laboured long in their compilation. Errors which may have occurred in subsequent efforts
to transcribe the engines under each shed should be laid at the authors' door.

[Allocation = 1st January of each year. Superscripts indicate month of arrival of
individual engines not present at that time.]

1925 ALLOCATIONS

OLD OAK COMMON

'Metro' 2–4–0T	3567, 3568, 3570, 3586, 3591, 3592
'645' 0–6–0T	651
'655' 0–6–0T	1789
'1076' 0–6–0T	731, 740, 748, 1081, 1175, 1230, 1248, 1639, 1651, 1659
'850' 0–6–0T	852, 861, 868, 870, 992, 1217, 1226, 1901, 1903, 1908, 1938, 1940, 1945, 1946, 1961, 1969, 1975, 1983, 1987, 1994, 1996, 2008, 2014
'1016' 0–6–0T	1064
'1854' 0–6–0T	1725, 1793, 1857, 1870, 1877, 1898
'1813' 0–6–0T	1848, 1850
'2021' 0–6–0T	2026, 2046, 2083
'Dean Goods' 0–6–0	2409, 2433, 2447, 2455, 2484, 2514, 2515
'26XX' 2–6–0	2662
'2721' 0–6–0T	2792
'28XX' 2–8–0	2800, 2817, 2837, 2844, 2846, 2857, 2860, 2870
'Saint' 4–6–0	2953, 2989
'30XX' 2–8–0	3023[5], 3032[5], 3044[6]
'31XX' 2–6–2T	3117, 3118, 3128, 3146
'Bulldog' 4–4–0	3330, 3360, 3429
'Star' 4–6–0	4000, 4002, 4003, 4005, 4007, 4008, 4011, 4013, 4015, 4016, 4021, 4024, 4026, 4029, 4033, 4037, 4040, 4042, 4045, 4049, 4051, 4052, 4055, 4056, 4057, 4059, 4061, 4062, 4071, 4072
'Castle' 4–6–0	4073, 4074, 4075, 4076, 4078, 4079, 4081, 4082, 4083[5], 4089[7], 4090[8], 4091[8], 4092[8], 111 (Rebuilt 9/24)
'43XX' 2–6–0	4303, 4310, 4328, 4371, 4383, 4396, 5300, 5306, 5341, 5354, 5364, 5367, 5373, 5384, 6306, 6309, 6314, 6326, 6327, 6329, 6330, 6333, 6344, 6355, 6357, 6365[10], 6380, 6386, 6395, 7300
'4700' 2–8–0	4701, 4705, 4708
'119' 0–6–0ST	124
'633' 0–6–0T	633, 634, 635, 641, 642, 643
'1661' 0–6–0T	1682
'2221' 4–4–2T	2221, 2226, 2235, 2236, 2241, 2245, 2246, 2247, 2249
'36XX' 2–4–2T	3600, 3602, 3615, 3619
'City' 4–4–0	3718
'Atbara' 4–4–0	4138

SOUTHALL

'Metro' 2–4–0T	972, 1404, 1407, 1415, 1416, 1417, 1418, 1420, 3500, 3562, 3566, 3582, 3583, 3585, 3587, 3590, 3598, 3599
'517' 0–4–2T	216, 518, 547, 575, 848, 1163, 1435, 1444, 1470
'1076' 0–6–0T	956, 1171, 1282, 1634
'1854' 0–6–0T	1869, 1872, 1880, 1881
'1813' 0–6–0T	1843
'2021' 0–6–0T	2054, 2070, 2072, 2081, 2101, 2117
'2361' 0–6–0 (OSF)	2370
'Dean Goods' 0–6–0	2430, 2472, 2474, 2556
'2721' 0–6–0T	2752
'28XX' 2–8–0	2810, 2825
'Bulldog' 4–4–0	3436
'43XX' 2–6–0	4331, 6308, 6332
'1661' 0–6–0T	1678, 1680, 1687
Steam Railmotors	41, 61, 62[6]

STAINES

'517' 0–4–2T	222

SLOUGH

'Metro' 2–4–0T	1406, 1408, 1409, 3561, 3563, 3565, 3569, 3581, 3596, 3597
'1076' 0–6–0T	1179
'2021' 0–6–0T	2103, 2121
'2361' 0–6–0 (OSF)	2361
'Dean Goods' 0–6–0	2427, 2551
'2221' 4–4–2T	2222, 2223, 2227, 2228, 2229, 2231, 2233, 2237, 2239, 2242, 2243, 2248, 2250
'3232' 2–4–0	3238
'36XX' 2–4–2T	3601, 3626

MARLOW

'Metro' 2–4–0T	3594

WATLINGTON

'2021' 0–6–0T	2159

AYLESBURY

'Metro' 2–4–0T	1403
'517' 0–4–2T	524
'2221' 4–4–2T	2225, 2230, 2232

READING

'Metro' 2–4–0T	1459, 3564, 3593
'655' 0–6–0T	1781
'1076' 0–6–0T	1172, 1241, 1293, 1567
'1016' 0–6–0T	1026
'1854' 0–6–0T	1770
'2021' 0–6–0T	2086, 2112
'Dean Goods' 0–6–0	2304, 2305, 2312, 2340, 2463, 2471, 2479, 2489, 2512, 2561, 2572
'2361' 0–6–0 (OSF)	2362, 2369, 2540
'2721' 0–6–0T	2757, 2768
'28XX' 2–8–0	2874
'30XX' 2–8–0	3033[6]
'31XX' 2–6–2T	3148
'Duke' 4–4–0	3254, 3267, 3275, 3284, 3286
'Bulldog' 4–4–0	3346, 3367, 3386, 3388, 3390, 3394, 3405, 3407, 3413, 3423, 3434, 3446, 3448
'43XX' 2–6–0	4343, 5318, 5361, 6352, 6354, 6356
'1661' 0–6–0T	1681
'2221' 4–4–2T	2224, 2234, 2238, 2240
'3232' 2–4–0	3236, 3242, 3250, 3251
'36XX' 2–4–2T	3614
'City' 4–4–0	3705
'County' 4–4–0	3813, 3820, 3821
Steam Railmotors	72, 85, 87

HENLEY-ON-THAMES

'Metro' 2–4–0T	469, 615

BASINGSTOKE

'Metro' 2–4–0T	3589
'Dean Goods' 0–6–0	2546
'43XX' 2–6–0	4321, 6346, 6366[10], 6389
'2221' 4–4–2T	2244

LAMBOURN

'850' 0–6–0T	1912

WALLINGFORD

'517' 0–4–2T	519

DIDCOT

'517' 0–4–2T	1484
'645' 0–6–0T	645
'1076' 0–6–0T	950, 1257, 1601
'850' 0–6–0T	1921, 1953, 2003
'1334' 2–4–0 (ex MSWJ)	1334, 1335
'Dean Goods' 0–6–0	2397, 2516, 2523
'Duke' 4–4–0	3255, 3263, 3282
'Bulldog' 4–4–0	3334, 3356
'Standard Goods' 0–6–0	407
'302' 0–6–0ST	307
'360' 0–6–0	369
'Stella' 2–4–0	3502, 3506, 3513, 3515
'Barnum' 2–4–0	3214
'3232' 2–4–0	3241, 3249
'3521' 4–4–0	3543, 3549
'Badminton' 4–4–0	4119
'Atbara' 4–4–0	4129

NEWBURY

'Dean Goods' 0–6–0	2481

WINCHESTER

'3232' 2–4–0	3233, 3245, 3249

OXFORD

'Metro' 2–4–0T	616, 626, 1493
'517' 0–4–2T	541
'1076' 0–6–0T	1249, 1294
'850' 0–6–0T	1935
'1016' 0–6–0T	1044
'1854' 0–6–0T	1854, 1866
'1813' 0–6–0T	1836
'2021' 0–6–0T	2036
'Dean Goods' 0–6–0	2343, 2429
'26XX' 2–6–0	2630, 2640, 2652
'28XX' 2–8–0	2827
'Bulldog' 4–4–0	3320, 3326, 3331, 3351, 3385
'Standard Goods' 0–6–0	1203
'De Glehn' 4–4–2	102, 103, 104
'1661' 0–6–0T	1664, 1665
'3232' 2–4–0	3247
'City' 4–4–0	3702, 3709, 3714, 3715
'Badminton' 4–4–0	4102, 4110
'Atbara' 4–4–0	4130, 4141
'Flower' 4–4–0	4153

ABINGDON

'517' 0–4–2T	1443

FAIRFORD

'Metro' 2–4–0T	1461, 1498

1930 ALLOCATIONS

OLD OAK COMMON

'Metro' 2–4–0T	3567, 3568, 3570, 3585, 3586, 3591, 3592
'1076' 0–6–0T	1081, 1152, 1175, 1257, 1651
'850' 0–6–0T	852, 1217, 1903, 1946, 1969, 1996
'1016' 0–6–0T	1060, 1062
'1854' 0–6–0T	1857, 1872
'1813' 0–6–0T	1817, 1836
'2021' 0–6–0T	2038, 2046, 2081, 2083
'2361' 0–6–0 (OSF)	2362, 2370
'Dean Goods' 0–6–0	2484, 2515
'Aberdare' 2–6–0	2611, 2626, 2653
'2721' 0–6–0T	2752
'28XX' 2–8–0	2805, 2816, 2820, 2846, 2847, 2864, 2867, 2879
'Saint' 4–6–0	2952, 2980
'30XX' 2–8–0	3020, 3023, 3047
'Duke' 4–4–0	3274
'Bulldog' 4–4–0	3341, 3374, 3407, 3429
'Star' 4–6–0	4005, 4007, 4017, 4020, 4038, 4041, 4043, 4046, 4053, 4054, 4055, 4059, 4064, 4072
'Castle' 4–6–0	4073, 4074, 4076, 4078, 4079, 4081, 4083, 4089, 4090, 4091, 4092, 4093, 4099, 111 (rebuilt 1924), 4037, 5000, 5001, 5003, 5005, 5006, 5009, 5010
'43XX' 2–6–0	4331, 4365, 4382, 4384, 4396, 5321, 5380, 6310, 6318, 6330, 6332, 6354, 6362, 6367, 6373, 6378, 6388, 6392, 7312, 7319, 7321, 8304, 8333, 8360, 8365, 8366, 8387
'45XX' 2–6–2T	4519, 4521, 4522, 4557, 4563, 4567, 4568, 4571
'4700' 2–8–0	4701, 4702, 4703, 4705, 4708
'Hall' 4–6–0	4900, 4921, 4922, 4924, 4925, 4926, 4927, 4943, 4944, 4951, 4968, 4969, 4970, 4971[1], 4972[1]
'51XX' 2–6–2T	5119, 5123, 5141, 5149
'57XX' 0–6–0T	5715, 5717, 5737, 5745, 5750, 5751, 5752, 5753, 5754, 5757, 5758, 5759, 5760, 5761, 5762, 5763, 5764, 5765, 5766, 5767, 5772, 5773, 5779, 5798[11], 5799[11], 7708[5], 7709[4], 7710[5], 7711[5], 7712[5], 7713[5], 7717[5], 7718[6], 7731, 7732[2], 7733[2], 7734[2], 7750[12], 7778[12], 7779[12], 7788[12], 7789[12], 7791[12]
'King' 4–6–0	6000, 6001, 6003, 6005, 6007, 6009, 6011, 6013, 6015, 6021[9], 6025[8], 6026[8], 6027[9], 6028[8], 6029[10]
Departmental Loco 0–4–0T (vertical boiler)	13
'633' 0–6–0T	633, 634, 641, 642, 643
'2221' 4–4–2T	2224, 2230, 2232, 2234, 2235, 2236, 2244, 2247, 2248
'36XX' 2–4–2T	3612, 3619, 3626

SOUTHALL

'Metro' 2–4–0T	976, 982, 1404, 1409, 1416, 1453, 3562, 3565, 3566, 3583, 3598
'517' 0–4–2T	526, 554, 828, 830, 1159, 1160, 1438, 1470, 1484
'645' 0–6–0T	1538
'1076' 0–6–0T	1237, 1282, 1659
'850' 0–6–0T	1994
'1854' 0–6–0T	1727, 1793, 1880
'1813' 0–6–0T	1848, 1850
'2021' 0–6–0T	2072
'2361' 0–6–0 (OSF)	2361, 2374
'Dean Goods' 0–6–0	2393, 2489, 2556
'28XX' 2–8–0	2843, 2844, 2851
'Bulldog' 4–4–0	3389
'45XX' 2–6–2T	4593, 4594, 5500
'57XX' 0–6–0T	5727, 5744
'43XX' 2–6–0	6307, 6382, 6391
'1661' 0–6–0T	1696
'39XX' 2–6–2T	3902, 3919
Steam Railmotors	74, 96

STAINES

'517' 0–4–2T	575

SLOUGH

'Metro' 2–4–0T	972, 1403, 1407, 1497, 3500, 3563, 3564, 3569, 3588, 3589, 3595
'2021' 0–6–0T	2026, 2069, 2087, 2112
'Dean Goods' 0–6–0	2312
'2721' 0–6–0T	2787
'Bulldog' 4–4–0	3410
'56XX' 0–6–2T	6670, 6671
'2221' 4–4–2T	2222, 2223, 2225, 2226, 2227, 2228, 2231, 2238, 2239, 2240, 2241, 2242, 2243, 2245
'36XX' 2–4–2T	3601, 3617
'39XX' 2–6–2T	3907
Steam Railmotors	55, 64

MARLOW

'Metro' 2–4–0T	3596

WATLINGTON

'2021' 0–6–0T	2074

AYLESBURY

'517' 0–4–2T	1156
'2221' 4–4–2T	2221, 2246, 2250
'39XX' 2–6–2T	3906

READING

'Metro' 2–4–0T	615, 1415, 3599
'517' 0–4–2T	568, 1430
'655' 0–6–0T	1743
'1076' 0–6–0T	956, 1240, 1248, 1295
'1016' 0–6–0T	1066
'1334' 2–4–0 (ex MSWJ)	1336
'1854' 0–6–0T	1797, 1877
'1813' 0–6–0T	1832
'2251' 0–6–0	2253[4], 2264[5]
'Dean Goods' 0–6–0	2305, 2343, 2447, 2471, 2479, 2512, 2572
'2361' 0–6–0 (OSF)	2369, 2376
'Aberdare' 2–6–0	2609
'2721' 0–6–0T	2757, 2784
'Saint' 4–6–0	2926, 2981
'30XX' 2–8–0	3025, 3026
'3150' 2–6–2T	3166
'Duke' 4–4–0	3285, 3286, 3290
'Bulldog' 4–4–0	3302, 3319, 3323, 3325, 3326, 3350, 3364, 3382, 3390, 3394, 3404, 3411, 3427, 3434, 3448, 3450, 3458
'43XX' 2–6–0	4359, 4364, 4375, 6312, 6315, 6345, 6356, 6380, 8305, 8308, 8313, 8338, 8383
'5101' 2–6–2T	5147, 5168[12]
'57XX' 0–6–0T	7754[12]
'2221' 4–4–2T	2229, 2233, 2237, 2249
'36XX' 2–4–2T	3600, 3610
'City' 4–4–0	3712
'County' 4–4–0	3813, 3820, 3825, 3830
Steam Railmotors	88[1]

HENLEY-ON-THAMES

'Metro' 2–4–0T	616

BASINGSTOKE

'Dean Goods' 0–6–0	2404
'Hall' 4–6–0	4966

LAMBOURN

'850' 0–6–0T	1921

WALLINGFORD

'517' 0–4–2T	1469

DIDCOT

'645' 0–6–0T	645
'1076' 0–6–0T	1263, 1601, 1610
'850' 0–6–0T	1912
'1334' 2–4–0 (ex MSWJ)	1334, 1335
'2021' 0–6–0T	2045
'2251' 0–6–0	2254[4], 2259[4]
'Dean Goods' 0–6–0	2303, 2405, 2430, 2528, 2547, 2561, 2570
'Duke' 4–4–0	3254, 3255, 3265
'Bulldog' 4–4–0	3361, 3385, 3454
'302' 0–6–0ST	307
'36XX' 2–4–2T	3605, 3614
'County' 4–4–0	3807
Badminton 4–4–0	4113
'Atbara' 4–4–0	4124, 4130
'Flower' 4–4–0	4150

NEWBURY

'Dean Goods' 0–6–0	2427

WINCHESTER

'Dean Goods' 0–6–0	2397, 2463

OXFORD

'Metro' 2–4–0T	457, 626, 1413, 1492, 1473
'1076' 0–6–0T	1134, 1294, 1569
'850' 0–6–0T	1935, 1976
'1016' 0–6–0T	1026
'1854' 0–6–0T	1898
'Dean Goods' 0–6–0	2344, 2429
'Aberdare' 2–6–0	2646
'28XX' 2–8–0	2863
'Saint' 4–6–0	2902, 2920
'Bulldog' 4–4–0	3356
'51XX' 2–6–2T	5125, 5133
'5101' 2–6–2T	5169[12]
'1661' 0–6–0T	1688
'County' 4–4–0	3803, 3804, 3811, 3814, 3821, 3826, 3827, 3828, 3829, 3832, 3835
'Badminton' 4–4–0	4101

ABINGDON

'517' 0–4–2T	1466

FAIRFORD

'Metro' 2–4–0T	1461, 1498

1936 ALLOCATIONS

OLD OAK COMMON

'850' 0–6–0	1976
'2361' (OSF)	2376
'Dean Goods' 0–6–0	2443
'26XX' 2–6–0	2637
'28XX' 2–8–0	2801, 2808, 2818, 2840, 2845, 2847, 2848, 2855, 2856, 2863, 2865, 2879, 2881
'57XX' 0–6–0T	3710[12]
'Star' 4–6–0	4021
'Castle' 4–6–0	4073, 4075, 4084, 4087, 4090, 4099, 111 (rebuilt 9/24) 4037 (rebuilt 6/26) 5004, 5005, 5006, 5008, 5014, 5018, 5022, 5023, 5025, 5027, 5029, 5037, 5038, 5039, 5040, 5043[4], 5044[4], 5045[4], 5054[6], 5055[6], 5056[6]
'43XX' 2–6–0	4320, 4356, 5375, 5380, 6312, 6364, 6366, 6398, 8373, 9301, 9303, 9304, 9305, 9306, 9308, 9312, 9313, 9314, 9318
'4700' 2–8–0	4700, 4701, 4702, 4705, 4707
'Hall' 4–6–0	4900, 4938, 4962, 4972, 4977, 4984, 4995, 4998, 4999, 5910, 5923, 5925, 5934, 5936, 5937, 5938, 5940, 5941, 5948, 5950, 5954, 5962[7]
'54XX' 0–6–0T	5400
'57XX' 0–6–0T	5715, 5717, 5737, 5745, 5750, 5751, 5752, 5754, 5755, 5757, 5759, 5761, 5764, 5765, 5773, 5779, 5783, 5799, 7709, 7713, 7734, 7754, 8750, 8751, 8752, 8753, 8754, 8755, 8756, 8759, 8760, 8761, 8762, 8763, 8764, 8765, 8766, 8767, 8768, 8769, 8770, 8771, 8773, 9700, 9701, 9702, 9703, 9704, 9705, 9706, 9707, 9708, 9709, 9710, 9725, 9726, 9751, 9754, 9762, 9763, 9789[4], 9791[6]
'King' 4–6–0	6000, 6001, 6003, 6007, 6009, 6011, 6013, 6014, 6015, 6021, 6025, 6027, 6028, 6029
'61XX' 2–6–2T	6103, 6107, 6108, 6120, 6121, 6122, 6126, 6130, 6133, 6134, 6135, 6137, 6141, 6143, 6144, 6166, 6168, 6169
'Grange' 4–6–0	6802[10], 6809[10]
Departmental 0–4–0T (vertical boiler)	13

SOUTHALL

'Metro' 2–4–0T	3500
'850' 0–6–0T	1912, 1935, 1969
'1854' 0–6–0T	1716, 1765, 1861
'2021' 0–6–0T	2079
'Dean Goods' 0–6–0	2441, 2535, 2547
'2721' 0–6–0T	2765, 2787
'28XX' 2–8–0	2843, 2859, 2867, 2868
'48XX' 0–4–2T	4808, 4826, 4848
'54XX' 0–6–0T	5401, 5405, 5408, 5409, 5410, 5412, 5413, 5414, 5415, 5416, 5417, 5418, 5420, 5421, 5422
'57XX' 0–6–0T	3704[10], 5744, 5758, 5762, 8757, 8758, 8772, 8774, 9749, 9755, 9757
'61XX' 2–6–2T	6112, 6125, 6128, 6132, 6139, 6147, 6148, 6153, 6156, 6159, 6161, 6162, 6163
'43XX' 2–6–0	9310, 9311

STAINES

'48XX' 0–4–2T	4825

SLOUGH

'Metro' 2–4–0T	3568
'1854' 0–6–0T	1767
'1813' 0–6–0T	1836
'2021' 0–6–0T	2026, 2046, 2087, 2098, 2112
'57XX' 0–6–0T	5727, 7731
'61XX' 2–6–2T	6101, 6102, 6104, 6105, 6113, 6114, 6119, 6123, 6124, 6127, 6129, 6136, 6142, 6145, 6146, 6149, 6150, 6152, 6155, 6157, 6158, 6160, 6167

MARLOW

'Metro' 2–4–0T	3592
'48XX' 0–4–2T	4847

WATLINGTON

'2021' 0–6–0T	2074

AYLESBURY

'54XX' 0–6–0T	5407
'61XX' 2–6–2T	6111, 6116, 6151

READING

'Metro' 2–4–0T	3585
'517' 0–4–2T	216, 1163
'1334' 2–4–0 (ex MSWJ)	1335, 1336
'2251' 0–6–0	2253, 2264, 2276
'Dean Goods' 0–6–0	2346, 2405, 2459, 2489, 2553, 2561
'2361' 0–6–0 (OSF)	2369
'2721' 0–6–0T	2747, 2774, 2784
'29XX' 4–6–0	2937
'30XX' 2–8–0	3025, 3026
'Duke' 4–4–0	3286
'33XX' 4–4–0	3341, 3377, 3382, 3404
'43XX' 2–6–0	4341, 4373, 5312, 5339, 5385, 6313, 6359, 7312, 7318, 9300, 9302, 9309, 9315, 9317, 9319
'48XX' 0–4–2T	4807, 4838, 4844, 4862[3]
'Hall' 4–6–0	4912, 4914, 4975, 4994, 5935, 5942, 5959[2]
'57XX' 0–6–0T	5735, 5766, 5772, 7708, 7732, 7777, 7788, 9722, 9758
'61XX' 2–6–2T	6100, 6109, 6110, 6117, 6118, 6131, 6140, 6154, 6165

HENLEY-ON-THAMES

'57XX' 0–6–0	5763

BASINGSTOKE

'43XX' 2–6–0	4345
'Hall' 4–6–0	5901, 5933
'61XX' 2–6–2T	6115

LAMBOURN

'1334' 2–4–0 (ex MSWJ)	1334

WALLINGFORD

'48XX' 0–4–2T	4842

DIDCOT

'655' 0–6–0T	1743
'1076' 0–6–0T	1565
'850' 0–6–0T	1925, 1990, 2007
'2021' 0–6–0T	2045, 2076
'2251' 0–6–0	2254, 2259, 2280, 2282[2], 2285[2]
'Dean Goods' 0–6–0	2354, 2395, 2430, 2463, 2512, 2532, 2533, 2566, 2571
'Dukedog' 4–4–0	3206[12]
'Duke' 4–4–0	3254, 3256, 3267, 3280, 3282
'33XX' 4–4–0	3375, 3380, 3420, 3434, 3448, 3454
'Hall' 4–6–0	5939
'61XX' 2–6–2T	6106
'74XX' 0–6–0T	7407[9]
'43XX' 2–6–0	9307

NEWBURY

'Dean Goods' 0–6–0	2549

WINCHESTER

'Duke' 4–4–0	3266

OXFORD

'Metro' 2–4–0T	3565, 3588, 3589
'645' 0–6–0T	1548
'1076' 0–6–0T	1574
'850' 0–6–0T	1958
'1854' 0–6–0T	1751
'1813' 0–6–0T	1850
'Dean Goods' 0–6–0	2332, 2393, 2429
'26XX' 2–6–0	2668, 2676
'30XX' 2–8–0	3008, 3047
'33XX' 4–4–0	3415
'Star' 4–6–0	4004, 4057
'48XX' 0–4–2T	4843, 4850
'Hall' 4–6–0	4902, 4903, 4905, 4920, 4921, 4922, 4933, 4936, 4955, 4961, 4974, 5931, 5960[2]
'57XX' 0–6–0T	5767, 7710
'61XX' 2–6–2T	6138
'43XX' 2–6–0	6388, 8379, 9316
'56XX' 0–6–2T	6631

ABINGDON

'517' 0–4–2T	1159

FAIRFORD

'Metro' 2–4–0T	3564, 3583

1940 ALLOCATIONS

OLD OAK COMMON

'850' 0–6–0T	1912, 1969
'2361' 0–6–0 (OSF)	2381
'2301' 0–6–0	2395
'28XX' 2–8–0	2826, 2840, 2843, 2848, 2850, 2855, 2863, 2868, 2875, 2881
'57XX' 0–6–0T	3600, 3618, 3619, 3635, 3642, 3644, 3646, 3648, 3652[1], 3659[3], 3672[6], 3710, 3734, 3738, 3754, 3766, 5717, 5750, 5751, 5752, 5753, 5764, 5765, 5779, 5799, 7713, 7734, 7754, 7760, 8707, 8750, 8751, 8753, 8754, 8756, 8757, 8759, 8760, 8761, 8762, 8763, 8765, 8767, 8768, 8769, 8770, 8771, 8772, 8773, 9700, 9701, 9702, 9703, 9704, 9705, 9706, 9707, 9708, 9709, 9710, 9725, 9726, 9749, 9751, 9754, 9758, 9784
'Castle' 4–6–0	4073, 4075, 4082, 4091, 100 A1 (rebuilt 4/25), 111 (rebuilt 9/24) 4037 (rebuilt 6/26) 5000, 5004, 5005, 5008, 5018, 5019, 5022, 5023, 5027, 5029, 5036, 5037, 5038, 5039, 5040, 5043, 5044, 5045, 5055, 5056, 5066, 5067, 5069, 5079, 5080, 5085, 5093
'4700' 2–8–0	4700, 4701, 4702, 4705, 4707
'Hall' 4–6–0	4900, 4907, 4935, 4936, 4938, 4943, 4961, 4973, 4978, 4981, 4985, 4998, 5903, 5922, 5931, 5934, 5936, 5937, 5938, 5939, 5940, 5941, 5950, 5954, 5955, 5962, 5978, 5985, 5987, 5996[7], 6900[7], 6902[7]
'43XX' 2–6–0	5321, 6388, 9302, 9306, 9307, 9308, 9311
'King' 4–6–0	6001, 6003, 6007, 6009, 6013, 6014, 6015, 6021, 6025, 6027, 6028
'61XX' 2–6–2T	6107, 6111, 6120, 6121, 6132, 6134, 6137, 6141, 6142, 6144, 6155, 6166
'Grange' 4–6–0	6802, 6809, 6826, 6864, 6865
Departmental 0–4–0T (vertical boiler)	13

SOUTHALL

'Metro' 2–4–0T	3585, 3596
'2251' 0–6–0	2285
'28XX' 2–8–0	2845, 2856, 2858
'57XX' 0–6–0T	3620, 3704, 3750, 3799, 5727, 5737, 5755, 7710, 7730, 7731, 7732, 8752, 8755, 8758, 8764, 8774, 9731, 9755
'48XX' 0–4–2T	4826
'54XX' 0–6–0T	5401, 5405, 5408, 5409, 5410, 5411, 5413, 5414, 5415, 5416, 5417, 5418, 5420, 5421
'61XX' 2–6–2T	6110, 6112, 6115, 6118, 6125, 6128, 6139, 6146, 6147, 6148, 6156, 6169
'43XX' 2–6–0	9300, 9301, 9304, 9310

STAINES

'48XX' 0–4–2T	4826

SLOUGH

'2021' 0–6–0T	2078
'2721' 0–6–0T	2747, 2757
'57XX' 0–6–0T	3681[8], 3769, 5715, 5783, 9763, 9789
'48XX' 0–4–2T	4807, 4831
'61XX' 2–6–2T	6101, 6102, 6104, 6105, 6108, 6113, 6114, 6116, 6119, 6123, 6124, 6126, 6127, 6133, 6143, 6145, 6149, 6150, 6151, 6152, 6157, 6160, 6161, 6164, 6167

MARLOW

'48XX' 0–4–2T	4862

WATLINGTON

'2021' 0–6–0T	2112

AYLESBURY

'61XX' 2–6–2T	6129, 6135, 6158, 6168

READING

'1334' 2–4–0 (ex MSWJ)	1335, 1336
'2021' 0–6–0T	2055
'2251' 0–6–0	2208, 2252, 2264, 2299
'2301' 0–6–0	2559
'30XX' 2–8–0	3025, 3026, 3047
'33XX' 4–4–0	3386, 3418, 3419, 3426
'57XX' 0–6–0T	3663[3], 3715, 3727, 3783, 5761, 5762, 5763, 5766, 5772, 7708, 7777, 7788, 9722, 9791
'Star' 4–6–0	4052
'Castle' 4–6–0	4085
'48XX' 0–4–2T	4844, 4847, 4848
'Hall' 4–6–0	4931, 4989, 4992, 4994, 4995, 5901, 5933, 5948, 5959, 5973, 5986
'43XX' 2–6–0	5356, 5375, 5380, 5385, 6312, 6313, 6320, 6359, 6383, 6393, 7318, 9309, 9313, 9315, 9317, 9318, 9319
'61XX' 2–6–2T	6100, 6109, 6117, 6131, 6136, 6140, 6153, 6154, 6159, 6162, 6163, 6165

HENLEY ON THAMES

'48XX' 0–4–2T	4809, 4837

BASINGSTOKE

'57XX' 0–6–0T	3770
'Hall' 4–6–0	4914
'61XX' 2–6–2T	6130
'43XX' 2–6–0	6363, 9305

WALLINGFORD

'48XX' 0–4–2T	4842

DIDCOT

'655' 0–6–0T	1742
'850' 0–6–0T	1925, 2007
'1334' 2–4–0 (ex MSWJ)	1334
'1854' 0–6–0T	907, 1861
'2021' 0–6–0T	2076
'2251' 0–6–0	2202, 2226[10], 2227[10], 2276, 2282, 2289
'2301' 0–6–0	2530, 2552
'2721' 0–6–0	2765, 2783, 2784, 2787
'Dukedog' 4–4–0	3206, 3215, 3283
'33XX' 4–4–0	3376, 3408, 3430, 3448
'57XX' 0–6–0T	3622, 3677[7], 5710, 5735, 5744, 7709
'Hall' 4–6–0	5935
'61XX' 2–6–2T	6106
'43XX' 2–6–0	6379, 9312, 9314

NEWBURY

'2301' 0–6–0	2573

WINCHESTER

'2251' 0–6–0	2221[10], 2222[9], 2280

OXFORD

'Metro' 2–4–0T	3500, 3564, 3568, 3588
'517' 0–4–2T	1159
'645' 0–6–0T	1531
'655' 0–6–0T	1743, 1785
'850' 0–6–0T	1935
'30XX' 2–8–0	3031
'57XX' 0–6–0T	3608, 3721, 3722, 3723, 3741, 3781, 3798
'Star' 4–6–0	4004, 4021
'48XX' 0–4–2T	4850
'Hall' 4–6–0	4902, 4903, 4905, 4921, 4922, 4928, 5904, 5960
'54XX' 0–6–0T	5400
'61XX' 2–6–2T	6103, 6122, 6138
'43XX' 2–6–0	6366, 9303, 9316

ABINGDON

'48XX' 0–4–2T	4843

FAIRFORD

'Metro' 2–4–0T	3583, 3589

UTILIZATION OF LOCOMOTIVE POWER

Summary of Special Return showing how every engine belonging to the company was occupied during six days ended November 16th 1912

Locomotive Station	No. of engines allocated to shed during the whole or portion of the week	Total time in hands of Traffic or other Department				Time on Shed for Locomotive Purposes						Repairs						Cleaning		Standing idle		Total engine hours
		At work		Standing		Waiting attention other than cleaning or repairing		Washing out, tube cleaning, coaling, steam raising, preparing, etc.		Waiting to go to works		Waiting for Repairs at shed or for material		Being Repaired		Night time and meal hours of workmen*						
		Hours	Per cent to total hours	Hours	Per cent to total hours	Hours	Per cent to total hours	Hours	Per cent to total hours	Hours	Per cent to total hours	Hours	Per cent to total hours	Hours	Per cent to total hours	Hours	Per cent to total hours	Hours	Per cent to total hours	Hours	Per cent to total hours	
Aylesbury	4	132	22.9	55	9.5	19	3.3	73	12.7					22	3.8	2	0.3	90	15.7	183	31.8	576
Basingstoke	4	153	26.6	38	6.6	20	3.5	66	11.4			54	9.4	22	3.8	26	4.5	72	12.5	125	21.7	576
Henley	2	57	19.8	69	23.9			26	9.0					2	0.7	1	0.4	30	10.4	103	35.8	288
Marlow	1	41	28.5	57	39.6	1	0.7	18	12.5									23	16.0	4	2.7	144
Old Oak Common	151	7091	32.6	2112	9.7	1225	5.6	2498	11.5	66	0.3	360	1.7	1415	6.5	583	2.7	898	4.1	5505	25.3	21753
Reading	53	2338	30.6	566	7.4	138	1.8	744	9.8	143	1.9	285	3.8	344	4.5	97	1.2	379	4.9	2607	34.1	7642
Slough	32	1409	30.6	716	15.5	96	2.1	478	10.4			344	7.5	282	6.1	112	2.4	240	5.2	931	20.2	4608
Southall	35	1890	37.5	799	15.8	89	1.8	485	9.6			139	2.8	335	6.6	195	3.9	169	3.4	939	18.6	5040
Staines	1	51	35.4	53	36.8	1	0.2	12	8.4									16	11.1	11	7.6	144
Watlington	2	4	1.4					5	1.7	96	33.3			6	2.1	1	0.3	3	1.1	173	60.1	288
	285	13166	32.1	4465	10.9	1589	3.8	4405	10.7	305	0.7	1183	2.9	2428	5.9	1017	2.6	1920	4.6	10581	25.8	41059

*when repairs are suspended

G.W.R. CHIEF MECHANICAL ENGINEER'S DEPARTMENT.

Form "B" (7346)

SUMMARY OF ALLOCATION OF ENGINES FOR ALL PURPOSES

SOUTHALL & OUTSTATIONS. Station. Date MARCH 5th, 1938.

Wheel Arrangement and Class. (1)	Group as per Service Book (2)	Pass. (3)	Goods (4)	Shunting (5)	Banking (6)	Pilot (7)	Special Work (8)	Total (9)	Allocated to Depot (10)	In for General Repairs and not replaced (11)	Over 2 weeks repair (12)	Under 2 weeks repair (13)	At Depot in working order (14)	In excess of requirements Col.9 (15)	Short of requirements Col.9 (16)
0-4-0T Metro	-	-	-	1	-	-	-	1	2	1	-	-	2	1	X
0-4-2T 48XX Auto	A	1	-	-	-	-	-	1½	2	1	1	-	1	3	X
0-6-0T 54XX Auto	A	10	-	-	-	-	-	10	15	1	1	A	13	3	X
0-6-0T 4'1½"	A	1	1	-	-	-	-	1	1	-	1	-	1	-	-
0-6-0T 4'7½" Yellow	A	-	-	-	-	-	-	-	4	1	-	-	3	3	X
0-6-0T 4'7½" Blue	A	-	-	-	-	-	-	3	3½	2	-	-	3	X	X
1-6-0 Standard Gds.	A	-	3	-	-	-	-	3	3	-	-	-	2	1	X
0-6-0T 57XX	C	-	2	9½	-	-	1	12½	10	-	1	1	9	1	X
0-6-0T 87XX	C	-	-	2	-	-	-	2	5	-	-	1	4	2	X
2-6-0 93XX	D	-	5	-	-	-	-	5	8	1	-	-	8	2	X
2-6-2T 61XX	D	9	-	-	-	-	-	9	12	-	-	B.	11	2	X
2-8-0 28XX	E	-	4	-	-	-	-	4	4	1	-	C.	4	-	X
DIESEL CAR	E	4	-	-	-	-	-	4	4	-	-	-	4	-	-
TOTALS		20	14	11½	-	-	1	46½	45	6	2	1	56	13	6½

$ T A I N E S.

| 0-4-2T 48XX Auto | - | 1 | - | - | - | - | - | 1 | 1 | - | - | - | 1 | - | ✓ |

TOTAL ..

A. Two engines replaced not sent In.
B. One engine loaned to Oxford.
C. One engine loaned from O.O.C.

* Column 14 to include Engines undergoing ordinary Running Repairs, Boilerwashing, Examinations, etc.

G.W.R. CHIEF MECHANICAL ENGINEER'S DEPARTMENT.

Form "B" (7346)

SUMMARY OF ALLOCATION OF ENGINES FOR ALL PURPOSES

OLD OAK COMMON. Station. Date MARCH 5th, 1938.

Wheel Arrangement and Class. (1)	Group as per Service Book (2)	Pass. (3)	Goods (4)	Shunting (5)	Banking (6)	Pilot (7)	Special Work (8)	Total (9)	Allocated to Depot (10)	In for General Repairs and not replaced (11)	Over 2 weeks repair (12)	Under 2 weeks repair (13)	At Depot in working order (14)	In excess of requirements Col.9 (15)	Short of requirements Col.9 (16)
0-6-0 Standard Gds.	A	-	2	-	-	-	1	3	1	-	-	-	1	-	X
0-6-0 Standard Gds.	B	-	-	-	-	-	-	-	2	-	-	-	1	1	X
0-6-0T 57XX	C	10½	-	24½	-	-	1	36	31	2	-	-	39	5	X
0-6-0T 87XX	C	2	13	3	-	-	-	18	21	3	1	A.19	-	X	X
0-6-0T 97XX Smithfield	C	1	5	-	-	-	-	6	11	3	-	-	9	5	X
4-6-0 King	D	7	-	-	-	1	1	9	14	1	-	-	15	5	X
4-6-0 Castle	D	20	1	-	-	2	3	26	23	5	1	-	26	-	X
4-6-2T 61XX	D	9	1	-	-	-	-	10	15	3	-	-	12	2	X
4-6-0 43XX	D	-	-	-	-	-	-	7B	1	-	-	7	-	X
2-6-0 83XX	D	3	10	-	-	-	-	15	7	3	-	-	5	2	X
4-6-0 93XX	D	-	-	-	-	-	-	-	5	-	-	-	4	3	X
4-6-0 68XX	E	-	-	-	-	-	-	-	1B	-	-	-	1	1	X
4-6-0 Manor	D	3	1	-	-	-	-	4	24	5	-	-	19	-	X
4-6-0 49XX	D	-	4	-	-	-	-	4	5	-	-	-	5	1	X
4-6-0 47XX	E	10	-	-	-	-	-	10	14	-	-	-	13	-	X
2-8-0 28XX	E	-	-	-	-	-	-	-	1	-	-	-	1	1	X
DIESEL ELECTRIC	-	1	-	1	-	-	1	1	1	-	-	-	1	-	X

| TOTAL .. | | 54 | 85 | 27½ | - | 2 | 12 | 160 | 189 | 25 | 1 | 1 | 168 | 12 | 30 |

A. One engine replaced not sent In.
B. One engine replaced by "Manor" Class.
C. One engine loaned to Southall.

* Column 14 to include Engines undergoing ordinary Running Repairs, Boilerwashing, Examinations, etc.

13

Form "B" (7346)

G.W.R. CHIEF MECHANICAL ENGINEER'S DEPARTMENT.

SUMMARY OF ALLOCATION OF ENGINES FOR ALL PURPOSES

SLOUGH &OUTSTATIONS. Station. Date MARCH 5th, 1938.

ENGINES: Wheel Arrangement and Class. (1)	Group as per Service Book. (2)	Number of Turns: Pass. (3)	Goods (4)	Shunting (5)	Banking (6)	Pilot (7)	Special Work (8)	TOTAL (9)	Number of Engines: Allocated to Depot (10)	In Factory for General Repairs and not replaced (11)	In Local Repairing Shops: Over 2 weeks repairs (12)	Under 2 weeks repairs (13)	At Depot in working order * (14)	In excess of requirements Col. 9 (15)	Short of requirements Col. 9 (16)
0-6-0T. 4'1½"	A	-	-	-	-	-	-	-	3	-	-	A.	4	4	-
0-6-0T. 4'7½"	A	-	-	3½	-	-	-	3½	2	-	-	B.	3	-	½
0-6-0 Standard Gds.	A	-	1	-	-	-	-	1	1	-	-	-	1	-	-
0-6-0T. 57XX.	C	-	1	1½	-	-	1	3½	3	-	1	C.	3	-	½
2-6-2T. 61XX.	D	17	2	-	-	-	2	21	25	2	-	D1	21	-	-
TOTALS.	-	17	4	5	-	-	3	29	34	2	1	1	32	4	1

A. One engine replaced not sent In.
B. do
C. One engine loaned from Oxford.
D. One engine loaned to Didcot.

AYLESBURY.

2-6-2T. 61XX	D	3	-	-	-	-	-	3	3	-	-	-	3	-	-

Watlington

0-6-0T. 4'1½"	A	1	-	-	-	-	-	1	1	-	-	-	1	/	/

TOTAL ..

* Column 14 to include Engines undergoing ordinary Running Repairs, Boilerwashing, Examinations, etc.

3,500—N.3. 12-35—(17).

14

Form "B" (7346)

G.W.R. CHIEF MECHANICAL ENGINEER'S DEPARTMENT.

SUMMARY OF ALLOCATION OF ENGINES FOR ALL PURPOSES

READING & OUTSTATIONS. Station. Date MARCH 5th, 1938.

ENGINES: Wheel Arrangement and Class. (1)	Group as per Service Book. (2)	Number of Turns: Pass. (3)	Goods (4)	Shunting (5)	Banking (6)	Pilot (7)	Special Work (8)	TOTAL (9)	Number of Engines: Allocated to Depot (10)	In Factory for General Repairs and not replaced (11)	In Local Repairing Shops: Over 2 weeks repairs (12)	Under 2 weeks repairs (13)	At Depot in working order * (14)	In excess of requirements Col. 9 (15)	Short of requirements Col. 9 (16)
2-4-0T. Metro	A	-	-	-	-	-	-	-	1	-	-	-	1	1	-
0-6-0 Standard Gds.	A	1	3	-	-	-	1	5	6	-	-	-	6	1	-
2-4-0 13XX *M.S.W*	A	1	-	-	-	-	-	1	1	-	-	-	1	-	-
0-6-0T. 4'7½ Blue	A	-	-	-	-	-	-	-	1	-	-	-	1	1	-
0-4-2T. Auto *48XX*	~~A~~	2	-	-	-	-	-	2	6	-	-	-	A 5	3	-
0-6-0 Standard Gds.	B	-	-	-	-	-	-	-	1	1	-	-	-	-	-
0-6-0 " 22XX	B	-	2	-	-	-	-	2	3	1	-	-	2	-	-
4-4-0 Bulldog.	B	-	-	-	-	-	-	-	~~2~~	~~2~~	-	-	-	-	-
4-4-0 Dukes	B	-	-	-	-	-	-	-	1	-	-	-	1	1	-
4-6-0 29XX.	C	-	-	-	-	-	-	-	1	-	-	-	1	1	-
0-6-0T 57XX.	C	-	1	10	-	-	-	11	11	2	-	-	9	-	2
2-6-0 43XX	D)							-	10	2	-	-	8)		*9*
2-6-0 83XX	D	9	5	-	-	-	3	17	-	-	-	-	B~~8~~	-	-
2-6-0 93XX.	D)								7	-	-	-	7)	*7*	
2-8-0 R.O.D.	D	-	2	-	-	-	-	2	3	-	-	-	3	1	-
2-6-2T. 61XX.	D	5	4	-	-	-	-	9	11	1	1	-	9	-	-
4-6-0 49XX.	D	2	-	-	-	2	3	7	9	-	-	-	9	2	-
4-6-0 40XX.	D	1	-	-	-	-	-	1	*1*	*1*	-	-	-	-	1
DiESEL CAR	-	~~2~~	-	-	-	-	-	~~2~~	~~2~~	-	-	-	~~2~~	-	-
TOTALS.	-	~~22~~ *21*	17	10	-	2	7	~~38~~ *37*	~~75~~ *73*	~~9~~ *8*	1	-	~~66~~ *63*	~~17~~ *18*	~~3~~ *12*

WALLINGFORD.

4-2 ~~0-6-0T~~ Auto *48XX*	-	1	-	-	-	-	-	1	1	-	-	-	1	-	-

MARLOW.

0-4-2.T. Auto *48XX*	-	1	-	-	-	-	-	1	1	-	-	-	1	-	-

HENLEY.

0-6-0T. 57XX.	C	1	-	-	-	-	-	1	1	-	-	-	1	-	-

BASINGSTOKE.

2-6-2T 61XX.	D	1	-	-	-	-	-	1	1	-	-	-	1	-	-
2-6-0 43XX.	D	-	1	-	-	-	-	1	1	-	-	-	1	-	-
4-6-0 49XC	D	-	1	-	-	-	-	1	1	-	-	-	1		
TOTALS.	-	1	2	-	-	-	-	3	3	-	-	-	3	-	-

A. One engine loaned to Oxford.
B. Two engines loaned from Swindon.

TOTAL ..

* Column 14 to include Engines undergoing ordinary Running Repairs, Boilerwashing, Examinations, etc.

3,500—N.3. 12-35—(17).

G.W.R. CHIEF MECHANICAL ENGINEER'S DEPARTMENT.

Form "B" (7346)

SUMMARY OF ALLOCATION OF ENGINES FOR ALL PURPOSES

OXFORD & OUTSTATION.   Station. – Date   MARCH 5th, 1938

ENGINES		NUMBER OF TURNS							NUMBER OF ENGINES						
Wheel Arrangement and Class.	Group as per Service Book.	Pass.	Goods	Shunt-ing	Bank-ing	Pilot	Special Work	TOTAL	Allo-cated to Depot	In scurry for General Repairs and not re-placed	In Local Repairing Shops Over 2 weeks repairs	Under 2 weeks repairs	At Depot in work-ing order	In excess of require-ments Col.9	Short of require-ments Col.9
1	2	3	4	5	6	7	8	9	10	11	12	13	14	15	16
Metro	–	1						1	3	1			2	1	X
4175" Yellow	A	1	3					5	4	1			4	1	
4175" Blue	A	1						1	1				1	1	X
41½"	A	1						1	1				1	1	X
Standard Gds.	A		3					3	4				4		X
57XX	C			4		1		5	5			A.	4	1	X
43XX	D					2	1	1	1					3	X
93XX	D		2				1	3	3	2	1		1		X
49XX	D	6			2		1	9	10	2	1		8		X
40XX	D	2					1	3	3				3	1	X
R.O.D.	D		1					1	1	1		B.	1	1	X
61XX	D	3	1						2	2	1	1	3	2	X
Auto 48XX	–	3							2	1	1			1	X
DIESEL CAR	–														X
TOTALS.		11	11	4	2	2	2	30	38	5		1	33	9	6

F A I R F O R D.   A. One engine loaned to Slough.

A B I N G D O N.   B. One engine loaned from Southall.

| Metro | – | 2 | | | | | | | 2 | | | | 2 | | X |
| Auto | – | 1 | | | | | | | 1 | | | | 1 | | X |

A. One engine loaned to Slough.
B. One engine loaned from Southall.
C. One engine loaned from Reading.

TOTAL ...

* Column 14 to include Engines undergoing ordinary Running Repairs, Boilerwashing, Examinations, etc.

G.W.R. CHIEF MECHANICAL ENGINEER'S DEPARTMENT.

Form "B" (7346)

SUMMARY OF ALLOCATION OF ENGINES FOR ALL PURPOSES

DIDCOT & OUTSTATIONS.   Station.   Date   MARCH 5th, 1938.

ENGINES		NUMBER OF TURNS							NUMBER OF ENGINES						
Wheel Arrangement and Class.	Group as per Service Book.	Pass.	Goods	Shunt-ing	Bank-ing	Pilot	Special Work	TOTAL	Allo-cated to Depot	In scurry for General Repairs and not re-placed	In Local Repairing Shops Over 2 weeks repairs	Under 2 weeks repairs	At Depot in work-ing order	In excess of require-ments Col.9	Short of require-ments Col.9
1	2	3	4	5	6	7	8	9	10	11	12	13	14	15	16
13XX. W.S.W.	A	4					1	1	3	1			1	1	X
Standard Goods	A	1	4				2	7	6	1			5	2	X
4175" Yellow	A	1		2				5	5				5	3	X
4175" Blue	A			3			1	3	1	1			1	1	X
41½"	A						4	5	4				4	4	X
Standard Gds 23XX	B		2					2	2	1			3	1	X
Bulldog	B	3						3	3	1			5	2	X
Dukes 32XX	B	3						3	4	2			2	2	X
61XX	D	1					1	2	2			B	1	1	X
49XX	D	1					1	2	2	1			1	1	X
93XX Cam	D							1					1	1	X
TOTALS.	–	10	6	5			4	25	36	6		–	29	10	6

W I N C H E S T E R.

| Standard Gds. | A | 2 | | | | | | 2 | 2 | | | | 2 | – | X |

A. One engine replaced by 40XX to Old Oak Common.
B. One engine loaned from Slough.

TOTAL ...

* Column 14 to include Engines undergoing ordinary Running Repairs, Boilerwashing, Examination, etc.

374

Appendix 5 – TURNTABLES

Appendix 4
Some London Division details, extracted from the 'Map of System' December 1929

	No. of Engines	Turntable	Engine Hoist
Winchester	1	42 ft	–
Newbury	–	65 ft	–
Basingstoke	5	–	–
Reading	94	65 ft	50T electric crane
Slough	48	45 ft	–
Staines	1	–	–
Southall	70	65 ft	20T hydraulic crane
Ranelagh Bridge	–	65 ft	–
Old Oak Common	211	4 x 65 ft + 70 ft in carriage yard	Not listed
Marlow	1	–	–
Henley	1	55 ft	–
Watlington	1	–	–
Wallingford	1	–	–
Aylesbury	2	–	–
Oxford	60	65 ft	50T electric crane
Abingdon	1	–	–
Didcot	50	65 ft	50T electric crane
Fairford	2	–	–
Yarnton	–	65 ft	–
Lambourn	[blank]		

No. 111 on the Reading 'table, 26th September 1925. Swindon policy towards turntables has always been slightly confusing. The distinctive overgirder type is generally regarded as synonymous with Great Western practice (though the LSWR employed a very similar arrangement) but undergirder units, from outside manufacturers, were commonplace. The overgirder type was considered something of a hindrance to workings in the new roundhouses and conventional 'tables, boarded over, were put in, purchased from Cowans Sheldon and Ransomes & Rapier. The boarding over the Reading 'table is an incidental reminder of the original plans for a new roundhouse.

R. S. Carpenter

The overgirder type (right) had the advantage of a very shallow pit but the earlier examples were narrow and confining; hence the awkward 'escape ladder'. They looked markedly odd inside round-houses such as Croes Newydd and were too small at 55 ft. Extension to 65 ft took place frequently but the balance was never quite as satisfactory.

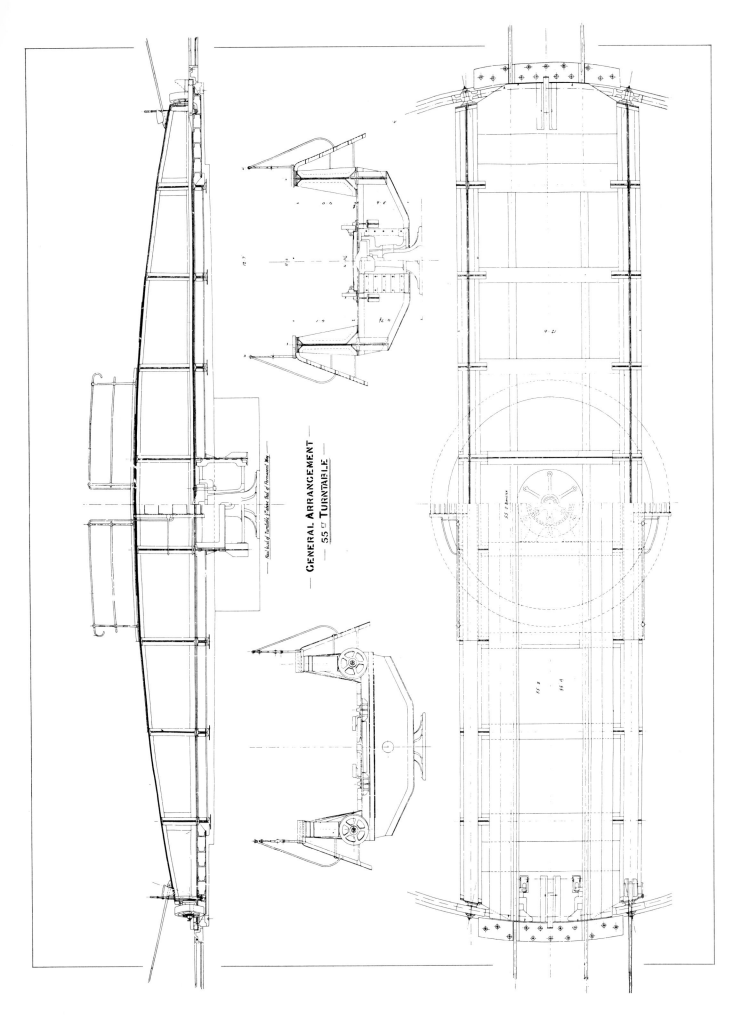

— GENERAL ARRANGEMENT —
— 55 ᵗᵒⁿ TURNTABLE —

The wider, 65 ft 'table was an improvement over the earlier type and appeared, according to notes on this drawing, from at least 1904. It was quite possible, and safe, to walk along these units whilst occupied by a locomotive. Their massive girdering imparted an effect of great power and strength and, it might be added, absolute immobility.

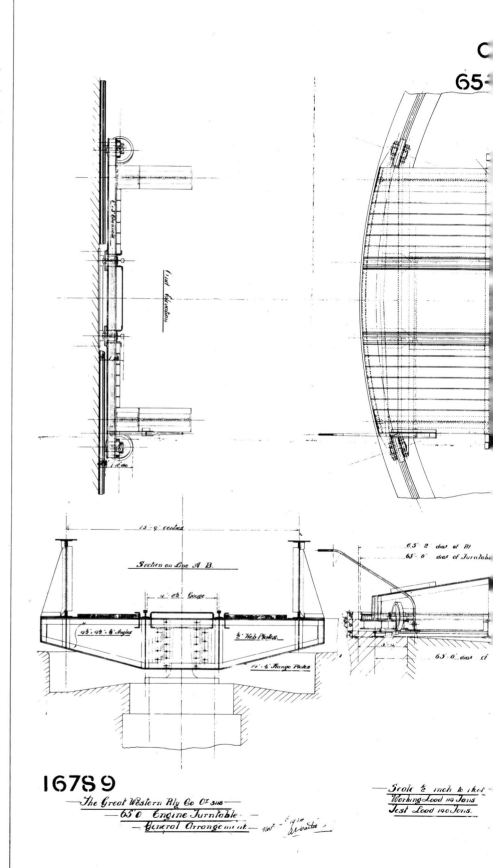

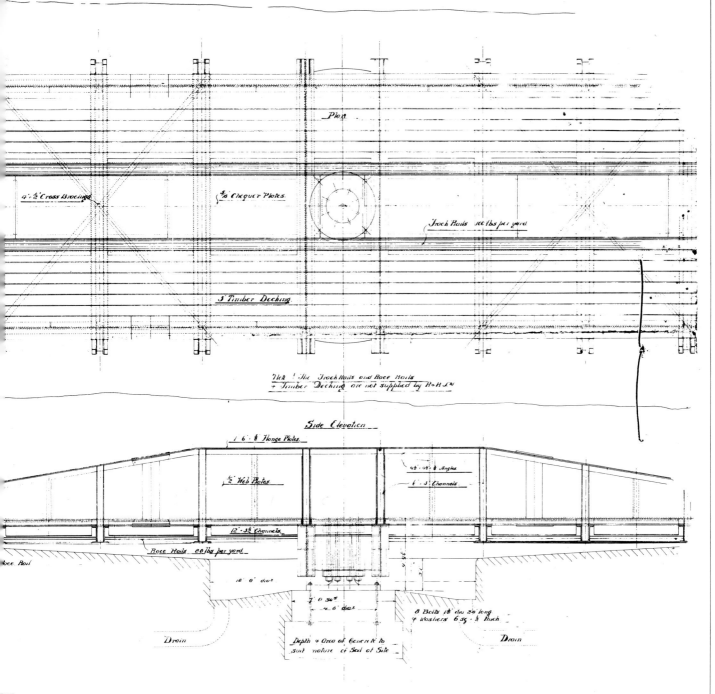

GREAT WESTERN RLY CO

O" ENGINE TURNTABLE.

DRAWING Nº 167 9

Plan

4'·½" Cross Bracings

⅝" Chequer Plates.

Track Rails 100 lbs per yard

3" Timber Decking

Note: The Track Rails and Race Rails
& Timber Decking are not supplied by R & R Ltd

Side Elevation

1'·6"·⅝" Flange Plates.

½" Web Plates.

4½"·4½"·⅝" Angles.

6"·3" Channels.

12"·3½" Channels.

Race Rails 80 lbs per yard

Race Rail

18'·0" dia

7'·0·50" dia
4'·0" dia

8 Bolts 1⅛" dia 2'0 long
& Washers 6 sq·½" thick

Drain

Depth & Area of Concrete to
suit nature of Soil of Site

Drain

Drawing labelled Ransomes & Rapier

ACKNOWLEDGEMENTS

Emerging blinking into the sunlight, this book is made reality only through the labours of many. In some respects it has been a journalistic exercise, a record of the experience of others wedded to archive and secondary sources. The story has been long in the making, its abiding pleasure the almost endless series of evenings, afternoons and weekends spent in discussion, always enlightening and invariably amusing. The world that emerged was one of gloom and murk, The War, the firepit and the flarelamp, 'Double Homes' and endless shifts, and choking dust, coal, oil and water. The job of an engineman was among the hardest, leavened by an anarchic humour and remembered now with some (but not too much) affection.

"As a class enginemen and firemen know less of the amenities of life than any other section of the community."

This book is dedicated in part to that great host of workers in and about the engine sheds who endured awful conditions right into the 1960s, long after others had rejected such work.

Bill Pedlar provided some of the keenest insights into engine shed work on the Great Western, with a surpassing cheerfulness and hospitality, and Alec Swain went to some considerable personal effort to assist the compilation of the book. Alec became well known to enginemen through his duties, particularly in the early 'sixties, and it is a pleasure to note the universal respect and affection in which he is held. Many groups of enginemen (long engaged in different careers) continue to meet informally, recalling many good memories of sheds long demolished or changed out of all recognition. John Church was an enormous help and together with Gerry Coleman enlightened and amused from a great anecdotal storehouse. Charles Turner endured a considerable correspondence without complaint and Mr. Trethewey received us with great kindness. Pete Wadley provided help and encouragement of an exceptional kind and went to some effort to organise a wider discussion, consenting to oddly-timed 'supplementaries' at some personal inconvenience. Harold Sawyer, Rodney Bailey and Ron Durman enlivened the discussions at '94' and Reg Warr was a source of further valuable material. Ken Bowler, with great good humour, endured an afternoon of questioning at a time of personal sadness, and to him must be expressed a special thanks. Tony MacDonald, with hospitality and great interest pursued a variety of obscure and otherwise impenetrable points, again an effort for which there must be a special appreciation. Cyril Slade and Roy Sharpe gave their time with enthusiasm and a fondness for the best parts of times long gone.

Douglas Quaterman, together with his wife, provided a most hospitable welcome, bringing together a lively enthusiasm and a sharply focused recollection.

Chris Turner, head figuratively shaking in some disbelief, was ever a source of advice, assistance and encouragement; V. R. Webster commented to great effect on aspects of the text; similarly Mike Romans. Special thanks are due to Ian Coulson and to his colleague Lenny Lean for help of an absolutely invaluable nature over a lengthy period — a good-humoured co-operation, the importance of which is difficult to overstate. Gerry Beale pursued many aspects of the text and had a hand in the final shaping of the book. Roger Carpenter went to much effort in pursuit of photographs and Reg Randell made available some obscure plans. Peter Winding, with unique hospitality and great charm, provided some photographs of a particularly unusual nature and his collection has enhanced the photographic content considerably. W. A. Camwell is also owed a special thanks.

Many other individuals and institutions were involved in the making of this book, some centrally, some very much at the periphery — Michael Max, John Hooper, Laurence Waters, Uxbridge Library, British Library Map Room, British Railways, Mrs. Webb and Laurie Webb, R. C. Riley, Brian Hilton, Ken Fairey, The Great Western Society, The National Railway Museum at York, J. E. Kite, H. C. Casserley, R. M. Casserley, W. Potter, Tony Wright, Eric Mountford, S. W. Baker, P. J. Kelley, Maurice Deane, J. L. Smith, Harold White, A. W. Croughton, Merchant Navy Preservation Society, C. C. B. Herbert, C. L. Turner, G. H. Daventry, Lens of Sutton, Locomotive Club of Great Britain, Pendon Museum, H. F. Wheeller, R. F. Roberts, S. J. Dickson, P. J. Garland, A. Attewell, Mrs. Collins, R. E. Gilbert, J. H. Ahern, F. J. Agar, J. H. Venn, Roye England, E. Wilmshurst, R. H. G. Simpson, I. D. Beale, Railway Correspondence & Travel Society, L. W. Perkins, Dr. I. C. Allen, J. W. Sparrowe, E. Eggleton, L. Ward, F. M. Gates, M. W. Earley, N. E. Preedy, W. Turner, M. Light, J. H. Meredith, J. H. Russell, R. C. Chown, J. J. Davis and Harrow Library.

The burden of logistics was more than ever a joint effort; thanks again to Paul and June and, of course, Beverly (and Anna) and Wendy.